BARRON'S

ACT®
MATH AND SCIENCE
WORKBOOK

Roselyn Teukolsky, M.S.
Ithaca High School
Ithaca, New York

BARRON'S

About the Author

Roselyn Teukolsky has an M.S. degree from Cornell University and is a math and computer science teacher at Ithaca High School in Ithaca, New York. She has taught physics, chemistry, biology, ecology, and oceanography. She has published articles in *The Mathematics Teacher* and in the National Council of Teachers of Mathematics *Yearbook*. She is the author of Barron's *AP Computer Science* review book and coauthor of Barron's *SAT 2400: Aiming for the Perfect Score*. She has received the Edyth May Sliffe Award for Distinguished Mathematics Teaching and the Alfred Kalfus Distinguished Coach Award from the New York State Math League (NYSML).

Acknowledgments

I owe thanks to many people who helped in the creation of this book.

I am especially grateful to the Science Department at Ithaca High School, who were exceptionally generous in offering me use of their science materials. Special thanks to Ann Bronson, Pat Dutt, Kate Gefell, Carlan Gray, Linda Knewstub, Deborah Lynn, Mark Nelson, Brenda Smith, Vivian Smith, Hallie Snowman, and Bob Tuori. Not only were all these teachers generous with their materials, they were also helpful with explanations and suggestions when I asked for them.

Thanks also to Edith Cassel for sharing her lab materials.

I am grateful to my students Jennifer Kenkel and Seth Wraight, who checked the science section and made some excellent suggestions for improvement.

Many thanks to my student Rachel Zax, who checked the entire manuscript and provided great alternative solutions to some of the math problems. Her help to me was invaluable.

A special thank you to Linda Carnevale, who taught me to lighten up a bit and use student-friendly icons and humorous advice.

I am extremely grateful to my editor at Barron's, Pat Hunter, for her gentle guidance and moral support throughout this project. Thanks, too, to my excellent copyeditor, Michele Sandifer, and to the entire production team at Barron's who brought the book to fruition. I also want to thank Wayne Barr for his faith in me as author of this workbook.

My husband, Saul, has helped me tremendously—reading and checking the manuscript, and giving me advice and every kind of support. My daughters, Rachel and Lauren, have helped me by being wonderful and encouraging every step of the way. I dedicate the book to my family.

Roselyn Teukolsky
Ithaca, NY

10%
POST-CONSUMER
WASTE
Paper contains a minimum of 10% post-consumer waste (PCW). Paper used in this book was derived from certified, sustainable forestlands.

All inquiries should be addressed to:
Barron's Educational Series, Inc.
250 Wireless Boulevard
Hauppauge, New York 11788
www.barronseduc.com

ISBN-13: 978-0-7641-4034-1
ISBN-10: 0-7641-4034-5

Library of Congress Catalog Card Number: 2009000363

Library of Congress Cataloging-in-Publication Data
Teukolsky, Roselyn.
ACT math and science workbook / Roselyn Teukolsky.
   p. cm.
   ISBN-13: 978-0-7641-4034-1
   ISBN-10: 0-7641-4034-5
   1. Mathematics—Examinations, questions, etc.--Study guides. 2. Science—Examinations, questions, etc.—Study guides. 3. ACT Assessment—Study guides. I.Title.

QA43.T446 2009
510.76—dc22   2009000363

Printed in the United States of America

9 8 7

Contents

PART 3: MODEL ACT TESTS

APPENDIXES

ACT Overview
and Strategies

CHAPTER GOALS
• Description of the test
• Your ACT score
• Questions to consider
• Why use a math and science workbook?
• Test day
• Strategies for the ACT

If your life plan includes going to the college of your choice, then acing the ACT is a huge step forward in achieving your dreams. Welcome!

You probably already know that thousands upon thousands of students apply for top colleges every year, and many suffer the agonies of rejection. For example, Harvard and Yale each have an acceptance rate of about 8 percent, while Columbia University's rate is not much better at 12 percent. Pomona College in California is at 18 percent, while Williams College in Massachusetts is at 19 percent. Many, many colleges have an acceptance rate of less than 25 percent.

What you clearly need is an edge. Being an A student at your school and an upstanding citizen in your community all count in your favor, no question about it. Few things shine as brightly for an admissions committee, though, as the sparkling gem of a great ACT score.

DESCRIPTION OF THE TEST

By now you probably know what the ACT Test looks like, but here is a quick overview. The test time is 2 hours and 55 minutes, but you must add half an hour if you take the optional Writing Test. The four subject tests are, in the order you will take them, English, Math, Reading, and Science. When you take the test, you will be given a short, 10- to 15-minute break between the Math and Reading Tests.

All questions are multiple choice, except for the Writing. Here is the breakdown of the first four tests:

English	45 minutes	75 questions
Math	60 minutes	60 questions
Reading	35 minutes	40 questions
Science	35 minutes	40 questions
Total	175 minutes	215 questions

That means you have less than a minute per question—yikes! Stay calm. Many of the questions are easy, and you will zip right through them.

YOUR ACT SCORE

Your *raw score* is the total number of multiple-choice questions you got right. Your *scaled score* is the score from 1–36, a composite of all your scores, the all-important score that goes to colleges. This is the score you will tell people (or not) when they ask you what you got on the ACT.

For each of the four subjects you will receive a scaled score from 1–36. Within each subject—except for Science—you will get a further breakdown of subscores. For example, in Math you will receive three subscores:

Precalculus/Elementary Algebra	1–18
Algebra/Coordinate Geometry	1–18
Plane Geometry/Trigonometry	1–18

These scores are meaningful only if you know where you fall compared with other students. About half of all students taking the ACT have scores between 17 and 23. A score of 17 places you in the 28th percentile, which means that you scored better than just 28 percent of all students who took the ACT. Clearly, if you score 17, you have your work cut out for you. On the other hand, a score of 23 places you in the 76th percentile—not bad!

You should know that many top colleges will eliminate you if your ACT score is lower than 22. You will, however, be in the top 5 percent of all students if you have a score of 28 and the top 1 percent if you score 31.

QUESTIONS TO CONSIDER

ACT or SAT?

Colleges claim that they do not play favorites, that the ACT and SAT tests are given equal weight. So how do you choose which one to take? The time factor is an obvious difference. The ACT lasts 2 hours and 55 minutes plus an additional half hour if you take the writing section. The SAT lasts 3 hours and 45 minutes. Other obvious differences between the ACT and SAT are that the ACT tests science and trigonometry, while the SAT does not.

Less obvious is the fact that the ACT is more knowledge based than the SAT. The ACT measures math and English skills that are part of rigorous college-prep high school courses. The SAT is trickier somehow, more akin to puzzle solving. In this sense, the ACT is a fairer test of your high school achievement.

Here is something purely anecdotal. Both test publishers will say that students who have done well in school will do well on their tests.

Junior or Senior?

OK, it is a good bet that you have already decided whether to take the ACT as a junior or senior. Still, if you are a junior and are debating whether to take the test this year, you should know that there are several advantages to taking the ACT as a junior:

- If you are in a rigorous college-prep program with accelerated and AP courses, the ACT material will still be relatively fresh in your memory when you take the test.
- You are likely to have just completed a good precalculus course, which contains most of the coursework required for the ACT Math Test.
- If you think you can improve your score, you get more opportunities to have another shot at the ACT.
- Your ACT score gives you an additional guide to selecting colleges.

WHY USE A MATH AND SCIENCE WORKBOOK?

The Math Section

First consider the math. Most test takers can get the easy questions right, those straight-forward questions that ask you to perform the type of simple computations you've been doing in your sleep since middle school. Many test takers can handle the no-frill elementary algebra questions. Let's face it, you have been solving linear equations for a long time.

However, to attain a score that impresses admissions and scholarship committees, you need to crack a good number of the harder questions. The ACT Math Test calls on you to have at your fingertips topics from your rigorous algebra 2 and trigonometry courses, the courses where you dealt with complex numbers, trig equations, matrices, and conic sections, among other enticing goodies. This workbook will help you brush up on all of these topics as well as give you lots of practice ACT questions based solely on the harder stuff.

In the math part of this workbook, you will find a topic-by-topic review of the more challenging math content that you should know, with lots of practice in solving problems that require specialized knowledge. For the tricky math questions that cut across single-topic lines, some "nonclassroom" strategies will show you how to achieve fast, successful results. Cracking a good number of harder math questions on the ACT is a good part of getting the edge you need.

A complete practice Math Test with detailed explanations to all questions will help you to assess your progress.

As you work through the math section, you will spot several icons, each of which provides a useful test-taking tip:

Time saver: Look for this icon to learn a shortcut—how to speed up without losing accuracy. High scorers on the ACT know that time is of the essence.

Gold star: Here you will find a tried-and-true technique that would earn you a gold star from your math teacher. Believe it or not, such techniques are sometimes the best approach.

Neat trick: For some problems, a nifty maneuver will pull the answer out of a hat. Knowing tricks like these helps give you the edge that you need.

Active pencil: With pencil in hand you can often work wonders as you mull over a problem. Smart test takers stay on top of their tasks by writing as they think. This helps them to stay focused.

Calculator: Look for this icon to find an alternative route to the solution. Judicious use of your calculator can save you time and effort on many questions.

The Science Section

It is a sad fact but true: the ACT Science Test is a source of particular anxiety for many students who are otherwise quite confident about the ACT. There is, however, lots of good news about the Science Test:

- Unlike the Math Test, the Science Test is *not* content based. You do not need to know all of high school science. All you need to bring to this test are your common sense, your ability to focus, and a can-do attitude.
- The format of the test is unvarying and therefore predictable. It *can* be learned!

The science part of this workbook will teach you about the three distinct types of science passages that appear on the ACT Test and the best way to approach each type. Before you jump into any actual ACT passages, however, you will:

- Become an expert in reading graphs and tables.
- Nail down the scientific method and how to interpret experiments.
- Learn specific four-step drills to help automate your approach to tackling a science passage.

In short, this section of the workbook will teach you the Science Test. As you know from previous experience in test taking, knowing the test is half the battle. There is a complete practice Science Test at the end of this workbook, with answers and explanations. Use this to assess your progress after you have tackled the passages in the focus chapters.

TIP

Smart test takers know the tricks of the trade and apply them accordingly.

Throughout the science section, you will find:

- ACE tips that will remind you how to do well on the Science ACT.
- Coaching on the side to keep you on track as you proceed through a science passage.
- Warm-up passages that will give you a gentle introduction to sample ACT passages.
- Drills that you should use to focus your thinking.
- Sample jottings you might make to nail the content of each passage.

Wait and see—practice will boost your confidence and, more importantly, your ACT score.

TEST DAY

It is not enough to bring your wits to this test. The ACT Test is demanding and requires mental and physical stamina. You must come prepared. This is a big and important day for you, and you want to guarantee that everything goes smoothly. You don't want any unanticipated disasters—like losing a contact lens—to sap your mental energy and put you in a funk before you even get started.

Think of each of the following the night before the test:

- What to wear? If they forgot to turn on the heating or air-conditioning in your testing room because it is a Saturday, you should not be one of those who notices it. Plan to wear comfortable clothes with plenty of layers.
- What to eat? Not a breakfast person? Well, tomorrow is the day to make an exception. Eat a healthy power breakfast! You will not be allowed to eat or drink in the testing room.
- What time to rise and shine? You need to be at your test center at 8 A.M. Late-comers will not be admitted. It is crucial that you set a reliable alarm clock and arrange for backup from a family member. Don't forget to build in time for breakfast and negotiating traffic. It goes without saying that you know ahead of time exactly where the testing site is.
- Pre-ACT party? Forget about it! You need a good night's sleep.
- What to take to the test tomorrow? Here is a checklist:

  ✔ Your admission ticket.
  ✔ Proper ID, like a driver's license or student ID.
  ✔ Several sharpened #2 pencils with good erasers that leave no marks.
  ✔ Your favorite calculator with *fresh* batteries for the Math Test. (See the next chapter for a description of allowable calculators for the ACT.)
  ✔ A spare calculator, if possible.
  ✔ A spare pair of glasses or contact lenses if you wear them.
  ✔ A watch. Not all testing rooms have wall clocks.
  ✔ A snack and drink for the break. (Have them outside the testing room!)
  ✔ A small pack of tissues.

Do not bring books, notes, scratch paper, highlighters, dictionaries, and so on. They will not be allowed in the testing room.

> **TIP**
>
> Test erasers ahead of time. It is important that the computerized scoring machine does not pick up stray marks.

A special note about your cell phone—you know, that little gizmo that you can't live without? *It needs to be turned off.* If it goes off anywhere near you during the test, you will be disqualified and sent home. Ouch!

STRATEGIES FOR THE ACT

By now you know that the ACT is a tough test, and you need to be prepared. In this book, you will find tips and strategies specifically geared toward the Math and Science Tests. This particular section, however, deals with general strategies that apply to all tests on the ACT. Remember, you are a smart person, and you can crack this nut.

Before the Test

- Find out about the test. Get up-to-date information about the ACT at its official web site, *www.actstudent.org.* You should also speak to teachers and counselors who know about this test and to students who have taken it. Their insights could be invaluable to you.
- Familiarize yourself with the format of each individual test. This book will help you in math and science. There are similar books with practice in English, reading, and writing.
- Plan on taking the ACT plus Writing Test because some schools require a writing score. The last thing you need is to have to retake the entire ACT test because you later decided to apply to a school that required the writing score.
- Become familiar with the instructions *for each test.* Yes, you will be given time to read these on the test day before the actual test, but knowing them in advance is helpful and comforting.
- Practice! The really good news is that the test does not vary in its format—same types of questions, same approaches to passages, same number of questions in certain topics. Just as you break the code for any of your teachers, so you can learn this particular test. You are doing exactly the right thing, working through a book such as this. Practice may not make perfect, but it sure as heck will improve your score.
- Learn the material that you need to know. This means that you should refresh your knowledge and skills in the math and English content areas. This book will help you do that in math.
- Set aside a regular time for ACT study. You probably have an insanely busy life with extracurricular activities, sports, 12 hours of homework every night, plus social dates. If you do not build ACT study time into your schedule, it is just not going to happen.
- Learn how to pace yourself during an ACT Test. This is a critical skill that you can develop by taking timed tests when you practice. The different nature of the various ACT tests calls for different time strategies.

NOTE

If you find that much of the course content in math is unfamiliar to you, you may want to postpone taking the ACT for a year while you take an Algebra 2 and Trigonometry course. This is much more effective than a cram course in trig, for example.

Five Minutes Before the Test

Use the bathroom, even if you think you do not need to go!

During the Test

Here are several different strategies that will serve you well, no matter which of the multiple-choice tests you are taking.

ANSWER EVERY QUESTION!

There is no penalty for guessing. Notice that this is different from "solve every problem." Do your best and, if necessary, guess. Resist the impulse to leave a question that you have no clue about blank. The ACT Test is different from tests at school, and you must adjust your strategy accordingly. Often you will be able to eliminate some of the choices, which improves your shot at the right answer.

If you are going to run out of time, take a few seconds to bubble in answers to *all* of the remaining questions. Remember, the hard questions are worth the same as the easy ones, so answer them all.

TACKLE THE EASY QUESTIONS FIRST

It is human nature to start at question 1 and proceed sequentially through the set of questions. This makes sense if the questions are in increasing order of difficulty. Unfortunately, this is not necessarily so on the ACT. You must adopt a strategy of skipping questions when a solution method is not immediately apparent to you.

Here is the strategy. Work quickly through the entire test, answering only questions that appear easy to you. (There will be many of these.) Skip the questions you do not like. Circle these in your test booklet so that you have a speedy way of coming back to them. After your first pass, go back and spend time on the harder questions. This approach has several advantages:

- The comforting feeling of solving many problems quickly will settle you down and boost your confidence. It is good to approach the more challenging questions with a positive mindset.
- You will avoid the tragedy of running out of time before getting to some doable questions toward the end of the test.

This approach does have potential disadvantages:

- Extra care is required to keep track of which questions must still be done.
- You encounter the danger of solving a question correctly and then filling in the wrong oval on the answer sheet (disaster!)

PACE YOURSELF

Timing is important, but do not let the time issue dominate your thinking. You must never lose sight of your main goal, which is to answer the questions correctly.

NOTE

The test proctor will give you a five-minute warning at the end of each test.

CHECK YOUR TEST

Any time left over should be used to check your test. It is not the time for meditation, yoga exercises, or a quick nap. You need to take advantage of every minute of time allotted for each test. You are not allowed to proceed to the next test. So use leftover time to go back and check the current test.

- Check that you have marked only one answer per question on your answer sheet.
- Check that you have answered every question on the test.

YOUR TEST BOOKLET

Use your test booklet wisely. It is yours for the duration of the test, and you can write in it.

- Circle the questions that you must return to.
- Underline important points in the passages.
- Mark up graphs and diagrams to clarify the passages or questions.
- Jot down any helpful thoughts and conclusions. The science and math sections of this workbook will have more specifics on how you can use your test booklet to great advantage.

> **NOTE**
>
> If you are not taking the test in the U.S., you may not be allowed to write in the test booklet.

THE ANSWER SHEET

Take great care with how you mark your answer sheet. The oval for your answer choice should be completely filled in and should not overlap with the adjacent ovals. To change an answer, you need to erase thoroughly without leaving stray marks on the sheet. Remember, these sheets are electronically scored. Careless bubbling in of answers may cost you precious points that you did not deserve to lose.

USE CAUTION

Be aware of subtle differences in multiple-choice questions from test to test. The Math Test asks you for the "correct" answer, while the English, Reading, and Science Tests ask for the "best" answer. This is less clear cut. An answer choice may be quite reasonable within the context of a passage; nevertheless, it may be wrong in the context of the ACT test, because it is not the *best* answer! In the science section of this workbook are several examples of such questions.

CONCENTRATE

Concentrate on the task at hand. When a test on the ACT is over, it is over. You cannot go back to it. It is history. Do not obsess about the questions you could not do on the last test. Focus your mental energy on the questions that you will now tackle, on the current test. Smart people do not worry about stuff that they cannot change.

Here's a final thought. The English, Math, Reading, and Science Tests are all multiple choice. In other words, they are giving you the right answer! You just need to select it.

PART 1

THE MATH
SECTION

Overview of the Math Test

CHAPTER 1

CHAPTER GOALS

- What topics are on the test?
- Question types
- Calculators

As is true of the Science Test, the Math Test on the ACT follows a predictable format, right down to the expected number of questions per topic!

WHAT TOPICS ARE ON THE TEST?

By now you know that the Math Test contains 60 multiple-choice questions for which you will be given 60 minutes. Each question will present 5 answer choices, either A, B, C, D, E or F, G, H, J, K, in alternating questions. This is to help prevent entering a choice for the wrong question. Math is the second test in the ACT sequence of tests, following English. Reading comes next. Once you have started tackling the Reading Test, you will not be allowed to go back to math.

The ACT test is based on the algebra and geometry courses that you took (or are currently taking) in high school. If you are not sure how your high school stacks up compared to the typical high school or, for that matter, how you stack up, here is a breakdown of topics on ACT math:

- Pre-algebra
- Elementary algebra
- Intermediate algebra
- Coordinate geometry
- Plane geometry
- Trigonometry

PRE-ALGEBRA: 14 QUESTIONS (24 PERCENT)

You must know all the early topics in arithmetic: numbers, fractions, decimals, positive powers, square roots, ratios and proportions, percents, multiples, factors, absolute value, order, simple equations, probability, counting, and simple statistics.

ELEMENTARY ALGEBRA: 9 QUESTIONS (15 PERCENT)

You must know topics from your earliest algebra course: variables, substitution, simple operations on polynomials, factoring, quadratic equations solved by factoring, linear equations, inequalities, exponents, and square roots.

INTERMEDIATE ALGEBRA: 9 QUESTIONS (15 PERCENT)

You must know harder algebra: the quadratic formula, rational expressions, radicals, inequalities, absolute value, sequences, simultaneous equations, quadratic inequalities, functions, matrices, roots of polynomials, complex numbers, and functions.

COORDINATE GEOMETRY: 9 QUESTIONS (15 PERCENT)

You will be asked about the number line, *xy*-plane, graphs of polynomials, circles, curves in the *xy*-plane, equations, slopes, parallel and perpendicular lines, distances, midpoints, transformations, and conic sections.

PLANE GEOMETRY: 14 QUESTIONS (24 PERCENT)

You need to know information from your favorite high school geometry course: triangles, rectangles, parallelograms, circles, angles, parallel and perpendicular lines, transformations, techniques of proof, simple three-dimensional geometry, perimeter, area, and volume.

TRIGONOMETRY: 4 QUESTIONS (7 PERCENT)

You will encounter a small section about right triangle trigonometry, radians, graphs, identities, equations, and problems that require you to use the sine or cosine rule.

Did your entire mathematical life just flash before your eyes? Never fear—all topics will be reviewed in these pages, so you can set your mind at ease.

According to ACT spokespeople, their test favors the student with a good grasp of material taught in rigorous high school courses. If you are insecure about the extent of your grasp, practicing the typical ACT-like math problems presented in this workbook will bring you up to snuff. As with every skill you aspire to excel at, the buzzword is practice!

What Is Not on the Test?

Something you should not expect to find is a bunch of formulas at the start of the ACT math test (as is provided on that other test, the SAT). You are expected to know basic formulas and relationships, like areas of triangles and circles and also the side ratios of special triangles.

If a question requires you to use a particular formula, the ACT often provides it in the question. Having said that, you should know that most of the problems on the Math ACT depend on basic formulas and skills rather than complex formulas and extensive computation. Many questions emphasize reasoning applied in practical situations. In fact, if you find yourself stuck in an endless forest of calculations for a given question, chances are good that you are on the wrong path and need to move on.

QUESTION TYPES

Easy Questions

Here is some good news: there are many easy questions on the math ACT, questions that you will answer in a flash. Be aware, however, that questions range from easy through challenging within each category. (Yes, there are hard pre-algebra questions!) The 60 questions on the ACT are not necessarily in increasing order of difficulty. "Easy" and "hard" are subjective terms. Someone who starred in algebra but hated geometry may have a different view from the High School Geometry Queen about what is easy or hard. Nevertheless, the easiest questions typically use few words and cut to the chase, for example, "Solve $x + x + x = ...$" or "Find the average of ...." These questions are topic based, easily recognizable as a type. The challenging problems will often test your understanding and logical reasoning ability. They may also stray across different mathematical categories.

Some of the ACT questions will be placed in a setting, which means that you will need to extract the math problem from a story. Typically, you will find that the solution to the problem is straightforward. The difficulty comes from analyzing the setup. As is true of all ACT questions, those placed in a setting can be easy, medium, or hard.

Here are some examples of easy questions, the type that you should be able to solve without breaking a sweat.

Questions

1. Which of the following is the graph of the solution set of $3x < 6$?

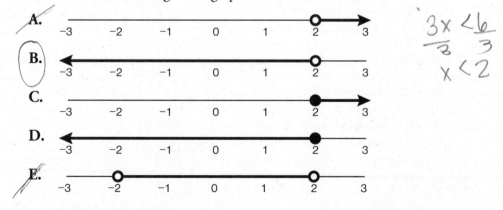

$$\frac{3x}{3} < \frac{6}{3}$$

$$x < 2$$

2. In the figure below, $\angle B$ is a right angle, and the measure of $\angle C$ is 30°. If $\overline{AC}$ is 8 units long, then how many units long is $\overline{BC}$?

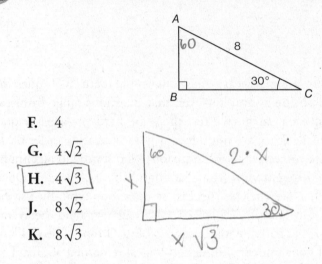

  F.   4

  G. $4\sqrt{2}$

  H. $4\sqrt{3}$

  J. $8\sqrt{2}$

  K. $8\sqrt{3}$

3. Slips of paper numbered 1 through 100 are placed into a hat. The first number drawn is 45 and wins a prize for its holder. The slip of paper with this number is discarded, and a second number is drawn. What is the probability that the second number drawn is 27?

  A. $\dfrac{1}{99}$

  B. $\dfrac{1}{100}$

  C. $\dfrac{2}{99}$

  D. $\dfrac{1}{25}$

  E. $\dfrac{1}{49}$

4. Which of the following is the equation of a line that contains the point $(0, 4)$ and has slope $\dfrac{1}{3}$?

  F. $4y = 3x$

  G. $3y = 12x + 1$

  H. $y = 3x + 4$

  J. $3y = x + 12$

  K. $3y = x + 4$

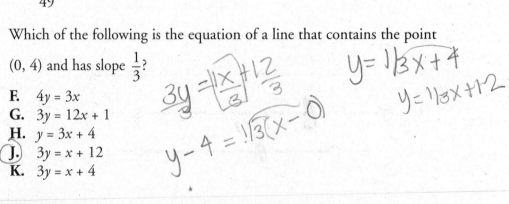

SOLUTIONS

  1. **(B)**   2. **(H)**   3. **(A)**   4. **(J)**

1. **(B)** This is the simplest type of inequality question that you can get. Divide both sides by 3 to get the correct range for x.

   $3x < 6 \Rightarrow x < 2$

   Strictly, "less than 2" means that you should use an open circle on 2. For this reason you can eliminate choices (C) and (D) immediately. The other choices do not work either:

   (A) This represents the set $x > 2$.
   (E) This represents the set $-2 < x < 2$.

2. **(H)** Recognize this immediately as a 30°-60°-90° triangle, where the relationships between sides are shown below:

   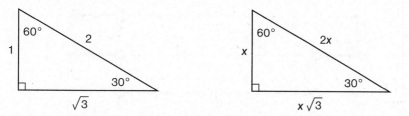

   For the given triangle, 8 is the hypotenuse. Therefore, the length opposite the 30° angle is 4, and the length opposite the 60° angle is $4\sqrt{3}$.

3. **(A)** Here is a question in a setting. Can you extract the simple probability problem? The slip with 45 on it is thrown away, leaving 99 numbers in the hat. What is the probability of drawing the number 27? Since all 99 numbers are equally likely to be drawn, the answer is $\dfrac{1}{99}$.

4. **(J)** In this equation, you are given the slope, $\dfrac{1}{3}$, and the y-intercept, 4.

   Thus, the required equation is $y = \dfrac{1}{3}x + 4$. To get the form of the answer choices, multiply both sides by 3, yielding the correct answer: $3y = x + 12$.

   Recall that the slope-intercept form of a linear equation is $y = mx + b$, where m is the slope and b is the y-intercept.

   An alternate solution is to notice that only the last two choices have a slope of $\dfrac{1}{3}$. Of these, only $3y = x + 12$ works for the ordered pair (0, 4).

What makes these questions easy is that you can quickly recognize each of them as one clearly defined topic. They each cover something easy that you probably mastered a long time ago: simple linear inequalities, special right triangles, simple probability, and the slope-intercept form of a linear equation.

Medium Questions

Here are four questions that are similar to those above; but these require additional steps to solve them. They are not especially easy, but neither are they particularly challenging. The topics are easy to recognize, but you will need extra steps to solve the problems. See how well you do.

Questions

$|3x| < -6$

$\dfrac{3x}{3} < \dfrac{6}{3}$

$x < 2$

$x < -2$

1. Which of the following is the graph of the solution set of $|3x| < 6$?

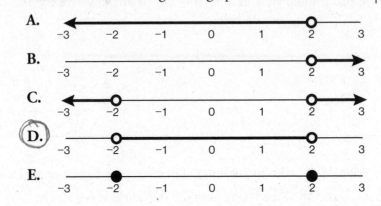

2. In the figure shown below, given that $\overline{AC} \cong \overline{DC}$, what is the value of x?

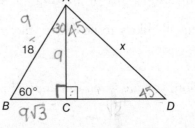

    F. $18\sqrt{6}$

    G. $18\sqrt{2}$

    H. $9\sqrt{2}$

    J. $9\sqrt{3}$

    K. $9\sqrt{6}$

3. Suppose that the probability of rain in City A is $\frac{2}{3}$ and the probability of

rain in City B is $\frac{1}{6}$. What is the probability that it will rain in *neither* city?

You may assume that rain in City A and rain in City B are independent events.

A. $\frac{1}{6}$

B. $\frac{5}{18}$

C. $\frac{1}{2}$

D. $\frac{2}{3}$

E. $\frac{5}{6}$

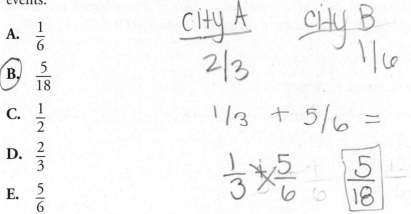

4. Which of the following is the equation of a line that contains the point $(1, -3)$ and is perpendicular to the line $3x - 6y = 4$?

F. $y + 2x + 5 = 0$

G. $y + 2x + 1 = 0$

H. $y - 2x + 5 = 0$

J. $2y + x + 5 = 0$

K. $2y - x - 7 = 0$

SOLUTIONS

1. **(D)**   2. **(K)**   3. **(B)**   4. **(G)**

1. **(D)** This is an absolute value inequality. It looks simple, but you need to recognize it as a compound inequality.

The three general forms for absolute value are:

$|x| = k \Rightarrow x = -k$ or $x = k$

$|x| < k \Rightarrow -k < x < k$

$|x| > k \Rightarrow x < -k$ or $x > k$

where k represents a nonnegative number.

For the inequality given in this question,

$$|3x| < 6 \Rightarrow 3|x| < 6$$
$$\Rightarrow |x| < 2$$
$$\Rightarrow -2 < x < 2$$

This means that the solution set consists of all *x*-values strictly between –2 and 2, which corresponds to the graph in choice (D).

2. **(K)** $\triangle ABC$ is a 30°-60°-90° triangle.

$\therefore BC = 9$ and $AC = 9\sqrt{3}$.

$\triangle ABC$ is a 45°-45°-90° triangle (isosceles triangle with a right angle)

$\therefore AD = AC\sqrt{2} = (9\sqrt{3})\sqrt{2} = 9\sqrt{6}$

> **TIP**
>
> When you take the ACT, know those special right triangles like the back of your hand.

3. **(B)**

P(rain in neither City A nor City B)

= P(no rain in City A *and* no rain in City B)

= [1 – P(rain in City A)][1 – P(rain in City B)]

= $\left(\dfrac{1}{3}\right)\left(\dfrac{5}{6}\right)$

= $\dfrac{5}{18}$

This solution uses two facts that you should know.

 The complement rule: If $P(E)$ is the probability of an event, then $P(\text{not } E)$ equals $1 - P(E)$.

 The product rule: If A and B are independent events, then $P(A \text{ and } B)$ equals $P(A)P(B)$.

Here is an alternative solution.

P(rain in neither City A nor City B)

= 1 – P (rain in City A or rain in City B)

= $1 - \left[\dfrac{2}{3} + \dfrac{1}{6} - \left(\dfrac{2}{3} \cdot \dfrac{1}{6}\right)\right]$

= $1 - \dfrac{3}{18}$

= $\dfrac{5}{18}$

This solution uses both the complement rule and the following rule:

> If A and B are two events, then $P(A \text{ or } B)$ equals
> $P(A) + P(B) - P(A \text{ and } B)$.

Notice that in the given problem, the two events, rain in City A and rain in City B, are not *mutually exclusive*. This means that it could rain in both cities simultaneously. Therefore, in the second solution, you must subtract that probability from the sum of the probabilities to avoid overcounting.

4. **(G)** First find the slope of the given line by writing it in slope-intercept form:

$$3x - 6y = 4 \Rightarrow 6y = 3x - 4 \Rightarrow y = \frac{1}{2}x - \frac{2}{3}$$

Thus, slope = $\frac{1}{2}$.

Since the required line is perpendicular to the given line, the slope of the required line is the negative reciprocal of $\frac{1}{2}$, namely -2. Now the problem boils down to finding the equation of a line with slope -2 and containing point $(1, -3)$.

> The equation of a line, given the slope and a point on the line, is $y - y_P = m(x - x_P)$, where m is the slope and (x_P, y_P) is a point on the line.

In the given problem:

$$y - (-3) = -2(x - 1) \Rightarrow y + 3 = -2x + 2 \Rightarrow y + 2x + 1 = 0$$

The above set of problems is harder than the previous set. In question 1, you are required to know how to solve an absolute value inequality. A bell must go off in your head, signaling that this is not a simple inequality but a compound one. $|3x| < 6$ is equivalent to two inequalities: $3x > -6$ and $3x < 6$, which simplifies to the region $-2 < x < 2$.

Question 2 uses both a 30°-60°-90° triangle and a 45°-45°-90° triangle in its solution. You are also expected to know the law of radicals that states $\sqrt{a}\sqrt{b} = \sqrt{ab}$, where $\sqrt{a}$ and $\sqrt{b}$ are nonnegative real numbers. Thus, $(9\sqrt{3})\sqrt{2} = 9\sqrt{6}$.

Question 3 is tricky but easily recognizable. If you have practiced this type of probability question, you can solve it. Just make sure that you know the three probability rules described in the solution.

Question 4 is straightforward, but it does need several steps. First you must find the slope of the given line using the slope-intercept form of a linear equation. Then you must get the slope of the required line by taking the negative reciprocal of the slope of the perpendicular line. Now you must find the equation of the required line, given that you know its slope and a point on the line. Again, if you have practiced this type of question before, it is easily recognizable and you should have no difficulty with it.

Challenging Questions

The difficult questions do not necessarily require more steps than the so-called "easy" and "medium" questions. Sometimes challenging questions simply probe your understanding of a tricky concept or test your reasoning ability when you are outside of the typical textbook-type questions. Try your hand at the following.

Questions

1. The graph of $f(x) = \dfrac{4}{x-1}$ is shown below.

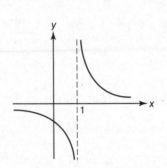

Among the following, which best represents $g(x) = \dfrac{4}{|x-1|}$?

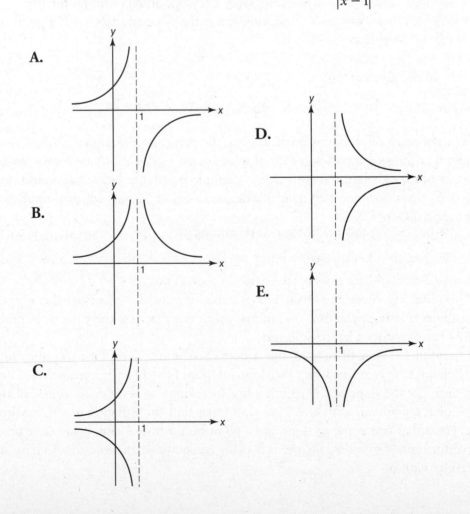

2. In the standard (x, y) coordinate plane, a circle with center $(6, 0)$ is tangent to the line $y = x$. What is the area of this circle, expressed in square coordinate units?

    F. 9π
    G. 12π
    H. 18π
    J. 27π
    K. 36π

3. Suppose that someone must get from point K to point L, shown in the figure below, by going only north and east (up and right). For example, one possible path is to go 3 steps east and then 3 steps north.

    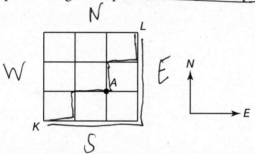

    How many possible paths are there that do *not* include point A?

    A. 22
    B. 20
    C. 16
    D. 14
    E. 11

4. Consider this repeating decimal:

    0.102003000400005…80000000090000000001020030004…

    What will be the 118th digit of this number?

    F. 4
    G. 6
    H. 8
    J. 0
    K. 2

SOLUTIONS

1. **(B)**   2. **(H)**   3. **(E)**   4. **(F)**

1. **(B)** At first glance, this is a tricky question, an unfamiliar function. The solution, however, is not hard to find if you understand that because of the absolute value in the denominator, $\dfrac{4}{|x-1|}$ is positive for all x. This means that there are no negative y values! This realization immediately eliminates all choices except for (B).

Another quick way to find this answer (if you do not have the insight needed for the solution above) is to get the graph of $g(x)$ using your graphing calculator:

$$\boxed{y=}\ \ 4/\text{abs}(x-1)$$

This will immediately sketch the correct graph for you.

 To get abs: $\boxed{\text{MATH}}$ num abs

2. **(H)**

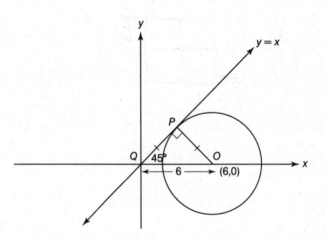

 A picture here is crucial; be sure to draw in the radius to the point of tangency.

The key to this problem is seeing that $\triangle PQO$ is a 45°-45°-90° triangle. This is because the line $y = x$ makes a 45° angle with each axis. Also, in the triangle, $\angle P$ is a right angle since a radius drawn to a tangent at the point of tangency is perpendicular to the tangent. This leaves 45° for the third angle in $\triangle PQO$.

$$\therefore PO = \frac{6}{\sqrt{2}} = 3\sqrt{2}$$

The area of the circle $= \pi r^2 = \pi(3\sqrt{2})^2 = 18\pi$.

3. **(E)**
Method 1: Combinations and permutations
Number of paths from K to L, excluding those that contain A
= (total number of paths from K to L) – (number of paths that include A).

To find the total number of paths from K to L:

You need to go east (E) 3 times and north (N) 3 times. Here are 2 different ways you can do this: EEENNN, NENENE. Think of this as being the number of arrangements of 3 E's and 3 N's. There are 6 slots. The correct answer, however, is not 6!—that is (6)(5)(4)(3)(2)(1)—since the E's are indistinguishable from each other, as are the N's. You must divide by the number of arrangements of those 3 E's and the 3 N's.

$\therefore$ total number of paths from K to L is $\dfrac{6!}{3!3!} = \dfrac{(6)(5)(4)(3)(2)(1)}{(3)(2)(3)(2)} = 20$

Now the number of paths that include A:

There are 3 ways to get to A before proceeding to L.

EEN_ _ _
ENE_ _ _
NEE_ _ _

To get from A to L, you must fill the other 3 slots with the remaining 1 E and 2 N's.

Number of arrangements of 1 E and 2 N's = $\dfrac{3!}{2!1!} = \dfrac{(3)(2)}{(2)} = 3$

This must be multiplied by those 3 ways to get to A.
$\therefore$ number of paths from K to L that include A = (3)(3) = 9
$\therefore$ number of paths from K to L that exclude A = 20 – 9 = 11
So the final answer is 11. Whew!

Method 2: Just counting
Here is a neat, quick, intuitive way to solve this problem. Start at the end-point, L, and count paths working backward, 1 cell at a time, until you reach the starting point K. When you get to K, you should have the total possible number of paths. Got it? Here is the basic strategy:

There is just one way to get to the end (point L) from the point just below it and also the point to the left of it. Label these with a 1 as shown:

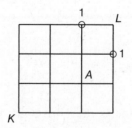

From the point directly below or left of any labeled point, there is just one way to get to the labeled point. So for any point that has upper and right neighbors labeled, label that point with the sum of its upper and right neighbors. For any point that is outside the grid, pretend that it is labeled with a 0. Each label represents the total number of paths to point L from that grid point.

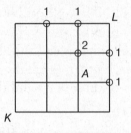

Continue with this labeling scheme, making sure to omit point A, which cannot be crossed. The final diagram, on the right below, shows that there are 11 paths starting at point K.

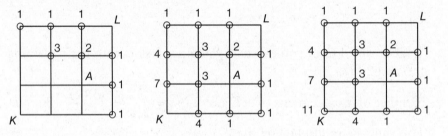

 In a path-counting problem, starting at the endpoint and working backward often leads to a fast and accurate solution.

4. **(F)**

Number of 0's in one cycle = $1 + 2 + 3 + \ldots + 9 = \dfrac{(9)(10)}{2} = 45$.

∴ number of digits in one cycle = $45 + 9 = 54$.
∴ number of digits in two cycles = 108.

$$1 \quad 0 \quad 2 \quad 0 \quad 0 \quad 3 \quad 0 \quad 0 \quad 0 \quad 4$$

$$\uparrow \qquad\qquad\qquad\qquad \uparrow \qquad\qquad\qquad\qquad \uparrow$$

$$109 \qquad\qquad\qquad\quad 114 \qquad\qquad\qquad 118$$

∴ the 118th digit is the same as the 10th digit, which is 4.

The above problems are hard because they do not broadcast what you must do to solve them. Question 1 needs a conceptual insight about the nature of absolute value when used in an expression. Alternatively, it requires an appreciation of how your graphing calculator can be invaluable when you are given a formula for a graph.

Question 2 requires good visualization about where, exactly, the given circle is on the graph. It also goes without saying that you need to draw a diagram to help see what is where. What makes this problem tricky is that the key to solving it, the 45°-45°-90° triangle, is not specifically indicated in the statement of the problem. This is an insight that you have to have, unaided. Once you notice the special triangle, the rest of the problem is routine.

Question 3 is particularly challenging because counting problems can be challenging. You have to avoid counting the same path twice. The trick in the first solution is representing each path as a sequence of E's and N's and then finding the number of arrangements of 3 E's and 3 N's needed to go from point K to point L. The trick in the second solution is to start at the end position and do a cell-by-cell count of total paths as you work your way backward toward the starting point.

 A "how many paths . . .?" question can often be rewritten as a "find the number of permutations (arrangements). . ." question.

Question 4 is a challenging problem in pre-algebra. It does not fall into any category. You cannot use your calculator because the number is too big. You have to bring along your brain power, plain and simple. The question shows that just as you can get an easy question in the trigonometry part of the ACT test, you can also get a zinger in pre-algebra!

Questions in Settings

A question in a setting usually describes a real-life situation from which you must extract and solve a math problem. You have solved many problems like these before. They are the familiar word problems that so many students love to hate.

As is true of every question on the ACT math test, a question in a setting can lie anywhere in the spectrum, from easy to hard. Solving it sometimes takes no more than a good diagram. In all such questions, you need to strip away the packaging and rephrase the problem as a straightforward math question.

Here are two sample questions to try.

Questions

1. Lauren rode her bike from her house to a friend's house $3\frac{1}{2}$ miles away.

   On the first leg of her trip, she rode uphill at 3 miles per hour. The second part of the trip covered a larger distance but was downhill, and Lauren rode at 5 miles per hour. If the downhill part of the ride took half an hour, how many minutes was the uphill part of the ride?

   A. 9
   B. 20
   C. 27
   D. 40
   E. 60

2. A can contains $\frac{1}{4}$ of a pound of cashews. A mixture that has equal weights of cashews, pecans, and walnuts is added to fill the can. If the final weight is 1 pound, what fraction of the final nut mixture are the cashews?

   F. $\frac{1}{4}$

   G. $\frac{1}{3}$

   H. $\frac{1}{2}$

   J. $\frac{2}{3}$

   K. $\frac{3}{4}$

SOLUTIONS

1. **(B)**   2. **(H)**

1. **(B)**

   Draw a picture showing the trip.

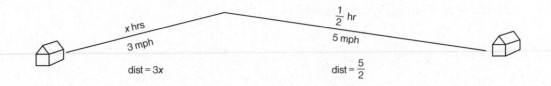

Let x be the time in hours for the uphill part of the trip.

⭐ Be sure to remember this formula: distance = speed × time

Distance for first part = $3x$

Distance for second part = $(5)\left(\dfrac{1}{2}\right) = 2\dfrac{1}{2}$

Total distance = $3\dfrac{1}{2}$

∴ Distance for first part of trip = $3\dfrac{1}{2} - 2\dfrac{1}{2} = 1$

∴ $3x = 1$

∴ $x = \dfrac{1}{3}$ hours = 20 minutes.

2. **(H)**

Mixture problems are usually no more and no less than adding and subtracting fractions. Amount of mixture added = final weight – original weight = $1 - \dfrac{1}{4} = \dfrac{3}{4}$ pound. Equal weights of cashews, pecans, and walnuts means that $\dfrac{1}{4}$ pound of each was added. Since the can already contained $\dfrac{1}{4}$ pound of cashews, the final weight of cashews = $\dfrac{1}{4} + \dfrac{1}{4} = \dfrac{1}{2}$ pound. This is $\dfrac{1}{2}$ the final mixture.

Question Sets

The ACT Math Test usually has two sets of questions that refer to the same initial information contained in a paragraph and followed by a graph or diagram. There can be two to four questions in each set. The questions can be easy, medium, or hard within a given set.

Here is an example of a question set.

Refer to the graph below for questions 1 and 2. The graph shows the enrollment of students in Scripture classes at a small college from the years 1998 until 2002.

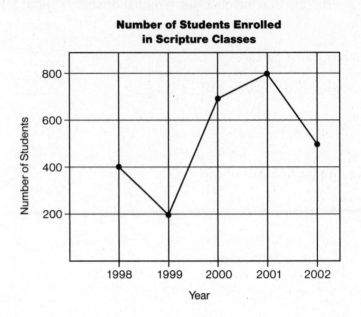

1. The percent increase in students enrolled in Scripture class from 1999 to 2000 exceeded the percent increase from 2000 to 2001 by approximately what percent?

    A. 300%
    B. 250%
    C. 236%
    D. 100%
    E. 14%

2. The enrollment in Scripture class for 2007 was projected to be down 40 percent from 2002. How many students were expected to enroll in 2007?

    F. 500
    G. 460
    H. 340
    J. 300
    K. 200

SOLUTIONS

1. **(C)**   2. **(J)**

1. **(C)**

 Percent increase equals the change divided by the original amount, multiplied by 100.

% increase from 1999 to 2000 = $\dfrac{700 - 200}{200} \cdot 100 = 250\%$

% increase from 2000 to 2001 = $\dfrac{800 - 700}{700} \cdot 100 \approx 14\%$

250 exceeds 14 by 236.

2. **(J)**
2002 enrollment = 500

40% of 500 = $\dfrac{40}{100} \cdot 500 = 200$

Therefore, enrollment in 2007 is expected to be 200 fewer than 500, namely 300. In this question, as in all others, you must be careful to answer the question asked!

Too Much or Too Little Information

Did you ever read an Agatha Christie mystery where that creepy butler did so many weird things that you became convinced that he was the murderer? Then, in the end, the murderer turned out to be that nice, quiet neighbor living down the road?

Well, the butler was a red herring in the story, put there to lead you astray. Certainly, as it turned out, all that information about the butler was extraneous, not at all relevant to solving the mystery.

For most math questions on the ACT Test, you will need all the given information to solve the questions. Be warned, however. The occasional question will contain extraneous information. Do not be led astray.

Occasionally, one of the answer choices will be "Cannot be determined from the given information." Some people assume that this must be the correct answer whenever it appears in a question. Their assumption would be wrong. Be careful.

Questions

1. If the measure of an angle is 59.5°, as shown in the figure below, what is the measure of its supplement?

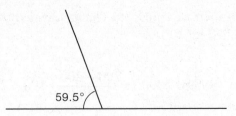

   A. 30.5°
   B. 120.5°
   C. 121.5°
   D. 180°
   E. Cannot be determined from the given information

2. If the measure of an angle is 59.5°, as shown in the figure below, what is the measure of its complement?

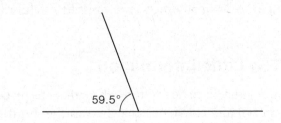

   F. 30.5°
   G. 120.5°
   H. 121.5°
   J. 180°
   K. Cannot be determined from the given information

SOLUTIONS

   1. **(B)**   2. **(F)**

1. **(B)** The measure of the supplement of any ∠A equals 180° – measure of ∠A.

   Therefore, the supplement of 59.5° is 180° – 59.5° = 120.5°. Notice that you are actually given too much information here. You did not need the picture! The picture helps jog your memory, perhaps, because adjacent angles on a straight line are supplementary.

2. **(F)** The measure of the complement of any $\angle A$ equals 90° – measure of $\angle A$.

Therefore, the complement of 59.5° is 90° – 59.5° = 30.5°. Notice that the picture in this case is not only unnecessary. Is it also a red herring? Did the misleading picture cause you to pick choice (K) as the answer? Remember, the measure of the complement of an angle is independent of where the angle is situated.

CALCULATORS

Some Friendly Advice

When you read the ACT literature, you will be told that all of the ACT math problems can be solved without a calculator. You are not even required to have a calculator, the publishers say.

You should know, however, that you do yourself a great disservice to show up for the ACT Math Test *without* a calculator. Most, if not all, of the other test takers will have one. Why put yourself at a disadvantage? Make no mistake—that familiar graphing calculator that you have been using in class during these past couple of years will be a huge asset. For certain types of questions, it can save you time and effort. It can also be used to check answers if you have time left at the end.

If you have not used a graphing calculator before, do *not* borrow one from a friend. The ACT Math Test is not the place to train yourself in the use of a new graphing calculator. You will be much better off using the scientific calculator that you are used to using.

One of the things that you must do long before test day is check that your calculator is one that is allowed on the ACT Test. See the list of prohibited calculators at the end of this section. Also check the list of calculators permitted with modification. It is critically important to check this ahead of time. Imagine how distressed you will be if you are disqualified from the test because you were found to be using an "illegal" calculator!

Once you've checked out your calculator, use it on all of the practice tests, so that you get a feel for when you should and should not use it. Train yourself to use it wisely; overuse can eat up valuable time. Prudent use can save you time and help pile on those points.

When you do use your calculator, make sure that your answer makes sense. Do not ever let the calculator short-circuit your brain! Remember—the calculator is not the final authority on the answer to any question.

How to Use the Graphing Calculator

The discussion below refers to the TI-84 Plus graphing calculator. All graphing calculators, however, have similar features. Be sure to know your own calculator!

What follows is not a comprehensive manual. It assumes you are familiar with your own graphing calculator and summarizes features that may be useful for the ACT Test. You probably know a lot more than what is shown here!

> **REMEMBER**
>
> Bring and use the graphing calculator that you are used to using.

1. The MODE button shows all the default settings highlighted on the left. Please take note of whether Degree or Radian is selected for the angle mode. On the ACT, the questions may use either radians or degrees.

2. The "top" level of the calculator is where you will do arithmetic calculations and work with trig functions.

3. The $y =$ button gets you to the window where you will type the formulas for functions whose graphs you want to view. The functions must be in the form $y =$. For example, if you want to graph $2x - y = 5$, you need to rewrite it as $y = 2x - 5$ before you can type it in. You must use the X,T,θ,n button for x and the $-$ button for subtraction. The (–) is for negation. Example: Here is how you would type in $y = -(x - 4)^2$:

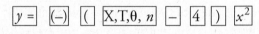

4. The 2nd button allows you to access the "blue" functions. Thus 2nd x^2 gets you the radical sign, $\sqrt{}$, since it is in blue above the x^2 button. For example, here is how you would enter $y = \sqrt{2x - 3}$:

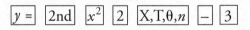

No closing parenthesis is required.

5. The GRAPH button gives you the graphing window, with both x- and y-axes ranging from –10 to 10. Your graph should appear.

6. The WINDOW button allows you to change the range of numbers on the x- and y-axes. Be sure to use the negation key, (–), for negative numbers.

7. The TRACE button allows you to use the right- and left-arrow keys to get the coordinates of points on the graph.

8. The CALC menu allows some very useful operations after you have sketched a graph. Since CALC is in blue above the TRACE button, you must press 2nd TRACE. Here is what the CALC menu allows:

value If you enter any x, you will get the corresponding y value.

zero This gives a zero of the function, that is, an x-intercept of the graph. Use the left- and right-arrow keys to bracket the root. Just to the left of the root, hit ENTER. Move just to the right, and hit ENTER twice. The graphing calculator will give you that x-intercept.

minimum and maximum This gives any minimum or maximum point on the graph. Again, you bracket the desired point. Get close to it on the left, press ENTER, get close to it on the right, press ENTER twice, and the calculator will give you an estimate of the coordinates of the desired point.

9. The MATH menu allows you to get cubes, cube roots, and absolute value. For example, to find $\sqrt[3]{625}$, go to the top level of the calculator. (2nd MODE is the way to QUIT and go there.) Then MATH 4 selects $\sqrt[3]{}$. Now type 625 ENTER, and you will get the answer 8.549879733. For example, to graph $y = |x + 4|$, MATH NUM abs gets you $y =$ abs (, and you can now enter $x + 4$.

Prohibited Calculators

Here is the list of calculators that you may not use.

- All Texas Instruments with model numbers that start with **TI-89** or **TI-92**
- Texas Instruments **TI-Nspire CAS** (Note that the **TI-Nspire** non-**CAS** *is* allowed)
- Hewlett-Packard with model numbers that start with **hp 40G**, **hp 49G**, or **hp 50G**
- Hewlett-Packard **hp 48GII**
- Casio with model numbers that start with **CFX-9970G**
- Casio **Algebra fx 2.0**
- Casio **ClassPad 300**
- Calculators with built-in computer algebra systems
- Pocket organizers
- Laptop or handheld computers
- Electronic writing pads or pen-input devices (Note that the **Sharp EL 9600** *is* allowed)
- Cell phone calculators
- Calculators whose keys are in QWERTY format (Note that calculators with letter keys not in QWERTY format *are* allowed)

Calculators Permitted with Modification

If you modify your calculator as described below, then it will be allowed.

- For calculators with paper tape, remove the tape.
- For calculators that make noise, turn off the sound.
- If your calculator can communicate wirelessly with other calculators, completely cover the infrared data port with heavy opaque material, such as duct tape.
- For calculators with power cords, remove all power and electrical cords.

Here is a final note to ponder. Make sure that your calculator works on the day of the ACT Test. This is serious. Not even the finest calculator will work without reliable batteries.

Pre-Algebra

CHAPTER 2

> ## CHAPTER GOALS
>
> - What you should expect
> - Specific strategies
> - Using a calculator
> - Topics in pre-algebra
> - Ace the ACT! Sample pre-algebra questions

WHAT SHOULD YOU EXPECT?

Almost one-fourth of the 60 multiple-choice questions on the ACT Math Test deal with basic math and arithmetic that you learned when you were in the cradle (OK, when you were in elementary or middle school). Do not start celebrating. As with all ACT topics, these questions can range from easy to hard. In many of the questions, tried-and-true school techniques will not necessarily lead to the solutions. Some questions will need no more than a little imagination and a lot of common sense.

What will you be tested on in these questions? The answer is just about all the math you learned before high school: number sets, fractions, decimals, powers, square roots, ratios, percents, prime numbers, factors, multiples, scientific notation, absolute value, and ordering of numbers. You will also see simple linear equations in one variable; simple counting and probability; interpretation of straightforward graphs; and simple statistics, namely mean, median, mode, and weighted averages. Whew! Quite a list. Chances are good that you have at least a passing familiarity with these topics.

SPECIFIC STRATEGIES

Here are some nonclassroom strategies that work well for certain types of problems.

Pick a Number

The perfect candidates for this strategy are percent problems and problems with fractions. What does it mean to pick a number, and which numbers should you pick? Pick a hypothetical starting amount and solve the problem using that amount. You may be surprised at how often this technique leads you straight to the answer.

- For percent problems, start with 100.
- For problems with fractions, pick the least common denominator (LCD) of the fractions.

Example 1

In a certain election, several students collected signatures to place a candidate on the ballot. Unfortunately, 25% of the signatures were thrown out for being invalid. Then a further 20% of those remaining were thrown out. What percent of the original signatures was left?

A. 40%
B. 45%
C. 50%
D. 55%
E. 60%

SOLUTION

(E) This is a percent problem, so assume that you start with 100 signatures. 25% of 100 thrown out means 25 are thrown out and 75 are left. 20% of 75 thrown out means 15 are thrown out and 60 are left. Therefore, 60 out of the original 100 are left, which is 60%.

Example 2

Mary has d dollars to spend and goes on a shopping spree. First she spends $\frac{2}{5}$ of her money on shoes. Then she spends $\frac{3}{4}$ of what is left on books.

Finally, she buys a raffle ticket that costs $\frac{1}{3}$ of her remaining dollars. What fraction of d is left?

F. $\frac{1}{10}$

G. $\frac{3}{20}$

H. $\frac{1}{5}$

J. $\frac{3}{10}$

K. $\frac{23}{60}$

SOLUTION

(F) This is similar to the percent problem in example 1, but now fractions are used. So you should pick the LCD of the fractions to replace *d*, the original amount of dollars. The LCD of 3, 4, and 5 is 60.

$\frac{2}{5}$ of 60, namely 24, is spent, which leaves 36.

$\frac{3}{4}$ of 36, namely 27, is then spent, which leaves 9.

$\frac{1}{3}$ of 9 is then spent, which leaves 6.

$\frac{6}{60} = \frac{1}{10}$ is the fraction of the original amount left.

 The pick-a-number strategy is a neat trick that should pop into your head whenever there is a tricky-sounding question in a setting that involves percents or fractions.

Memorize Some Common Values

In this day and age, memorizing stuff for tests is *so* nineteenth century. Still, you should know the following by heart since they come up so often on the ACT Test. You know most of them anyway.

$$\frac{1}{2} = 0.5 = 50\%$$

$$\frac{1}{3} = 0.\overline{3} = 33\frac{1}{3}\%$$

$$\frac{1}{4} = 0.25 = 25\%$$

$$\frac{1}{5} = 0.2 = 20\%$$

$$\frac{1}{10} = 0.1 = 10\%$$

$$\frac{2}{3} = 0.\overline{6} = 66\frac{2}{3}\%$$

$$\frac{3}{4} = 0.75 = 75\%$$

 Save time by having the commonly used values at your fingertips.

Calculations with Decimals

 Use the calculator!

Fraction Tricks

Here is a well-kept secret.

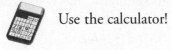 Your graphing calculator has some neat fraction tricks up its sleeve.

Reduce a fraction When big numbers are involved, this is really helpful. For example, it is not apparent at a glance that $\frac{85}{102}$ can be reduced. Use the frac feature on the graphing calculator as follows: Type in 85/102 [MATH] frac [ENTER], and you will see the answer, 5/6, displayed.

Convert a decimal to a fraction Type the decimal or if you already have it displayed as the answer to a calculation, follow the decimal with [MATH] frac [ENTER], and you'll see the equivalent fraction displayed on the screen.

Convert a fraction to a decimal Just type in the fraction and hit [ENTER]. Voila!

Convert a repeating decimal to a fraction To change a repeating decimal, such as $0.\overline{6}$, type two rows of 6s after the decimal. Then type [MATH] frac [ENTER] .

USING A CALCULATOR

 Use the calculator wisely. Each push of a button takes up valuable time.

If you use your graphing calculator for arithmetic, use the top level. For a calculation that involves more than one step, store intermediate results on the way to the answer. Either write these down or use the storage capacity of the calculator. Here is how: [STO] [ALPHA] [A] stores the current value in the key labeled A. To retrieve the value in key A, press [ALPHA] [A] [ENTER] . You can similarly store values in slots B, C, D, and so on.

Comparing Numbers

To compare two decimals, do a digit-by-digit comparison, starting on the left. For example, to compare 0.124 and 0.$\overline{12}$,

$$0 . 1\ 2\ ④ \qquad 0 . 1\ 2\ ①\ 2\ 1\ 2$$

Since 4 > 2, 0.124 > 0.$\overline{12}$.

To compare two fractions, for example $\frac{3}{4}$ and $\frac{2}{3}$, you can use two different methods.

Method 1: Common Denominators

The least common denominator of $\frac{3}{4}$ and $\frac{2}{3}$ is 12. Since $\frac{3}{4} = \frac{9}{12}$ and $\frac{2}{3} = \frac{8}{12}$,

the given problem is equivalent to comparing $\frac{9}{12}$ and $\frac{8}{12}$. Since 9 > 8, $\frac{3}{4} > \frac{2}{3}$.

Method 2: Decimals

Convert each fraction to a decimal and then compare the two decimals as shown above:

$$\frac{3}{4} = 0.75 \text{ and } \frac{2}{3} = 0.666666 \ldots$$

Since 0.75 > 0.66666 ..., $\frac{3}{4} > \frac{2}{3}$.

LCM and GCD

 Consider using your graphing calculator if the answer is not immediately apparent.

The *least common multiple* (LCM) of two numbers is the smallest integer that both divide into exactly. For example, the LCM of 8 and 12 is 24. You do not need a calculator for that. The *greatest common divisor* (GCD) of two numbers is the largest integer that goes exactly into both numbers. For example, the GCD of 20 and 28 is 4.

Suppose you need to find the LCM of 16 and 28. Here is how your graphing calculator can find it for you: MATH num lcm (16, 28) ENTER shows 112 as the answer. If you are finding the GCD, select it from the num menu as shown above for LCM. To get the screen with lcm and gcf in the num menu, press the up-arrow key, [^].

Miscellaneous Strategies

- Always—but especially if you use the calculator—ask yourself if your answer makes sense. Is it in the ballpark?
- Use your *head*! It is a great tool. Often in these pre-algebra problems, applying common sense leads directly to the answer.

Here is a final thought to chew on. Notice that your school test-taking strategies are turned upside down on the ACT:

- Do *not* show your work!
- Careless mistakes *do* matter.

What follows is a summary of pre-algebra topics for the ACT. If you are confident about these early topics, skip the summary and go straight to the practice problems at the end of the chapter.

TOPICS IN PRE-ALGEBRA

Sets of Numbers

Many ACT questions involve nothing more than manipulation of numbers. Yet these questions can be tricky. For starters, you need to be clear about which numbers belong to which sets:

Integers	$\{\ldots -4, -3, -2, -1, 0, 1, 2, 3, 4, \ldots\}$
Nonnegative integers	$\{0, 1, 2, 3, 4, \ldots\}$
Positive integers	$\{1, 2, 3, 4, \ldots\}$
Negative integers	$\{\ldots -4, -3, -2, -1\}$
Even integers	$\{\ldots -4, -2, 0, 2, 4, \ldots\}$
Odd integers	$\{\ldots -5, -3, -1, 1, 3, 5, \ldots\}$

Consecutive Integers

Consecutive integers are two or more integers that directly follow each other. For example, 10, 11, 12 are consecutive integers. If n is an even integer, then n, $n + 2$, $n + 4$, are *consecutive even integers*. Notice that if n is odd, then n, $n + 2$, $n + 4$, represent *consecutive odd integers*.

Factors and Multiples

The *factors* of a positive integer n are the positive integers that can be divided into n without a remainder. For example, the factors of 18 are 1, 2, 3, 6, 9, 18. The *multiples* of n are the positive integers that have n as a factor. For example, the multiples of 7 are 7, 14, 21, 28, 35, ...

> ## DIVISIBILITY RULES
> - A number is divisible by 2 if it is even.
> - A number is divisible by 3 if the sum of its digits is divisible by 3.
> - A number is divisible by 4 if its last two digits are a number divisible by 4.
> - A number is divisible by 5 if it ends in a 5 or 0.
> - A number is divisible by 6 if it is even and the sum of its digits is divisible by 3. This means that the number must be divisible by 2 and by 3.
> - There is no good rule for 7. Sorry!
> - A number is divisible by 8 if its last three digits are a number divisible by 8.
> - A number is divisible by 9 if the sum of its digits is divisible by 9.
> - A number is divisible by 12 if it is divisible by both 3 and 4.

For example, the number 21618

- Is divisible by 2 because it is even.
- Is divisible by 3 and by 9 because 2 + 1 + 6 + 1 + 8 = 18, which is divisible by both 3 and 9.
- Is divisible by 6 because it is divisible by both 2 and 3.

None of the other divisibility rules work for 21618. Try them!

Example 3

A four-digit integer is divisible by 12. If the first two digits of the integer are 32, what must the last two digits be?

A. 00
B. 08
C. 44
D. 46
E. 64

SOLUTION

(E) According to choice (E), the four-digit integer is 3264. You are given that the number is divisible by 12, which means that it must be divisible by both 3 and 4. Therefore, the sum of the digits must be divisible by 3 and the last two digits must be divisible by 4. Eliminate choice (D), 46, which is not divisible by 4. You can also eliminate choices (A), (B), and (C), because the sum of the digits of each resulting number is not divisible by 3. For example, look at choice (C). The number cannot be 3244 because 3 + 2 + 4 + 4 = 13, which is not divisible by 3.

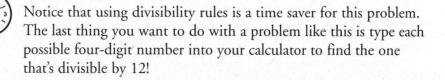 Notice that using divisibility rules is a time saver for this problem. The last thing you want to do with a problem like this is type each possible four-digit number into your calculator to find the one that's divisible by 12!

Prime Numbers

A *prime number* has exactly two factors, 1 and itself. This means that the number 1 is not prime. (It has just one factor!) The number 2 is the only even prime number.

The *prime factorization* of an integer is the product of its prime factors. For example, the prime factorization of 45 is $3^2 \times 5$.

Rational Numbers

The *set of rational numbers* is the set of all numbers that can be written as a fraction $\frac{a}{b}$, where *a* and *b* are integers and $b \neq 0$.

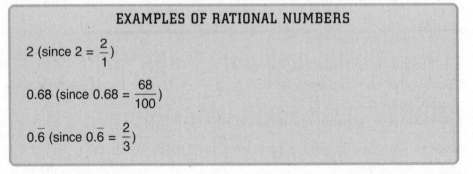

EXAMPLES OF RATIONAL NUMBERS

2 (since $2 = \frac{2}{1}$)

0.68 (since $0.68 = \frac{68}{100}$)

$0.\overline{6}$ (since $0.\overline{6} = \frac{2}{3}$)

 Notice that the *decimal equivalent* of a fraction can be obtained by dividing the numerator (top) by the denominator. Your calculator will do this for you in the blink of an eye.

> **TIP**
>
> Every integer, terminating decimal, and nonterminating *repeating* decimal is a rational number.

Example 4

Which digit is in the 60th decimal place of the decimal equivalent of $\frac{5}{11}$?

F. 1
G. 2
H. 3
J. 4
K. 5

SOLUTION

(K) Your calculator tells you that $\frac{5}{11} = 0.45454545\ldots$

Notice that there is a 4 in decimal places 1, 3, 5, 7, and so on, and a 5 in decimal places 2, 4, 6, 8, . . ., 60. The answer is 5.

Calculations with Fractions

ADDITION AND SUBTRACTION

> **QUICK AND EASY**
> - To get the denominator of the answer, multiply the denominators.
> - To get the numerator of the answer, take the sum (or difference for subtraction) of the "cross" products.
> - Reduce your answer.

For example, $\dfrac{3}{10} + \dfrac{4}{7} = \dfrac{40+21}{70} = \dfrac{61}{70}$.

Note that the "cross" products in this case are (10×4) and (7×3).

A note about subtraction. The order of subtraction matters. If the first fraction is larger than the second fraction, you get a positive answer. If it is smaller, the answer is negative.

MULTIPLICATION

> **MULTIPLYING TWO FRACTIONS**
> - To get the denominator of the answer, multiply the denominators.
> - To get the numerator of the answer, multiply the numerators.
> - Reduce your answer.

For example, $\dfrac{3}{10} \cdot \dfrac{4}{7} = \dfrac{3 \times 4}{10 \times 7} = \dfrac{12}{70} = \dfrac{6}{35}$.

Note that you could cancel first, dividing 2 into both 4 and 10, and then multiply.

DIVISION

To divide one fraction by another simply multiply the first fraction by the reciprocal of the second. For example,

$$\frac{3}{10} \div \frac{4}{7} = \frac{3}{10} \cdot \frac{7}{4} = \frac{3 \times 7}{10 \times 4} = \frac{21}{40}$$

COMPOUND FRACTIONS

How would you simplify this? $\dfrac{\dfrac{4}{5} - \dfrac{3}{8}}{\dfrac{11}{20}}$

Method 1

Calculate the numerator and denominator separately. Then divide.

$$\frac{\dfrac{4}{5}-\dfrac{3}{8}}{\dfrac{11}{20}} = \frac{\dfrac{32-15}{40}}{\dfrac{11}{20}} = \frac{17}{40} \div \frac{11}{20} = \frac{17}{40} \cdot \frac{20}{11} = \frac{17}{22}$$

Method 2

Multiply each fraction by the LCD of the fractions.

The LCD of 5, 8, and 20 is 40. Multiply the numerator and denominator of the compound fraction by 40. You must then be sure to multiply each of the fractions by 40.

$$\frac{\dfrac{4}{5}-\dfrac{3}{8}}{\dfrac{11}{20}} = \frac{40\left(\dfrac{4}{5}-\dfrac{3}{8}\right)}{40\left(\dfrac{11}{20}\right)} = \frac{32-15}{40} = \frac{17}{22}$$

Example 5

A farmer buys $96\dfrac{3}{4}$ pounds of chicken feed. If one chicken on his farm eats $2\dfrac{3}{5}$ pounds of feed, what is the maximum number of chickens that can be fed with this purchase?

A. 37
B. 38
C. 42
D. 43
E. 48

SOLUTION

(A) Number of chickens = $\dfrac{96\dfrac{3}{4}}{2\dfrac{3}{5}}$. By far the easiest and fastest route to the answer is to use your calculator and the knowledge that $\dfrac{3}{4} = 0.75$ and $\dfrac{3}{5} = 0.6$.

$$\frac{96\dfrac{3}{4}}{2\dfrac{3}{5}} = \frac{96.75}{2.6} = 37.21153846$$

Ignore the decimal part of the answer. The maximum number of whole chickens is 37.

Powers/Exponents

MEANING

"The fourth power of 3" is equal to $3 \times 3 \times 3 \times 3$ and can be written 3^4. The *base* is 3 and *exponent* is 4.

MULTIPLYING POWERS

When multiplying powers with the same base, add the exponents. For example,

$$6^4 \times 6^3 = 6^{4+3} = 6^7.$$

$$x^m \times x^n = x^{m+n}$$

DIVIDING POWERS

When dividing powers with the same base, subtract the exponents. For example,

$$2^4 \div 2^2 = \frac{2^4}{2^2} = 2^{4-2} = 2^2 = 4.$$

$$x^m \div x^n = \frac{x^m}{x^n} = x^{m-n}$$

RAISING A POWER TO A POWER

When raising a power to a power, multiply the exponents. For example,

$$(3^2)^4 = 3^{2 \times 4} = 3^8$$

$$(x^m)^n = x^{mn}$$

THE ZERO POWER

Any number or expression raised to the zero power equals one. For example,

$$4^0 = 1$$

$$x^0 = 1, x \neq 0$$

NEGATIVE POWERS

A number raised to a negative power is the reciprocal of the number raised to the positive power.

For example, $2^{-3} = \dfrac{1}{2^3}$, and $\dfrac{1}{3^{-2}} = 3^2$.

$$x^{-m} = \frac{1}{x^m}$$

$$\frac{1}{x^{-n}} = x^n$$

FRACTIONAL POWERS

A number raised to the fractional power $\dfrac{m}{n}$ is the nth root of the number raised to the mth power.

For example, $25^{\frac{1}{2}} = \sqrt{25} = 5$ and $27^{\frac{2}{3}} = \left(\sqrt[3]{27}\right)^2 = 3^2 = 9$.

$$x^{\frac{1}{n}} = \sqrt[n]{x}$$

$$x^{\frac{m}{n}} = \left(\sqrt[n]{x}\right)^m = \sqrt[n]{x^m}$$

Squares and Square Roots

Perfect squares pop up frequently on the ACT. Even though your calculator can help you here, you should recognize the first twenty perfect squares: 1, 4, 9, 16, 25, 36, 49, 64, 81, 100, 121, 144, 169, 196, 225, 256, 289, 324, 361, 400. Every positive number has two *square roots*, a positive and a negative number. Thus the square root of 64 can be 8 or −8. The symbol $\sqrt{64}$ represents the positive square root, 8, while $-\sqrt{64}$ represents the negative square root, −8.

MULTIPLYING AND DIVIDING SQUARE ROOTS

Simply multiply or divide the numbers under the radical sign.

For example, $\sqrt{6}\sqrt{7} = \sqrt{6 \times 7} = \sqrt{42}$, and $\sqrt{\dfrac{7}{4}} = \dfrac{\sqrt{7}}{\sqrt{4}} = \dfrac{\sqrt{7}}{2}$.

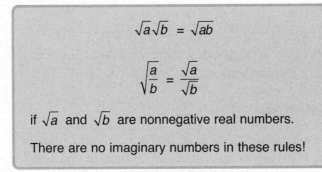

$$\sqrt{a}\sqrt{b} = \sqrt{ab}$$

$$\sqrt{\frac{a}{b}} = \frac{\sqrt{a}}{\sqrt{b}}$$

if $\sqrt{a}$ and $\sqrt{b}$ are nonnegative real numbers.

There are no imaginary numbers in these rules!

SIMPLIFYING RADICALS

In the radical $\sqrt{20}$, 20 is called the *radicand*. A radical is in *simple form* if the radicand has no perfect squares as factors. For example, $\sqrt{20}$ is not in simple form because 20 has 4 as a factor. To simplify: $\sqrt{20} = \sqrt{4 \times 5} = \sqrt{4}\sqrt{5} = 2\sqrt{5}$.

A fraction with radicals is in simple form if there are no radicals in the denominator. To simplify, multiply the fraction by 1 in a creative way. For example, $\dfrac{3}{\sqrt{2}}$ is not in simple form. To simplify:

$$\frac{3}{\sqrt{2}} = \frac{3}{\sqrt{2}} \cdot \frac{\sqrt{2}}{\sqrt{2}} = \frac{3\sqrt{2}}{\sqrt{2}}, \text{ since } \sqrt{2}\sqrt{2} = \sqrt{4} = 2.$$

 Your calculator can find powers and roots for you.

- For square roots, $\boxed{\text{2nd}}\ \boxed{x^2}$ is the square root function.

  For example, to find $\sqrt{289}$, $\boxed{\text{2nd}}\ \boxed{x^2}$ 289 $\boxed{\text{ENTER}}$ gives 17.

- For cube roots, use $\boxed{\text{MATH}}\ \sqrt[3]{\ }$.

  For example, to find $\sqrt[3]{216}$, $\boxed{\text{MATH}}\ \sqrt[3]{\ }$ 216 $\boxed{\text{ENTER}}$ gives 6.

  $\therefore \sqrt[3]{216} = 6$.

- For powers in general, use the $\boxed{\wedge}$ button. Be sure to put the exponent in brackets if it is a fraction because raising to an exponent has higher precedence than division. For example, take an expression that you have seen recently, $27^{\frac{2}{3}}$.

From the laws of exponents, you know that this is equal to $\left(\sqrt[3]{27}\right)^2 = 3^2 = 9$. However, if you type into your calculator 27 $\boxed{\wedge}$ 2 / 3, you get 243. Disaster! Here is what your calculator did: $(27^2) \div 3 = 729 \div 3 = 243$.

What you needed to type in the first place was actually

27 $\boxed{\wedge}$ (2 / 3).

 If you use your graphing calculator for exponents, put the exponents in parentheses.

Scientific Notation

Scientific notation is a convenient way of representing very small or very large numbers. The number is written as a number greater than or equal to 1 and less than 10 and is multiplied by a power of 10. For example,

$6.235 \times 10^6 = 6235000$ (move the decimal point 6 places to the right)
$2.08 \times 10^{-4} = 0.000208$ (move the decimal point 4 places to the left)

Example 6

If $x = 2.4 \times 10^6$ and $y = 6.0 \times 10^{-8}$, express xy, the product of x and y, in scientific notation.

F. 1.44×10^{-1}
G. 14.4×10^{-2}
H. 1.44×10^{-2}
J. 1.44×10^{-3}
K. 14.4×10^{-3}

SOLUTION

(F) 1.44×10^{-1}

Method 1: Rearrange terms and combine powers of 10.

$$xy = (2.4 \times 10^6)(6.0 \times 10^{-8})$$
$$= (2.4 \times 6.0)(10^6 \times 10^{-8})$$
$$= 14.4 \times 10^{-2}$$

If it looks to you like choice (G) is the correct answer, look again! In scientific notation, the number preceding the power of 10 must be greater than or equal to 1 and less than 10. You need to rewrite 14.4×10^{-2} as $(1.44 \times 10^1) \times 10^{-2} = 1.44 \times 10^{-1}$.

Method 2: Graphing calculator.

Set the $\boxed{\text{MODE}}$ to sci (Scientific Notation) and type in $2.4 \times 10\char`\^6 \times 6.0 \times 10\char`\^(^-8)$. Your calculator will tell you that the answer is 1.44E⁻1, which means 1.44×10^{-1}. If you do not use scientific notation mode, you will need to convert the decimal answer, .144, to scientific notation, namely 1.44×10^{-1}.

Ratios, Proportions, and Percents

RATIO

A *ratio* is a quotient of two quantities. For example, suppose the ratio of boys to girls at a school is 4 to 5. This means that for every 4 boys, there are 5 girls. Another way of saying this is:

$$\frac{\text{Number of boys}}{\text{Number of girls}} = \frac{4}{5}$$

The ratio can also be denoted as:

$$\text{Number of boys : Number of girls} = 4 : 5$$

PERCENT

A *percent* is a ratio in which the second quantity is 100. For example,

$$23\% = \frac{23}{100} = 0.23.$$

PROPORTION

A *proportion* is an equation that sets two ratios equal to each other. For example, $\frac{2}{5} = \frac{6}{15}$. Proportions are often used in the solution of ACT problems.

Example 7

The price of a toaster was originally marked at x dollars. The toaster went on sale at a 20% discount and was eventually sold for $50.40 after an additional 10% discount off the sale price. What was x, the original price of the toaster, in dollars?

A. $63
B. $70
C. $72
D. $168
E. $201

SOLUTION

(B) This is a tricky problem that can be simplified using the pick-a-number strategy. Instead of working backward from the actual price, note that the problem deals with percents. So start with $x = \$100$.

A 20% discount leaves a sale price of $80.

An additional 10% discount leaves a final price of $72, which is 72% of $100.

Therefore $50.40, the actual final price paid, was 72% of x, the original price.

Set up the following proportion: $\dfrac{72}{100} = \dfrac{50.40}{x}$

Cross multiply to solve for x: $x = \dfrac{(50.40)(100)}{72} = \$70$.

PERCENT INCREASE AND DECREASE

Some of the more challenging problems on the ACT involve *percent increase* or *percent decrease.* The percent increase of a quantity equals

$$\frac{\text{amount of increase}}{\text{original amount}} \cdot \frac{100}{1}.$$

The percent decrease of a quantity equals

$$\frac{\text{amount of decrease}}{\text{original amount}} \cdot \frac{100}{1}.$$

Example 8

The following chart shows the cost of one DVD player at a discount store during the first six months of the year.

Month	Jan.	Feb.	March	April	May	June
Cost	$200.99	$195.99	$150.00	$150.00	$135.99	$120.85

Which of the following is closest to the percent decrease in the cost of the DVD player from January to June?

F. 12%
G. 40%
H. 50%
J. 60%
K. 66%

SOLUTION

(G) Actual decrease = cost in Jan. − cost in June = \$200.99 − \$120.85 = \$80.14.

Percent decrease = $\dfrac{80.14}{200.99} \cdot 100 \approx 40\%$

 Don't waste time using a calculator for the final calculation.

You can see that the fraction is approximately $\dfrac{80}{200}$ which is

$\dfrac{40}{100}$ or 40%.

Counting, Permutations, Combinations, and Probability

COUNTING

To answer the question "How many ways can . . .?" sounds simple. You just count. These problems, however, can be tricky.

The basic rule of counting says that if event 1 can happen *k* different ways and an independent event, event 2, can happen *m* different ways, then the total number of ways both events can happen is *km*. A typical problem is the clothing problem. If you have 3 pairs of jeans and 10 T-shirts, you have a choice of 3 × 10 = 30 different outfits, where an outfit consists of a pair of jeans and a T-shirt.

Note that this rule can be extended to more than two events. If, in addition to your jeans and T-shirts, you have 4 hats, the number of different possible outfits goes up to 10 × 3 × 4 = 120, where an outfit consists of a pair of jeans, a T-shirt, and a hat.

PERMUTATIONS AND COMBINATIONS

A *permutation* is the number of arrangements of *n* objects, where each different ordering of the objects counts as one permutation. The order of the objects is important. For example, how many arrangements are there of the letters E, X, A, M? Imagine having four slots:

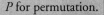

REMEMBER
P for permutation.
P for particular.
A permutation depends on the particular order of the objects.

You have 4 choices for the first slot, 3 choices for the second slot, and 2 choices for the third slot. By the time you get to the fourth slot, there is no choice. Just one letter is left. Therefore, the total number of permutations is 4 × 3 × 2 × 1 = 24. It is important to understand that EXAM and MAXE, for example, are different permutations.

Contrast this with the problem of calculating the number of three-person committees that can be formed from six people who are willing to serve. There are $6 \times 5 \times 4$ ways of selecting three people. If the order of their selection, however, is irrelevant—Mary-Tom-Nick is the same committee as Nick-Mary-Tom—you must divide by $3 \times 2 \times 1$ because each group of three can be chosen six different ways. When the order of choosing is not important, each arrangement is called a *combination*.

PROBABILITY

Events

Suppose an experiment is performed. An *event E* is a set of particular outcomes of this experiment. If set *S* is the set of all possible outcomes of the experiment, then *E* is a subset of *S*. For example, consider the experiment of flipping a fair coin and tossing a fair six-sided die. The set *S* of all possible outcomes is

$$S = \{1H, 2H, 3H, 4H, 5H, 6H, 1T, 2T, 3T, 4T, 5T, 6T\}.$$

Here are some events for the above experiment:

A = {Getting a prime number and tails} = {2T, 3T, 5T}.
B = {Getting heads on the coin }= {1H, 2H, 3H, 4H, 5H, 6H}.
C = {Getting a 4 on the die} = {4H, 4T}.

The Probability of an Event

The *probability* of an event E, $P(E)$, is given as follows. If E can occur in m ways out of a total of n equally likely ways,

$$P(E) = \frac{m}{n} = \frac{\text{Number of outcomes in event } E}{\text{Total number of possible outcomes}}$$

For the coin/die experiment above, all 12 outcomes in set S are equally likely. The probabilities of events A, B, and C (given above) are

$$P(A) = \frac{3}{12} = \frac{1}{4}, P(B) = \frac{6}{12} = \frac{1}{2}, P(C) = \frac{2}{12} = \frac{1}{6}.$$

In the coin/die experiment, the probability of getting a 4 on the die, $P(C)$, is $\frac{1}{6}$.

The probability of *not* getting a 4 on the die = $P(C') = 1 - P(C) = 1 - \frac{1}{6} = \frac{5}{6}$.

PROBABILITY REMINDERS

- If event E is an empty set, it represents an *impossible event*. $P(E) = 0$.
- If $E = S$, it represents a *certain event*. $P(E) = 1$.
- If E is a nonempty, nonequal subset of S, then $0 < P(E) < 1$.
- E', the *complement* of E, is the set containing all the elements of S that are not in E. Thus the probability that event E will *not* happen is given by $P(E') = 1 - P(E)$.

Example 9

The spinner in the diagram randomly stops in any of the numbered regions shown. Given that the spinner is equally likely to land in any of the regions, what is the probability that the spinner will land on 2, 3, or 4?

A. $\dfrac{1}{512}$

B. $\dfrac{1}{4}$

C. $\dfrac{1}{2}$

D. $\dfrac{3}{8}$

E. $\dfrac{1}{3}$

SOLUTION

(D) Notice that there are 3 regions with a successful outcome: 2, 3, and 4. Since the total number of possible outcomes is 8, $P(2, 3, \text{ or } 4)$ is $\dfrac{3}{8}$.

Alternatively, for any one region, the probability that the spinner will land there is $\dfrac{1}{8}$, since each of the 8 regions is equally likely.

$$P(2, 3, \text{ or } 4) = P(2) + P(3) + P(4)$$
$$= \dfrac{1}{8} + \dfrac{1}{8} + \dfrac{1}{8}$$
$$= \dfrac{3}{8}$$

Simple Statistics

ARITHMETIC MEAN

The *arithmetic mean* (or the average) of n values $= \dfrac{\text{sum of } n \text{ values}}{n}$.

For example, a strong ACT student has the following test scores in math (so far): 98, 94, 98, 78, 82, 80, 92.

$$\text{The arithmetic mean of his scores} = \frac{98 + 94 + 98 + 78 + 82 + 80 + 92}{7}$$

$$\approx 88.9$$

MEDIAN

To find the *median* of n values, arrange the numbers in order. If n is odd, the median is the middle number. If n is even, the median is the arithmetic mean of the two middle numbers. For example, to find the median of those test scores above, arrange them in order: 78, 80, 82, $\boxed{92}$, 94, 98, 98. The median score is 92.

Suppose the same student takes another test and has a really bad day, scoring 70. His scores, in order, are now 70, 78, 80, $\boxed{82, 92}$, 94, 98, 98. The number of scores is even, and the median equals $\dfrac{82 + 92}{2} = 87$.

MODE

The *mode* of a list of values is the value that occurs the most often. Look at these test scores: 70, 78, 80, 82, 92, 94, 98, 98. The mode is 98 since 98 is the only value that appears more than once. It is possible to have more than one mode in a list. For example, the list 1, 1, 6, 6, 6, 9, 9, 10, 11, 11, 11, 14, 16, 20, 20, 20 has three modes: 6, 11, and 20.

It is also possible for a list to have no mode if each of the values appears exactly the same number of times as each of the other values. For example, the list 2, 2, 2, 4, 4, 4, 9, 9, 9 has no mode.

WEIGHTED AVERAGE

A *weighted average* is the average of two or more sets of values in which the sets do not all have the same size. For example, if a class is divided into three groups:

- Group A, with 10 students, has a test average of 65.
- Group B, with 5 students, has a test average of 90.
- Group C, with 7 students, has a test average of 80.

To find the class average, you should know that what you *cannot* do is find $\dfrac{65 + 90 + 80}{3}$. What you have to do is weight each score by multiplying by the

> **REMEMBER**
>
> When an ACT question asks for the average, it is asking you to find the arithmetic mean.

number of students in each group. Find the sum of the results and divide by 22, the total number of students.

$$\therefore \text{Arithmetic mean of scores } \frac{(65)(10) + (90)(5) + (80)(7)}{22} \approx 75.5$$

Example 10

The Hadleys took a car trip to visit relatives. Mr. Hadley drove for 2 hours and covered 100 miles. For the last 60 miles, their teenage son, Hank, drove. He took 1 hour to complete this leg of the trip. What was the average speed, in miles per hour, for the trip?

F. 50

G. $53\frac{1}{3}$

H. 55

J. $56\frac{2}{3}$

K. 60

SOLUTION

(G) The average speed is $53\frac{1}{3}$ mph.

You are asked for the average speed, which means that you must find the arithmetic mean of the speeds.

The family drove 2 hours at $\frac{100}{2} = 50$ mph.

The family drove 1 hour at $\frac{60}{1} = 60$ mph.

The average to be found is a weighted average.

$$\therefore \text{Average speed} = \frac{(50)(2) + (60)(1)}{3} = \frac{160}{3} = 53\frac{1}{3} \text{ mph.}$$

Another way to think of this is Average speed $= \dfrac{\text{Total distance}}{\text{Total time}}$.

Charts and Graphs

TABLES

On the ACT, you will be asked to interpret information that is presented in tables and graphs. Sometimes you will be asked to do calculations based on that information.

Example 11

In a certain school district, teachers are allowed to take 3 personal days, at full pay, during one school year. Here is a summary of the number of personal days taken by teachers in 2007–2008.

Number of Personal Days Available to Teachers	Number of Teachers Who Took Personal Days
0	Fewer than 10
1	50
2	200
3	85

From this table, you can accurately find the

   I. arithmetic mean of personal days taken
  II. median number of personal days taken
 III. mode of the number of personal days taken

A. I only
B. II only
C. III only
D. II and III only
E. I, II, and III

SOLUTION

(D) Think of the data laid out, in order, like this:

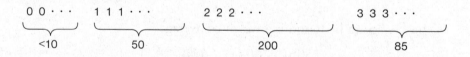

It is not possible to find the arithmetic mean because you do not know how many items are in the list. "Fewer than 10" is too vague. (What will the denominator be?) You can see, however, that 2 is the middle number, whether 0 occurs zero times or nine times. Therefore, the median is 2. You can also find the mode: 2 occurs more often than the other numbers.

GRAPHS

Circle Graphs

In a *circle graph* or *pie chart*, the size of the wedges is proportional to the size of the numbers represented.

Example 12

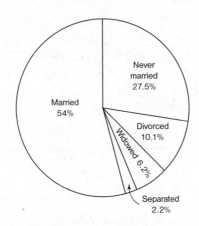

The graph shows the marital status of U.S. citizens over age 15 in 2003. If the total number of U.S. citizens over age 15 was approximately 222 million in 2003, how many, to the nearest million, were divorced or separated?

F. 2 million
G. 3 million
H. 10 million
J. 22 million
K. 27 million

SOLUTION

(K) The pie chart shows that the number divorced or separated add up to 10.1% + 2.2% =12.3%.

12.3% of 222 million ≈ 27 million.

 Don't waste time using your calculator here. 10% of 222 ≈ 22, so you should pick the only answer choice that is greater than 22.

Line Graphs

A *line graph* or *time plot* is a good way to examine trends over a given time period. Here is a double-line graph that shows the life expectancy at birth for males born in the U.S. between 1920 and 2000.

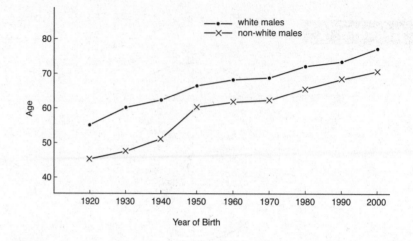

From this graph, you can see many trends:

- The life expectancy of men in the U.S. has increased from 1920–2000.
- The life expectancy of white males in the U.S. has been greater than that of nonwhite males from 1920–2000.
- From 1920–2000, the greatest difference in life expectancy between white and nonwhite males occurred in 1930, a difference of about 13 years.

Bar Graphs

Another way to display data is in a *bar graph*. Each bar represents a different category. The height of the bar represents a numerical value for that category. The bar graph shown compares the percents of several age groups who have completed four or more years of college:

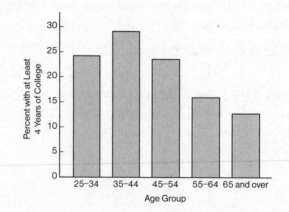

The graph shows that almost 30 percent of people aged 35–44 have completed at least four years of college. Also, at a glance, you can see that older people are less likely to have completed four years of college.

Pictographs

A *pictograph* presents data using pictorial symbols. Typically, one symbol represents a fixed number of items. The pictograph below shows the number of students who graduated each year from a small college.

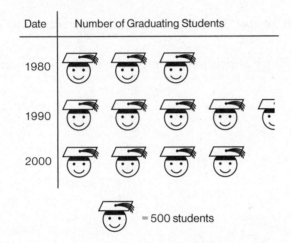

Date	Number of Graduating Students

= 500 students

From the graph you can see that about 2250 students graduated in 1990. But there were only 1500 graduates in 1980.

Scatter Plots

A *scatter plot* is a graph of ordered pairs (x, y) that assists in finding a relationship between the variables x and y. Often, but not always, the variable along the x-axis is a predictor for the variable along the y-axis. For example, if the scatter plot shows the height of people (x-axis) plotted against their weight (y-axis), one might expect taller people to weigh more.

On the ACT, you may be asked a question about the *line of best fit* for a scatter plot. This is a straight line that passes through the arithmetic means of the x and y variables. Roughly speaking, this line has the same number of points on either side of it. Sometimes called the trend line, the line of best fit indicates the correlation between the variables. If the slope is positive, there is a *positive correlation* between the variables. This means that as one variable increases, so does the other. If the slope is negative, the correlation between the variables is negative. This means that as one variable increases, the other decreases. For example, a scatter plot of GPAs of high school students versus the number of hours per day they spend reading would be expected to show a positive correlation. (See the left diagram on the next page.) On the other hand, a scatter plot of GPAs of high school students versus number of hours per day they spend watching television would be expected to show a negative correlation (as in the diagram on the right).

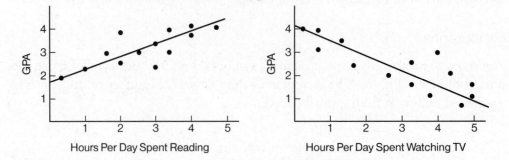

Hours Per Day Spent Reading   Hours Per Day Spent Watching TV

Are you ready to try a mixture of sample pre-algebra ACT questions?

Ace the ACT!
Sample Pre-Algebra Questions

1. How many prime numbers are between 20 and 30?

   A. 1
   B. 2
   C. 3
   D. 4
   E. 5

2. A candy jar contains 20 candies: 8 are orange, 7 are green, and 5 are red. Two candies are picked at random and eaten. If both of these are orange, what is the probability that the next candy, picked at random, is also orange?

   F. $\dfrac{3}{20}$

   G. $\dfrac{1}{4}$

   H. $\dfrac{3}{10}$

   J. $\dfrac{1}{3}$

   K. $\dfrac{2}{5}$

3. In a shipment of 10,000 headlights, 5% are defective. What is the ratio of defective headlights to nondefective headlights?

   A. $\dfrac{1}{19}$

   B. $\dfrac{1}{20}$

   C. $\dfrac{19}{1}$

   D. $\dfrac{20}{1}$

   E. $\dfrac{1}{5}$

4. Which of the following is equal to $\sqrt{20}\,\sqrt{3}$?

   F. $2\sqrt{30}$

   G. $2\sqrt{15}$

   H. $4\sqrt{15}$

   J. $3\sqrt{10}$

   K. $20\sqrt{3}$

5. If you travel 6.2 miles in 15 minutes, what was your average speed in miles per hour?

   A. 1.55
   B. 15.5
   C. 18.6
   D. 24.8
   E. 93.0

6. If $\dfrac{\frac{5}{8}}{0.25}$ is expressed as a fraction in lowest terms, what number will be in the denominator?

   F. 2
   G. 4
   H. 5
   J. 8
   K. 32

7. The choices for an ice cream sundae are as follows: chocolate or vanilla ice cream; hot fudge, strawberry, or butterscotch topping; and toasted almonds, cherry, or sprinkles as decoration. If you know that your sundae will have one ice cream, one topping, and one decoration, how many different choices for a sundae do you have?

   A. 6
   B. 8
   C. 9
   D. 12
   E. 18

8.

Population in Region *R* by Town		
σ = 10,000 people		
Town *A*	σ σ	
Town *B*	σ σ σ σ	
Town *C*	σ σ σ σ σ	
Town *D*	σ σ σ σ σ σ σ σ σ	

   If the four towns shown in the graph are the only towns in Region *R*, the total of which two towns account for exactly 45% of the population of Region *R*?

   F. Towns *A* and *B*
   G. Towns *B* and *C*
   H. Towns *A* and *C*
   J. Towns *A* and *D*
   K. Towns *B* and *D*

9. Let *A* = the set of all 3-digit positive integers with the digit 1 in the ones place, and let *B* = the set of all 3-digit positive integers with the digit 2 in the tens place. How many positive 3-digit integers are there that are in either *A* or *B* but not in both *A* and *B*?

   A. 162
   B. 171
   C. 180
   D. 182
   E. 191

10. Yan needs $2.37 in postage to mail a letter. If he has 60-cent, 37-cent, 23-cent, 5-cent and 1-cent stamps, at least 10 of each, what is the smallest number of stamps he can use that will get him the exact postage he needs?

   F. 6
   G. 7
   H. 8
   J. 9
   K. 13

11. The table below gives the number of questions answered correctly on the 20-question written section of a drivers' education test.

Number Correct	12	13	14	15	16	17	18	19	20
Frequency	2	3	0	3	3	5	5	6	4

What is the mode of the data?

A. 3
B. 6
C. 18
D. 19
E. 20

12. A typing class in elementary school is divided into 3 groups. The Red Robins, with 6 students, has an average typing speed of 60 words per minute. The Blue Wax Bills, with 10 students, has an average typing speed of 45 words per minute. The Gold Finches, with 16 students, has an average typing speed of 30 words per minute. Which of the following is closest to the average (arithmetic mean) of the typing speeds, in words per minute, for the class?

F. 27.8
G. 32.0
H. 40.3
J. 45.0
K. 55.7

Solutions and Explanations

1. **(B)**	4. **(G)**	7. **(E)**	10. **(H)**
2. **(J)**	5. **(D)**	8. **(G)**	11. **(D)**
3. **(A)**	6. **(F)**	9. **(A)**	12. **(H)**

1. **(B)** Recall that a prime number has exactly two factors, 1 and itself. Eliminate the even numbers, 22, 24, 26, and 28, since they are divisible by 2. Eliminate 21, 24, and 27, because they are divisible by 3. Eliminate 25 because it is divisible by 5. That leaves 23 and 29, the only two prime numbers between 20 and 30.

2. **(J)** After 2 orange candies are eaten, the jar contains 18 candies: 6 orange, 7 green, and 5 red. Thus, the probability of picking another orange candy is $\frac{6}{18} = \frac{1}{3}$.

3. **(A)** Did you notice that 10,000 was a red herring? You can solve the problem without it! Given that 5% are defective, for every 100 headlights, 5 are defective and 95 are OK. Therefore, the ratio of defective to nondefective headlights is $\frac{5}{95} = \frac{1}{19}$.

4. **(G)**
$$\sqrt{20}\,\sqrt{3} = \sqrt{20 \times 3}$$
$$= \sqrt{60}$$
$$= \sqrt{4 \times 15}$$
$$= \sqrt{4}\sqrt{15}$$
$$= 2\sqrt{15}$$

5. **(D)** 6.2 miles in 15 minutes

$\Rightarrow$ 6.2 miles in $\frac{1}{4}$ hour

$\Rightarrow (4)(6.2) = 24.8$ miles in 1 hour
The average speed = 24.8 miles per hour.

6. **(F)**

   Method 1: Recognize $0.25 = \dfrac{1}{4}$

   $$\frac{\frac{5}{8}}{0.25} = \frac{\frac{5}{8}}{\frac{1}{4}} = \frac{5}{8} \times \frac{4}{1} = \frac{5}{2}$$

   This shows that there is a 2 in the denominator.

   Method 2: Rewrite $\dfrac{5}{8}$ as 0.625

   $$\frac{\frac{5}{8}}{0.25} = \frac{0.625}{0.25} = 2.5 = 2\frac{1}{2} = \frac{5}{2}$$

7. **(E)** There are 2 choices for ice cream.
   There are 3 choices for topping.
   There are 3 choices for decoration.
   Each choice can go with each of the others.
   $2 \times 3 \times 3 = 18$ choices altogether.

8. **(G)** Since each little picture represents the same number of people, you can simplify the problem. Which combination of two towns accounts for 45% of the pictures? You do not need to multiply by 10,000 at any stage! Count the number of pictures: 20. 45% of 20 = $0.45 \times 20 = 9$. The only two towns that have a total of 9 pictures are towns B and C.

9. **(A)** Draw a picture of a 3-digit integer in set A.

H	T	O
		1

   There are 9 choices for the hundreds place, and 10 choices for the tens place. (Remember, the number cannot start with 0.) The ones place must contain 1, according to the information given. Therefore the number of permutations = $(9)(10)(1) = 90$ elements in A.

   Now draw a picture of a 3-digit integer in set B.

H	T	O
	2	

There are 9 choices for the hundreds place, 1 choice for the tens place, and 10 choices for the ones place. (Again, remember, the number cannot start with 0.) Therefore, the number of permutations = (9)(1)(10) = 90 elements in *B*. Thus, the number of integers in *A* or *B* is 90 + 90 = 180.

You must now count how many positive 3-digit integers have both a 1 in the ones place and a 2 in the tens place: 121, 221, 321, . . ., 921. There are just 9 elements! These 9 elements are in both *A* and *B* and must therefore be subtracted twice from 180. Thus, the required number of elements is 180 − 2(9) = 162.

10. **(G)** The fewest number of stamps is seven:

$$2(60 \text{ c}) + 3(37 \text{ c}) + 1(5 \text{ c}) + 1(1 \text{ c})$$

Notice that if Yan uses three 60-cent stamps, there is a remainder of 57 cents. He will then need eight stamps:

$$3(60 \text{ c}) + 1(37 \text{ c}) + 4(5 \text{ c})$$

OR

$$3(60 \text{ c}) + 2(23 \text{ c}) + 2(5 \text{ c}) + (1(1 \text{ c})$$

If Yan uses one 60-cent stamp or no 60-cent stamps, he will need at least eight stamps. Try it!

11. **(D)** The data items are the numbers of questions answered correctly. The mode is the value that occurs most frequently. Since the highest frequency is 6, the mode is 19.

12. **(H)** Recognize this as a weighted-average problem. Find the average of these typing speeds:

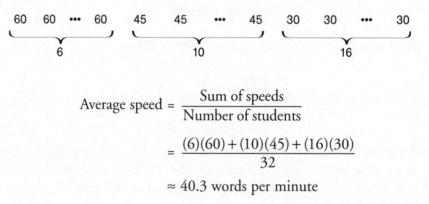

$$\text{Average speed} = \frac{\text{Sum of speeds}}{\text{Number of students}}$$

$$= \frac{(6)(60) + (10)(45) + (16)(30)}{32}$$

$$\approx 40.3 \text{ words per minute}$$

Elementary Algebra

CHAPTER GOALS
• Specific strategies • Topics in elementary algebra • Ace the ACT! Sample elementary algebra questions

About 9 (15%) of the 60 multiple-choice questions on the ACT Math Test involve topics and skills that you have been using for quite a while:

- Linear equations and inequalities
- Simple operations on polynomials
- Factoring polynomials
- Solving quadratic equations by factoring
- Translating English into algebra

Many of the questions, because of their familiarity, will be easy for you. Make no mistake, this section contains difficult questions too.

SPECIFIC STRATEGIES

Some of the same strategies that work well for arithmetic questions can be applied to problems that involve variables.

Plug In

In its simplest form, plugging in works whenever you are asked to find a specific value and you are given five numbers from which to choose. Instead of solving the problem from scratch and then optimistically seeking your answer among the choices, try plugging the given values into the problem to find the one that works. Remember, one of these choices is the right answer! Your job is to use an efficient method to find it.

Example 1

If $4x + 3 = 127$, then $x = ?$

A. 25
B. 31
C. 33
D. 41
E. 120

SOLUTION

(B) Notice that the answer choices are given in increasing order. A good idea is to start by plugging in the middle value, because you may be able to eliminate either the larger or the smaller answer choices. The idea is that if the middle value is too small, the numbers that are less than it will definitely be too small! Using choice (C) and plugging in 33 gives

$$4(33) + 3 = 132 + 3 = 135$$

This tells you that 33 is too big, which means that 41 and 120 are *way* too big, and can be eliminated. You are down to choosing between choices (A) and (B). Trying $x = 31$ yields the correct answer:

$$4(31) + 3 = 124 + 3 = 127$$

You will need to use your judgment about when to use a plug-in strategy. In the actual problem, if the equation is really simple, it will be quicker and easier just to solve the equation! You must be the judge.

Example 2

Which is a solution to $(8^x)(2^4) = \left(\dfrac{1}{2}\right)^x$?

F. -2
G. -1
H. $-\dfrac{1}{12}$
J. 0
K. $\dfrac{1}{2}$

SOLUTION

(G) A solution to the equation will give a true statement when you plug it in. Starting with choice (H) here is not wise. Plugging in $-\dfrac{1}{12}$ is much harder than plugging in 0 or –1. If choice (H) does not work, can you really tell whether to make x bigger or smaller? So start with choice (J) and plug in 0, an easy number. Recall that $a^0 = 1$.

$$(8^0)(2^4) \overset{?}{=} \left(\frac{1}{2}\right)^0$$

$$\Rightarrow (1)(16) \overset{?}{=} 1 \quad \text{False}$$

Try choice (G) and plug in –1. Recall that $a^{-1} = \dfrac{1}{a}$ and $\left(\dfrac{1}{a}\right)^{-1} = a$.

$$(8^{-1})(2^4) \overset{?}{=} \left(\frac{1}{2}\right)^{-1}$$

$$\Rightarrow \left(\frac{1}{8}\right)(16) \overset{?}{=} 2 \quad \text{True!}$$

No rule says you cannot use algebra if you know how to do it. When using an algebraic solution, write everything with the same base, in this case 2:

$$(8^x)(2^4) = \left(\frac{1}{2}\right)^x$$

$$\Rightarrow (2^3)^x 2^4 = (2^{-1})^x$$
$$\Rightarrow 2^{3x} \cdot 2^4 = 2^{-x}$$
$$\Rightarrow 2^{3x+4} = 2^{-x}$$
$$\Rightarrow 3x + 4 = -x$$
$$\Rightarrow x = -1$$

 To solve an exponential equation, write all factors in the problem as powers with the same base.

Pick a Number

Yes, the same pick-a-number strategy that works so well in many arithmetic problems works here too. Use it for problems that involve variables and for any problem in which your math teacher would suggest that you select variables and translate the English into algebra.

Example 3

If $a = b^2c$, where $a \neq 0$ and $b \neq 0$, then $\dfrac{b}{c} = ?$

A. $\dfrac{a}{c}$

B. $\dfrac{a}{b}$

C. $\dfrac{a}{bc}$

D. $\dfrac{a}{b^2c}$

E. $\dfrac{a}{bc^2}$

SOLUTION

(E) Suppose you pick $b = 2$ and $c = 3$. Then a must be 12 since $a = 2^2(3)$. Therefore, $\dfrac{b}{c} = \dfrac{2}{3}$. This is what you must get when you plug your values into the answer choices.

A. $\dfrac{a}{c} = \dfrac{12}{3} = 4$ No

B. $\dfrac{a}{b} = \dfrac{12}{2} = 6$ No

C. $\dfrac{a}{bc} = \dfrac{12}{6} = 2$ No

D. $\dfrac{a}{b^2c} = \dfrac{12}{12} = 1$ No

E. $\dfrac{a}{bc^2} = \dfrac{12}{18} = \dfrac{2}{3}$ Yes!

Example 4

A man has x dollars to be divided equally among p people. If n new people join the group, then each person gets how many fewer dollars than the original people would have received?

F. $\dfrac{xn}{p+n}$

G. $\dfrac{x}{p+n}$

H. $\dfrac{xn}{p^2+pn}$

J. $\dfrac{-xn}{p^2+pn}$

K. $\dfrac{-xn}{p+n}$

SOLUTION

(H) The key to doing this problem by plugging in numbers is to realize that x dollars are going to be divided among various numbers of people, so pick x to be a number with lots of factors. 36 is a good choice, and so is 20. Try $x = 20$, $p = 4$ (the original number of people), and $n = 6$ (the additional people). When \$20 is divided by 4, each person will get \$5. When \$20 is divided by (6 + 4), each person will get \$2. The answer to the question is \$5 – \$2 = \$3. Now plug your numbers into the answer choices to see which gives you 3.

F. $\dfrac{xn}{p+n} = \dfrac{(20)(6)}{10} = 12$ No

G. $\dfrac{x}{p+n} = \dfrac{20}{10} = 2$ No

H. $\dfrac{xn}{p^2+pn} = \dfrac{(20)(6)}{16+24} = 3$ Yes!

Did you notice that you could eliminate choices (J) and (K) without plugging in? The statement of the problem calls for a positive answer. You can see at a glance that the expressions in (J) and (K) are negative.

  Always be on the lookout for impossible answers that you can eliminate immediately.

The algebraic solution of the problem is to say that p people would each get $\dfrac{x}{p}$ dollars while $p + n$ people would each get $\dfrac{x}{p+n}$. The difference is $\dfrac{x}{p} - \dfrac{x}{p+n}$.

You now must use the lowest common denominator (LCD) of the fractions, which is $p(p + n)$, to find the answer:

$$\frac{x}{p} - \frac{x}{p+n} = \frac{x(p+n) - xp}{p(p+n)} = \frac{xn}{p^2 + pn}$$

TIP

A question that seems abstract is often simplified when you substitute numbers to make the problem concrete.

Addition or Subtraction

The notion of addition or subtraction as a strategy may seem strange to you. However, a certain type of ACT algebra question calls for this strategy. Typically, you are given two or more equations that express relationships between variables. You are then asked to find yet another relationship. The problem looks tricky because you do not know the values of the variables. If, however, you are aware of addition or subtraction as a strategy, the problem becomes very simple. Look at the following example.

Example 5

If $2x + y = 6$ and $x + 3y = -2$, then $x - 2y = $?

A. -12
B. 0
C. 4
D. 8
E. 12

SOLUTION

(D)
$2x + y = 6$ (Equation 1)
$x + 3y = -2$ (Equation 2)

Equation 1 $-$ Equation 2 gives:

$$x - 2y = 6 - (-2)$$
$$= 6 + 2$$
$$= 8$$

The solution to this problem uses the following algebraic fact:

If $a = b$ and $c = d$, then $a - c = b - d$ and $a + c = b + d$

What this means in practical terms is that whenever you are given two (or more) equations, you can set the sum (or difference) of the left sides equal to the sum (or difference) of the right sides.

Example 6

Suppose x, y, and z are three quantities such that $4x + 4y + 3z = 30$ and $3x + 3y + 2z = 10$. What is the average of x, y, and z?

F. $6\frac{2}{3}$

G. $7\frac{1}{2}$

H. 8

J. 10

K. $13\frac{1}{3}$

SOLUTION

(F) Recall that the average of x, y, and z is given by $\frac{x + y + z}{3}$. The point of this problem is to find this average without knowing the values of x, y, and z. Use the subtraction strategy.

$4x + 4y + 3z = 30$ (Equation 1)
$3x + 3y + 2z = 10$ (Equation 2)

Equation 1 – Equation 2 gives $x + y + z = 20$.

Average of x, y, and z equals $\frac{x + y + z}{3} = \frac{20}{3} = 6\frac{2}{3}$.

The sum or difference of equations often yields a desired relationship without calculating the actual values of the variables.

TOPICS IN ELEMENTARY ALGEBRA

This section summarizes the elementary algebra topics that you should know for the ACT Test.

Linear Equations and Inequalities

Your basic technique in solving all linear equations and inequalities should be to get all terms with variables on the left side and all numbers on the right. The laws of algebra allow you to add (or subtract) the same quantity to each side or multiply (or divide) both sides by the same quantity. There is, however, a wrinkle for inequalities.

When you multiply or divide both sides of an inequality by a negative quantity, the inequality sign flips around.

For example, if $-3x < 9$, then $x > -3$, since both sides were multiplied by $-\frac{1}{3}$.

Example 7

Which of the following statements completely describes the solution set for the inequality $2(x - 3) > 3(x + 4)$?

A. $x < -18$ only
B. $x < 18$ only
C. $x > 18$ only
D. $x > -18$ only
E. There are no solutions for x

SOLUTION

(A)

$2(x - 3) > 3(x + 4)$
$\Rightarrow 2x - 6 > 3x + 12$
$\Rightarrow -x > 18$
$\Rightarrow x < -18$

Polynomials

A *monomial* has one term, a *binomial* has two terms, and a *trinomial* has three terms.

SIMPLIFYING

You need to be able to perform simple operations on polynomials. For example, to simplify $(2x^2)^3$:

$$(2x^2)^3 = 2^3 \cdot (x^2)^3 = 8x^6$$

Don't forget that each factor in the monomial must be raised to the third power. You must also be careful when there are minus signs in front of brackets. For example, to simplify $2x^2 - 4x + 8 - 2(x^2 + 3x - 4)$:

$$2x^2 - 4x + 8 - 2(x^2 + 3x - 4)$$
$$= 2x^2 - 4x + 8 - 2x^2 - 6x + 8$$
$$= -10x + 16$$

Be sure that you use the correct laws of exponents when you multiply monomials. For example, to simplify $(3x^2y)(2x^4y^7)$:

$$(3x^2y)(2x^4y^7) = 6x^{2+4}y^{1+7} = 6x^6y^8$$

Example 8

If $x^2b^4 = ab^{-1}$, what is a in terms of b and x?

F. x^2b^3
G. x^2b^5
H. x^2b^{-3}
J. x^2b^{-5}
K. x^2b^4

SOLUTION

(G) The question means you must solve for a.

$x^2b^4 = ab^{-1}$

$\Rightarrow x^2b^4 = \dfrac{a}{b}$

$\Rightarrow \dfrac{a}{b} = x^2b^4$

$\Rightarrow a = x^2b^5$ (multiply both sides by b)

FACTORING

You need to know the following *factored forms* or products:

> Difference of perfect squares: $x^2 - y^2 = (x + y)(x - y)$
> Perfect square trinomial: $x^2 + 2xy + y^2 = (x + y)^2$
> Perfect square trinomial: $x^2 - 2xy + y^2 = (x - y)^2$

You may be expected to factor simple trinomials, for example,

$$x^2 - x - 12 = (x \quad)(x \quad)$$

To figure out what numbers go in the parentheses, you must find numbers whose product is -12 and whose sum equals the middle coefficient, namely -1.

$$\text{Answer: } x^2 - x - 12 = (x - 4)(x + 3)$$

Notice that you can check whether this is correct by multiplying $(x - 4)$ by $(x + 3)$. Do you remember FOIL? Use it to multiply two binomials. Remember to multiply in the correct order so you can keep track of the terms.

FOIL $(x - 4)(x + 3)$	
First terms	$(x)(x) = x^2$
Outer terms	$(x)(3) = 3x$
Inner terms	$(-4)(x) = -4x$
Last terms	$(-4)(3) = -12$

TIP

Do not make careless mistakes when factoring. Check your factored form by taking a minute to multiply mentally the two binomials of your answer. The result must equal the given trinomial.

Put it all together and collect like terms:

$$x^2 + 3x - 4x - 12 = x^2 - x - 12$$

Yes! This was the original polynomial, so the factoring was correct.

Here is an example of a tricky ACT problem that uses simple factoring and operations on monomials and binomials.

Example 9

If $x^2 - y^2 = 40$, and $x - y = 4$, then $x^2 + y^2 = ?$

A. $2xy$
B. $-2xy$
C. $100 - 2xy$
D. $100 + 2xy$
E. $10 - xy$

SOLUTION

(C) $100 - 2xy$

Method 1: Algebra

$x^2 - y^2 = (x + y)(x - y)$
$\Rightarrow 40 = 4(x + y)$
$\Rightarrow x + y = 10$

Now square both sides.

$x^2 + 2xy + y^2 = 100$
$\Rightarrow x^2 + y^2 = 100 - 2xy$

Method 2: Pick some numbers

The numbers are small enough to find values of x and y that satisfy the given equations $x^2 - y^2 = 40$, and $x - y = 4$.

Taking a moment to try some of the perfect squares under 100 hits the jackpot with $x = 7$ and $y = 3$. (Check that these numbers work: $49 - 9 = 40$ and $7 - 3 = 4$.) You can now calculate that $x^2 + y^2 = 49 + 9 = 58$. Plugging in to the choices shows that (C) gives the right value: $100 - 2xy = 100 - 2(7)(3) = 100 - 42 = 58$.

Method 3: Algebra *and* pick some numbers

$x + y = 10$ (see Method 1)
$x - y = 4$ (given)
$\therefore 2x = 14$ (add the equations)
$\therefore x = 7$ and $y = 3$

Once you have x and y, proceed with a plug-in strategy, as shown in Method 2.

Quadratic Equations

A quadratic equation has the form $ax^2 + bx + c = 0$, where $a \neq 0$ and a, b, and c are real numbers.

If $b = 0$, you get a rather simple-looking equation with x^2. Don't forget that the equation has *two* roots, one positive and one negative. For example, to solve $x^2 - 16 = 0$, $x^2 - 16 = 0 \Rightarrow x^2 = 16 \Rightarrow x = \pm 4$.

Many quadratic equations on the ACT can be solved by factoring.

Example 10

Find the larger root of $x^2 + 11x + 30 = 0$.

F. -2
G. -3
H. -5
J. -6
K. -10

SOLUTION

(H) -5

$x^2 + 11x + 30 = 0$
$\Rightarrow (x + 6)(x + 5) = 0$
$\Rightarrow x = -6$ or $x = -5$

Beware! $-5 > -6$
Therefore, the larger root is -5.

Example 11

A rectangular garden plot has dimensions $x - 1$ feet by $x + 3$ feet and has area 32 square feet. What is the length, in feet, of the larger side of the plot?

A. 4
B. 5
C. 7
D. 8
E. .10

SOLUTION

(D) 8

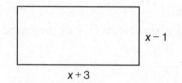

A picture of the setting is shown. You can assume that x is positive because the plot should have positive values for its dimensions. Thus, $x + 3$ is the length. Since you are given that the area is 32 square feet, you can write the following equation:

$$(x + 3)(x - 1) = 32$$

This is a quadratic equation, which you should solve by rewriting it in standard form:

$(x + 3)(x - 1) = 32$
$\Rightarrow x^2 + 2x - 3 = 32$
$\Rightarrow x^2 + 2x - 35 = 0$
$\Rightarrow (x - 5)(x + 7) = 0$
$\Rightarrow x = 5$ or $x = -7$

Reject -7 since length and width must be positive.

Be careful that you do not select 5, choice (B), as the answer. You are asked to find *length*, not x.

Length $= x + 3 = 5 + 3 = 8$ feet.

English into Algebra

On the ACT, many problems in settings require you to translate an English sentence into an algebraic equation that you can then solve. Since the translating is often trickier than the solving, you should have each of the following at your fingertips.

English	Algebra
A certain number	x
The product of two numbers is	$xy =$
The sum of two numbers is	$x + y =$
The difference between two numbers is	$|x - y| =$
5 times a number	$5x$
The cost of a ticket and dinner is	$t + d =$
Pat ate 5 candies for every 2 that Marvin ate	$\dfrac{p}{m} = \dfrac{5}{2}$
The difference between Sara's salary and Pat's salary is $100.	$|s - p| = 100$
Peter is 4 years older than Lauren	$p = l + 4$
The discount is 25% off price p	$d = 0.25p$
What percent is	$\dfrac{x}{100} =$
3 consecutive integers	$x, x + 1, x + 2$
3 consecutive even integers	$x, x + 2, x + 4$
3 consecutive odd integers	$x, x + 2, x + 4$

From the chart above, you can get the idea of the types of English-to-algebra translations you should be able to make.

Example 12

Three consecutive odd integers are such that 3 times the middle integer is 25 more than the sum of the smallest and largest. Find the largest of the integers.

F. 23
G. 24
H. 25
J. 26
K. 27

SOLUTION

(K) 27

Method 1: Algebra

Be sure to let x be the number asked for, namely the biggest of the three odd numbers. Then the consecutive odd numbers, in increasing order, are $x - 4$, $x - 2$, and x. Now translate into math "3 times the middle integer is 25 more than the sum of the smallest and largest."

$3(x - 2) = 25 + (x - 4 + x)$
$\Rightarrow 3x - 6 = 25 + 2x - 4$
$\Rightarrow x = 27$

Method 2: Plug in

Using algebra, as shown above, is probably the quickest way to solve this problem. However, do not forget the alternative route. When you are given numerical answer choices, you can always plug those into the problem to see which works. For example, when you try choice (F), the consecutive odd numbers are 19, 21, and 23.

(F): $3(21) \overset{?}{=} 25 + 19 + 23$
$\Rightarrow 63 \overset{?}{=} 67$ False

When you try choice (K), the consecutive odd numbers are 23, 25, and 27.

(K): $3(25) \overset{?}{=} 25 + 23 + 27$.
$\Rightarrow 75 \overset{?}{=} 75$ True!

Example 13

Jack has a job that pays p dollars per hour. On any day that he works for more than 8 hours, he gets paid an additional n dollars for each hour over 8 hours. The following chart shows the hours he worked for one week.

Day	Number of Hours
Mon.	4
Tue.	10
Wed.	1
Thur.	8
Fri.	12

In terms of n and p, how many dollars did Jack earn for the week?

A. $29p + 6n$
B. $29n + 6p$
C. $35(p + n)$
D. $35n + 6p$
E. $35p + 6n$

SOLUTION

(E) $35p + 6n$

Total number of hours worked = 35
Regular pay for 35 hours = $35p$
Number of overtime hours = $(10 - 8) + (12 - 8) = 6$
Overtime pay = $6n$
Total pay = $35p + 6n$

Now try your hand at a mixture of elementary algebra problems.

Ace the ACT!
Sample Elementary Algebra Questions

1. For all y, $(y-2)(y-4) = $?

   A. $y^2 + 8$
   B. $y^2 - 8$
   C. $y^2 - 6y - 8$
   D. $y^2 + 6y - 8$
   E. $y^2 - 6y + 8$

2. If $2x - 3y = 9$, and $x - y = 4$, then $y = $?

   F. 3
   G. 1
   H. 0
   J. -1
   K. -3

3. If $-3 < a < -1$, which of the following inequalities is *false*?

   A. $\dfrac{1}{a} < a$

   B. $\dfrac{1}{a} < a^2$

   C. $\dfrac{1}{a} > a$

   D. $a < a^2$

   E. $a < \dfrac{1}{a^2}$

4. The relationship between temperature expressed in degrees Celsius (C) and degrees Fahrenheit (F) is given by the formula

   $$C = \frac{5}{9}(F - 32)$$

   If the temperature is -10 degrees Celsius, what is it in degrees Fahrenheit?

   F. -50
   G. 14
   H. $23\dfrac{1}{3}$
   J. $27\dfrac{4}{9}$
   K. 46

5. What is the smallest value of x that satisfies the equation $2x^2 - 9x - 5 = 0$?

   A. -5
   B. -1
   C. $-\dfrac{1}{2}$
   D. $\dfrac{1}{2}$
   E. 5

6. Which of the following is equivalent to $2x^2 + 8 - (x^2 + 4)$?

   F. $3x^2 - 4$
   G. $3x^2 + 4$
   H. $x^2 + 12$
   J. $x^2 - 4$
   K. $x^2 + 4$

7. There are k students in a school. Of these, $n\%$ take at least one foreign language. Which of the following expressions represents the number of students who do *not* take a foreign language?

    A. $(1 - n)k$

    B. $(100 - n)k$

    C. $\dfrac{(1 - n)k}{100}$

    D. $\dfrac{(100 - n)k}{100}$

    E. $\dfrac{nk}{100}$

8. If the expression $x^2 - 3px - 2 = 10$ when $x = -1$, what is the value of p?

    F. $\dfrac{11}{3}$

    G. $-\dfrac{11}{3}$

    H. $\dfrac{13}{3}$

    J. $-\dfrac{13}{3}$

    K. 11

9. If the arithmetic mean of four consecutive integers is 14.5, what is the smallest integer?

    A. 11
    B. 12
    C. 13
    D. 14
    E. 15

10. The sides of a triangle are in the ratio 4:3:2. If the perimeter of the triangle is 792, what is the length of the smallest side?

    F. 88
    G. 176
    H. 200
    J. 264
    K. 352

Solutions and Explanations

1. **(E)**	3. **(A)**	5. **(C)**	7. **(D)**	9. **(C)**
2. **(J)**	4. **(G)**	6. **(K)**	8. **(F)**	10. **(G)**

1. **(E)** Use FOIL to multiply (**F**irst, **O**uter, **I**nner, **L**ast).

   $(y - 2)(y - 4)$
   $= y^2 - 4y - 2y + 8$
   $= y^2 - 6y + 8$

2. **(J)** You need to eliminate x from the equations. Do not waste time by eliminating y, solving for x, and then substituting to find y.

   $2x - 3y = 9$ (Equation 1)
   $x - y = 4$ (Equation 2)

   From Equation 2, $x = y + 4$

   Substitute x in Equation 1 and solve for y:

   $2(y + 4) - 3y = 9$
   $\Rightarrow 2y + 8 - 3y = 9$
   $\Rightarrow y = -1$

3. **(A)** Whenever you see a problem like this, take an actual value. Often it will lead you right to the answer. You are given that $-3 < a < -1$, so try -2. When you plug -2 into choice (A), you immediately see that the result is false:

   $\dfrac{1}{a} < a$

   $\Rightarrow \dfrac{1}{-2} < -2$ False!

Notice that every other choice results in a true statement:

   (B): $\dfrac{1}{a} < a^2$

   $\Rightarrow \dfrac{1}{-2} < 4$ True!

   (C): $\dfrac{1}{a} > a$

   $\Rightarrow \dfrac{1}{-2} > -2$ True!

(D): $a < a^2$

$\Rightarrow -2 < 4$ True!

(E): $a < \dfrac{1}{a^2}$

$\Rightarrow -2 < \dfrac{1}{4}$ True!

4. **(G)** You must substitute -10 for C and solve for F:

$$C = \frac{5}{9}(F - 32)$$

$$\Rightarrow -10 = \frac{5}{9}(F - 32)$$

Now multiply both sides by $\dfrac{9}{5}$. You want to get F on its own, on one side.

$$\therefore \frac{-90}{5} = F - 32$$

$$\Rightarrow -18 + 32 = F$$
$$\Rightarrow F = 14$$

5. **(C)**

$2x^2 - 9x - 5 = 0$
$\Rightarrow (2x + 1)(x - 5) = 0$

At this stage, you must multiply back and check that your factoring is correct!

$(2x + 1)(x - 5) = 0$
$\Rightarrow 2x + 1 = 0 \text{ or } x - 5 = 0$

$\Rightarrow x = -\dfrac{1}{2} \text{ or } x = 5$

The smallest value of x that satisfies the equation is $-\dfrac{1}{2}$.

6. **(K)**

$2x^2 + 8 - (x^2 + 4)$
$= 2x^2 + 8 - x^2 - 4$
$= x^2 + 4$

7. **(D)** Given that n% take a foreign language, $(100 - n)$% do not. The problem wants you to find $(100 - n)$% of k. The answer is $\dfrac{(100 - n)k}{100}$.

   This is another example of a problem where you can make it concrete by using actual numbers, the pick-a-number strategy. Pretend that 40% take a foreign language. Then 60% do not. (How did you get that? $100 - 40 = 60$.)

   So you want to find 60% of k. How would you do that? $\dfrac{60}{100}k$.

8. **(F)** You must substitute $x = -1$ and then solve for p.

$$x^2 - 3px - 2 = 10$$
$$\Rightarrow (-1)^2 - 3p(-1) - 2 = 10$$
$$\Rightarrow 1 + 3p - 2 = 10$$
$$\Rightarrow 3p = 11$$
$$\Rightarrow p = \frac{11}{3}$$

9. **(C)** 13.

   Method 1: Algebra

   Let x be the smallest integer. The other consecutive integers are $x + 1$, $x + 2$, and $x + 3$. You are given that the arithmetic mean is 14.5:

$$\therefore \frac{x + (x + 1) + (x + 2) + (x + 3)}{4} = 14.5$$
$$\Rightarrow \frac{4x + 6}{4} = \frac{2(2x + 3)}{4} = 14.5$$
$$\Rightarrow \frac{2x + 3}{2} = 14.5$$
$$\Rightarrow 2x + 3 = 29$$
$$\Rightarrow 2x = 26$$
$$\Rightarrow x = 13$$

   Method 2: Plug in

   In each answer choice, the smallest of the consecutive integers is given.

   Choice (A): If the integers are 11, 12, 13, and 14, the arithmetic mean is 12.5. Can you see that the arithmetic mean of four consecutive integers will always be the number that is midway between the second and third integers? Thus, the arithmetic mean of four consecutive integers will be 14.5 if the second and third integers are 14 and 15. Therefore, the numbers must be 13, 14, 15, and 16, choice (C).

10. **(G)** 176

Method 1: Plug in

You are given a choice of five numbers, so start with choice (H). The smallest side is 200. The biggest side is double this, 400. The middle side is somewhere between these. Even if you assume the middle side is close to 200, you get a perimeter over 800, which is too big. This lets you also eliminate choices (H) and (K). If 200 is too big, then 264 and 352 are even bigger! You can eliminate choice (F) with similar reasoning. If the smallest side is approximately 90, then the biggest side is 180 and the middle side is somewhere in between. The perimeter you get is quite a bit less than 792, the given perimeter. So the answer must be choice (G).

Method 2: Algebra

This is a case where a direct solution may actually be easier. If the sides are in the ratio 4:3:2, you can think of the sides as being $4x$, $3x$, and $2x$, which equal 9 "parts." If the perimeter is 792, then $4x + 3x + 2x = 792$. This means that $9x = 792$, and each "part," x, is 88. The smallest side is $2x = 2(88) = 176$.

Intermediate Algebra

CHAPTER 4

> ## CHAPTER GOALS
>
> - Specific strategies
> - Topics in intermediate algebra
> - Ace the ACT! Sample intermediate algebra questions

About 9 questions, or 15% of the 60 multiple-choice questions on the ACT Math Test, are on the more advanced algebra topics. You will probably recognize most of these from your school algebra course:

- Quadratic equations and inequalities
- Equations with radicals
- Linear functions
- Quadratic functions
- Functions as models
- Rational expressions
- Matrices
- Systems of equations and inequalities
- Sequences
- Complex numbers
- Logarithms

The list of topics is broad, covering quite a vast terrain. The really, really good news is that the ACT has its favorites, and the same types of questions occur again and again.

This chapter will touch on all of these topics. It strongly focuses on the frequently asked types of questions. Some more good news is that many of the intermediate algebra questions are straightforward, with solutions that come right out of your math textbook.

SPECIFIC STRATEGIES

Some strategies in previous chapters work with intermediate algebra questions.

Pick a Number

Here is a textbook problem that can be solved in a decidedly nontextbook way.

Example 1

If x is not equal to 2 or –2, what is equivalent to $\dfrac{3x^2 - 8x + 4}{x^2 - 4}$?

A. $3 - 8x$

B. $4 - 2x$

C. $\dfrac{3x - 2}{x - 2}$

D. $\dfrac{3x + 2}{x + 2}$

E. $\dfrac{3x - 2}{x + 2}$

SOLUTION

(E) You are given that x can be any number except 2 or –2. Nothing in the problem suggests that x cannot be 0. Since 0 is an easy number to substitute, try it. In the given fraction,

$$\frac{3x^2 - 8x + 4}{x^2 - 4} = \frac{3(0)^2 - 8(0) + 4}{(0)^2 - 4} = \frac{4}{-4} = -1$$

Now plug $x = 0$ into the answer choices and find which choice equals –1.

(A): $3 - 8x = 3$ No

(B): $4 - 2x = 4$ No

(C): $\dfrac{3x - 2}{x - 2} = 1$ No

(D): $\dfrac{3x + 2}{x + 2} = 1$ No

(E): $\dfrac{3x - 2}{x + 2} = -1$ Yes!

If you are good at algebra, you can do this algebraically by factoring the numerator and denominator and then canceling:

$$\frac{3x^2 - 8x + 4}{x^2 - 4} = \frac{(x - 2)(3x - 2)}{(x - 2)(x + 2)} = \frac{3x - 2}{x + 2}, \text{ choice (E).}$$

Graphing Calculator

You do not want to overuse your graphing calculator since each push of a button takes time. Still, be aware that for some questions that involve graphs, the graphing calculator can give you the answer immediately.

Example 2

Which is the graph of $y = -(x - 2)^2$?

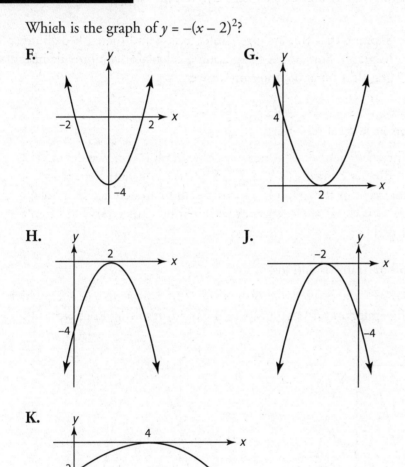

SOLUTION

(**H**) is correct.

Method 1: Graphing calculator

Use the graphing calculator to sketch the graph of $y = -(x - 2)^2$. The graphing window clearly shows a graph that matches choice (H). End of story.
  Of course, there are ways to solve this without a graphing calculator.

 Suppose that you are given an equation and then asked about its graph. Sometimes the graphing calculator can provide instant gratification and an instant answer.

Method 2: Logical reasoning

Since the coefficient of x^2 is negative, the graph is concave down. This eliminates choices (F) and (G). Since the constant term is –4, the y-intercept of the graph is –4, which eliminates choice (K). Solving $-(x - 2)^2 = 0$ yields $x = 2$ as a root, eliminating choice (J). Therefore the answer is (H).

Method 3: Transformations

If $f(x) = -x^2$, the given equation $y = -(x - 2)^2$ represents $f(x - 2)$, which shifts the graph of $f(x)$ two units to the right, resulting in choice (H).

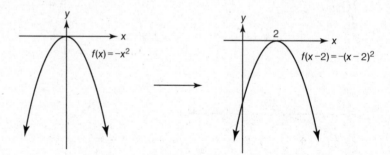

Plug In

Here is another familiar strategy that works well whenever you are given actual numbers in the answer choices.

Example 3

Find the points at which the graphs of $y = \frac{1}{2}x^2 - 3$ and $y = x + 1$ intersect.

A. $(-2, -3)$ $(4, 5)$
B. $(-1, -2)$ $(5, 4)$
C. $(-4, -3)$ $(-2, 4)$
D. $(-4, -3)$ $(2, 3)$
E. $(-2, -1)$ $(4, 5)$

SOLUTION

(E)

$(-2, -1)$ $(4, 5)$

Method 1: Plug in

Since a point of intersection lies on both graphs, its coordinates must satisfy both equations. Go through each answer choice, plugging in the coordinates until you find the points that satisfy both equations. If you start at (A) and go down the choices, you will find that you need to go all the way to choice (H):

$(-2, -1)$	$(4, 5)$
Plug into $y = \frac{1}{2}x^2 - 3$:	Plug into $y = \frac{1}{2}x^2 - 3$:
$-1 = \frac{1}{2}(-2)^2 - 3$	$5 = \frac{1}{2}(4)^2 - 3$
$\Rightarrow -1 = 2 - 3$ True	$\Rightarrow 5 = 8 - 3$ True
Plug into $y = x + 1$:	Plug into $y = x + 1$:
$-1 = -2 + 1$ True	$5 = 4 + 1$ True

Method 2: Graphing calculator

Graph $y_1 = \frac{1}{2}x^2 - 3$ and $y_2 = x + 1$ on the graphing calculator.

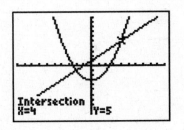

Either ⎡TRACE⎤ to get the coordinates of the points of intersection, or use the intersect option in the ⎡CALC⎤ menu to yield the required points. The answer is (**E**).

Method 3: Algebra

Solve $y = \frac{1}{2}x^2 - 3$ and $y = x + 1$ simultaneously. Substitute $x + 1$ for y in the first equation:

$$x + 1 = \frac{1}{2}x^2 - 3$$
$$\Rightarrow 2x + 2 = x^2 - 6$$
$$\Rightarrow x^2 - 2x - 8 = 0$$
$$\Rightarrow x = 4 \text{ or } -2$$

Substituting $x = 4$ into $y = x + 1$ yields $y = 5$. Substituting $x = -2$ yields $y = -1$. Thus the coordinates where the graphs intersect are $(-2, -1)$ and $(4, 5)$, answer choice (**E**).

 On the ACT, avoid solving complex systems of equations from scratch. Plugging in or using the graphing calculator always provides faster routes to the answer.

TOPICS IN INTERMEDIATE ALGEBRA

Which topics in algebra should you review? The field is broad. The following is a brief summary, with special attention paid to the types of questions you are sure to encounter.

Equations with Radicals

To solve equations with radicals, isolate the radical. This means get the radical on its own on one side. Then square both sides. For example,

$$\sqrt{x} - 5 = 2$$
$$\Rightarrow \sqrt{x} = 7$$
$$\Rightarrow (\sqrt{x})^2 = 7^2$$
$$\Rightarrow x = 49$$

Quadratic Equations, Revisited

Most quadratic equations on the ACT Test can be solved by factoring. Still, it's good to know that the quadratic formula always gives the correct solutions!

For the equation $ax^2 + bx + c = 0$ where a, b, c are real numbers and $a \neq 0$:

Quadratic formula: $x = \dfrac{-b \pm \sqrt{b^2 - 4ac}}{2a}$

Sum of the roots: $-\dfrac{b}{a}$

Product of the roots: $\dfrac{c}{a}$

Example 4

What is the sum of the two real solutions to the equation $x^2 + 3x = 7$?

F. 3

G. $\dfrac{3}{2}$

H. $-\dfrac{3}{2}$

J. -3

K. -7

SOLUTION

(J) Write the equation in standard quadratic form:

$x^2 + 3x - 7 = 0$

Sum of roots $= -\dfrac{b}{a} = -\dfrac{3}{1} = -3.$

Notice how much work you must do if you do not know the formula for the sum of the roots. You will need to solve the equation and then add the roots. To add insult to injury, this quadratic does not factor, which means you must use the formula:

$$x = \frac{-b \pm \sqrt{b^2 - 4ac}}{2a}$$

$$= \frac{-3 \pm \sqrt{(3)^2 - (4)(1)(-7)}}{2(1)}$$

$$= \frac{-3 \pm \sqrt{37}}{2}$$

$$\text{Sum of roots} = \frac{-3+\sqrt{37}}{2} + \frac{-3-\sqrt{37}}{2}$$

$$= \frac{-6}{2}$$

$$= -3$$

 Knowing the formulas for the sum and product of the roots of a quadratic equation can save you precious minutes.

Rational Expressions

A *rational expression* is an algebraic fraction in which both the numerator and denominator are polynomials. Some examples are $\frac{1}{x-7}$, $\frac{x^2+4x-4}{x}$, and $\frac{(x+3)(x-4)}{(1-x)^2}$.

SIMPLIFYING

To simplify a rational expression, factor the numerator and denominator. Then cancel if possible. The following type of question is a favorite on the ACT.

Example 5

For all x for which it is defined, $\dfrac{x^3-9x}{2x^2-3x-9}$ simplifies to:

A. $\dfrac{x^2+3x+9}{2x+3}$

B. $\dfrac{x(x-3)}{2x-9}$

C. $\dfrac{x(x+3)}{2x+3}$

D. $\dfrac{x^2(x+3)}{2x+3}$

E. $\dfrac{x(x-3)}{2x-3}$

SOLUTION

(C) Notice that the numerator has a common factor, x. When you factor it out, you have a difference of squares, $x^2 - 9$, that can be factored further. The denominator is a quadratic trinomial that you should multiply back to check your factoring.

$$\frac{x^3 - 9x}{2x^2 - 3x - 9} = \frac{x(x^2 - 9)}{(2x - 3)(x - 3)}$$

$$= \frac{x(x + 3)(x - 3)}{(2x + 3)(x - 3)}$$

$$= \frac{x(x + 3)}{2x + 3}$$

GRAPHS OF RATIONAL EXPRESSIONS

Many ACT questions test your understanding of the fact that a rational expression is undefined at any x value that produces 0 in the denominator. For example, $\frac{1}{x - 7}$ is undefined at $x = 7$, $\frac{x^2 + x}{x}$ is undefined at $x = 0$, and $\frac{x^3 + x^2 + x^1}{x^2 - 4}$ is undefined at $x = \pm 2$. A value at which a rational expression is undefined shows up as a discontinuity (break) in the graph.

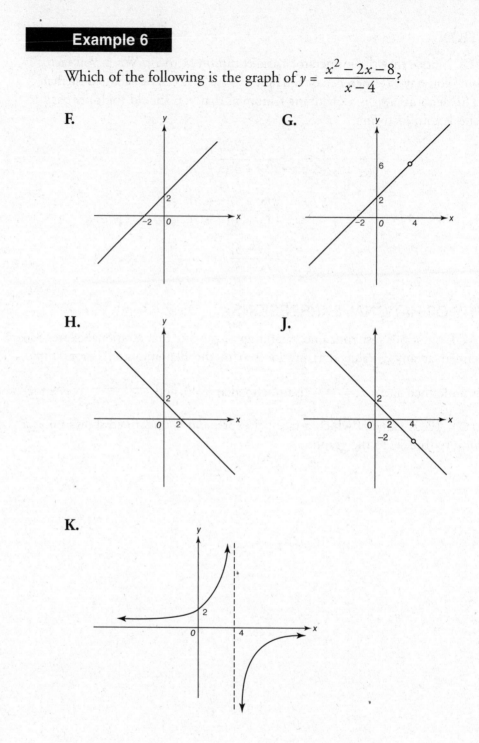

Example 6

Which of the following is the graph of $y = \dfrac{x^2 - 2x - 8}{x - 4}$?

F.

G.

H.

J.

K.

SOLUTION

(G) You first need to simplify $y = \dfrac{x^2 - 2x - 8}{x - 4}$. Factor the numerator, and then cancel.

$$y = \frac{x^2 - 2x - 8}{x - 4}$$

$$= \frac{(x - 4)(x + 2)}{(x - 4)}$$

$$\Rightarrow y = x + 2$$

In a vacuum, if you plot $y = x + 2$, you get the line shown in choice (F): slope 1 and y-intercept 2. Remember, however, that $y = \dfrac{x^2 - 2x - 8}{x - 4}$ is undefined at $x = 4$. This shows up as a "hole" in the graph at the point (4, 6).

 If a factor of the denominator of a rational expression cancels out when the expression is simplified, the graph will have a hole in it at the x-value for which the expression is undefined.

What happens if the factor containing an x-value for which the expression is undefined does *not* cancel out, namely a value that gives you 0 in the denominator? Well, instead of a hole, the graph will have a vertical asymptote at that value. An asymptote is a line that the graph approaches but never reaches. For example, here are the graphs of $y = \dfrac{1}{x}$, and $y = -\dfrac{1}{x}$, both of which are undefined at $x = 0$.

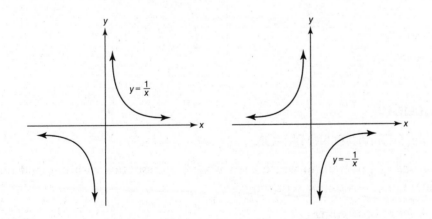

Example 7

If (a, b) is a point on the graph of $y = -\dfrac{5}{x-1}$, which of the following must be true?

A. $a \neq -5$
B. $b \neq 1$
C. $a \neq -1$
D. $a \neq 1$
E. $b \neq -1$

SOLUTION

(D) The expression $-\dfrac{5}{x-1}$ is undefined for $x = 1$. This means that any point on the graph cannot have 1 as an x-coordinate. Therefore, $a \neq 1$.

This is what the graph of $y = -\dfrac{5}{x-1}$ looks like:

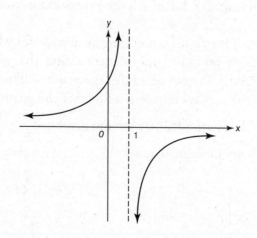

Functions

DEFINITION AND NOTATION

A *function* is a relation in which each x-value corresponds with one and only one y-value. Functions can be represented as:

- A set of ordered pairs.
- An equation in terms of x and y.
- A graph.

From the definition, you should see that a function cannot have two (or more) ordered pairs that start with the same x-value.

Here are two examples of functions:

1. $y = x + 4$

2.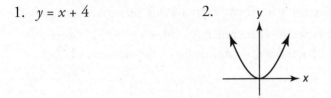

A function can be represented with $f(x)$ notation. For instance, $f(x) = (x - 3)^2$ is equivalent to $y = (x - 3)^2$. To evaluate $f(5)$ means to find the value of $(x - 3)^2$ when $x = 5$. So $f(5) = f(5 - 3)^2 = 4$. Similarly $f(-1) = (-1 - 3)^2 = 16$ and $f(a) = (a - 3)^2$.

Example 8

If $f(x) = x^2 + h^2$, then $f(x - h) = $?

F. $x^2 - 2xh$
G. $x^2 + 2xh$
H. $x^2 - 2xh + h^4$
J. $x^2 - 2xh + 2h^4$
K. $x^2 - 2xh + 2h^2$

SOLUTION:

(K) $f(x - h)$ means "Replace x with $x - h$."

$$f(x - h) = (x - h)^2 + h^2$$
$$= x^2 - 2xh + h^2 + h^2$$
$$= x^2 - 2xh + 2h^2$$

DOMAIN AND RANGE

The *domain* of a function is the set of all x-values for which the function is defined. The *range* of the function is the set of corresponding y-values produced by the function. Think of the domain as being the set of real numbers that are allowable x-values. Which values are *not* allowed?

- Any value that produces 0 in the denominator (undefined expression).
- Any value that produces negative values in a radical (imaginary number).

Example 9

Which value is *not* in the domain of $f(x) = \sqrt{x - 5}$?

A. 4
B. 5
C. 6
D. 7
E. 8.5

SOLUTION

(A) Plug in each choice for x until you find a value that gives a negative radicand. You hit the jackpot with choice A: $\sqrt{4-5} = \sqrt{-1}$. Since the radicand, $x - 5$, can't be negative, 4 cannot be in the domain of $f(x)$.

Example 10

What is the range of $f(x) = -(x - 2)^2 - 4$?

F. All real numbers
G. $y \geq -8$
H. $y \leq -8$
J. $y \geq -4$
K. $y \leq -4$

SOLUTION

(K) $y \leq -4$

Method 1: Graphing calculator

Graph $y = -(x - 2)^2 - 4$ on the graphing calculator. The graphing window shows that the graph exists only where $y \leq -4$. Therefore the answer is choice (K).

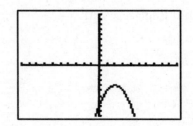

Method 2: Algebra

When a quadratic function is written as $f(x) = a(x - h)^2 + k$, the vertex is (h, k). Therefore, in the given problem, the vertex is $(2, -4)$. Also, since the coefficient of x^2 is negative, the curve is concave down and the function has a maximum. (Note that if the coefficient of x^2 is positive, the function has a minimum.) Since the maximum value of y is -4, the range is all $y \leq -4$.

THE LINEAR FUNCTION

A *linear function* is one whose graph is a straight line. The *slope-intercept* form of the equation is $y = mx + b$, where m represents the slope of the line and b the y-intercept.

Here are two other facts about the graphs of linear functions:

- Parallel lines have the same slope.
- Perpendicular lines have slopes that are negative reciprocals of each other.

A favorite on the ACT is to give you a linear equation that is not in slope-intercept form and then to ask you to find the slope or y-intercept of the line with that equation. This is an easy question, as long as you remember to start by writing it in slope-intercept form!

Example 11

The slope of the line with equation $2x - 2y = 7$ is

A. -1
B. 1
C. $\dfrac{7}{2}$
D. $-\dfrac{7}{2}$
E. 2

SOLUTION

(B) Get the equation into slope-intercept form: $2x - 2y = 7 \Rightarrow 2y = 2x - 7 \Rightarrow$ $y = x - \dfrac{7}{2}$.

Slope = coefficient of x, which equals 1.

Example 12

The equations below represent lines in the standard (x, y) coordinate plane.

$2x + 2y + 7 = 0$
$2x + 2y + 11 = 0$

Which of the following is a true statement about the lines?

F. The lines are parallel.
G. The lines are perpendicular.
H. The lines coincide.
J. The lines are not perpendicular but do intersect at exactly one point.
K. The lines are neither parallel nor do they intersect.

SOLUTION

(F) Notice that if you were to solve each equation for y, the coefficient of x would be the same in each case, -1.

$$2x + 2y + 7 = 0 \Rightarrow y = -x - \frac{7}{2}$$

$$2x + 2y + 11 = 0 \Rightarrow y = -x - \frac{11}{2}$$

Since the slope of each line is -1, the lines are parallel. Note that if both the slopes and y-intercepts were the same, the lines would coincide. They would be the same line.

THE QUADRATIC FUNCTION

A *quadratic function* is one whose graph is a parabola. The standard form of the equation is $y = ax^2 + bx + c$, $a \neq 0$. The axis of symmetry of the graph is given by $x = -\frac{b}{2a}$. The constant term c represents the y-intercept. If the coefficient of x^2, a, is positive, the graph is concave up. Otherwise, it is concave down.

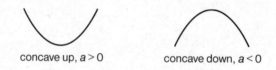

concave up, $a > 0$ concave down, $a < 0$

The value of a controls the width of the parabola. The bigger the magnitude of a, the narrower the parabola is.

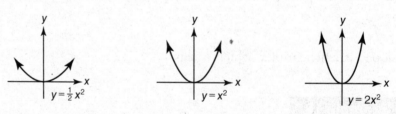

FACTS ABOUT THE QUADRATIC FUNCTION

1. Roots (x-intercepts):   Factor $ax^2 + bx + c = 0$

2. Roots (x-intercepts):   Solve the quadratic formula

$$x = \frac{-b \pm \sqrt{b^2 - 4ac}}{2a}$$

3. Sum of the Roots: $-\dfrac{b}{a}$

4. Product of the roots: $\dfrac{c}{a}$

5. Axis of symmetry: $-\dfrac{b}{2a}$ when in the form $ax^2 + bx + c = 0$

6. Axis of symmetry $x = h$ when in the form $y = a(x - h)^2 + k$

7. Vertex: (h, k) when in the form $y = a(x - h)^2 + k$

Example 13

Which could be the graph of $y = x^2 + 3x + k$, where k is an integer?

A.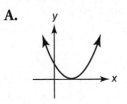

B.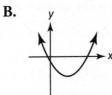

C.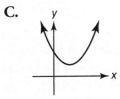

D.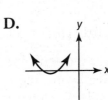

E.

SOLUTION

(D) Since the coefficient of x^2 is positive, the graph must be concave up, so eliminate choice (E). The axis of symmetry is $x = -\dfrac{b}{2a} = -\dfrac{3}{2}$, which is to the left of the y-axis; so eliminate all but choice (D) .

Example 14

$f(x) = ax^2 + bx + c$, $a \neq 0$, has the sum of its roots equal to the product of its roots. Which could be $f(x)$?

F. $x^2 + x + 2$
G. $x^2 - 2x + 1$
H. $x^2 - 4x + 4$
J. $x^2 + 3x - 6$
K. $x^2 + x + 1$

SOLUTION

(H) Notice that sum of roots = product of roots.

$$\Rightarrow -\frac{b}{a} = \frac{c}{a}$$

$$\Rightarrow -b = c$$

Go through each choice and see which expression has $-b = c$.

Choice (H) is the only one that does.

 When solving a problem like example 14, one that involves the sum and product of roots, don't even *think* of solving each equation and then checking if the product of the roots equals the sum.

QUADRATIC INEQUALITIES

The first step in solving a quadratic inequality is to recognize that it is not linear! A linear inequality is solved by moving all variable terms to one side and all numerical terms to the other side. In contrast, quadratic inequality is solved by factoring and inspecting the graph. For example,

$$x^2 - 6x + 8 = 0 \Rightarrow (x - 4)(x - 2) = 0$$
$$\Rightarrow x = 4 \text{ or } 2$$

To solve $x^2 - 6x + 8 > 0$:

$x^2 - 6x + 8 > 0$

$\Rightarrow (x - 4)(x - 2) > 0$

The roots are 2 and 4.

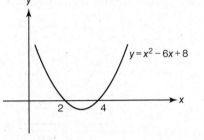

Notice that the y-values in the graph are positive outside of the roots. Thus, the answer is $x < 2$ or $x > 4$. If you were asked to solve $x^2 - 6x + 8 < 0$, note that y is negative for x values *between* the roots, namely $2 < x < 4$.

Transformations

The following table summarizes different transformations and their effects on the graph of $f(x)$. Given the graph of $f(x)$, you should know which transformation produces which related graph. In the table, assume $k > 0$ is a constant.

Related Function	Resulting Transformation of $f(x)$
$f(x) + k$	Vertical shift, k units up
$f(x) - k$	Vertical shift, k units down
$f(x + k)$	Horizontal shift, k units to the left
$f(x - k)$	Horizontal shift, k units to the right
$-f(x)$	Reflection across the x-axis
$f(-x)$	Reflection across the y-axis
$kf(x)$	Vertical dilation from the x-axis by a factor of k
$f(kx)$	Horizontal dilation from the y-axis by a factor of $\dfrac{1}{k}$

For example, suppose $f(x) = x^2$.

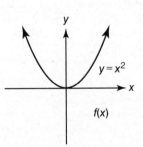

Shown below are the related graphs.

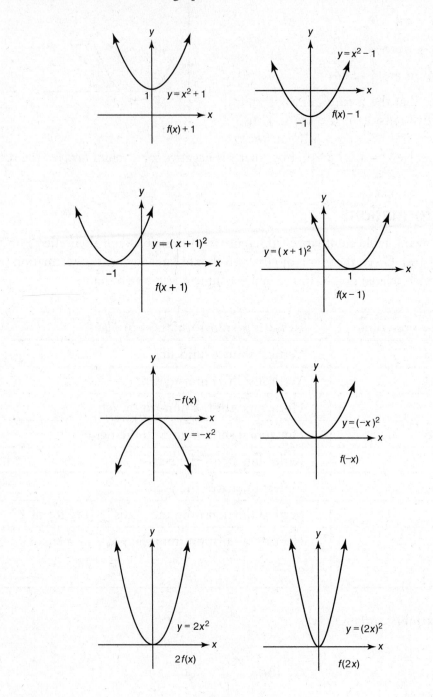

Example 15

If $f(x) = -x^2$, which represents the graph of $f(x) + 3$?

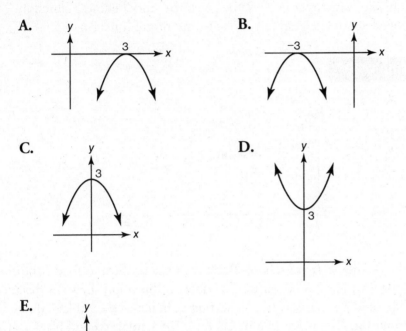

A.

B.

C.

D.

E.

SOLUTION

(**C**) is the answer.

Method 1: Graphing calculator

Using a calculator makes the problem trivial. Graph $y = -x^2 + 3$, and note that choice (C) matches the graph shown in the graphing window. End of story.

Method 2: Transformation of $f(x) = -x^2$

The graph of $f(x) = -x^2$ is one you've memorized by now:

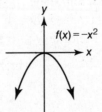

The required graph is the graph of $f(x)$ shifted vertically 3 units up—choice (C).

Functions as Models

On the ACT Test, you are often given a formula for a function and asked about its graph, or vice versa. As you know, however, real-world situations can be modeled using functions. So sometimes you will be given the story behind a function. Then you will be asked about the graph or the equation of the function.

Example 16

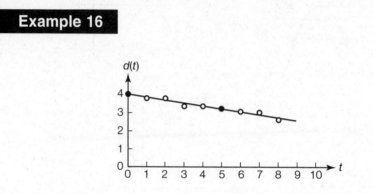

Joe bikes 4 kilometers to school. Because of the traffic and road conditions along the way, Joe's speed varies. The dots on the graph show his distance from the school at various times, starting at home at $t = 0$ (black dot). After 5 minutes, he is 3.2 kilometers from the school (second black dot). The data show that Joe's speed is almost constant, and his distance from the school can be approximated by a straight line. The graph of the function that models Joe's distance from school as a function of time in minutes is shown as a solid line. Which of the following equations best represents this function?

F. $d(t) = -0.5t + 4$
G. $d(t) = -6.25t + 4$
H. $d(t) = -0.16t + 4$
J. $d(t) = 0.16t + 4$
K. $d(t) = 0.5t + 4$

SOLUTION

(H) The given function is linear and has the form $d = mt + 4$. The slope m differs in each answer choice. The line shown has negative slope, so eliminate choices (J) and (K). The slope in the given graph is small, close to 0. The slope of -6.25 in (G) is too steep. Eliminate choice (G). You must now choose between choices (F) and (H). Even though you are given points $(0, 4)$ and $(5, 3.2)$ on the line, do not waste time with the slope formula. Get this answer quickly by noticing that $\frac{\text{rise}}{\text{run}} \approx \frac{-1}{5}$ which is closer to -0.16 than -0.5.

 Always be on the lookout for quick approximations that lead to the answer without using formulas.

Systems of Linear Equations and Inequalities

You may be asked to solve a system of equations in two variables, for example

$$2y + x = 22 \quad \text{(Equation 1)}$$
$$3y - 2x = -2 \quad \text{(Equation 2)}$$

Eliminate one of the variables:

Rewrite Equation 1 as $x = 22 - 2y$ and substitute in Equation 2.

$$3y - 2(22 - 2y) = -2$$
$$\Rightarrow 3y - 44 + 4y = -2$$
$$\Rightarrow 7y = 42$$
$$\Rightarrow y = 6$$

Substituting $y = 6$ into either of the above equations gives $x = 10$.

Solution: $x = 10$ and $y = 6$

 Using an algebraic solution is seldom the quickest way of solving a system of equations on the ACT.

Example 17

Where do the graphs of $y = 2x - 5$ and $x + 3y = -1$ intersect?

A. (−1, 2)
B. (−2, −1)
C. (2, −1)
D. (−2, 1)
E. (1, −2)

SOLUTION

(C) is the answer.

Method 1: Plug in

The ordered pair in the answer must satisfy both equations. Plug in each answer choice until you find one that works. The numbers are easy. You should quickly be able to reject those that do not work. Notice that choice (C) works: $-1 = 2(2) - 5$ and $2 + 3(-1) = -1$.

Method 2: Graphing calculator

Plot $y = 2x - 5$ and $x + 3y = -1$ on the calculator. Be sure to rewrite the second equation as $y = \dfrac{-x - 1}{3}$. A quick look at the point of intersection on the graph tells you that choice (C) is the answer.

To solve a *system of linear inequalities* means to find the region on a graph that satisfies both inequalities. To find a correct solution:

1. Write each inequality in a standard form:

$$y < mx + b, \ y \leq mx + b, \ y > mx + b, \ \text{or} \ y \geq mx + b.$$

2. For each inequality, sketch the line $y = mx + b$. Draw a solid line if the inequality is $\leq$ or $\geq$, and draw a dotted line for $<$ or $>$.

3. For each inequality, shade the region above the line if the inequality is $>$ or $\geq$. Shade below the line if the inequality is $<$ or $\leq$.

4. The solution set for the system of inequalities is the intersection of the regions, where the regions overlap.

For example, to find the solution set for this system:

$$4 - 2y \leq x \ \text{and} \ 3y - 4x > 12.$$

Step 1:

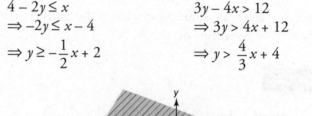

Step 2: Sketch $y = -\dfrac{1}{2}x + 2$ (solid line).

Sketch $y = \dfrac{4}{3}x + 4$ (dotted line).

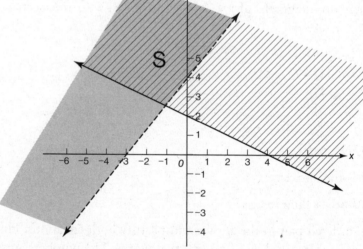

Step 3: Shade above $y = -\dfrac{1}{2}x + 2$ and above $y = \dfrac{4}{3}x + 4$.

Step 4: Region *S*, where the two shaded regions overlap, is the solution set.

Matrices

A matrix is a two-dimensional array of numbers. For example, here is a matrix with two rows and three columns, a 2×3 matrix.

$$\begin{bmatrix} 2 & 7 & 1 \\ 4 & 3 & 5 \end{bmatrix}$$

Matrices with the same dimensions can be added to or subtracted from each other by adding or subtracting the elements in corresponding positions. For example,

$$\begin{bmatrix} 2 & 7 & 1 \\ 4 & 3 & 5 \end{bmatrix} + \begin{bmatrix} 6 & 8 & 10 \\ 7 & 1 & 5 \end{bmatrix} = \begin{bmatrix} 8 & 15 & 11 \\ 11 & 4 & 10 \end{bmatrix}$$

Note that the sum or difference of two $m \times n$ matrices is an $m \times n$ matrix.

The ACT Test frequently features a question that involves matrix multiplication. Two matrices can be multiplied if and only if the number of columns of the first matrix equals the number of rows of the second. Also, the product matrix when an $m \times n$ matrix is multiplied by an $n \times p$ matrix is an $m \times p$ matrix. For example,

$$[1 \quad -3 \quad 4] \begin{bmatrix} 2 & 4 \\ 0 & 6 \\ -1 & 5 \end{bmatrix} = [-2 \quad 6]$$

This shows a 1×3 matrix multiplied by a 3×2 matrix. Where did the answer come from? Remember, the product must be a 1×2 matrix. Call it $[a \quad b]$. To get a, the element in the first row and first column, multiply each element of row 1 in the first matrix (the only row in this case) by each element of column 1 of the second, and add the products together:

$$a = (1)(2) + (-3)(0) + (4)(-1) = -2$$

To get b, the element in the first row and second column of the answer, multiply each element of row 1 in the first matrix by each element of column 2 in the second. Add the products as before:

$$b = (1)(4) + (-3)(6) + (4)(5) = 6$$

The final answer is $[-2 \quad 6]$.

Information presented in a table can be extracted as a matrix.

Example 18

The following table represents sales of T-shirts for a high school booster club.

Sleeve/Size	Small	Medium	Large
Short	1	5	3
Long	4	6	2

The cost of T-shirts is shown below:

Sleeve Type	Cost ($)
Short	6
Long	8

Which of the following matrix products could be used to find the total costs for each of the three sizes of T-shirts?

F. $\begin{bmatrix} 6 \\ 8 \end{bmatrix} \begin{bmatrix} 1 & 5 & 3 & 4 & 6 & 2 \end{bmatrix}$

G. $\begin{bmatrix} 6 & 8 \end{bmatrix} \begin{bmatrix} 1 & 4 \\ 5 & 6 \\ 3 & 2 \end{bmatrix}$

H. $\begin{bmatrix} 6 & 8 \end{bmatrix} \begin{bmatrix} 1 & 5 & 3 \\ 4 & 6 & 2 \end{bmatrix}$

J. $\begin{bmatrix} 1 & 5 & 3 \\ 4 & 6 & 2 \end{bmatrix} \begin{bmatrix} 6 & 8 \end{bmatrix}$

K. $\begin{bmatrix} 1 & 5 & 3 \\ 4 & 6 & 2 \end{bmatrix} \begin{bmatrix} 6 \\ 8 \end{bmatrix}$

SOLUTION

(H) Matrix multiplication is defined only if the number of columns of the first matrix equals the number of rows of the second. So you can eliminate choices (G), (J), and (K). The correct product is one that multiplies each of the quantities of short-sleeved shirts by 6 and each of the quantities of long-sleeved shirts by 8. Choice (H), which will result in a 1×3 matrix, does this. The product (which you are not asked to find) will be:

$$[(6)(1) + (8)(4) \quad (6)(5) + (8)(6) \quad (6)(3) + (8)(2)] = [38 \quad 78 \quad 34]$$

Are you able to interpret the resulting matrix? It means the amount of money collected for small T-shirts was $38, for medium T-shirts was $78, and for large T-shirts was $34.

The other matrix-related question that crops up occasionally on the ACT Test is a straightforward question about the *determinant* of a matrix. The determinant is a unique number associated with only a square matrix. The ACT questions always deal with the determinant for a 2×2 matrix.

The determinant of $\begin{bmatrix} a & b \\ c & d \end{bmatrix}$ is denoted $\begin{vmatrix} a & b \\ c & d \end{vmatrix}$ and is defined as $ad - bc$.

For example, $\begin{vmatrix} 3 & -1 \\ 2 & 4 \end{vmatrix} = (3)(4) - (-1)(2) = 14$

Example 19

By definition, the determinant $\begin{vmatrix} a & b \\ c & d \end{vmatrix} = ad - bc$. What is the value of

$\begin{vmatrix} 4p & -3q \\ -3p & 2q \end{vmatrix}$ when $p = -2$ and $q = -1$?

A. -2
B. 2
C. -34
D. 34
E. 42

SOLUTION

(A) The easiest way to do this is to start by substituting the given values into the determinant:

$$\begin{vmatrix} 4p & -3q \\ -3p & 2q \end{vmatrix} = \begin{vmatrix} -8 & 3 \\ 6 & -2 \end{vmatrix}$$

Now use the definition of the determinant:

$$\begin{vmatrix} -8 & 3 \\ 6 & -2 \end{vmatrix} = (-8)(-2) - (3)(6) = 16 - 18 = -2$$

Complex Numbers

You should know several facts about complex numbers.

$$i = \sqrt{-1}$$

$$i^2 = -1$$

$$(1 + i)(1 - i) = 1 - i^2 = 1 - (-1) = 2$$

For example, to simplify $\dfrac{i}{2-i} \cdot \dfrac{3}{2+i}$, notice that the product of the denominators is a difference of perfect squares:

$$\frac{i}{2-i} \cdot \frac{3}{2+i} = \frac{3i}{4-i^2} = \frac{3i}{4-(-1)} = \frac{3i}{5}$$

Example 20

$3i(1 - i) = ?$

F. 2
G. 6
H. $6i$
J. $3 - 3i$
K. $3 + 3i$

SOLUTION

(K) Use the distributive property to multiply and the fact that $i^2 = -1$:

$$3i(1 - i) = 3i - 3i^2$$
$$= 3i - 3(-1)$$
$$= 3i + 3 \text{ or } 3 + 3i$$

Logarithms

Occasionally the Act Test will include a question on logarithms.

DEFINITION OF LOGARITHM

$$\log_b a = x$$

$$b^x = a$$

The *exponential form* is $b^x = a$. It is equivalent to the *logarithmic form*, $\log_b = a$. This means that each form can be written the other way. Often, that is all it takes to solve the problem. Notice that the logarithm, x, is simply an exponent.

Example 21

$\log_{25} 5 =?$

A. -2

B. $-\dfrac{1}{2}$

C. $\dfrac{1}{2}$

D. 2

E. 5

SOLUTION

(C) Let the expression equal x. Then rewrite the statement in exponential form and solve for x.

Let $\log_{25} 5 = x$.

$25^x = 5$

$\therefore (5^2)^x = 5^1$

$\therefore 5^{2x} = 5^1$

$\therefore 2x = 1$

$\therefore x = \dfrac{1}{2}$

When asked to simplify an expression with logs, try to write the expression in exponential form.

LAWS OF LOGARITHMS

- Product rule: $\log_b mn = \log_b m + \log_b n$

- Quotient rule: $\log_b \dfrac{m}{n} = \log_b m - \log_b n$

- Power rule: $\log_b m^n = n \log_b m$

> **Example 22**

If $\log_b 3 = x$ and $\log_b 5 = y$, then $\log_b 45 = ?$

F. $2x + y$
G. $x + 2y$
H. $2xy$
J. $2x^2y$
K. x^2y

SOLUTION

(F) is correct.

$$
\begin{aligned}
\log_b 45 &= \log_b [(9)(5)] \\
&= \log_b 9 + \log_b 5 \text{ (product rule)} \\
&= \log_b 3^2 + \log_b 5 \\
&= 2\log_b 3 + \log_b 5 \text{ (power rule for } \log_b 3^2) \\
&= 2x + y
\end{aligned}
$$

Sequences

A sequence is a list of numbers that generally follow a pattern. For example,

$$2, 5, 10, 17, 26, \ldots$$

The pattern for the kth term is "square k and add 1." Thus, the next term in the sequence is 37.

There are two particular types of sequences that you should know: arithmetic and geometric.

An *arithmetic sequence* generates its next term by adding a *common difference* to the preceding term. For example,

$-2, 2, 6, 10, \ldots$ Common difference = 4
$10, 8, 6, 4, \ldots$ Common difference = -2

Notice that the nth term of the first sequence is $-2 + (n - 1)4$. The nth term of the second sequence is $10 + (n - 1)(-2)$. The nth term of an arithmetic sequence is always the first term plus $(n - 1)$ common differences.

A *geometric sequence* generates its next term by multiplying the preceding term by the same number, called a *common ratio*. For example,

$3, 9, 27, 81, \ldots$ Common ratio = 3
$4, \dfrac{4}{3}, \dfrac{4}{9}, \dfrac{4}{27}, \ldots$ Common ratio = $\dfrac{1}{3}$

Notice that the nth term of the first sequence is $(3)(3)^{n-1}$. The nth term of the second sequence is $(4)\left(\dfrac{1}{3}\right)^{n-1}$. The nth term of a geometric sequence is always the first term multiplied by the $(n-1)$th power of the common ratio.

Example 23

In the triangle shown below, each row has two more asterisks than the previous row.

```
*
***
*****
*******
```

. . .

If the triangle continues with the same pattern, how many asterisks will be in the 50th row?

A. 151
B. 121
C. 99
D. 98
E. 97

SOLUTION

(C) Notice that the number of asterisks in the rows can be represented as a sequence, where the kth term in the sequence is the number of asterisks in the kth row:

$$1, 3, 5, 7, \ldots$$

This is an arithmetic sequence with a common difference of 2. You are asked to find the number of asterisks in the 50th row, which is the 50th term in the sequence.

$a_{50} = 1 + 49d$, where d is the common difference.

$\therefore a_{50} = 1 + 49(2) = 99$

Example 24

One-third of the air in a tank is removed with each stroke of a pump. To the nearest percent, what percent of the original amount of air remains in the tank after 5 strokes?

F. 1
G. 13
H. 20
J. 33
K. 40

SOLUTION

(G) After 1 stroke, $\frac{2}{3}$ of the air is left.

After 2 strokes, $\left(\frac{2}{3}\right)$ of $\left(\frac{2}{3}\right)$, namely $\left(\frac{2}{3}\right)^2$ of the air is left. Notice the pattern.

After 5 strokes, $\left(\frac{2}{3}\right)^5$ of the air is left.

$$\left(\frac{2}{3}\right)^5 = \frac{32}{243}$$

As a percent, $\frac{32}{243} \cdot 100 \approx 13.1687\% \approx 13\%$

Now you can practice a mixture of problems.

Ace the ACT!
Sample Intermediate Algebra Questions

1. $2i^4 - i^6 = ?$

   A. $i - 1$
   B. $i + 1$
   C. -3
   D. -2
   E. 3

2. If $f(x) = \dfrac{x}{x^2 + 1}$, which of the following statements is (are) true?

   I. The domain of $f(x)$ consists of all real numbers.
   II. The point $(0, 0)$ lies on the graph of $f(x)$.
   III. For all $x < 0$, $f(x) < 0$.

   F. I only
   G. II only
   H. III only
   J. I and II only
   K. I, II, and III

3. What is the matrix product

   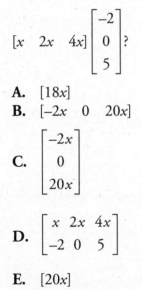

   $$[x \quad 2x \quad 4x]\begin{bmatrix} -2 \\ 0 \\ 5 \end{bmatrix}?$$

   A. $[18x]$
   B. $[-2x \quad 0 \quad 20x]$
   C. $\begin{bmatrix} -2x \\ 0 \\ 20x \end{bmatrix}$
   D. $\begin{bmatrix} x & 2x & 4x \\ -2 & 0 & 5 \end{bmatrix}$
   E. $[20x]$

4. If $p + 2\sqrt{x - 1} = q$ and $q > p$, what is $x - 1$ in terms of p and q?

   F. $\dfrac{\sqrt{q - p}}{2}$
   G. $\sqrt{\dfrac{q - p}{2}}$
   H. $\dfrac{q - p}{2}$
   J. $\dfrac{(q - p)^2}{2}$
   K. $\dfrac{(q - p)^2}{4}$

5. The table of values shown is for some linear function $f(x)$. Find $f(10)$.

x	y
-2	-11
-1	-7
0	-3
1	1

   A. 7
   B. 10
   C. 21
   D. 37
   E. 43

6. If $f(x) = ax^2 + bx + c$, $a \neq 0$, and a, b, and c are all negative, which could be the graph of $f(x)$?

   F.

   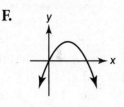

   G.

   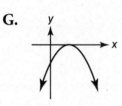

   H.

   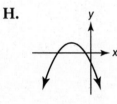

   J.

   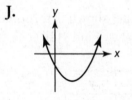

   K.

   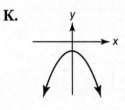

7. A stone projected vertically upward with an initial velocity of 112 feet per second moves according to the equation $s = 112t - 16t^2$, where s is the distance from the ground in feet and t is the time in seconds. What is the maximum height reached by the stone?

   A. 16 feet
   B. 96 feet
   C. 112 feet
   D. 196 feet
   E. 672 feet

8. The graph of $f(x)$ is shown below.

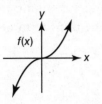

Which of the following represents the graph of $f(x - 3)$?

F.

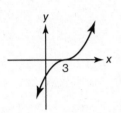

G.

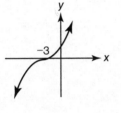

H.

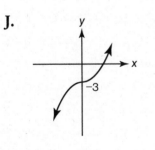

J.

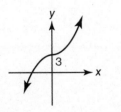

K.

9. Which of the following systems of inequalities is represented by the shaded region of the graph below?

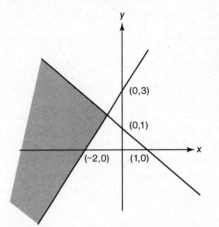

A. $y \leq -x + 1$ and $y \geq \dfrac{3}{2}x + 3$

B. $y \leq -x + 1$ or $y \geq \dfrac{3}{2}x + 3$

C. $y \geq -x + 1$ and $y \leq \dfrac{3}{2}x + 3$

D. $y \geq -x + 1$ or $y \leq \dfrac{3}{2}x + 3$

E. $y \leq x - 1$ and $y \geq \dfrac{2}{3}x + 3$

10. Which of the following is the solution set for the inequality $x^2 \leq 4$?

    F. $x \leq -2$ or $x \geq 2$
    G. $-2 \leq x \leq 2$
    H. $x \leq 2$
    J. $x \geq -2$
    K. $x \leq \pm 2$

11. A geometric sequence has a first term of $x - y$ and a common ratio of $x + y$. What is the third term of the sequence?

    A. $x^3 + 2x^2y - y^3$
    B. $x^3 + x^2y - xy^2 - y^3$
    C. $x^3 - y^3$
    D. $x^2 - y^2$
    E. $x^2 + y^2$

Solutions and Explanations

1. **(E)**	4. **(K)**	7. **(D)**	10. **(G)**
2. **(K)**	5. **(D)**	8. **(F)**	11. **(B)**
3. **(A)**	6. **(H)**	9. **(A)**	

1. **(E)** Remember that $i^2 = -1$.
   Then $i^3 = (i^2)i = -i$,
   and $i^4 = (i^3)i = (-i)i = -i^2 = -(-1) = 1$
   $\therefore 2i^4 - i^6 = 2(1) - (i^4)(i^2)$
   $= 2 - (1)(-1)$
   $= 3$

2. **(K)** All are true!
   I. There are no values of x for which the denominator is 0. This means that $f(x)$ is defined for all x.
   II. Test whether $(0, 0)$ satisfies the equation:

   $$0 \stackrel{?}{=} \frac{0}{(0)^2 + 1}$$

   $$\Rightarrow 0 \stackrel{?}{=} \frac{0}{1} \quad \text{True!}$$

   Since $(0, 0)$ satisfies the equation, $(0, 0)$ is a point on the graph of $f(x)$.
   III. If $x < 0$, $x^2 + 1$ is positive since $x^2 > 0$. The numerator, however, is negative. A negative numerator divided by a positive denominator equals a negative value. Thus, for all $x < 0$, $f(x) < 0$.

3. **(A)** You are asked for the product of a 1×3 and a 3×1 matrix. The product, therefore, must be a 1×1 matrix. This narrows down your choices to (A) or (E). The only element in the product is obtained as follows:

   $(x)(-2) + (2x)(0) + (4x)(5)$
   $= -2x + 0 + 20x$
   $= 18x$

4. **(K)** This is an equation with a radical and so your plan should be to isolate the radical and then square both sides.

   $$p + 2\sqrt{x-1} = q$$

   $$\Rightarrow 2\sqrt{x-1} = q - p$$

   $$\Rightarrow \sqrt{x-1} = \frac{q-p}{2}$$

   $$\Rightarrow x - 1 = \frac{(q-p)^2}{4}$$

5. **(D)** Whichever method you choose to solve this problem, it will probably involve using the slope-intercept form of the linear equation, $y = mx + b$.

   Method 1: y-intercept and slope
   Since $(0, -3)$ is a point on the graph, the y-intercept, b, is -3.
   Since the y-values go up 4 units for every 1 that x goes up, the slope, m, is 4.
   $\therefore$ Equation of $f(x)$ is $y = 4x - 3$.
   $\therefore f(10) = 4(10) - 3 = 37$.

   Method 2: y-intercept and plug in
   Since -3 is the y-intercept, the equation of $f(x)$ is $y = mx - 3$. Now plug in any point from the table to find m. Plugging in $(1, 1)$ gives $1 = m - 3$ or $m = 4$. Therefore, the equation is $y = 4x - 3$, and $f(10) = 4(10) - 3 = 37$.

   Method 3: Arithmetic sequence
   Did you notice that the y-values in the table are an arithmetic sequence with a common difference of 4? If you did, there is a nifty solution that reduces the problem as follows: Find the 10th term, which would be $f(10)$ of an arithmetic sequence with the first term equal to 1 and a common difference of 4.

   $f(10) = 1 + 9(4) = 37$.

6. **(H)** Since $a < 0$, the graph must be concave down, so eliminate choice (J).
   Since $c < 0$, the y-intercept must be negative, so eliminate choice (F).
   Since $a < 0$ and $b < 0$, the axis of symmetry must be $x = $ a negative number,

   because $x = -\dfrac{b}{2a}$. The only choice that satisfies this is choice (H).

7. **(D)**

   Method 1: Graphing calculator
   Graph $y = 112x - 16x^2$. Note that you must adjust the $\boxed{\text{WINDOW}}$ to fit the whole graph on the screen. The large coefficient of x suggests that you try 150, 200, and so on for Ymax. Setting Ymax equal to 200 works quite well. Notice that the vertex of the parabola is close to 200. Therefore, the answer must be choice (D), 196 feet. You can check using $\boxed{\text{TRACE}}$ but should not waste the time. None of the other answer choices are close!

   Method 2: Axis of symmetry
   The maximum value is on the axis of symmetry, which is given by

   $$t = \frac{-112}{2(-16)} = 3.5$$

   $\therefore s = 112(3.5) - 16(3.5)^2 = 196$

   This calculation will take you no time with the calculator. Notice that you have enough information to solve the problem without using the initial velocity, which is a piece of extraneous information.

8. **(F)** $f(x - 3)$ is produced when $f(x)$ is shifted horizontally 3 units to the right, as shown in choice (F).

9. **(A)** The equation of the line containing (0, 1) and (1, 0) is (slope -1 and y-intercept 1).

The equation of the line containing (0, 3) and (–2, 0) is $y = \frac{3}{2}x + 3$ (slope $\frac{3}{2}$ and y-intercept 3). Eliminate choice (E) immediately, because it has the wrong lines.

The region that represents $y \leq -x + 1$ lies below the line $y = -x + 1$. Call it Region 1.

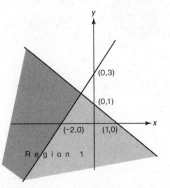

The region that represents $y \geq \frac{3}{2}x + 3$ lies above the line $y = \frac{3}{2}x + 3$. Call it Region 2.

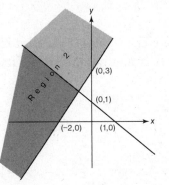

The shaded region shown in the question is the intersection of Regions 1 and 2. Since this area is an intersection, "and" should link the inequalities.

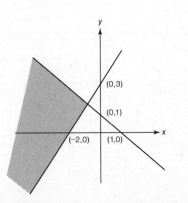

Notice that if the region shaded had included all of Regions 1 and 2, with only the "bottom" fourth of the graph (toward the right) unshaded, the correct answer would have been choice (B). This large shaded region would represent the *union* of the two regions, and "or" should have linked the inequalities.

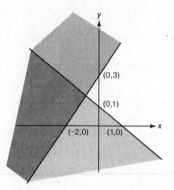

10. **(G)**   Recognize $x^2 \le 4$ as a quadratic inequality. Did a bell go off?

$x^2 \le 4$
$\Rightarrow x^2 - 4 \le 0$
$\Rightarrow (x - 2)(x + 2) \le 0$

The roots are -2 and 2.
The parabola $y = x^2 - 4$ has negative
y values when x is between -2 and 2.
Therefore, $x^2 \le 4 \Rightarrow -2 \le x \le 2$

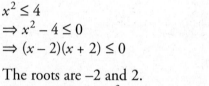

11. **(B)**   In a geometric sequence, you get the next term by multiplying the previous term by the common ratio. Here are the first three terms of the given sequence:

1st term: $x - y$ (given)
2nd term: $(x - y)(x + y) = x^2 - y^2$ (difference of two perfect squares!)
3rd term: $(x^2 - y^2)(x + y)$

Use FOIL to multiply. You get $x^3 + x^2 y - xy^2 - y^3$.
Notice that $x^2 y$ and $-xy^2$ are not like terms and therefore cannot be combined into one term.

Plane and Solid Geometry

CHAPTER 5

CHAPTER GOALS

- Specific strategies
- Topics in plane and solid geometry
- Ace the ACT! Sample plane and solid geometry questions

Of the 60 multiple-choice questions in the ACT Mathematics Test, about one-fourth of them are on plane and solid geometry. This is a hefty chunk!

Everything in your high school geometry career is fair game—properties of plane figures, symmetry, simple 3-D geometry, and measurements. You will need to have at your fingertips the special properties of triangles, parallelograms, rectangles, squares, rhombi, polygons, and circles. By the time you sit down to take the ACT, perimeters, areas, and volumes must be part of your bloodstream.

Here is the good news: since the questions are all multiple-choice, you won't be asked to provide formal proofs on the ACT. Nevertheless, you will need to be able to apply logic to geometric scenarios, and also reach reasonable conclusions.

As is true of all the math questions on the ACT, the geometry questions will range in difficulty from easy to complex. Some will be in the context of a setting, which means that the problem will be embedded in a story. Many of the questions will be accompanied by a diagram. Several will not. Some of the diagrams will be drawn to scale. Some will not.

SPECIFIC STRATEGIES

Irrespective of the type of geometry question, there is one main strategy to follow: FOCUS, with pencil in hand!

Active Pencil

- If there is no diagram, draw one. This will help you absorb the details as you go.
- Mark your diagram to show everything that is given in the question—congruent line segments, congruent angles, lengths, angle measures, arc measures, parallel lines, perpendicular lines, and so on.

- If the solution still eludes you, add some line segments of your own to the picture—join points, extend line segments, and drop perpendiculars.
- On the ACT, geometric diagrams are not guaranteed to be drawn to scale. So it sometimes helps to redraw the figure to scale. Beware—those test writers are tricky, and the information needed to draw the diagram to scale may be missing. For example, suppose they tell you that $\triangle ABC$ is isosceles, with $\overline{AB}$ congruent to $\overline{AC}$, and they helpfully give you this picture:

Don't be fooled. You *cannot* conclude that $BC < AB$. Here is another picture that satisfies the given information:

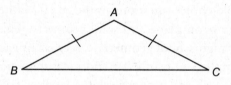

Diagram for Question in Setting

Read carefully if the problem is in a setting. Draw a diagram to represent the setup if one is not already provided. Often a simple problem will emerge from the thicket of words. Some problems just turn out to be easier than they look.

Take a minute to check that you found the correct quantity. Bubbling in a correct answer for the area of Jan's patio will not help you when, in fact, the volume of the swimming pool was required!

If your answer is the size of some real-life quantity, take a minute to check whether it makes sense in the context of the problem. The length of that swimming pool is unlikely to be 2 yards.

Plug In

Unconventional (nonschool) ways of solving problems often work for ACT geometry questions. Start with the answer choices, and work backward. Plug each choice into the problem, and see which one is consistent with the given quantities. You will be surprised at how often this approach works.

Formulas

Most of the time, when you need a formula to solve an ACT geometry problem, the formula will be provided in the question. Still, before the test, you should check that you know the old familiar, easy formulas—area of a circle, area of a parallelogram, and so on—by heart. They are provided in this chapter and at the end of the book, so you have no excuse.

Although many of your teachers (and you too!) may frown upon rote learning, just remember that the ACT Test is not the place to reinvent the geometric wheel and derive formulas that have slipped your mind. Don't ever forget—time is of the essence.

The following pages give you a terse, concise summary of the geometry facts you should know for the ACT. If you are the type whose eyes glaze over at the sight of bulleted facts, why not skip straight to the numbered examples scattered throughout this section? You can always go back to review the particular areas (no pun intended) that need work.

TOPICS IN PLANE AND SOLID GEOMETRY

Points, Lines, Angles

You should know the correct notation for geometric quantities.

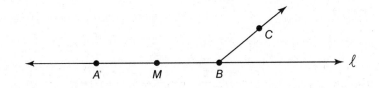

- $\overleftrightarrow{AB}$, $\overleftrightarrow{MB}$, and $\overleftrightarrow{AM}$ all denote *line l*, the line containing points *A*, *M*, and *B*.
- $\overline{AM}$ is the *line segment* with endpoints *A* and *M*. It does not contain point *B*.
- *AM* is the length of $\overline{AM}$.
- $\overrightarrow{BC}$ is the *ray* with endpoint *B* that contains *C*. Notice that ray $\overrightarrow{MA}$ does not contain *B*, but ray $\overrightarrow{AM}$ does.
- $\angle CBA$ is the *angle* formed by rays $\overrightarrow{BC}$ and $\overrightarrow{BA}$.
- $m\angle CBA$ is the measure of $\angle CBA$.
- *M* is the *midpoint* of $\overline{AB}$ if and only if $\overline{AM}$ is congruent to $\overline{BM}$, denoted $\overline{AM} \cong \overline{BM}$. This implies that *AM* = *BM*.

> **TIP**
>
> Knowing the correct notation helps you read geometry questions with greater understanding.

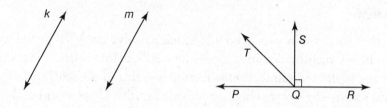

- Line *k* is *parallel* to line *m*. Denote this *k* ∥ *m*.
- Line $\overleftrightarrow{PR}$ is *perpendicular* to ray $\overrightarrow{QS}$, denoted $\overleftrightarrow{PR} \perp \overrightarrow{QS}$. If $\overleftrightarrow{PR} \perp \overrightarrow{QS}$, ∠*SQR* and ∠*SQP* are *right angles* and therefore measure 90°.
- ∠*TQP* is an *acute angle* since the measure of ∠*TQP* is less than 90°.
- ∠*TQR* is an *obtuse angle* since the measure of ∠*TQR* is between 90° and 180°.
- ∠*TQP* and ∠*TQS* are *complementary angles*, i.e., their sum is 90°.
- Two angles are *supplementary* if their sum is 180°. Two adjacent angles on a line are supplementary. Thus the following pairs of angles are supplementary: ∠*PQT* and ∠*TQR*; and ∠*PQS* and ∠*RQS*.

Parallel Lines

You should know the angle relationships when parallel lines are cut by a transversal and when two lines intersect:

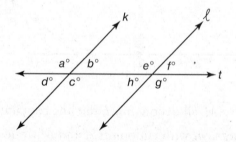

GIVEN *k*∥*l*, CUT BY TRANSVERSAL *t*:

- *Corresponding angles* are congruent.

  ∴ *a* = *e*, *b* = *f*, *d* = *h*, and *c* = *g*

- *Alternate interior angles* are congruent.

  ∴ *c* = *e* and *b* = *h*

- *Interior angles on the same side of a transversal* are supplementary.

  ∴ *b* + *e* = 180° and *c* + *h* = 180°

- *Vertical angles* are formed when two lines intersect. Vertical angles are congruent.

  ∴ *a* = *c*, *b* = *d*, *e* = *g*, and *f* = *h*

Example 1

Let *A, P, Q,* and *B* be points on $\overline{AB}$ as shown. If *AP*:*PQ* = 1:4, if *PQ*:*QB* = 8:3, and if *AP, PQ,* and *QB* are all integer lengths, which could be the length of $\overline{AB}$?

A. 61
B. 62
C. 63
D. 64
E. 65

SOLUTION

(E) 65

Method 1: Logical reasoning

Notice that *AP*:*PQ*:*QB* = 1:4:1.5. Since each length must be an integer, the lengths could be 2, 8, and 3. The total number of parts equals 2 + 8 + 3 = 13, so total length = 13 multiplied by an integer. Of the number choices given, only choice (E), 65, is a multiple of 13. Since 13 × 5 = 65, multiplying each of the lengths 2, 8, and 3 by 5 gives 10, 40, and 15, which add up to 65. Notice that 2, 8, and 3 can be scaled so that their sum is any of the answer choices, but only a multiple of 13 keeps the lengths as integers.

> In a ratio problem, add the numbers in the ratio to give you the number of "parts."

Method 2: Algebra

The ratio *AP*:*PQ*:*QB* = 2:8:3.

If *AP* = 2*x*, *PQ* = 8*x*, and *QB* = 3*x*.

∴ *AB* = 13*x*.

If you set 13*x* equal to any of the answer choices, you notice that 13*x* = 65 is the only case that gives integer values for each of the lengths.

Example 2

In the figure shown below, $\overrightarrow{BC}$ is parallel to $\overrightarrow{FG}$ and $\overrightarrow{BF}$ is parallel to $\overrightarrow{CG}$. If $\angle EFJ$ measures $3x + 5°$ and $\angle DCG$ measures $6x - 5°$, what is the measure, in degrees, of $\angle CBF$?

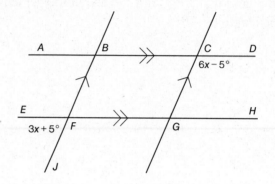

F. $13\dfrac{1}{3}$

G. 20

H. 55

J. $113\dfrac{2}{3}$

K. 115

SOLUTION

(K) 115°

Label $\angle BFG$ and $\angle CBF$ as shown: $\angle 1$ and $\angle 2$, respectively.

You are required to find the measure of $\angle 2$.

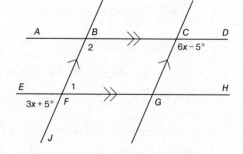

$\angle 1$ and $\angle EFJ$ are congruent vertical angles.

$\therefore \angle 1$ is $3x + 5°$.

$\angle 2$ and $\angle DCG$ are congruent corresponding angles ($\overrightarrow{BF} \parallel \overrightarrow{CG}$ cut by $\overrightarrow{AD}$).

$\therefore \angle 2$ is $6x - 5°$

$\angle 1$ and $\angle 2$ are interior angles on the same side of $\overrightarrow{BF}$.

$\therefore \angle 1$ and $\angle 2$ add up to $180°$ (since $\overrightarrow{BC} \parallel \overrightarrow{FG}$, interior angles supplementary)

$\therefore 3x + 5 + 6x - 5 = 180 \Rightarrow x = 20.$

Don't be careless; 20 is not the answer! You were asked to find the measure of ∠2, not of x. You must plug 20 into $6x - 5$, which gives 115 degrees.

Your technique in solving this (and any geometry) problem whose picture is drawn should be to fill in all the relevant quantities directly on the diagram in the test booklet.

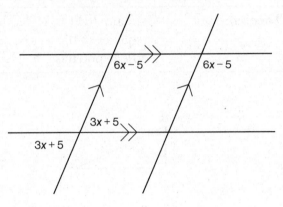

With this picture in front of you, you can quickly solve

$$3x + 5 + 6x - 5 = 180$$

Triangles

TYPES OF TRIANGLES

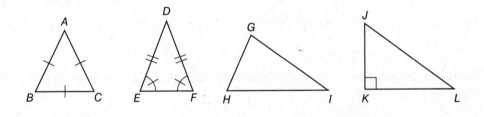

△*ABC* is *equilateral*.	All three sides are congruent, and all three angles measure 60°.
△*DEF* is *isosceles*.	Two sides, $\overline{DE}$ and $\overline{DF}$, are congruent. The third side, $\overline{EF}$ in the diagram above, is called the *base*. The *base angles*, ∠*E* and ∠*F*, are congruent.
△*GHI* is *scalene*.	All three sides have different lengths, and all three angles have different measures. The angle opposite the longest side has the greatest measure. The angle opposite the shortest side has the smallest measure.
△*JKL* is a *right triangle*.	$\overline{JK}$ and $\overline{KL}$ are the *legs*. $\overline{JL}$, the side opposite the right angle, is the *hypotenuse*.

SOME TRIANGLE FACTS

Triangle Inequality Theorem	The sum of the lengths of any two sides of a triangle is greater than the length of the third side.
Measure of Angles in a Triangle	The sum of the measure of the three angles in a triangle is 180°.
Pythagorean Theorem	In any right triangle, the sum of the squares of the legs equal the square of the hypotenuse. In $\triangle ABC$, $a^2 + b^2 = c^2$

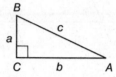

SPECIAL TRIANGLES

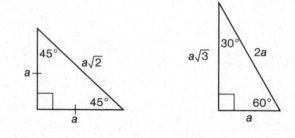

Know the lengths shown above! These nifty triangles often pop up on the ACT Math Test.

SIMILAR TRIANGLES

- Two triangles are *similar* if their sides are proportional. This means that the ratios of corresponding sides are equal.

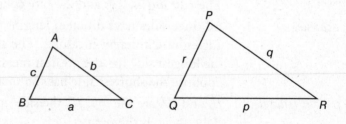

- Given that $\triangle ABC$ is similar to $\triangle PQR$, $\dfrac{a}{p} = \dfrac{b}{q} = \dfrac{c}{r}$.

- The corresponding angles in similar triangles are congruent.

- If two angles of one triangle are congruent to two angles of a second triangle, the triangles are similar.

- If two triangles are similar and the ratio of a pair of corresponding sides is $\dfrac{x}{y}$, then the ratio of their perimeters is $\dfrac{x}{y}$, the ratio of their altitudes is $\dfrac{x}{y}$, and the ratio of their areas is $\left(\dfrac{x}{y}\right)^2$. Remembering this cool fact can save you lots of steps.

Look at this example.

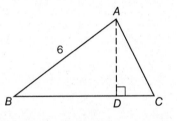 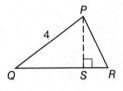

$\triangle ABC$ is similar to $\triangle PQR$.

$\dfrac{AB}{PQ} = \dfrac{3}{2},\ \dfrac{AD}{PS} = \dfrac{3}{2}$

$\dfrac{\text{Perimeter of } \triangle ABC}{\text{Perimeter of } \triangle PQR} = \dfrac{3}{2}$

$\dfrac{\text{Area of } \triangle ABC}{\text{Area of } \triangle PQR} = \left(\dfrac{3}{2}\right)^2 = \left(\dfrac{9}{4}\right)$

 For two similar figures, if the ratio of their sides is $\dfrac{x}{y}$, then the ratio of their areas is $\dfrac{x^2}{y^2}$ and the ratios of their volumes (if applicable) is $\dfrac{x^3}{y^3}$.

Example 3

In the diagram below, $\triangle ABC$ is similar to $\triangle PQR$.

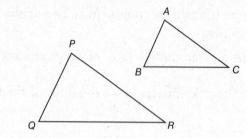

If the ratio of the area of $\triangle ABC$ to the area of $\triangle PQR$ is 8:18, then what is the ratio $AC:PR$?

A. 1:2
B. 2:3
C. 4:9
D. $2\sqrt{2}:3\sqrt{3}$
E. $2\sqrt{3}:3\sqrt{2}$

SOLUTION

(B) $\dfrac{AC}{PR} = \dfrac{x}{y}$

$\Rightarrow \dfrac{\text{Area of } \triangle ABC}{\text{Area of } \triangle PQR} = \dfrac{x^2}{y^2} = \dfrac{8}{18} = \dfrac{4}{9}$

$\therefore \dfrac{x}{y} = \dfrac{\sqrt{4}}{\sqrt{9}} = \dfrac{2}{3}$

Example 4

In the figure below, $\triangle PQR$ is a right triangle with the right angle at P. Line segment $\overline{PS}$ is an altitude, $PQ = 9$, and $PR = 12$. What is the area of $\triangle PQS$ to the nearest tenth of a square unit?

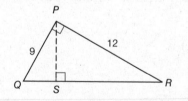

F. 19.4
G. 20.3
H. 24.6
J. 27.0
K. 60.0

SOLUTION

(F) Here is what this problem boils down to: Find the area of a triangle that is similar to a triangle whose area you know. Both $\triangle PQR$ and $\triangle PQS$ contain a right angle, and both contain $\angle Q$. Therefore, the triangles are similar. Picture them side by side:

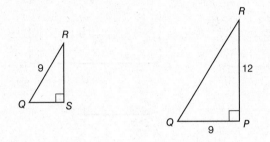

$\triangle PQS$ is similar to $\triangle RQP$.

Once you get this far, you can find the ratio $\dfrac{PQ}{RQ}$.

By the Pythagorean theorem, $RQ = 15$.

$$\therefore \frac{PQ}{RQ} = \frac{9}{15} = \frac{3}{5}$$

$$\therefore \frac{\text{Area of } \triangle PQS}{\text{Area of } \triangle RQP} = \left(\frac{3}{5}\right)^2$$

$$\therefore \frac{\text{Area of } \triangle PQS}{(1/2)(12)(9)} = \left(\frac{9}{25}\right)$$

$$\therefore \text{area of } \triangle PQS = \frac{(9)(54)}{25} \approx 19.4$$

Example 4 was a hard problem. The key to solving it was to draw the similar triangles side by side so the corresponding sides would be easy to identify.

Recognize this picture:

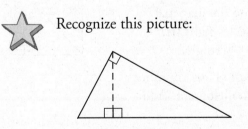

The three right triangles that you see are similar to each other.

> **TIP**
>
> Questions with similar triangles are always easier to solve if you have the similar triangles side by side in the same orientation.

Types of Quadrilaterals

This figure shows four familiar *quadrilaterals*: parallelogram, rectangle, square, and rhombus.

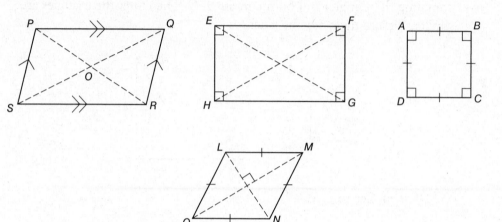

In parallelogram *PQRS*,

1. Opposite sides are parallel and congruent: $\overline{PQ} \parallel \overline{SR}$, $\overline{PS} \parallel \overline{QR}$, $\overline{PQ} \cong \overline{SR}$, and $\overline{PS} \cong \overline{QR}$.
2. Opposite angles are congruent: $\angle P \cong \angle R$ and $\angle S \cong \angle Q$.
3. The diagonals bisect each other: $\overline{PO} \cong \overline{RO}$ and $\overline{SO} \cong \overline{QO}$.

Every rectangle is also a parallelogram. Thus *EFGH* has all the properties of a parallelogram. Additionally, in a rectangle,

1. All four angles are right angles.
2. The diagonals are congruent: $\overline{EG} \cong \overline{HF}$.

Every square is also a rectangle. Therefore, *ABCD* has all the properties of a rectangle and of a parallelogram. Additionally, in a square,

1. All four sides are congruent.
2. The diagonals intersect at right angles.
3. The length of a diagonal is $x\sqrt{2}$, where x is the length of a side. This is because the diagonal splits the square into two isosceles right triangles, each a special 45°-45°-90° triangle.

Every rhombus is also a parallelogram. Thus rhombus *LMNO* has all the properties of a parallelogram. Additionally, in a rhombus,

1. All four sides are congruent.
2. The diagonals intersect at right angles.

Note that every square is a rhombus, but not every rhombus is a square!

Angles in a Quadrilateral

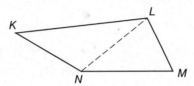

> The sum of the measures of the angles in a quadrilateral is 360°.

In quadrilateral *KLMN*, diagonal $\overline{LN}$ divides the figure into two triangles.

Sum of angles in $\triangle KLN$ = 180°
Sum of angles in $\triangle MLN$ = 180°
Sum of angles in *KLMN* = 360°

Polygons

The sum of the measures of the angles in a polygon is $(n - 2)180°$, where n is the number of sides in the polygon. You can see this if you pick any vertex and join it to each of the other vertices of the polygon.

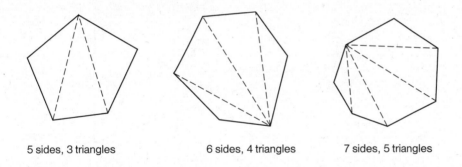

5 sides, 3 triangles   6 sides, 4 triangles   7 sides, 5 triangles

The sum of the angles in the polygon is the number of triangles multiplied by 180°, namely $(n - 2)180°$.

In a *regular polygon*, all the sides are congruent and all the angles are congruent.

The sum of the exterior angles for any polygon, one at each vertex, is 360°. Note that an exterior angle of a polygon is the angle between an extended side of the polygon and another, nonextended side. Shown below is a regular polygon and its five congruent exterior angles.

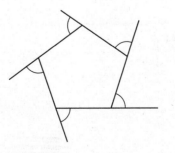

Example 5

What is the measure of one exterior angle of a regular polygon with 36 sides?

   A. 10°
   B. 20°
   C. 36°
   D. 136°
   E. 170°

SOLUTION

(A) The sum of the exterior angles of any polygon is 360°. Since there are 36 exterior angles in the polygon, each one measures $\dfrac{360}{36} = 10°$.

Example 6

In the figure below, what is the value of $x + y + z$?

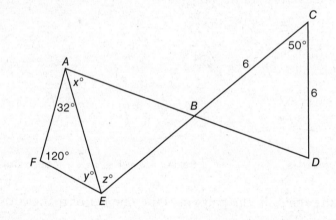

   F. 65
   G. 115
   H. 143
   J. 163
   K. 170

SOLUTION

(H) $\triangle CBD$ is isosceles. Therefore, the base angles are congruent.

Each measures 65° since the sum of the angle measures in a triangle = 180°.

There are congruent vertical angles at B, so $\angle ABE$ measures 65°.

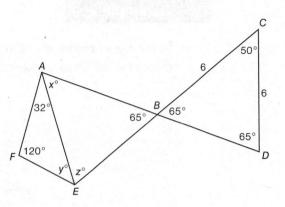

Method 1: Sum of angles in a triangle

In $\triangle ABE$, $x + z = 180° - 65° = 115°$

In $\triangle AFE$, $y = 180° - 152° = 28°$

$\therefore x + y + z = 115° + 28° = 143°$

Method 2: Sum of angles in a quadrilateral

In *FABE*, $120° + 32° + x + 65° + z + y = 360°$

$\therefore x + y + z = 360° - 217° = 143°$

Area

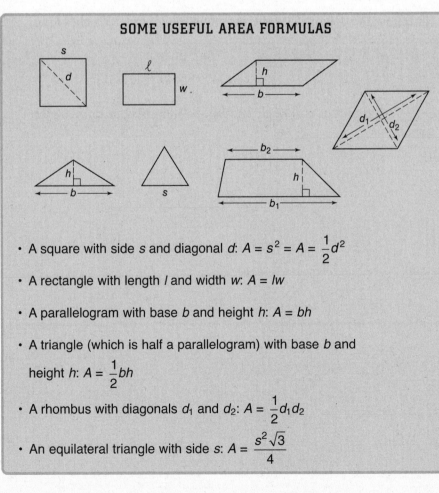

SOME USEFUL AREA FORMULAS

- A square with side s and diagonal d: $A = s^2 = A = \frac{1}{2}d^2$

- A rectangle with length l and width w: $A = lw$

- A parallelogram with base b and height h: $A = bh$

- A triangle (which is half a parallelogram) with base b and height h: $A = \frac{1}{2}bh$

- A rhombus with diagonals d_1 and d_2: $A = \frac{1}{2}d_1d_2$

- An equilateral triangle with side s: $A = \frac{s^2\sqrt{3}}{4}$

Example 7

In the figure below, the dimensions given are in inches. Find the area of rhombus *WXYZ* in square inches.

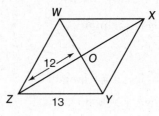

F. 30
G. 60
H. 78
J. 120
K. 240

SOLUTION

(J) Recall that the diagonals of a rhombus intersect at right angles.

Therefore right $\triangle OZY$ has $OY = 5$ (Pythagoras)

Therefore the diagonals of the rhombus are 24 and 10 inches long.

$\therefore$ Area of $WXYZ = \frac{1}{2}(24)(10) = 120$ sq. inches.

 A rhombus is special: Its diagonals intersect at right angles.

Perimeter

The *perimeter* of a polygon is the sum of the lengths of its sides.

Example 8

In the figure shown below, $\overline{WX}$ is parallel to $\overline{ZY}$. The base angles are as marked, and $\overline{WX}$ has a length of 10 feet. What is the perimeter, in feet, of quadrilateral *WXYZ*?

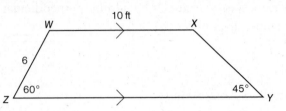

A. $29 + 3\sqrt{3} + 3\sqrt{6}$

B. $29 + 3\sqrt{3} + 3\sqrt{2}$

C. $29 + 6\sqrt{3} + 6\sqrt{6}$

D. $35 + 3\sqrt{2}$

E. $35 + 3\sqrt{6}$

SOLUTION

(A) Fill in all you can conclude on the diagram. The picture begs for altitudes; so draw $\overline{WK}$ and $\overline{XL}$.

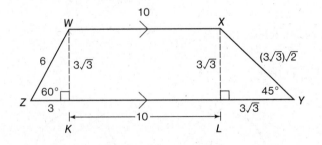

$\triangle WZK$ is a 30°-60°-90° triangle. $\therefore ZK = \dfrac{1}{2}$ the hypotenuse = 3.

Also, *WK*, the altitude, equals $\sqrt{3}$ times $ZK = 3\sqrt{3}$, $\therefore$ altitude $XL = 3\sqrt{3}$.

$\triangle XLY$ is a 45°-45°-90° triangle, $\therefore XL = LY = 3\sqrt{3}$

and $\therefore$ hypotenuse $XY = LY\sqrt{2} = 3\sqrt{3}\sqrt{2} = 3\sqrt{6}$.

$$\text{Perimeter of } WXYZ \quad = WX + WZ + ZY + YX$$
$$= WX + WZ + ZK + KL + LY + YX$$
$$= 10 + 6 + 3 + 10 + 3\sqrt{3} + 3\sqrt{6}$$
$$= 29 + 3\sqrt{3} + 3\sqrt{6}$$

Notice that quadrilateral *WXLK* is a rectangle.

 Angles of 30°, 60°, and 45° are magic numbers on the ACT. Create special triangles by adding perpendicular line segments to your diagram.

Circles

CIRCUMFERENCE AND AREA

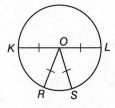

- All radii in a circle have the same length. Thus if *O* is the center, *OK* = *OL* = *OR* = *OS*.

- A radius is half the diameter. $\overline{KL}$ is a diameter and $OR = \frac{1}{2}KL$.

- The *circumference* of a circle is πd or $2\pi r$, where *d* is the diameter and *r* is the radius.

- The area of a circle is πr^2.

ARC AND SECTOR

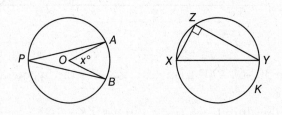

An angle whose vertex is the center of a circle is a *central angle*.

Central ∠*AOB* intercepts *arc AB*. The measure of *arc AB* is the measure of the central angle that intercepts it.

$$\therefore \text{measure of arc } AB = m\angle AOB = x°$$

Notice that $\angle APB$ also intercepts arc AB, where P is on the circumference. The measure of an angle whose vertex is on the circumference is one-half the measure of its intercepted arc.

$$m\angle APB = \frac{1}{2}m\angle AOB = \frac{x^\circ}{2}$$

The angle in a semicircle is a right angle. Thus, in the circle with diameter $\overline{XY}$,

$$m\angle XZY = \frac{1}{2}(\text{measure of arc } XKY) = \frac{1}{2}(180) = 90^\circ$$

You should be able to distinguish between the measure of an arc (in degrees) and the *length* of an arc. Since there are 360° in a circle, an arc of x° cuts off $\frac{x}{360}$ of the circumference. Let L be the arc length of an arc whose measure is x. Then $L = \frac{x}{360}2\pi r$. Note that L has the same units as r.

A *sector* is a region in a circle bounded by a central angle and the arc it intercepts. The area of sector AOB is $\frac{x}{360}\pi r^2$.

TIP

Knowing the vocabulary is half the battle in solving questions about arcs and sectors.

Example 9

In the circle below, the measure of $\angle PQR$ is 110°, and the measure of $\angle PRQ$ is 30°. Find the measure of arc QR.

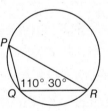

F. 20°
G. 30°
H. 40°
J. 60°
K. 80°

SOLUTION

(K) $m\angle P = 40^\circ$ (sum of angles in triangle $= 180^\circ$)

$\therefore$ measure of arc $QR = 80^\circ$ (angle at circumference $= \frac{1}{2}$ measure of intercepted arc)

Example 10

In the figure below, what is the area of the shaded region?

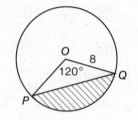

F. $\dfrac{16\pi}{3} - 16\sqrt{3}$

G. $\dfrac{16\pi}{3} - 16$

H. $\dfrac{16\pi}{3} - 64\sqrt{3}$

J. $\dfrac{64\pi}{3} - 32\sqrt{3}$

K. $\dfrac{64\pi}{3} - 16\sqrt{3}$

SOLUTION

(K) Finding shaded areas usually involves subtraction, and this problem is no exception.

Shaded area = Area of sector OPQ – Area of $\triangle OPQ$

To find the area of the triangle, draw in an altitude and fill in the lengths for the 30°-60°-90° triangle.

> **TIP**
>
> When you see "find the shaded area," think subtraction.

Since $OP = OQ$, $\triangle OPK \cong \triangle OQK$ and $PK = 4\sqrt{3}$.

$\therefore PQ = 8\sqrt{3}$.

Area of $\triangle OPQ = \dfrac{1}{2}(8\sqrt{3})(4) = 16\sqrt{3}$

Area of sector $OPQ = \dfrac{120}{360} \cdot \pi(8)^2 = \dfrac{64\pi}{3}$

$\therefore$ Shaded area $= \dfrac{64\pi}{3} - 16\sqrt{3}$

CHORDS

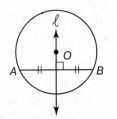

In the circle with center O, $\overline{AB}$ is a chord. Line l passes through the center of the circle.

> - A line through the center of a circle perpendicular to a chord bisects that chord.
> - A line through the center of a circle that bisects a chord is perpendicular to that chord.

TANGENTS

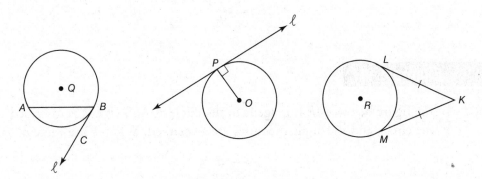

- In the circle with center O, line l is *tangent* to the circle at point P. This means that l intersects the circle in exactly one point, namely P. By the tangent-radius theorem, a tangent is perpendicular to a radius at the point of contact. $\therefore l \perp \overline{OP}$.
- In the circle with center Q, line l is *tangent* to the circle at point B. The measure of an angle formed by a tangent and chord is one-half the measure of its intercepted arc. Thus, $m\angle ABC = \frac{1}{2}$ measure of arc AB.

- In the circle with center R, $\overline{KL}$ and $\overline{KM}$ are tangent at L and M. Tangent segments to a circle from an outside point are congruent. Thus, $\overline{KL} \cong \overline{KM}$.

INSCRIBED CIRCLES AND POLYGONS

A circle is *inscribed* in a polygon if each side of the polygon is tangent to the circle. For example, circle *O* is inscribed in △*ABC*.

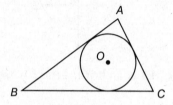

A polygon is inscribed in a circle if each vertex of the polygon is on the circle. For example, quadrilateral *FGHI* is inscribed in circle *O*.

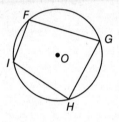

Example 11

In the figure below, $\overline{MR}$ is tangent to the circle at *M*. △*NLM* is inscribed in the circle, and the angle measures are as marked. What is the value of *y*?

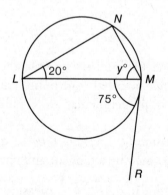

    F.   75°
    G.   80°
    H.   85°
    J.   90°
    K.   95°

SOLUTION

(H) The measure of arc *LM* is 150° since the angle formed by tangent and secant measures half of its intercepted arc.

∴m∠*LNM* = 75° (angle at circumference measures half its intercepted arc)

∴*y* = 85° (sum of angles in triangle is 180°)

Example 12

In the diagram below, circle center *O* is inscribed in equilateral △*BCD*. If the radius of the circle is 4, what is the ratio of the perimeter of △*BCD* to the area of △*BCD*? (Note: Ignore the units.)

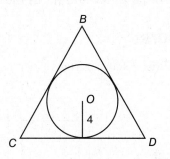

A. $1:2\sqrt{3}$
B. 1:2
C. $1:\sqrt{3}$
D. 1:4
E. $1:4\sqrt{3}$

SOLUTION

(B) 1:2

Draw in some line segments, as shown. By the tangent-radius theorem, each radius is perpendicular to a side of the triangle. Notice the symmetry of the picture. Each vertex of the given equilateral △*BCD* is bisected, giving an angle of 30° in each of the small triangles. All of those small triangles are congruent to each other, and each one is a 30°-60°-90° triangle. Label the sides in one of them, for example △*XOC*, as shown.

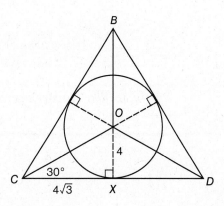

Perimeter of $\triangle BCD = 6(CX) = 24\sqrt{3}$

Area of $\triangle BCD = 6(\text{Area of } \triangle XOC) = 6\left(\frac{1}{2}\right)(4\sqrt{3})(4) = 48\sqrt{3}$

Alternatively,

Area of equilateral $\triangle BCD = \dfrac{s^2\sqrt{3}}{4} = \dfrac{(8\sqrt{3})^2\sqrt{3}}{4} = \dfrac{(64)(3)\sqrt{3}}{4} = 48\sqrt{3}$

$\therefore$ Perimeter: Area = 1:2

A problem with an inscribed circle often needs tangents and radii to solve it. However, what if no radii are in the picture? Draw them at the point of tangency and fill in those right angles!

Prisms and Cylinders

Do you recognize these solids? Each is a right prism.

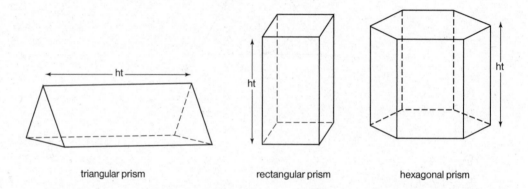

triangular prism   rectangular prism   hexagonal prism

A *right prism* has two congruent polygon bases connected by faces that are perpendicular to the bases. The name of the prism depends on the shape of the base. The height is the distance between the bases.

> The *volume* of a prism is (area of base) × (height).

A *right circular cylinder* resembles a right prism.

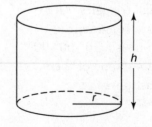

The bases are congruent circles, and the connecting curved surface is perpendicular to the bases. As with a prism, the height of a cylinder is the distance between bases.

Volume of a cylinder	$V = \pi r^2 h$ (area of base) × (height) where r = radius and h = height
Surface area of a cylinder	$S = 2\pi r^2 + 2\pi rh$ where r = radius and h = height
Surface area of a cube	$S = 6e^2$ where e = edge of cube
Surface area of a rectangle prism (box)	$S = 2(lw + lh + wh)$ where l = length, w = width, and h = height

Cones and Pyramids

You should also recognize a sphere, a right circular cone, and a pyramid.

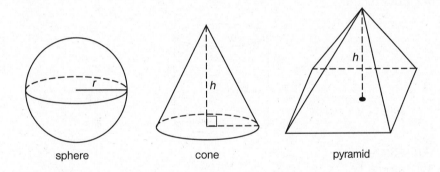

sphere   cone   pyramid

- A *sphere* is the set of points in space equidistant from the center. This distance from the center is r, the radius.
- A *right circular cone* has a circular base. The line connecting the vertex to the center of the base is perpendicular to the base.
- The base of a *pyramid* is a polygon. It is connected to the vertex by triangular faces. A *regular pyramid* is one whose base is a regular polygon and whose triangular faces are congruent, isosceles triangles.

- The volume of a cone with base radius r and height h is $V = \frac{1}{3}\pi r^2 h$.

- The volume of a pyramid with base area B and height h is $V = \frac{1}{3}Bh$.

- The surface area of a sphere with radius r is $S = 4\pi r^2$.

- The volume of a sphere with radius r is $V = \frac{4}{3}\pi r^3$.

> **TIP**
>
> Do not memorize the solid geometry formulas. If a formula is needed in a question, it will be provided in the question.

Questions about the surface area of solids can sometimes be solved using an "imaginary scissors" technique. Picture the solid as a hollow cardboard container.

Now cut it open and flatten it out to make a plane figure. For example, here is a rectangular solid that has been flattened out.

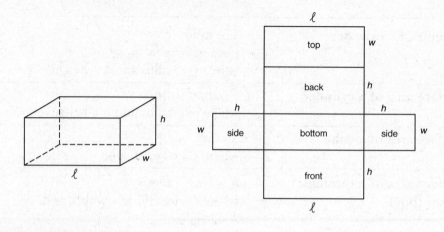

Example 13

What is the total surface area of the cylindrical can shown? The can includes its lid.

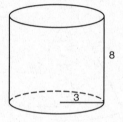

A. $18\pi + 64$

B. $48\pi + 18$

C. 57π

D. 66π

E. 90π

SOLUTION

(D) Use the imaginary scissors technique. Cut off the lid and base. Then cut the rest of the cylinder open and lay it flat.

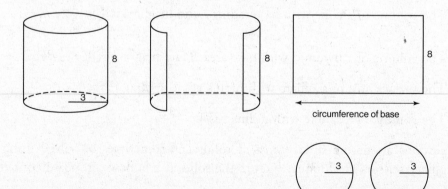

You can now see that the surface area, *SA*, is the area of two circles plus a rectangle whose length is the circumference of the base.

$$SA = 2\pi r^2 + 2\pi rh = 2\pi(9) + 2\pi(24) = 18\pi + 48\pi = 66\pi$$

Use the "imaginary scissors" technique whenever you want to picture a solid lying flat in a plane.

Example 14

The square pyramid shown below has an altitude of 6 feet and each side of its square base is 8 feet long. What is the area, in square feet, of one of the triangular faces of the pyramid?

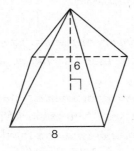

F. $8\sqrt{13}$
G. $16\sqrt{13}$
H. 24
J. 40
K. 80

SOLUTION

(F) $8\sqrt{13}$

Draw in some line segments on the given diagram. By visualizing the symmetry of the figure, you should see:

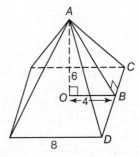

- $\overline{AB}$ is the height of $\triangle ADC$.
- O is the center of the square base.
- OB = half the side of the square base, namely 4 feet.

Use the Pythagorean theorem for $\triangle AOB$.

$AB^2 = 6^2 + 4^2$

$\therefore AB = \sqrt{52} = 2\sqrt{13}$

$\therefore$ Area of $\triangle ADC = \left(\frac{1}{2}\right)(DC)(AB) = \left(\frac{1}{2}\right)(8)(2\sqrt{13}) = 8\sqrt{13}$

Adding line segments works for 3-D diagrams too!

Symmetry

There are two types of symmetry that you should know, reflectional symmetry and rotational symmetry.

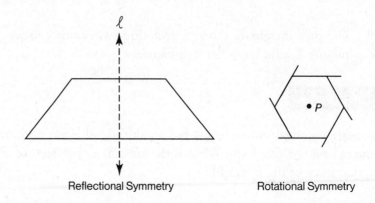

Reflectional Symmetry   Rotational Symmetry

A figure has *reflectional symmetry* or *symmetry about a line* if reflection across the line produces an identical figure. Line *l* is a *line of symmetry* for the trapezoid shown above.

A figure has *rotational symmetry* or *symmetry about a point P* if a rotation of *k* degrees, 0° < *k* < 360°, clockwise or counterclockwise, about *P* produces an identical figure. The point *P* is a *point of symmetry* for the figure. The angle of rotation could be 60°, 120°, 180°, 240°, or 300° for the figure on the right above.

The figure on the left above does not have symmetry about a point. The figure on the right above does not have symmetry about a line. Many figures have both types of symmetry.

Example 15

Which figure below has both symmetry about a line (reflectional) and symmetry about a point (rotational)?

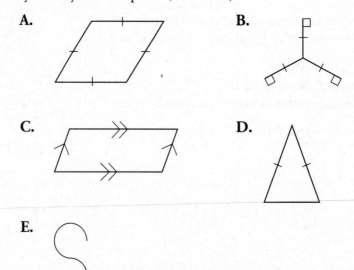

A.

B.

C.

D.

E.

SOLUTION

(A) The figure is a *rhombus,* a parallelogram with four congruent sides. Lines *k* and *l* are lines of symmetry. The rhombus also has 180° rotational symmetry about *P*. Choice (B) has no symmetry. Choice (C) has 180° rotational symmetry but no line symmetry. Choice (D) has line symmetry but no rotational symmetry. Choice (E) has only 180° rotational symmetry.

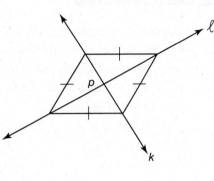

> **TIP**
>
> Always check diagonals for lines of symmetry.

Geometric Probability

A typical question involving geometic probability chooses a point at random in a geometric figure and you must find the probability that the point lies in a specified region.

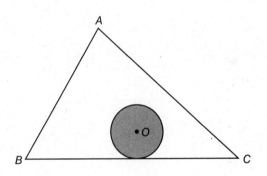

   For example, a point is chosen at random in △*ABC*. What is the probability that the point lands in circle *O*?

$$P(\text{point in circle}) = \frac{\text{Area of circle } O}{\text{Area of } \triangle ABC}$$

Example 16

In the circle shown below, O is the center and $\overline{AB}$ is a diameter. There are two semicircles with diameters $\overline{AO}$ and $\overline{BO}$. There are four smaller semicircles with congruent diameters $\overline{AC}$, $\overline{CO}$, $\overline{OD}$, and $\overline{DB}$. A point is picked at random in the large circle. What is the probability that it lands in a shaded region?

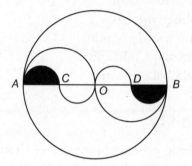

F. $\dfrac{1}{32}$

G. $\dfrac{1}{24}$

H. $\dfrac{1}{16}$

J. $\dfrac{1}{12}$

K. $\dfrac{1}{8}$

SOLUTION

(H) If you put the two little shaded semicircles together, you get one small circle whose radius is $\dfrac{1}{4}$ the radius of the given big circle.

$$P(\text{point in circle}) = \frac{\text{Area of small circle}}{\text{Area of big circle}} = \left(\frac{1}{4}\right)^2 = \frac{1}{16}$$

TIP

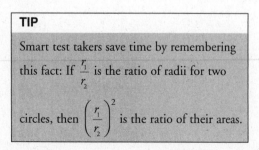

Smart test takers save time by remembering this fact: If $\dfrac{r_1}{r_2}$ is the ratio of radii for two circles, then $\left(\dfrac{r_1}{r_2}\right)^2$ is the ratio of their areas.

Ace the ACT!
Sample Plane and Solid Geometry Questions

1. In the diagram below, a chord of length 18 centimeters is bisected by a line segment that starts at the center and is 6 centimeters from the center. What is the radius of the circle in centimeters?

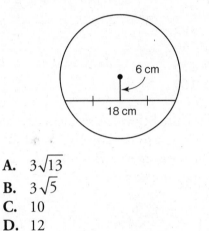

   A. $3\sqrt{13}$
   B. $3\sqrt{5}$
   C. 10
   D. 12
   E. 15

2. A rectangular aquarium 3 ft. × 2 ft. × 1 ft. is $\frac{2}{3}$ full of water. In cubic feet, how much water is in the tank?

   F. $14\frac{2}{3}$
   G. 11
   H. $7\frac{1}{3}$
   J. 6
   K. 4

3. Consider points A, B, C, and D as shown on line segment $\overline{AD}$ below.

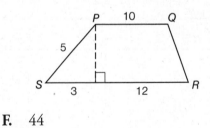

   If the ratio of AB to BC is 3:1 and the length of $\overline{AD}$ is 18 units, what is the length of $\overline{CD}$?

   A. 2
   B. 6
   C. 10
   D. 14
   E. Cannot be determined from the given information

4. In trapezoid $PQRS$, the lengths marked are in feet. What is the area of the trapezoid in square feet?

   F. 44
   G. 50
   H. 62.5
   J. 88
   K. 100

5. In the figure below, △*ABC* is similar to △*DEC*. If the angle measures are as marked, what is the measure of ∠*FEG*?

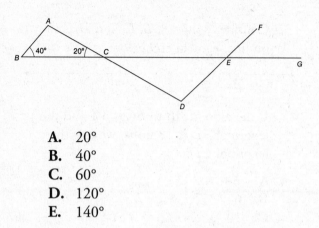

    A. 20°
    B. 40°
    C. 60°
    D. 120°
    E. 140°

6. In the figure below, $\overline{AB}$ is parallel to $\overline{ED}$, $\overline{AE}$ is parallel to $\overline{BD}$, and measure of ∠*A* is 130°. If △*BDC* is isosceles, with $\overline{BD}$ congruent to $\overline{BC}$, what is the measure of ∠*DBC*?

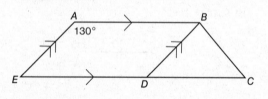

    F. 25°
    G. 50°
    H. 60°
    J. 80°
    K. Cannot be determined from the given information

7. A man who is 6 feet tall casts a shadow 10 feet long. At the same time, a tree casts a shadow 25 feet long. To the nearest foot, how tall is the tree?

    A. 10
    B. 15
    C. 18
    D. 20
    E. 40

8. In the figure below, the angles are as marked. What is *x*?

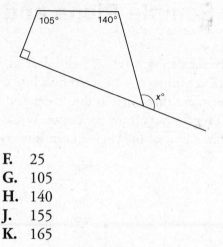

    F. 25
    G. 105
    H. 140
    J. 155
    K. 165

9. The figure below has segments $\overline{BA}$ and $\overline{BC}$ tangent to the circle at *A* and *C*. If the measure of ∠*B* is 30°, what is the measure of arc *ADC*?

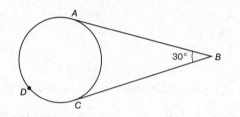

    A. 75°
    B. 150°
    C. 210°
    D. 300°
    E. 330°

10. In the diagram below, circle center O has diameter $\overline{AC}$, AO is 4 units long, and the measure of arc AB is 120°. What is the area of the shaded region?

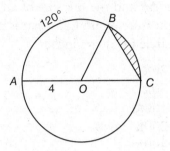

F. $\dfrac{16\pi}{3} - 8\sqrt{3}$

G. $\dfrac{8\pi}{3} - 2\sqrt{3}$

H. $\dfrac{8\pi}{3} - 4\sqrt{3}$

J. $\dfrac{8\pi}{3} - 8\sqrt{3}$

K. $\dfrac{4\pi}{3} - 4\sqrt{3}$

11. The figure below represents part of a regular polygon with n sides inscribed in a circle with center O. In terms of n, what is the degree measure of $\angle OBC$?

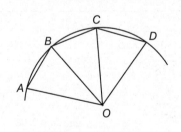

A. $90 - \dfrac{180}{n}$

B. $180 - n$

C. $180n - 360$

D. $180 - \dfrac{360}{n}$

E. $\dfrac{360}{n}$

12. M, N, and P are three points on a number line. $\overline{MN}$ is 7 units long, $\overline{NP}$ is 9 units long, and $\overline{MP}$ is 2 units long. Going from left to right, which of the following is a possible ordering of points on the line?

 I. M, N, P
 II. N, M, P
 III. P, M, N

F. I only
G. II only
H. III only
J. II and III only
K. I, II, and III

13. A line intersects two parallel lines, forming 8 angles. If one of the angles has measure $a°$, how many of the other 7 angles are supplementary to it?

A. 0
B. 1
C. 2
D. 3
E. 4

14. In the figure shown below, $\angle Q$ measures 70°, $\overline{PQ}$ is congruent to $\overline{PR}$, and $\overline{PQ}$ and $\overline{PR}$ are tangent at points A and B to circle center O. Find, in degrees, the measure of $\angle AOB$.

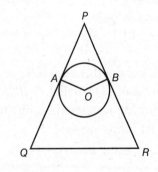

F. 140°
G. 135°
H. 130°
J. 125°
K. 120°

15. A rectangular box with length 22 inches, width 5 inches, and height 6 inches is to be packed with steel balls of radius 2 inches. What is the maximum number of balls that can fit into a box, given that balls should not protrude out of the box?

    A. 0
    B. 5
    C. 6
    D. 10
    E. 11

16. In △*PQR* below $\overline{PM}$ is a median.

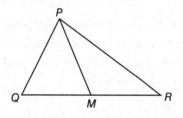

    Which of the following assertions is justifiable from the given information?

    I. ∠*QPM* is congruent to ∠*RPM*.
    II. Perimeter of △*PQM* equals perimeter of △*PRM*.
    III. Area of △*PQM* equals area of △*PRM*.

    F. I only
    G. II only
    H. III only
    J. I and II only
    K. II and III only

17. Quadrilateral *ABCD* has $\overline{AB}$ congruent to $\overline{DC}$, and has $\overline{AD}$ parallel to $\overline{BC}$. Which of the following statements is justifiable from the given information?

    A. $\overline{AB}$ is parallel to $\overline{DC}$.
    B. ∠*A* is congruent to ∠*C*.
    C. $\overline{AD}$ is congruent to $\overline{BC}$.
    D. ∠*A* and ∠*D* are supplementary.
    E. ∠*A* and ∠*B* are supplementary.

18. A quadrilateral *PQRS* is inscribed in a circle. The length of $\overline{PQ}$ is 16 inches, and the length of $\overline{PS}$ is 12 inches. Given that the measure of arc *PQ* equals the measure of arc *SR* and the measure of arc *PS* equals the measure of arc *QR*, what is the area of the circle in square inches?

    F. 20π
    G. 50π
    H. 100π
    J. 200π
    K. 400π

19. The triangles inside △*ABC*, shown below, are formed by joining the midpoints of the sides and then repeating the process. If a point is chosen at random inside △*ABC*, what is the probability that the point lies in the shaded region?

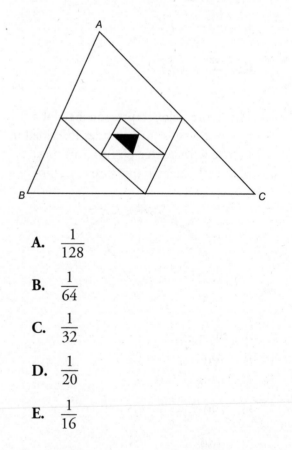

    A. $\dfrac{1}{128}$

    B. $\dfrac{1}{64}$

    C. $\dfrac{1}{32}$

    D. $\dfrac{1}{20}$

    E. $\dfrac{1}{16}$

20. In the figure below, circle with center O has radius 6, and circle with center P has radius 4. The circles are tangent to each other at point S. Line segment $\overline{OP}$ contains point S. If $\overline{RQ}$ is tangent to circle O at R and to circle P at Q, what is the length of $\overline{RQ}$?

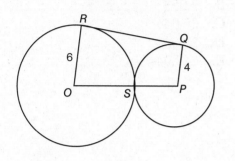

   F. $2\sqrt{21}$
   G. $4\sqrt{6}$
   H. 8
   J.   9
   K. 10

Use the following information to answer questions 21–23.

A grain silo, shown below, is in the shape of a cylinder with a half sphere on top. The radius of the base of the cylinder is 10 feet, and the height of the cylindrical part is 60 feet, as marked.

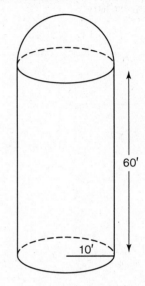

21. The silo, when full, can hold 2,100 bushels of wheat. On each of five consecutive days, the farmer sells 150 bushels from an initially full silo. After these sales, approximately what percent of the silo's capacity is still filled with wheat?

   A. 16
   B. 36
   C. 45
   D. 64
   E. 70

22. The farmer who owns the silo plans to apply a coat of paint to the cylindrical exterior. He is not going to paint the spherical top. A formula for the lateral surface area S of a cylinder with radius r and height h is $S = 2\pi rh$. If one can of paint covers 300 square feet of surface, what is the *fewest* number of cans that the farmer must buy?

    F. 9
    G. 10
    H. 11
    J. 12
    K. 13

23. The volume of a sphere with radius r is given by $V = \frac{4}{3}\pi r^3$. The volume of a cylinder with height h and base area A is given by $V = Ah$. What is the volume of the silo to the nearest cubic foot?

    A. 5,864
    B. 7,959
    C. 20,944
    D. 23,038
    E. 245,044

Solutions and Explanations

1. **(A)**	6. **(J)**	11. **(A)**	16. **(H)**	21. **(D)**
2. **(K)**	7. **(B)**	12. **(J)**	17. **(E)**	22. **(K)**
3. **(E)**	8. **(J)**	13. **(E)**	18. **(H)**	23. **(C)**
4. **(G)**	9. **(C)**	14. **(F)**	19. **(B)**	
5. **(B)**	10. **(H)**	15. **(B)**	20. **(G)**	

1. **(A)**

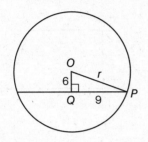

Draw radius r as shown.

$\triangle OPQ$ is a right triangle since a line through the center of a circle that bisects a chord is perpendicular to that chord.

In $\triangle OPQ$,

$$r^2 = 9^2 + 6^2$$
$$= 81 + 36$$
$$= 117$$
$$\therefore r = \sqrt{117} = \sqrt{9 \cdot 13} = 3\sqrt{13}$$

2. **(K)** Volume of rectangular prism = $(3)(2)(1) = 6$ cu. ft.

Two-thirds full means that the volume of water = $\frac{2}{3}(6) = 4$ cu. ft.

3. **(E)**

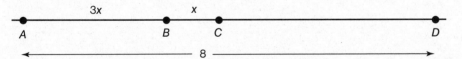

Let $BC = x$. Then $AB = 3x$.

You are given that $AB + BC + CD = 18$.

$\therefore 3x + x + CD = 18$, which implies that $CD = 18 - 4x$.

If $x = 1$, $CD = 14$, $BC = 1$, and $AB = 3$

If $x = 2$, $CD = 10$, $BC = 2$, and $AB = 6$

If $x = 3$, $CD = 6$, $BC = 3$, and $AB = 9$

If $x = 4$, $CD = 2$, $BC = 4$, and $AB = 12$

Notice that each set of values in the above examples is consistent with what is given. Notice also that you are not even told that the lengths must be integers, which means that there is an infinite number of possibilities for the length of *CD*. You therefore need additional information to find *CD* uniquely.

4. **(G)** Find the altitude of the trapezoid using the Pythagorean theorem in △*PSK*.

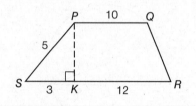

PK = 4

Since *PQRS* is a trapezoid,

$$\text{Area of } PQRS = \frac{1}{2}h(b_1 + b_2)$$

$$= \frac{1}{2}(4)(10 + 15)$$

$$= 50 \text{ sq. ft.}$$

5. **(B)** Since △*ABC* is similar to △*DEC* and vertical angles are congruent, you can fill in the following angle measures on the diagram:

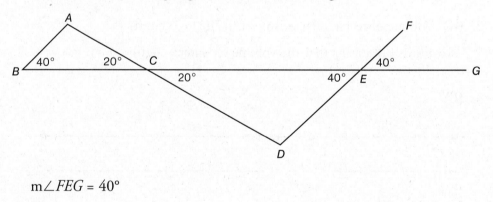

m∠*FEG* = 40°

6. **(J)**

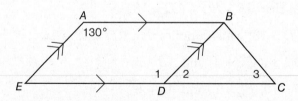

Using the angles labeled as shown:

Since *ABDE* is a parallelogram, m∠1 = 130° (opposite angles congruent)

∴m∠2 = 50° (adjacent angles on line supplementary)
∴m∠3 = 50° (base angles of isosceles triangle congruent)
∴m∠DBC = 80° (sum of angles in triangle = 180°)

7. **(B)** Make a little sketch:

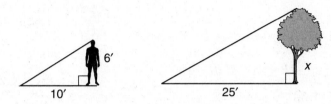

The key is to realize that these right triangles are similar because the angle of the sun's rays is the same at the same time of day.

$$\therefore \frac{x}{25} = \frac{6}{10} \Rightarrow x = \frac{(6)(25)}{10} = 15 \text{ ft.}$$

8. **(J)**

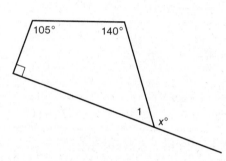

The sum of the angles in a quadrilateral = 360°.

$$\begin{aligned} m\angle 1 &= 360° - (105° + 140° + 90°) \\ &= 360° - 335° \\ &= 25° \end{aligned}$$

Don't be careless. You were asked for x, not for m∠1.

$$x = 180° - 25° = 155°$$

9. **(C)**

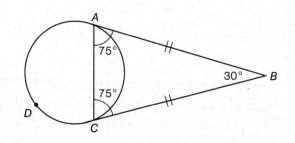

Draw chord $\overline{AC}$.

$\triangle ABC$ has $\overline{AB} \cong \overline{BC}$ since tangents from an external point to the circle are congruent.

$\therefore$ m$\angle BAC$ = m$\angle BCA$ = 75°(sum of angles in triangle = 180°)

$\therefore$ measure of arc AC = 150° (angle between tangent and secant = half intercepted arc)

$\therefore$ measure of arc ADC = 360° − 150° = 210°

10. **(H)**

    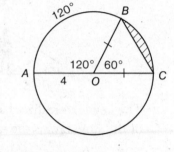

    Fill in all you know.

    Measure of arc AB = m$\angle AOB$ = 120°

    $\therefore$ m$\angle BOC$ = 60°

    $OB = OC = AO = 4$ (radii)

    $\therefore \triangle OBC$ is equilateral.

    Area of shaded region = Area of sector OBC − Area of equilateral $\triangle OBC$

    Area of sector OBC = $\dfrac{60}{360}\pi(4)^2 = \dfrac{8\pi}{3}$

    Area of $\triangle OBC$ = $\dfrac{s^2\sqrt{3}}{4} = 4\sqrt{3}$

    $\therefore$ Shaded area = $\dfrac{8\pi}{3} - 4\sqrt{3}$

11. **(A)** The sum of all angles in a polygon with n sides is $(n-2)180°$. Since there are n congruent angles in a regular polygon, each angle measures $\dfrac{(n-2)180}{n}$.

    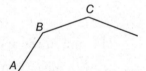

    Notice that $\angle ABC$ is one of these angles.

    From the symmetry,

    m$\angle OBC$ = $\dfrac{1}{2}$m$\angle ABC$

    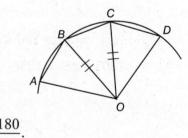

    $= \dfrac{(n-2)180}{2n} = \dfrac{(n-2)90}{n} = \dfrac{90n-180}{n} = 90 - \dfrac{180}{n}$.

12. **(J)** Don't put down that pencil—you need three sketches here. Your technique should be to place the first two points in each Roman numeral choice and then try to place the third point so that the length requirements are satisfied.

Choice I: Reject it since it is not possible to place point *P* to the right of *N* and get *MP* = 2.

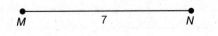

Choice II is possible:

Choice III is possible:

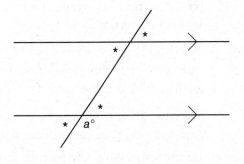

13. **(E)** A picture always helps. Two angles are supplementary if the sum of their measures is 180°. Either of the adjacent angles to the marked angle is supplementary to it. Mark those angles with an asterisk. Using the facts that corresponding angles are congruent, and alternate interior angles are congruent, mark all of the angles that are congruent to that "asterisk" angle, as shown. Altogether, four angles are congruent to each other and are supplementary to the angle with measure *a*°.

14. **(F)** Fill in everything you know on the diagram. The triangle is isosceles, so the base angles are congruent. The sum of the three angles in a triangle is 180°, so ∠*P* = 40°. Radii are perpendicular to tangents, so there are right angles at *A* and *B*. The problem is now easy to complete. *PAOB* is a quadrilateral; therefore the sum of its angles is 360°.

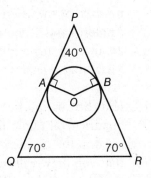

m∠*AOB* = 360° − (90° + 90° + 40°) = 140°.

15. **(B)**

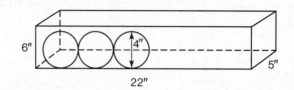

Some visualization is needed here. This is a long, skinny box. The diameter of each ball is 4 inches, so these balls will need to go one by one, lengthwise, to fit into the box. This is a question about length, not volume. Reduce the question to how many 4-inch diameters will fit into the 22-inch length. The answer is $\frac{22}{4}$ = 5, with a bit left over. There is not enough room to squeeze in another ball, so the answer is 5.

16. **(H)** Assertion I is wrong because, in general, a median does not bisect the angle at its vertex.

Assertion II will work only if $PQ = PR$, which is not necessarily true. (Notice that two out of the three sides of the inside triangles are equal: the common median $\overline{PM}$, and the bases $\overline{QM}$ and $\overline{RM}$.)

Assertion III is true because the area of each triangle depends on only the base and height of each. Because $\overline{PM}$ is a median, the bases $\overline{QM}$ and $\overline{RM}$ are the same. Also, the altitude from P to $\overline{QR}$ is the same for each triangle. Therefore, the areas are the same.

17. **(E)** The diagram on the right satisfies all of the given conditions and provides counterexamples for each of the assertions in the other choices. Angles A and B are supplementary because they are interior angles on the same side of a transversal that intersects two parallel lines.

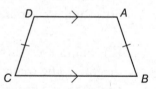

18. **(H)** Because of the pairs of congruent arcs, quadrilateral $PQRS$ must be a rectangle, centered in the circle as shown. (Any nonrectangle that you draw will not cut off the congruent arcs that are given. Try it!) Once you realize this, all that is needed to find the circle's area is to find its radius, which is half the diagonal of the rectangle.

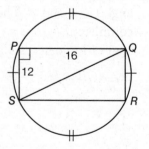

$SQ = 20$ (Pythagorean theorem)

∴ radius = 10 (half of diameter)

Area of circle = $\pi r^2 = 100\pi$

19. **(B)**

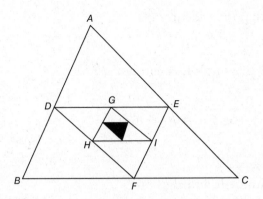

In the diagram, $\overline{DE} \parallel \overline{BFC}$, $\overline{EF} \parallel \overline{ADB}$, and $\overline{DF} \parallel \overline{AEC}$.

It can therefore be shown that $\triangle ADE \cong \triangle DBF \cong \triangle EFC \cong \triangle FED$.

$\therefore \triangle FED = \dfrac{1}{4}$ area $\triangle ABC$

Similarly, $\triangle GHI = \dfrac{1}{4}$ area $\triangle FED = \dfrac{1}{16}$ area $\triangle ABC$.

Here is the sequence of areas you get, compared with $\triangle ABC$:

$1, \dfrac{1}{4}, \dfrac{1}{16}, \dfrac{1}{64}, \ldots$ This is a geometric sequence with a common ratio of $\dfrac{1}{4}$.

Since the shaded region $= \dfrac{1}{64}$ area $\triangle ABC$, the probability of a random point

landing there is $\dfrac{1}{64}$.

20. **(G)**

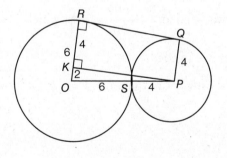

Fill in what you know so far: right angles at R and Q (tangent-radius theorem) and radii along $\overline{OP}$. This is a tough problem. Did you find the line segment that you need to solve it?

The secret is to drop a perpendicular $\overline{PK}$ from P to $\overline{RO}$, which forms rectangle $QPKR$. Since $RQ = KP$, the problem reduces to can you find KP.

In right $\triangle PKO$, $OP = 10$.

Also, $RK = 4$ (opposite side to $\overline{PQ}$).

$\therefore KO = 6 - 4 = 2$

Now use the Pythagorean theorem in $\triangle PKO$:

$KP^2 = 10^2 - 2^2 = 96$

$\therefore KP = \sqrt{96} = \sqrt{16 \cdot 6} = 4\sqrt{6} = RQ$

21. **(D)** 64

Method 1: Arithmetic and algebra
150 bushels a day for 5 days means that a total of 750 bushels were sold. The amount of wheat remaining is $2100 - 750 = 1350$ bushels. The problem now boils down to 1350 is what percent of 2100?

$$\frac{1350}{2100} = \frac{x}{100} \Rightarrow x = \frac{135000}{2100} \approx 64$$

Method 2: Quick estimation

750 is a little more than $\frac{1}{3}$ of 2100. This means that a little less than $\frac{2}{3}$, or $66\frac{2}{3}\%$, is left. The answer closest to this is 64%.

22. **(K)**

$S = 2\pi rh$
$\quad = 2\pi(10)(60)$
$\quad = 1200\pi$

The number of cans needed $= \dfrac{1200\pi}{300} = 4\pi$, which is approximately 12.5.

Therefore, 13 cans are needed.

Notice that 4π is a little more than $4 \times 3 = 12$. Don't waste your time using a calculator here!

23. **(C)**
Volume of cylinder $= \pi r^2 h$
$\qquad\qquad\qquad\quad = \pi(100)(60)$
$\qquad\qquad\qquad\quad = 6000\pi$

For the sphere, you need to realize that its radius is equal to the radius of the base of the cylinder, namely 10.

Volume of half sphere $= \dfrac{2}{3}\pi r^3$

$$= \dfrac{2}{3}\pi\,(1000)$$

$$= \dfrac{2000}{3}\pi$$

Total volume $= \pi\left(6000 + \dfrac{2000}{3}\right)$

$$= \pi\left(\dfrac{18000}{3} + \dfrac{2000}{3}\right)$$

$$= \dfrac{20000}{3}\pi$$

$$\approx 21{,}000$$

Notice that when you get as far as $\dfrac{20000}{3}\pi$, you should see that this is slightly more than 20,000. (When you are estimating, the 3 and π cancel each other). A glance at the answer choices will then tell you that choice (C), 20,944, is the correct answer.

Coordinate Geometry

CHAPTER GOALS

- Specific strategies
- Topics in coordinate geometry
- Ace the ACT! Sample coordinate geometry questions

The coordinate geometry section of the ACT is composed of about 9 questions, or 15% of the 60 multiple-choice questions on the ACT Math Test. Your math courses during high school will have introduced you to most of these topics:

- Number line graphs
- Lengths on the number line
- Points in the plane
- The distance and midpoint formulas
- Graphs of lines in the plane
- Graphs of circles
- Simple conics
- Transformations

In the discussions of these topics, the emphasis will again be on the frequently asked types of questions, the favorites of the ACT Math Test.

SPECIFIC STRATEGIES

Plug In

Use the plug-in strategy as described in previous chapters.

- Plug coordinates into an equation to check whether a point is on a curve.
- Plug coordinates into two equations to check if a point is the place where two lines intersect.

Try to work backward wherever possible. This method is often easier than solving from scratch.

Example 1

A line containing the point (2, 4) has slope 3. If point *P* lies on this line, which of the following could be point *P*?

  A. (1, 7)
  B. (2, 6)
  C. (2, 7)
  D. (3, –1)
  E. (3, 7)

SOLUTION

(E) The slope of the line is 3. Use the slope formula with the given point (2, 4) and each of the answer choices until you find a slope of 3 (plug-in strategy). Only one of the choices will work. The slope for (3, 7), choice (E), and (2, 4) is $\frac{(7-4)}{(3-2)} = 3$.

The numbers are easy. You should be able to zip through them, mentally applying the slope formula, until you find the answer. What you should *not* do is find the equation of the line containing (2, 4) with slope 3 and then plug in the coordinates of the given choices to see which satisfies the equation.

> **TIP**
>
> Always be on the lookout for plug-in shortcuts.

Accurate Sketch

Draw an accurate sketch when a picture is not provided. This will focus your mind and help you to "see" the answer.

Why must the sketch be accurate? If you are careless with your picture, you may introduce a special case or mental block that should not be there. For example, suppose you are told that a circle is tangent to the *y*-axis and its center is in the fourth quadrant. Here are two possible pictures you may draw, where each satisfies the requirements of the problem:

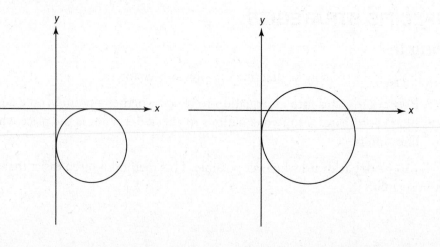

Both Figures 1 and 2 satisfy what is given. Figure 1, however, shows the circle as tangent to both the *x*- and *y*-axes. With this picture, you may be tempted to use the fact that the circle is tangent to the *x*-axis, which was not given. Figure 2 is a much better general representation of the given facts. While pondering this picture, you are unlikely to mistakenly use the fact that the circle is tangent to the *x*-axis.

Example 2

Line segment $\overline{AB}$ has midpoint $(7, -1)$. If point *A* has coordinates $(2, 6)$, then what are the coordinates of point *B*?

F. $\left(\dfrac{9}{2}, \dfrac{5}{2}\right)$

G. $\left(\dfrac{19}{2}, -\dfrac{9}{2}\right)$

H. $(12, -8)$

J. $(14, -8)$

K. $\left(12, \dfrac{5}{2}\right)$

SOLUTION

(H) Draw a picture. The coordinates of *M*, the midpoint of $\overline{AB}$, are given

by $\left(\dfrac{x_A + x_B}{2}, \dfrac{y_A + y_B}{2}\right)$.

Method 1: Plug in

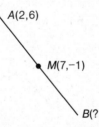

Notice that the average of the endpoints' *x*-coordinates gives 7, and the average of the endpoints' *y*-coordinates gives -1. Plug in the integer answer choices first. Start with choice (H). Point $B = (12, -8)$, and point $A = (2, 6)$.

$$M = \left(\dfrac{12 + 2}{2}, \dfrac{-8 + 6}{2}\right) = (7, -1), \text{ the given midpoint. It works!}$$

Method 2: Slope

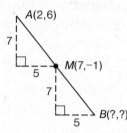

Notice that to get from point A (2, 6) to M (7, –1), the x-coordinate of A goes up 5 and the y-coordinate of A goes down 7:

$$2 + 5 = 7 \text{ and } 6 - 7 = -1.$$

The three points A, M, and B are collinear, and M is the midpoint of $\overline{AB}$.

Therefore, to get from M to B, the x-coordinate of M should go up 5, and the y-coordinate of M should go down 7:

$$7 + 5 = 12 \text{ and } -1 - 7 = -8$$

$\therefore B$ is the point (12, –8).

TOPICS IN COORDINATE GEOMETRY

The following sections describe the main topics in coordinate geometry that you should know. Again, the emphasis is on the ACT favorites.

Distance, Midpoints, Slope

You should have the following information at your fingertips. Refer to the following diagram for the facts about distance and slope.

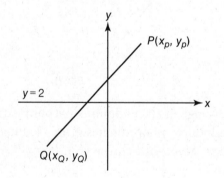

- The *distance* between two points $P(x_P, y_P)$ and $Q(x_Q, y_Q)$ in the (x, y) coordinate plane is $PQ = \sqrt{(x_P - x_Q)^2 + (y_P - y_Q)^2}$

- If P and Q are on the same horizontal line, you can subtract their x-coordinates to find PQ: $PQ = |x_P - x_Q| = |x_Q - x_P|$

- Similarly, if P and Q are on the same vertical line, $PQ = |y_P - y_Q| = |y_Q - y_P|$

- The *midpoint M* of $\overline{PQ}$ is $\left(\dfrac{x_P + x_Q}{2}, \dfrac{y_P + y_Q}{2} \right)$, which is the average of the x-coordinates and the average of the y-coordinates of the endpoints of the given segment.

- The *slope* of $\overrightarrow{PQ} = \dfrac{\text{change in } y}{\text{change in } x} = \dfrac{y_P - y_Q}{x_P - x_O} = \dfrac{y_Q - y_P}{x_Q - x_P}$.

- If $\overrightarrow{PQ}$ is a horizontal line, its slope is 0.

- If $\overrightarrow{PQ}$ is a vertical line, its slope is undefined.

- If two nonvertical lines are parallel, they have the same slope.

- If two lines are perpendicular and neither line is vertical nor horizontal, the product of their slopes is −1. This means that if $l_1 \perp l_2$ and l_1 has slope k, then l_2 has slope $-\dfrac{1}{k}$.)

Example 3

What is the distance in the standard (x, y) coordinate plane between the points $(7, 3)$ and $(1, -1)$?

A. $2\sqrt{10}$
B. $2\sqrt{13}$
C. $2\sqrt{17}$
D. $13\sqrt{2}$
E. $17\sqrt{2}$

SOLUTION

(B) Use the distance formula. Then write your answer in simple radical form.

$$\text{Distance} = \sqrt{(7-1)^2 + (3-(-1))^2}$$

$$= \sqrt{36 + 16}$$

$$= \sqrt{52} = \sqrt{4}\sqrt{13} = 2\sqrt{13}$$

Slope-Intercept Form of Lines

Two standard forms of a linear equation are very useful on the ACT. The *slope-intercept* form, which has popped up many times in this book, is $y = mx + b$, where m is the slope, and b the y-intercept.

Example 4

What is the slope of a line that passes through (–2, 5) and has y-intercept 4?

F. $-\dfrac{6}{5}$

G. $-\dfrac{5}{6}$

H. $-\dfrac{1}{2}$

J. $\dfrac{1}{2}$

K. 2

SOLUTION

(H) $-\dfrac{1}{2}$

Method 1: Slope-intercept form

Since the y-intercept is 4, the equation of the line is $y = mx + 4$. You are asked to find m, the slope of the line. Since the line contains (–2, 5), these values can be plugged into the equation, which can then be solved for m:

$5 = m(-2) + 4$

$\Rightarrow 2m = -1$

$\Rightarrow m = -\dfrac{1}{2}$

Method 2: Slope

Since the y-intercept is 4, the point (0, 4) lies on the line. Also, you are given that the line contains (–2, 5). Use the slope formula:

$\text{Slope} = \dfrac{5-4}{-2-0} = \dfrac{1}{-2} = -\dfrac{1}{2}$

Point-Slope Form of Lines

The other standard form of a linear equation that is useful on the ACT is the *slope-point form*. If you know the slope m of a line and one point on the line (x_1, y_1), the point-slope form of the equation of the line is:

$$y - y_1 = m(x - x_1)$$

For example, if the slope is 4 and the point on the line is (1, 3), the equation of the line is $y - 3 = 4(x - 1)$.

Circles

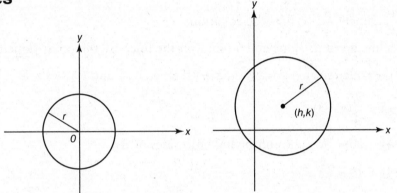

For a circle with radius r centered at the origin, as shown in the circle on the left above, the equation is:

$$x^2 + y^2 = r^2$$

If the circle with radius r is centered at (h, k), as shown in the circle on the right above, the equation is:

$$(x - h)^2 + (y - k)^2 = r^2$$

For example, a circle with equation $(x + 2)^2 + (y - 7)^2 = 36$ is a circle in the (x, y) coordinate plane with center $(-2, 7)$ and radius 6.

Example 5

In the (x, y) coordinate plane, what is the equation of a line that is tangent to the circle $x^2 + y^2 = 25$ at the point $(-3, 4)$?

A. $5y + x = 17$
B. $5y - x = 23$
C. $4y + 3x = 7$
D. $4y - 3x = 25$
E. $4y + 3x = 25$

SOLUTION

(D) The circle has center (0, 0) and radius 5. Denote the line containing the radius, k, and the line through the point of tangency, whose equation is required, l. Notice that the slope of k is $-\dfrac{4}{3}$. Since l is a tangent, $l \perp k$ at the point of tangency. Therefore, the slope of l is the negative reciprocal of $-\dfrac{4}{3}$, namely $\dfrac{3}{4}$. To find the equation

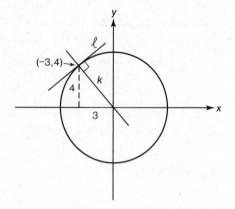

of a line given its slope and a point on the line, use the point-slope form of the equation: $y - y_1 = m(x - x_1)$, where $m = \dfrac{3}{4}$ and $(x_1, y_1) = (-3, 4)$.

$$y - 4 = \frac{3}{4}(x + 3)$$

$$\Rightarrow 4y - 16 = 3x + 9 \text{ (multiplying both sides by 4)}$$

$$\Rightarrow 4y - 3x = 25$$

Notice that an accurate sketch helps you visualize the problem and check your work as you go.

Example 6

A circle in the standard (x, y) coordinate plane is tangent to the x-axis at −10 and the y-axis at 10. Which of the following is an equation of the circle?

F. $(x - 10) + (y + 10) = 100$
G. $(x - 10)^2 + (y + 10)^2 = 100$
H. $(x - 10)^2 + (y - 10)^2 = 100$
J. $(x + 10)^2 + (y - 10)^2 = 100$
K. $(x + 10)^2 + (y + 10)^2 = 100$

SOLUTION

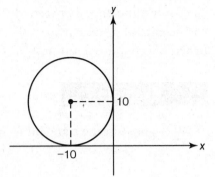

(J) From the picture, notice that the center of the circle is (–10, 10) and the radius is 10. To find the equation, use the standard form of the circle with center (*h*, *k*) and radius *r*, namely, $(x - h)^2 + (y - k)^2 = r^2$.

$$(x - (-10))^2 + (y - 10)^2 = 10^2$$
$$\Rightarrow (x + 10)^2 + (y - 10)^2 = 100$$

 Again, a sketch is worth a thousand words.

Conics

Occasionally, a question requires you to distinguish between equations and recognize the corresponding types of graphs. The ACT does not test an extensive knowledge of conic sections. You should, however, be able to identify the following graphs centered at the origin.

Conic Section	General Equation	Example Equation	Figure
Ellipse	$ax^2 + by^2 = c$ where $a \neq b$ and a, b, and c are all positive	$2x^2 + 3y^2 = 6$	
Hyperbola	$ax^2 - by^2 = c$ or $by^2 - ax^2 = c$ where $c \neq 0$ and a, b, and c are all positive	$2x^2 - 3y^2 = 6$	
Circle centered at the origin	$ax^2 + by^2 = c$ where $a = b$ and a, b, and c are all positive	$x^2 + y^2 = 6$	

Contrast the general equations for an ellipse and a hyperbola with that of a circle. The only difference between the equations of a circle an an ellipse is that the coefficients of x^2 and y^2 are the same for a circle. Notice that the equation for hyperbola contains a minus sign (–), while that for a circle contains a plus sign (+).

Example 7

A graph in the standard (x, y) coordinate plane is shown below.

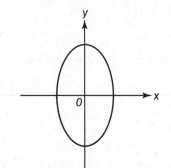

Which of the following could be the corresponding equation?

A. $6x^2 = 6 + y^2$
B. $6x^2 = 6 - y^2$
C. $6x^2 = 6 - 6y^2$
D. $6x^2 = 6 + y$
E. $6x^2 = -6 - y^2$

SOLUTION

(B) The graph shown is an ellipse centered at the origin. So you should look for an equation with the form $ax^2 + by^2 = c$, where a and b are different and c is positive. Choice (B) fits the bill. It can be written as $6x^2 + y^2 = 6$. None of the other equations represents an ellipse.

A. $6x^2 = 6 + y^2 \Rightarrow 6x^2 - y^2 = 6$, a hyperbola
C. $6x^2 = 6 - 6y^2 \Rightarrow x^2 + y^2 = 1$, a circle
D. $6x^2 = 6 + y \Rightarrow y = 6x^2 - 6$, a parabola (Surprise! Remember parabolas from page 104?)
E. $6x^2 = -6 - y^2 \Rightarrow 6x^2 + y^2 = -6$. If the right side were positive, the equation would represent an ellipse. As it is, however, there are no ordered pairs (x, y) such that the sum of their squares will produce a negative number. There is no graph in the (x, y) plane that corresponds to the equation in choice (E).

TIP

Give yourself an ACT edge by having at your fingertips the standard forms for lines, parabolas, ellipses, hyperbolas, and circles.

Transformations

A *translation* shifts all points of a figure horizontally and/or vertically. There is no rotation, reflection, or distortion of a figure when it is translated.

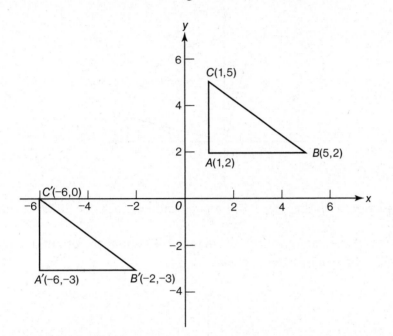

In the picture, $\triangle ABC$ is translated 7 units to the left and 5 units down. $\triangle A'B'C'$ is the image after translation.

A *reflection* produces a mirror image across a line. Every point of the original figure is the same distance from the line of reflection as its image.

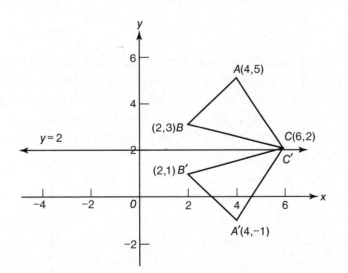

In the picture, $\triangle A'B'C'$ is the image of $\triangle ABC$ reflected across the line $y = 2$.

A *rotation* rotates a figure about a point, called the center of rotation. After rotation, the image of the point is the same distance from the point of rotation as was the original point.

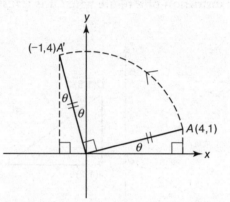

In the picture, *A′* is the image of *A* rotated counterclockwise 90° about the origin.

 When a point (a, b) is rotated 180° about the origin, its image has coordinates $(-a, -b)$.

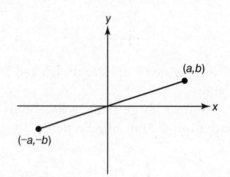

When (a, b) is rotated 90° about the origin, its image has coordinates (b, a), sort of. You need to find the signs of b and a by inspecting the image. For example, when the point $(3, -4)$ is rotated clockwise through 90°, its image has coordinates $(-4, -3)$, as shown in the figure on the left below. However, when the point $(3, -4)$ is rotated counterclockwise through 90°, its image has coordinates $(4, 3)$, as shown in the figure on the right below.

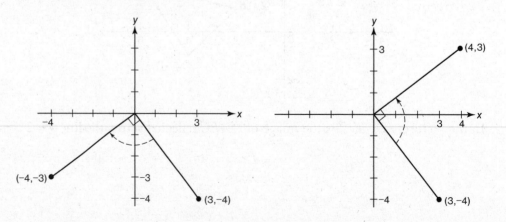

Example 8

In the figure below, $\triangle ABC$ is shown in the standard (x, y) coordinate plane.

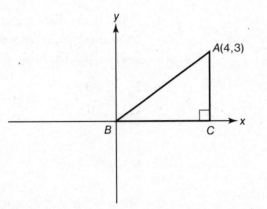

Suppose $\triangle ABC$ is rotated counterclockwise through 90° about the origin and its image is $\triangle A'B'C'$. What is the slope of $\overline{A'B'}$?

F. $\dfrac{3}{4}$

G. $\dfrac{4}{3}$

H. $-\dfrac{3}{4}$

J. $-\dfrac{4}{3}$

K. -3

SOLUTION

(J) Simplify the problem. $\overline{A'B'}$ is the image of the hypotenuse. Therefore, the rest of the triangle is irrelevant. You must rotate $\overline{AB}$ and find the slope of its image, $\overline{A'B'}$. $\overline{A'B'} \perp \overline{AB}$, so their slopes are negative reciprocals. The slope of $\overline{AB} = \dfrac{3}{4}$. Therefore, the slope of $\overline{A'B'} = -\dfrac{4}{3}$.

If a question asks about a piece of a figure, like a point or a line segment that is part of a larger figure that is being transformed, focus on the piece only. Ignore the rest of the figure. If possible, make a sketch that contains just the piece and its image.

The following contains a mixture of sample ACT problems in coordinate geometry.

Ace the ACT!
Sample Coordinate Geometry Questions

1. Which of the following is the equation of a circle in the standard (x, y) coordinate plane?

    A. $(x - 3) + (y + 6) = 100$
    B. $x^2 = y^2 + 25$
    C. $y = x^2 + 25$
    D. $x^2 = 36 - y^2$
    E. $2x^2 + y^2 = 50$

2. What is the distance in the standard (x, y) coordinate plane between the points $(-3, 6)$ and $(-2, -1)$?

    F. $\sqrt{26}$
    G. $\sqrt{74}$
    H. $2\sqrt{5}$
    J. $5\sqrt{10}$
    K. $5\sqrt{2}$

3. A circle with center $(5, -2)$ is tangent to the y-axis. What is the radius of the circle?

    A. 25
    B. 16
    C. 5
    D. 4
    E. 2

4. What is the distance in the standard (x, y) coordinate plane between the points $(-2, 6)$ and $(8, 6)$?

    F. $2\sqrt{3}$
    G. $\sqrt{10}$
    H. 6
    J. 8
    K. 10

5. What is the y-intercept of the line in the standard (x, y) coordinate plane that goes through the points $(4, 5)$ and $(-2, -7)$?

    A. -3
    B. -2
    C. $-\dfrac{1}{2}$
    D. 2
    E. 3

6. The graph shown below in the standard (x, y) coordinate plane is rotated 90° counterclockwise through the origin.

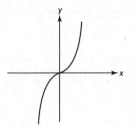

Which of the following graphs is the result of this rotation?

F.

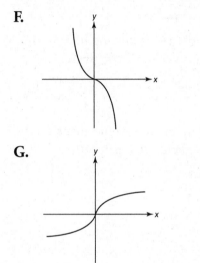

G.

H.

J.

K.

7. A line contains the points $(2, 4k)$ and $(k, -6)$. If the slope of the line is $\frac{2}{3}$, what is the value of k?

   A. $-\dfrac{8}{3}$

   B. $-\dfrac{7}{5}$

   C. $-\dfrac{2}{13}$

   D. -1

   E. 1

8. A triangle, $\triangle PQR$, shown in the diagram below, is translated 4 units to the right and 5 units down. The resulting triangle is then rotated 180° counterclockwise about the origin.

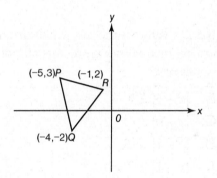

What is the final image of point P'' in the standard (x, y) coordinate plane?

   F. $(-1, -2)$
   G. $(1, 2)$
   H. $(2, 1)$
   J. $(-2, 1)$
   K. $(2, -1)$

9. In the standard (x, y) coordinate plane, points $A(2, 4)$ and $B(8, 4)$ are two vertices of a triangle, $\triangle ABC$. If the perimeter of the triangle is less than 12, which of the following points could be point C?

   I. (5, 4)
  II. (5, 5)
 III. (5, 8)

A. None
B. II only
C. III only
D. II and III only
E. I, II, and III

10. A set of real numbers is represented graphically as follows:

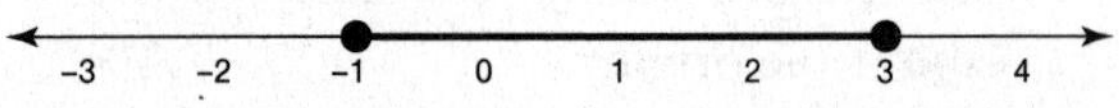

If x is a value in the set, which of the following inequalities represents all possible values of x?

F. $|x - 3| \leq 4$
G. $|x - 3| \geq 4$
H. $|x - 1| \leq 2$
J. $|x - 1| \geq 2$
K. $|x - 3| \leq 1$

11. In the figure below, D is the midpoint of $\overline{CE}$ and the ratio $AB:BC$ is 2:1.

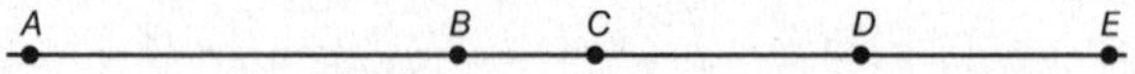

If the length of $\overline{BD}$ is 14 and the length of $\overline{AE}$ is 34, what is the length of $\overline{AB}$?

A. 6
B. 8
C. 12
D. 14
E. 16

12. Consider the following lines in the standard (x, y) coordinate plane:

$$3x + y = 10$$
$$y - kx = 4$$

What value of k would make the lines perpendicular to each other?

F. -3
G. $-\dfrac{1}{3}$
H. $\dfrac{1}{3}$
J. $\dfrac{2}{3}$
K. 3

Solutions and Explanations

1. **(D)**	4. **(K)**	7. **(D)**	10. **(H)**
2. **(K)**	5. **(A)**	8. **(G)**	11. **(C)**
3. **(C)**	6. **(H)**	9. **(A)**	12. **(H)**

1. **(D)** The standard form for a circle with radius r and centered at the origin is $x^2 + y^2 = r^2$. If the circle is centered at (h, k), the standard form is $(x - h)^2 + (y - k)^2 = r^2$. The equation in choice (D) can be written as $x^2 + y^2 = 36$.

   Eliminate choice (A) because it has no squared terms.

   Eliminate choice (B) because it can be written as $x^2 - y^2 = 25$, which is the equation of a hyperbola.

   Eliminate choice (C) because it does not have a y^2 term.

   Eliminate choice (E) because the coefficients of x^2 and y^2 are different. The equation in choice (E) represents an ellipse.

2. **(K)** This is a straightforward application of the distance formula. The distance between $(-3, 6)$ and $(-2, -1)$ is given by:

$$\sqrt{[-3 - (-2)]^2 + [6 - (-1)]^2}$$
$$= \sqrt{(-3 + 2)^2 + (6 + 1)^2}$$
$$= \sqrt{50}$$
$$= \sqrt{25}\sqrt{2}$$
$$= 5\sqrt{2}$$

3. **(C)**

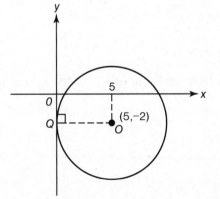

$\overline{QO}$ is a radius of the circle since O is the center and Q is on the circle. The length of $\overline{QO}$ equals 5, the x-coordinate of O. Thus, the radius is 5.

4. **(K)**

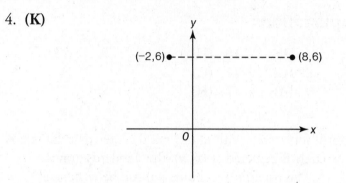

Notice that the points are on the same horizontal line. Therefore, the distance between them is the absolute value of the difference of the *x*-coordinates:

Distance = $|8 - (-2)| = 10$

 Don't use the distance formula for points on the same horizontal or vertical line.

5. **(A)** Your plan should be to find the equation of the line in slope-intercept form, from which you can easily get the *y*-intercept.

To find the slope of the line joining two points: $\dfrac{\text{difference in } y}{\text{difference in } x}$.

Slope $m = \dfrac{-7 - 5}{-2 - 4} = \dfrac{-12}{-6} = 2$

To find the equation of the line, use the point-slope form: $y - y_1 = m(x - x_1)$.

Using the point (4, 5), the equation is:

$y - 5 = 2(x - 4)$
$\therefore y - 5 = 2x - 8$
$\therefore y = 2x - 3$

Therefore, the *y*-intercept is –3.

Note that you could have used the other point, (–2, –7), to get the equation of the line.

TIP

When you have a choice of points to use in a calculation, choose the point that has no negative values. This cuts down on the chance of making careless mistakes.

6. **(H)** Mentally take one point on the given graph and picture where its image falls. For example, the point (2, 6) rotated 90° counterclockwise will land at (–6, 2). This tells you that the corresponding answer choice will have some of its graph in Quadrant II. You can therefore eliminate choices (G), (J), and (K). Eliminate choice (F) because by inspection, it is the wrong shape. Even if (F) were the right shape, the angle of rotation is less than 90°. This leaves choice (H) as the only possibility.

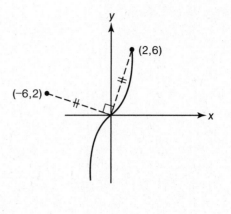

7. **(D)** Use the slope formula: slope = $\dfrac{\text{difference in } y}{\text{difference in } x}$.

∴ slope = $\dfrac{4k-(-6)}{2-k} = \dfrac{4k+6}{2-k} = \dfrac{2}{3}$.

$\Rightarrow 3(4k + 6) = 2(2 - k)$ (cross multiplication)
$\Rightarrow 12k + 18 = 4 - 2k$
$\Rightarrow 14k = -14$
$\Rightarrow k = -1$

8. **(G)** A careful reading of the problem tells you to reduce it to, where does point P'' land?

$P'(-1, -2)$ is the image of P after translating it 4 units right and 5 units down.

$P''(1, 2)$ is where P' lands after rotating it 180° through O.

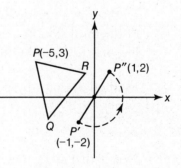

 If the rest of the figure is irrelevant, focus just on the point you need.

9. **(A)** None

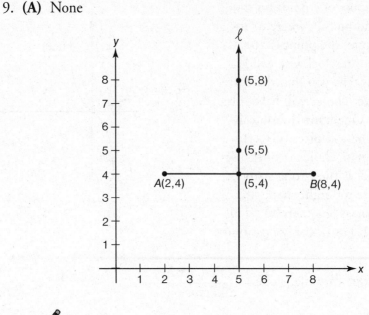

 No sketch in the problem? Provide one!

Method 1: Triangle inequality theorem

The length of $\overline{AB}$ is 8 – 2 = 6.

By the triangle inequality theorem, $AC + BC$ must be greater than 6, the length of the third side. You are told, however, that the perimeter of $\triangle ABC$ must be less than 12. You can therefore reject all given points for C!

Method 2: Point-by-point elimination

Clarify the situation by drawing a picture of $\overline{AB}$, with each of the three given points.

Notice that all of these points have x-coordinate 5 and therefore lie on line l, the perpendicular bisector of $\overline{AB}$. (The midpoint of $\overline{AB}$ is (5, 4).)

Option I: $C = (5, 4)$. Reject it because it lies on $\overline{AB}$ and therefore cannot be a vertex of $\triangle ABC$.

Option II: $C = (5, 5)$. Looks possible. Check the requirement that sum of sides <12.

$CA = \sqrt{(5-2)^2 + (5-4)^2} = \sqrt{10} = CB$, since (5, 5) is on the perpendicular bisector of $\overline{AB}$. $CA + CB = 2\sqrt{10}$, which is slightly greater than 6.

$AB = 8 - 2 = 6$
$\therefore AB + CA + CB > 12$

Therefore, reject (5, 5).

Option III: $C = (5, 8)$: Reject this point without wasting time checking it! From your sketch, you should be able to see that $AC + BC$ will be even larger than the value you got with option II.

 Did you notice the value of an accurate sketch?

10. **(H)** The given set is $-1 \le x \le 3$. Notice that subtracting 1 from each "piece" of the inequality gives $-2 \le x - 1 \le 2$, which is equivalent to $|x - 1| \le 2$. If you do not see this solution, eliminate choices (G) and (J), since these inequalities give two disjoint (separate) regions. Then solving each of the remaining choices leads to choice (H), because it is the only choice whose solution gives $-1 \le x \le 3$, which is the set given on the number line:

$|x - 1| \le 2$
$\Rightarrow x - 1 \ge -2$ and $x - 1 \le 2$
$\Rightarrow x \ge -1$ and $x \le 3$
$\Rightarrow -1 \le x \le 3$

11. **(C)** Label distances x and y as shown below.

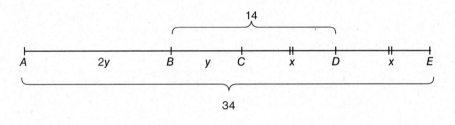

 Use variables on your sketch so that the relationships between lengths can be seen at a glance.

According to the sketch, you are required to find AB, which is $2y$. You must therefore make sure that you eliminate x, not y, when you solve the system of equations given:

$x + y = 14 \Rightarrow x = (14 - y)$
and $2x + 3y = 34$
$\therefore 2(14 - y) + 3y = 34$ (substitution)
$\Rightarrow 28 - 2y + 3y = 34$
$\Rightarrow y = 6$

Since AB is $2y$, the answer is 12.

 Don't waste time solving for other variables if you don't need them!

12. **(H)** Write the given equations in slope-intercept form since you will need to use the slopes in solving the problem:

$3x + y = 10 \Rightarrow y = -3x + 10$ (slope = -3)
$y - kx = 4 \Rightarrow y = kx + 4$ (slope = k)

For the lines to be perpendicular, the slopes should be negative reciprocals of each other. Therefore, $k = \dfrac{1}{3}$, the negative reciprocal of -3.

Trigonometry

> ## CHAPTER GOALS
>
> - The graphing calculator
> - Topics in trigonometry
> - Ace the ACT! Sample trigonometry questions

Even though a scant 7% of the ACT Math Test is devoted to trigonometry (trig)—just 4 questions—the topic is broad. The test can, and does, ask you questions from each of the following categories:

- Right triangle trigonometry
- Angles in radians
- Trig ratios in the four quadrants
- Graphs of trig functions
- Properties of trig functions
- Trig identities
- Trig equations
- Solution of triangles

Whew! Maybe your entire trigonometric life just passed before your eyes. The good news is that the trig questions tend to be straightforward. Yes, the ACT has its favorites here too, so you can focus on certain types of questions. If truth be told, however, you need to know your trig basics—no ifs, ands, or buts about it.

THE GRAPHING CALCULATOR

The main strategy that you should master is the use of your calculator. Both scientific and graphing calculators allow you to find the values of trig ratios and the angles that correspond to given ratios. At all times you must be aware of

> At all times be sure to check:
> Are you in degree or radian mode?
> What order of magnitude are you expecting in your answer?

The second point is true in all topics, on all questions. If a 20-foot ladder leans against a wall, as it often does in the ACT trig questions, be suspicious of an answer that tells you the ladder is 1000 feet from the wall!

Helpful Features

For the TI-84 Plus calculator, here are some simple features that are extremely helpful.

- The MODE button lets you select degree or radian mode.

 Think "MODE" before performing any trig calculation.

- To find the sine, cosine, or tangent of an angle, press the SIN, COS, or TAN button followed by the angle.
- To find the cosecant, secant, or cotangent of an angle, use the facts that

$$\csc x = \frac{1}{\sin x}, \sec x = \frac{1}{\cos x}, \text{ and } \cot x = \frac{1}{\tan x}.$$

- To find an angle whose sine, cosine, or tangent value is given, you need to use one of the inverse trig functions: $\sin^{-1}$, $\cos^{-1}$, or $\tan^{-1}$, respectively. Think of $\sin^{-1} x$ as "an angle whose sine is x."

Example 1

If the value to the nearest thousandth of $\cos \theta$ is -0.892, which of the following could be true about θ?

A. $0° \le \theta < 60°$
B. $60° \le \theta < 90°$
C. $90° \le \theta < 120°$
D. $120° \le \theta < 180°$
E. $270° \le \theta < 360°$

SOLUTION

(D) Put your calculator in degree mode. You want to find an angle whose cosine is -0.892. Press 2ND COS (–) 0.892 ENTER. You get 153.1256519. This is an angle between 120° and 180°, so you should select choice (D).

Drawing Trig Graphs

Your graphing calculator will draw excellent trig graphs for you. There are two steps you need to take.

1. Put the calculator in radian mode.
2. Press $\boxed{\text{ZOOM}}$ 7 to get into trig graphing mode. You can now enter into $\boxed{y =}$ any one of the trig functions: $y = \sin x$, $y = \cos x$, $y = \tan x$,

   $y = \dfrac{1}{\sin x}$ (for $y = \csc x$), $y = \dfrac{1}{\cos x}$ (for $y = \sec x$), or $y = \dfrac{1}{\tan x}$ (for $y = \cot x$).

   When you press the $\boxed{\text{GRAPH}}$ button, your calculator will draw you a lovely trig graph, with x-values from -2π to 2π, with the x-axis marked

   in intervals of $\dfrac{\pi}{2}$. Try it! Practice it.

The ability to inspect a graph at the touch of a button (or two) is a powerful strategy that can reveal many features of a trig function at a glance.

> **TIP**
>
> Check out how easy it is to draw trig graphs on your graphing calculator.

Example 2

For the function $y = 4 \sin 2x$, the x-axis can be partitioned into intervals, each of length p radians. The curve over any one interval is a repetition of the curve over each of the other intervals. What is the least possible value for p, the period of the function?

F. $\dfrac{\pi}{2}$

G. π

H. 2π

J. 3π

K. 4π

SOLUTION

(G) π

Method 1: Rule for finding period
The fundamental period of $y = \sin x$ is 2π. This you should already know.
The rule for finding the fundamental period of $y = \sin Bx$ is:

fundamental period $= \dfrac{2\pi}{|B|}$

In the given example, fundamental period $= \dfrac{2\pi}{|2|} = \pi$

Method 2: Graphing calculator
Suppose you forgot the fundamental period rule. Draw the graph of
$y = 4 \sin 2x$ on your graphing calculator:

Radian mode
Trig mode
$\boxed{y =}$ 4 sin 2x

Here is what you should see.

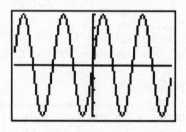

At a glance, you can see the familiar sine curve repeating in intervals of π.

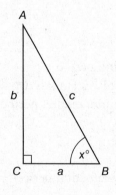

TOPICS IN TRIGONOMETRY

Here are the trig topics that you should know. Review them all thoroughly.

Right Triangle Trigonometry

Problems that require you to find missing lengths in right triangles can sometimes be solved using special triangles or the Pythagorean theorem. In general, you can also use one of the following trigonometric ratios:

$$\sin x = \frac{\text{opposite}}{\text{hypotenuse}} = \frac{b}{c} \text{ (soh)} \qquad \csc x = \frac{1}{\sin x} = \frac{c}{b}$$

$$\cos x = \frac{\text{adjacent}}{\text{hypotenuse}} = \frac{a}{c} \text{ (cah)} \qquad \sec x = \frac{1}{\cos x} = \frac{c}{a}$$

$$\tan x = \frac{\text{opposite}}{\text{adjacent}} = \frac{b}{a} \text{ (toa)} \qquad \cot x = \frac{1}{\tan x} = \frac{a}{b}$$

TIP

Ladders leaning against walls are an ACT favorite. You absolutely need to know how to solve these types of problems.

You are probably familiar with the words in parentheses, which give a simple way of remembering which sides correspond to sin x, cos x, and tan x.

Here is that ubiquitous ladder problem that the ACT is so fond of including on the test.

Example 3

A painter leans a 40-foot ladder against the wall of a building. The side of the building is perpendicular to the ground, and the bottom of the ladder is 15 feet from the base of the building. If θ is the angle that the ladder makes with the ground, which expression could be used to find θ?

A. $\sin \theta = \dfrac{15}{40}$

B. $\cos \theta = \dfrac{15}{40}$

C. $\tan \theta = \dfrac{5\sqrt{55}}{40}$

D. $\csc \theta = \dfrac{40}{5\sqrt{55}}$

E. $\cot \theta = \dfrac{40}{15}$

SOLUTION

(B) Since 15 feet is on the adjacent side to θ and 40 feet is the hypotenuse, you should use the cosine of θ to solve the problem: $\cos \theta = \dfrac{15}{40}$.

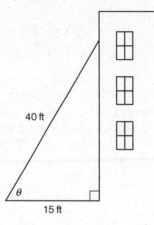

Example 4

The lengths in feet of the sides of right triangle *PQR* are as shown in the diagram below, with $x \geq 0$. What is the cosecant of *P* in terms of *x*?

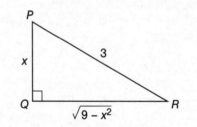

F. $\dfrac{3}{\sqrt{9-x^2}}$

G. $\dfrac{\sqrt{9-x^2}}{3}$

H. $\dfrac{3}{x}$

J. $\dfrac{x}{\sqrt{9-x^2}}$

K. $\dfrac{\sqrt{9-x^2}}{x}$

SOLUTION

(F)

$$\csc P = \frac{1}{\sin P} = \frac{\text{hypotenuse}}{\text{opposite}} = \frac{3}{\sqrt{9 - x^2}}$$

Be sure that you select the side opposite $\angle P$, not $\angle R$!

Example 5

If $\cot A = \dfrac{b}{a}$, $a > 0$, $b > 0$, and $0 < A < \dfrac{\pi}{2}$, what is $\cos A$?

A. $\dfrac{b}{a}$

B. $\dfrac{b}{\sqrt{a^2 + b^2}}$

C. $\dfrac{\sqrt{a^2 + b^2}}{a}$

D. $\dfrac{a}{\sqrt{a^2 - b^2}}$

E. $\dfrac{a}{\sqrt{a^2 + b^2}}$

> **TIP**
>
> In right triangle trigonometry, remember that what is "opposite" and "adjacent" for one of the acute angles is "adjacent" and "opposite" for the other!

SOLUTION

(B) Where did the right triangle come from? Well, whenever you are given an angle and a ratio, you can create your own right triangle. Notice that the range of values given for $\angle A$ tells you that $\angle A$ is acute. So just place it in a right triangle, as shown:

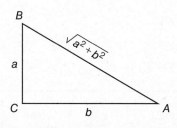

> **TIP**
>
> Remember, remember, remember: Drawing a good picture is often the key to unlocking a problem.

Use the Pythagorean theorem to find the hypotenuse. Then use the correct sides to find $\cos A$:

$$\cos A = \frac{\text{adjacent}}{\text{hypotenuse}} = \frac{b}{\sqrt{a^2 + b^2}}$$

Radians

Picture an angle at the center of a circle:

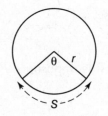

If the length of arc cut off by the angle is s and the radius of the circle is r, then the measure of θ in radians is defined as $\theta = \dfrac{s}{r}$.

If $s = r$, then $\theta = 1$. One radian is approximately $57°$.

Notice that if s, the arc length, is equal to the circumference of the circle, then

$$s = 2\pi r \text{ and } \theta = \frac{2\pi r}{r} = 2\pi$$

A rotation through the entire circle, 360°, is equivalent to 2π radians.

The key fact to remember about converting degrees to radians is that $180° = \pi$ radians.

You should easily be able to convert the familiar angles to radians:

$90° = \dfrac{\pi}{2}$ radians

$60° = \dfrac{\pi}{3}$ radians

$45° = \dfrac{\pi}{4}$ radians

$30° = \dfrac{\pi}{6}$ radians

Example 6

The equation of the circle shown below is $x^2 + y^2 = 36$.

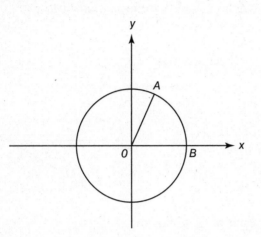

If the measure of $\angle AOB$ is 1.2 radians, what is the length of arc AB in coordinate units?

F. 3π
G. 6π
H. 6
J. 7.2
K. 43.2

SOLUTION

(J) From the equation of the circle, its radius is $\sqrt{36} = 6$.

Recall the definition of an angle in radians. If the vertex of an angle θ is the center of a circle radius r, then $\theta = \dfrac{s}{r}$, where s is the length of the arc cut off by the angle.

Therefore, $s = r\theta$. In the given picture, $s = 6(1.2) = 7.2$.

Trig Ratios in Four Quadrants

ANGLE IN STANDARD POSITION

In the figures below, angles α and β are in *standard position*:

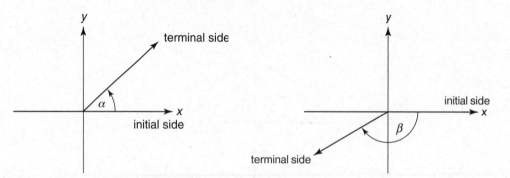

You should know each of the following.

- An angle is in standard position if its initial side is the positive *x*-axis and its vertex is at the origin.
- The quadrant that contains the terminal side determines the quadrant that the angle lies in. For example, α represents an angle in Quadrant I, while β is in Quadrant III.
- A positive angle is measured counterclockwise, while a negative angle is measured clockwise. Thus, α is positive, while β is negative.
- Every angle in standard position has a *reference angle*. The reference angle is the positive acute angle formed by the terminal side of the given angle and the *x*-axis. Some examples:

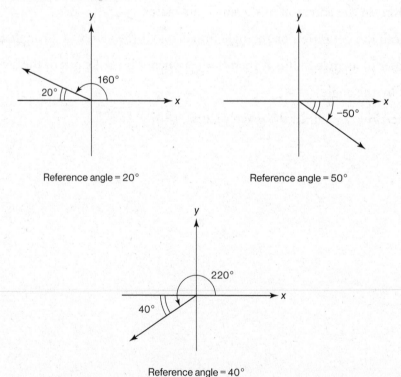

- If the terminal side of an angle in standard position is one of the axes, the angle is a *quadrantal angle*. For example, 90° and –180° are quadrantal angles.

TRIG RATIOS

You can get the trig ratios for any nonquadrantal angle as follows.

- Place the angle in standard position.
- Take any point (x, y) on the terminal side.
- Drop a perpendicular to the x-axis to form a right triangle.
- Label the hypotenuse r.
- Now use the familiar definitions from right triangle trig:

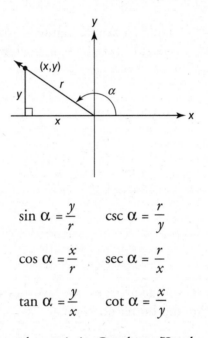

$$\sin \alpha = \frac{y}{r} \qquad \csc \alpha = \frac{r}{y}$$

$$\cos \alpha = \frac{x}{r} \qquad \sec \alpha = \frac{r}{x}$$

$$\tan \alpha = \frac{y}{x} \qquad \cot \alpha = \frac{x}{y}$$

Notice from the diagram that α is in Quadrant II, where $x < 0$ and $y > 0$ (r is always positive). Therefore, $\sin \alpha$ and $\csc \alpha$ are the only two ratios that are positive in Quadrant II. All the other ratios are negative. This is true for all Quadrant II angles. The same kind of reasoning can be used to show that all the ratios for a Quadrant I angle are positive. Here is something that you have seen before—a summary of which trig ratios are positive in the four quadrants.

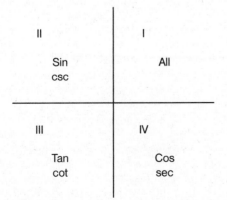

Here is a mnemonic to help you remember the positive signs of ratios in the four quadrants. Starting at Quadrant I: All Students Take Courses. ASTC: all, sine, tan, cosine.

1. ASTC tells you which ratios are positive. All other ratios are negative.
2. You need to remember which reciprocal functions go with each ratio. The trick helps only so much.

To find a trig ratio, find that ratio for the reference angle and affix the correct quadrant sign.

For example, tan 120° = –tan 60°. See the figure below on the left.
For example, cos 220° = –cos 40°. See the figure below on the right.

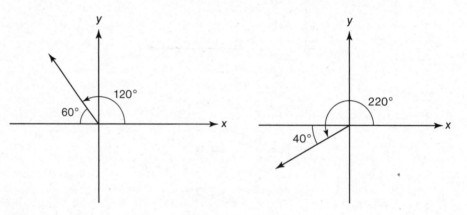

Questions about ratios and their signs are favorites on the ACT. Here is an example of a typical bread-and-butter question.

Example 7

If $\cos \theta = \dfrac{12}{13}$, and $\dfrac{3\pi}{2} \leq \theta < 2\pi$, then $\tan \theta = ?$

A. $-\dfrac{5}{13}$

B. $-\dfrac{5}{12}$

C. $-\dfrac{12}{5}$

D. $\dfrac{5}{12}$

E. $\dfrac{12}{5}$

SOLUTION

(B) Draw a picture of the angle in standard position, including the right triangle with lengths 12 and 13 correctly marked. Use the Pythagorean theorem to find the missing length, 5. You are required to find the tan of an angle in Quadrant IV, so your answer will be negative.

$$\tan \theta = -\frac{\text{opposite}}{\text{adjacent}} = -\frac{5}{12}$$

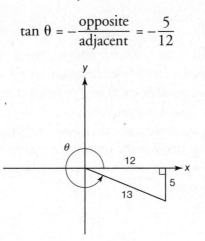

The Unit Circle

The *unit circle* has radius = 1. When finding trig ratios, if the point on the terminal side of an angle θ is also on the unit circle, then the coordinates of the point (x, y) are equivalent to (cos θ, sin θ). This is because $\cos \theta = \frac{x}{1} = x$ and $\sin \theta = \frac{y}{1} = y$.

Coordinates on the unit circle therefore show a way to see the sine and cosine of an angle at a glance.

Here are some familiar angles in radians, with their (cos θ, sin θ) values:

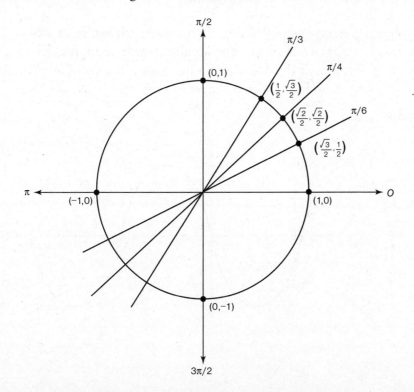

From this unit circle, you can see, for example, that $\cos 0 = 1$, $\sin 0 = 0$, $\cos \frac{\pi}{3} = \frac{1}{2}$, $\sin \frac{\pi}{3} = \frac{\sqrt{3}}{2}$, $\cos \pi = -1$, $\sin \pi = 0$, and so on.

Graphs of Trig Functions

Many properties of a trig function can be seen by examining its graph. Often just a peek at the graph will give you the answer to an ACT question.

All of the trig functions are *periodic*, which means that the graph repeats its pattern after some interval in x. Mathematically, $f(x + p) = f(x)$ for all x in the domain of f. The smallest possible value of p is called the *fundamental period* of the function, sometimes just called the *period*.

The sine and cosine graphs have an additional property, *amplitude*, which is half the distance from the crest (top) to the bottom of a wave. For a sine or cosine curve that has not been vertically translated, the amplitude is simply the distance from the x-axis to the crest of the wave.

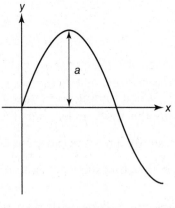

a = amplitude

The following are the graphs of the trig functions, shown from -2π to 2π. The domain, range, fundamental period, and amplitude (where applicable) are given for each function. Recall that the domain of a function is the set of all allowable real-number values for x, and the range is the set of values for y that you get.

y = sin x

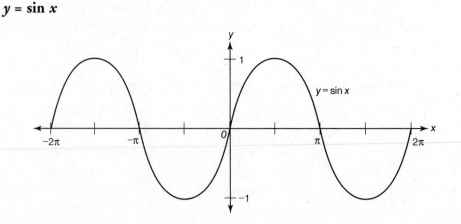

Domain: All real numbers
Range: All real numbers y such that $-1 \le y \le 1$
Fundamental period: 2π
Amplitude: 1

$y = \cos x$

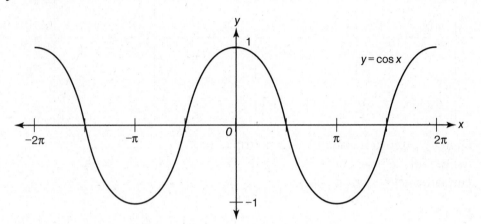

Domain: All real numbers
Range: All real numbers y such that $-1 \le y \le 1$
Fundamental period: 2π
Amplitude: 1

$y = \tan x$

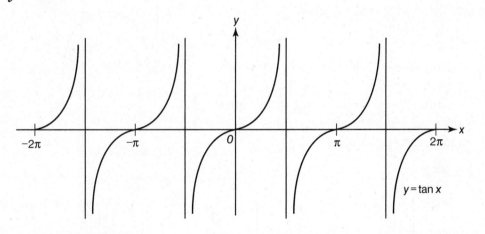

Domain: All real numbers x, $x \ne$ odd multiples of $\dfrac{\pi}{2}$.

Range: All real numbers
Fundamental period: π

$y = \cot x$

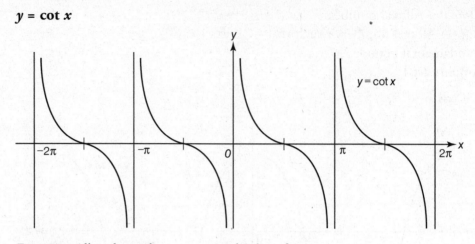

Domain: All real numbers x, $x \neq$ multiples of π.
Range: All real numbers
Fundamental period: π

$y = \csc x$

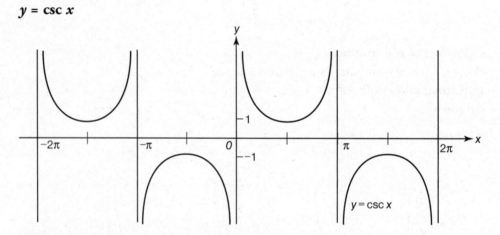

Domain: All real numbers x, $x \neq$ multiples of π.
Range: All real numbers y such that $y \leq -1$ or $y \geq 1$
Fundamental period: 2π

$y = \sec x$

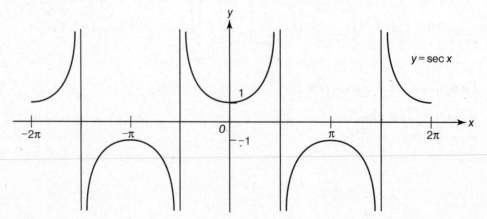

Domain: All real numbers x, $x \neq$ odd multiples of $\dfrac{\pi}{2}$.

Range: All real numbers y such that $y \leq -1$ or $y \geq 1$
Fundamental period: 2π

 Remember, you can generate each trig graph with your graphing calculator. (Radian mode, Trig mode, $\boxed{y=}$ ...)

The Graph of $y = A \sin Bx$ and $y = A \cos Bx$

> ### THE FUNDAMENTAL PERIOD AND AMPLITUDE
>
> • Fundamental period = $\dfrac{2\pi}{|B|}$
>
> • Amplitude = $|A|$

For example, the graph of the function $y = 4 \sin 3x$ has fundamental period $\dfrac{2\pi}{3}$ and amplitude 4. The graph of $y = -6 \cos \dfrac{1}{2}x$ has fundamental period 4π and amplitude 6.

Example 8

For the function graphed below, the x-axis can be partitioned into intervals, each of length k radians. The curve over any one interval is a repetition of the curve over each of the other intervals. What is the smallest-possible value for k, the period of the function?

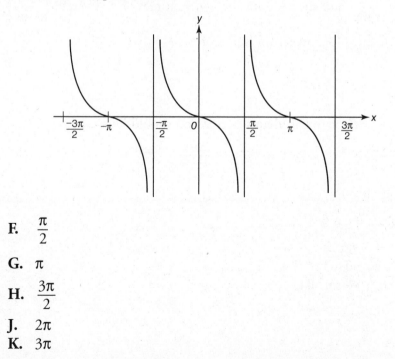

F. $\dfrac{\pi}{2}$

G. π

H. $\dfrac{3\pi}{2}$

J. 2π

K. 3π

SOLUTION

(G) Three repetitions are shown. For example, there is a complete repetition from $\frac{\pi}{2}$ to $\frac{3\pi}{2}$.

Therefore, the fundamental period $= \frac{3\pi}{2} - \frac{\pi}{2} = \frac{2\pi}{2} = \pi$

Example 9

Which of the following values is not in the domain of $f(x) = \csc x$?

A. $\dfrac{\pi}{2}$

B. $\dfrac{2\pi}{3}$

C. $\dfrac{5\pi}{6}$

D. $\dfrac{3\pi}{2}$

E. 3π

SOLUTION

(E) A glance at the graph will show you that there are asymptotes at -2π, $-\pi$, 0, π, and 2π, . . ., where the function is undefined. Recall that $\csc x = \dfrac{1}{\sin x}$, and $\sin x = 0$ for integer multiples of π. Therefore, $\dfrac{1}{\sin x}$ is not defined for integer multiples of π.

Identities

Here are some of the familiar identities that you should know:

$$\tan \theta = \frac{\sin \theta}{\cos \theta} \qquad \cot \theta = \frac{1}{\tan \theta} = \frac{\cos \theta}{\sin \theta}$$

$$\sin^2 \theta + \cos^2 \theta = 1$$

$$\sin 2\theta = 2 \sin \theta \cos \theta$$

$$\cos 2\theta = 1 - 2 \sin^2 \theta$$
$$= 2 \cos^2 \theta - 1$$
$$= \cos^2 \theta - \sin^2 \theta$$

$\sin(A + B) = \sin A \cos B + \cos A \sin B$

$\sin(A - B) = \sin A \cos B - \cos A \sin B$

$\cos(A + B) = \cos A \cos B - \sin A \sin B$

$\cos(A - B) = \cos A \cos B + \sin A \sin B$

 In the sum and difference formulas above, notice that SINE keeps its SIGN. (Cosine does not!)

The important thing about identities on the ACT is that you know how to use them. Many ACT questions actually provide the identities that you need in the question.

Example 10

What is $\cos \dfrac{5\pi}{12}$, given that $\dfrac{5\pi}{12} = \dfrac{\pi}{4} + \dfrac{\pi}{6}$ and that

$\cos(A + B) = (\cos A)(\cos B) - (\sin A)(\sin B)$?

You may use the following table of values:

θ	$\sin \theta$	$\cos \theta$
$\dfrac{\pi}{6}$	$\dfrac{1}{2}$	$\dfrac{\sqrt{3}}{2}$
$\dfrac{\pi}{4}$	$\dfrac{\sqrt{2}}{2}$	$\dfrac{\sqrt{2}}{2}$
$\dfrac{\pi}{3}$	$\dfrac{\sqrt{3}}{2}$	$\dfrac{1}{2}$

F. $\dfrac{\sqrt{2}+1}{2}$

G. $\dfrac{\sqrt{2}+\sqrt{3}}{2}$

H. $\dfrac{\sqrt{6}}{2}$

J. $\dfrac{\sqrt{3}}{4}$

K. $\dfrac{\sqrt{6}-\sqrt{2}}{4}$

SOLUTION

(K) Simply use the values that are given and plug into the formula that is provided:

$$\cos\frac{5\pi}{12} = \cos\left(\frac{\pi}{4}+\frac{\pi}{6}\right)$$

$$= \left(\cos\frac{\pi}{4}\right)\left(\cos\frac{\pi}{6}\right) - \left(\sin\frac{\pi}{4}\right)\left(\sin\frac{\pi}{6}\right)$$

$$= \frac{\sqrt{2}}{2}\cdot\frac{\sqrt{3}}{2} - \frac{\sqrt{2}}{2}\cdot\frac{1}{2}$$

$$= \frac{\sqrt{6}-\sqrt{2}}{4}$$

Example 11

Which of the following expressions is equal to $\dfrac{\cos\theta}{\sin\theta} + \dfrac{\sin\theta}{\cos\theta}$ for all

values of θ for which $\dfrac{\cos\theta}{\sin\theta} + \dfrac{\sin\theta}{\cos\theta}$ is defined?

A. $2\tan\theta$
B. $2\cot\theta$
C. $(\csc\theta)(\sec\theta)$
D. $2(\sin\theta)(\cos\theta)$
E. $\cot\theta + \tan\theta$

SOLUTION

(C) The least common denominator of the two given fractions is $\sin\theta\cos\theta$. You need this to add the fractions:

$$\frac{\cos\theta}{\sin\theta} + \frac{\sin\theta}{\cos\theta} = \frac{\cos\theta\cos\theta}{\sin\theta\cos\theta} + \frac{\sin\theta\sin\theta}{\sin\theta\cos\theta}$$

$$= \frac{\cos^2\theta+\sin^2\theta}{\sin\theta\cos\theta}$$

$$= \frac{1}{\sin\theta\cos\theta}$$

$$= \left(\frac{1}{\sin\theta}\right)\left(\frac{1}{\cos\theta}\right)$$

$$= \csc\theta\sec\theta$$

Trig Equations

On the ACT, you will not be asked to solve difficult trig equations. You could, however, be asked to solve fairly straightforward ones and be asked about solutions between 0 and 2π.

Example 12

Which of the following represents the complete solution set of the equation $\sin^2 \theta + \sin \theta = 0$, $0 \le \theta < 2\pi$?

You may use the following table of values:

θ	$\sin \theta$	$\cos \theta$
0	0	1
$\dfrac{\pi}{2}$	1	0
π	0	−1
$\dfrac{3\pi}{2}$	−1	0

F. $\dfrac{3\pi}{2}$

G. $0, \pi$

H. $0, \dfrac{\pi}{2}, \pi$

J. $\dfrac{\pi}{2}, \pi, \dfrac{3\pi}{2}$

K. $0, \pi, \dfrac{3\pi}{2}$

SOLUTION

(**K**) Your technique should always be to get all terms on the left side and then factor:

$\sin^2 \theta + \sin \theta = 0$
$\Rightarrow \sin \theta (\sin \theta + 1) = 0$

Now set each factor equal to 0, and solve for θ in the given range, $0 \le \theta < 2\pi$:

$\sin \theta = 0$	$\sin \theta + 1 = 0$
$\Rightarrow \theta = 0$ or π	$\Rightarrow \sin \theta = -1$
	$\Rightarrow \theta = \dfrac{3\pi}{2}$

Thus, the complete solution set in the range $0 \le \theta < 2\pi$ is 0, π, $\dfrac{3\pi}{2}$

⭐ To solve a trig equation, get all terms on one side, factor, and solve the equations you get when you set each factor equal to 0.

Solution of Triangles

An ACT trig question may give you a triangle, often described in a setting, and ask you how to find a missing side or angle. If the triangle is not a right triangle, you will need to use the law of sines or the law of cosines to find the missing piece.

You do not need to learn these laws by heart. Typically, an ACT question will provide the relevant formula and then ask you which expression will do the trick. So you do need to know how to use the formulas correctly.

THE LAW OF SINES

In any triangle, the ratio of the sine of an angle to the length of the opposite side is constant:

$$\frac{\sin A}{a} = \frac{\sin B}{b} = \frac{\sin C}{c}$$

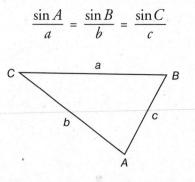

Use this formula to find a missing side or angle whenever you are given:

- Two angles and a side (SAA or ASA)
- Two sides and an angle opposite one of the sides (SSA)

The law of sines *cannot* be used for two sides and the included angle (SAS) because you need to have at least one of the angles opposite a given side. The ASA case works because you can find the third angle, which is opposite the given side.

THE LAW OF COSINES

There are two cases where the law of cosines applies.

- If given two sides and the included angle (SAS), you need to find the third side.
- If given three sides (SSS), you need to find one of the angles.

Refer to the previous figure.

The formulas for the laws of cosines are:

$$a^2 = b^2 + c^2 - 2bc \cos A$$

$$b^2 = a^2 + c^2 - 2ac \cos B$$

$$c^2 = a^2 + b^2 - 2ab \cos C$$

To find a missing angle when given three sides, you can solve the appropriate formula for $\cos A$, $\cos B$, or $\cos C$. For example, if you are given three sides in $\triangle ABC$ and need to find $\angle A$, use the following:

$$a^2 = b^2 + c^2 - 2bc \cos A$$

$$\Rightarrow 2bc \cos A = b^2 + c^2 - a^2$$

$$\Rightarrow \cos A = \frac{b^2 + c^2 - a^2}{2bc}$$

A numerical value on the right side would allow you to use your calculator to find the angle whose cosine is that value.

In practice, you will not need to do that much work. Here are some typical ACT questions that involve the solution of triangles.

Example 13

A tree stands on a hillside as shown below:

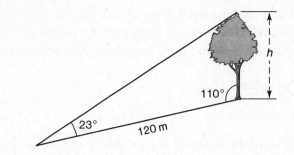

The angle formed by the tree and the ground is 110°, and the angle formed by the line from the bottom of the hill to the top of the tree is 23°. If the distance from the bottom of the hill to the foot of the tree is 120 meters, then *h*, the approximate height of the tree, is given by which of the following expressions?

A. $\dfrac{120\sin 23°}{\sin 47°}$

B. $\dfrac{120\sin 23°}{\sin 110°}$

C. $\dfrac{120\sin 47° \sin 23°}{\sin 110°}$

D. $\dfrac{120\sin 47°}{\sin 23°}$

E. $\dfrac{120\sin 110°}{\sin 23°}$

SOLUTION

(A) Notice how you are given ASA, two angles and an included side.
In order to use the law of sines, you need the angle opposite the given side, 120 meters. You can find this using the fact that the sum of three angles in a triangle is 180°. Thus, the angle opposite 120 is 180° − (110° + 23°) = 47°.

Now use the law of sines:

$$\frac{h}{\sin 23°} = \frac{120}{\sin 47°} = \Rightarrow h = \frac{120\sin 23°}{\sin 47°}$$

Example 14

.A cruise ship and a freighter leave port at the same time and follow straight line courses at 30 kilometers per hour and 10 kilometers per hour, respectively. Suppose the angle between their courses is 130°. Two hours after leaving port, the approximate distance between the two ships is given by which of the following expressions?

(Note: The law of cosines states that for any triangle with vertices A, B, and C and sides opposite those vertices with lengths a, b, and c respectively, $c^2 = a^2 + b^2 - 2ab \cos C$.)

F. $\sqrt{30^2 + 10^2 + 2(30)(10)\cos 50°}$

G. $\sqrt{60^2 + 20^2 - 2(60)(20)\cos 50°}$

H. $\sqrt{60^2 + 20^2 + 2(60)(20)\cos 50°}$

J. $\sqrt{60^2 + 20^2 + 2(60)(20)\cos 130°}$

K. $\sqrt{30^2 + 10^2 - 2(30)(10)\cos 130°}$

SOLUTION

(H) Were you careful to multiply each ship's speed by 2 to get its distance traveled in two hours?

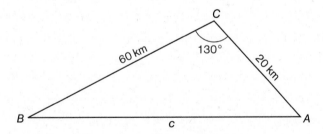

You are given SAS and need to find the third side, c.

$$c^2 = a^2 + b^2 - 2ab \cos C$$

$$= 60^2 + 20^2 - 2(60)(20)\cos 130°$$

$$\therefore c = \sqrt{60^2 + 20^2 - 2(60)(20)\cos 130°}$$

When you look at the answer choices, a shock may await you: your answer does not match any of the choices! Stay calm. Did you realize that cos 130° = −cos 50°, where 50° is the reference angle for the Quadrant II angle 130°? If you did, the above expression for side *c* becomes equivalent to choice (H):

$$c = \sqrt{60^2 + 20^2 - 2(60)(20)\cos 130°}$$

$$= \sqrt{60^2 + 20^2 - 2(60)(20)(-\cos 50°)}$$

$$= \sqrt{60^2 + 20^2 + 2(60)(20)(\cos 50°)}$$

If a trig problem does not give you a diagram, give yourself a diagram.

Here are some practice ACT trig questions.

Ace the ACT!
Sample Trigonometry Questions

1. The center pole of a tent is 8 feet tall, and a side of the tent is 12 feet long, as shown below.

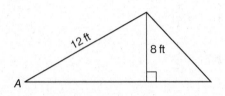

   Which of the following expressions could be used to find the measure of $\angle A$?

   A. $\cos A = \dfrac{8}{12}$

   B. $\sin A = \dfrac{8}{12}$

   C. $\tan A = \dfrac{8}{12}$

   D. $\sin A = \dfrac{4\sqrt{5}}{12}$

   E. $\tan A = \dfrac{4\sqrt{5}}{8}$

2. In which quadrant must θ lie if $\cos\theta > 0$ and $\sec\theta < 0$?

   F. I
   G. II
   H. III
   J. IV
   K. No such angle exists

3. Which of the following expressions is *not* equal to $\sin(-135°)$?

   A. $\sin 135°$
   B. $\cos 135°$
   C. $-\cos(-45°)$
   D. $\sin 225°$
   E. $\sin 315°$

4. In right $\triangle ABC$, if $\angle A$ and $\angle B$ are acute and if $\tan B = \dfrac{5}{4}$, what is the value of $\sin A$?

   F. $\dfrac{4}{5}$

   G. $\dfrac{4\sqrt{41}}{41}$

   H. $\dfrac{5\sqrt{41}}{41}$

   J. $\dfrac{\sqrt{41}}{4}$

   K. $\dfrac{\sqrt{41}}{5}$

5. Many functions are periodic. This means that for some p, $f(x + p) = f(x)$. The smallest value of p for which this is true is called the fundamental period of the function. Which of the following represents a function with fundamental period π?

A.

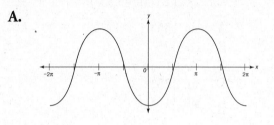

B.

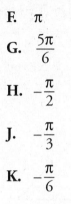

C.

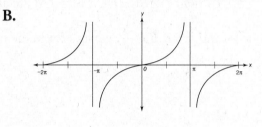

D.

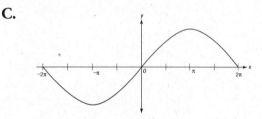

E.

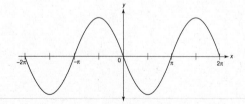

6. Which is a solution of the equation $2\sin^2\theta - \sin\theta - 1 = 0$?

F. π

G. $\dfrac{5\pi}{6}$

H. $-\dfrac{\pi}{2}$

J. $-\dfrac{\pi}{3}$

K. $-\dfrac{\pi}{6}$

7. Tom is standing 50 yards from a maple tree and 30 yards from an oak tree. His position is shown in the diagram below.

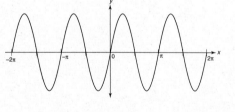

If he is facing the maple tree, he needs to turn his head 120° to look at the oak tree. Which of the following expressions represents the distance from the foot of the oak tree to the foot of the maple tree? You may wish to use the fact that in $\triangle ABC$ marked as shown:

$a^2 = b^2 + c^2 - 2bc \cos A$
$b^2 = a^2 + c^2 - 2ac \cos B$
$c^2 = a^2 + b^2 - 2ab \cos C$

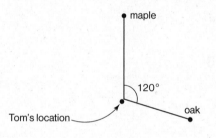

A. $\sqrt{50^2 + 30^2 + (50)(30)\sqrt{3}}$

B. $\sqrt{50^2 + 30^2 - (50)(30)\sqrt{3}}$

C. $\sqrt{50^2 + 30^2 - (50)(30)\sqrt{2}}$

D. $\sqrt{50^2 + 30^2 - (50)(30)}$

E. $\sqrt{50^2 + 30^2 + (50)(30)}$

8. If $\cos \alpha = \dfrac{5}{13}$ and $\dfrac{3\pi}{2} \leq \alpha < 2\pi$, what is $\tan \alpha$?

   F. $-\dfrac{12}{5}$

   G. $-\dfrac{12}{13}$

   H. $-\dfrac{5}{12}$

   J. $\dfrac{5}{12}$

   K. $\dfrac{12}{5}$

9. A right triangle that has its sides measured in the same units of length is shown below.

   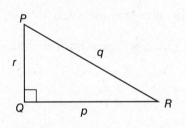

   For any such triangle, what is $(\cot P)(\csc R)$ equal to?

   A. $\dfrac{r}{p}$

   B. $\dfrac{p}{q}$

   C. $\dfrac{q}{p}$

   D. $\dfrac{pq}{r^2}$

   E. $\dfrac{r^2}{pq}$

10. For the angle α shown below, which of the following statements is true?

    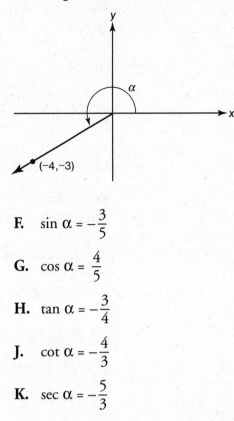

    F. $\sin \alpha = -\dfrac{3}{5}$

    G. $\cos \alpha = \dfrac{4}{5}$

    H. $\tan \alpha = -\dfrac{3}{4}$

    J. $\cot \alpha = -\dfrac{4}{3}$

    K. $\sec \alpha = -\dfrac{5}{3}$

Solutions and Explanations

1. **(B)**	3. **(A)**	5. **(D)**	7. **(E)**	9. **(C)**
2. **(K)**	4. **(G)**	6. **(K)**	8. **(F)**	10. **(F)**

1. **(B)** In the diagram, 8 feet is opposite $\angle A$, and 12 feet is the hypotenuse.

$$\sin A = \frac{\text{opposite}}{\text{hypotenuse}} = \frac{8}{12}$$

2. **(K)** Since $\sec \theta = \frac{1}{\cos \theta}$, $\sec \theta$ and $\cos \theta$ must have the same sign for all values of θ for which $\sec \theta$ is defined. It is therefore not possible for $\sec \theta$ and $\cos \theta$ to have opposite signs for any given θ.

 You absolutely need to know the reciprocals of the

trig ratios: $\csc \theta = \frac{1}{\sin \theta}$, $\sec \theta = \frac{1}{\cos \theta}$, and $\cot \theta = \frac{1}{\tan \theta}$.

3. **(A)** Note that each of the angles in the answer choices has 45° as a reference angle. Also, $\sin 45° = \cos 45° = \frac{1}{\sqrt{2}}$. Therefore, each answer choice is equal to $\pm \frac{1}{\sqrt{2}}$.

The question boils down to realizing that $\sin(-135°)$ is negative because $-135°$ is in Quadrant III. You must therefore find the answer choice that is positive.

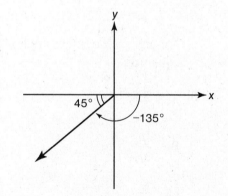

Choice (A): $\sin 135° = \sin 45°$, which is positive because 135° is in Quadrant II. This is the correct answer. All of the other answer choices represent a negative number:

Choice (B): $\cos 135° = -\cos 45°$
(cosine in Quadrant II is negative)

Choice (C): $-\cos(-45°) = -\cos 45°$ (cosine in Quadrant IV is positive)

Choice (D): $\sin 225° = -\sin 45°$ (sine in Quadrant III is negative)

Choice (E): $\sin 315° = -\sin 45°$ (sine in Quadrant IV is negative)

4. **(G)** Draw a right triangle with the given information marked on it.

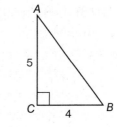

Since $\tan B = \dfrac{\text{opposite}}{\text{adjacent}}$, $\overline{AC}$, the side opposite $\angle B$, has length 5 and $\overline{BC}$, the side adjacent to $\angle B$, has length 4. You will need the hypotenuse to find $\sin A$. Use the Pythagorean theorem: $AB = \sqrt{5^2 + 4^2} = \sqrt{41}$.

Don't get your angles confused. Using $\angle A$ with its opposite side $\overline{BC}$ results in

$$\sin A = \frac{\text{opposite}}{\text{hypotenuse}} = \frac{BC}{AB} = \frac{4}{\sqrt{41}} = \frac{4\sqrt{41}}{\sqrt{41}\sqrt{41}} = \frac{4\sqrt{41}}{41}.$$

> **TIP**
>
> When you decide which side is opposite or adjacent, make sure you do it with respect to the correct angle.

5. **(D)** Notice that the sine curve pattern 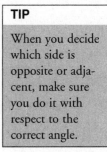 repeats itself in intervals of π, which was required. None of the other choices has a fundamental period of π. In choices (A), (B), and (E), the fundamental period is 2π. In choice (C), the fundamental period is 4π.

6. **(K)** The equation is quadratic and can be solved by factoring.

$2\sin^2\theta - \sin\theta - 1 = 0$
$\Rightarrow (2\sin\theta + 1)(\sin\theta - 1) = 0$
$\Rightarrow 2\sin\theta + 1 = 0$ or $\sin\theta - 1 = 0$
$\Rightarrow \sin\theta = -\dfrac{1}{2}$ or $\sin\theta = 1$

When $\sin\theta = -\dfrac{1}{2}$, θ is an angle in either Quadrant III or IV, with reference angle $\dfrac{\pi}{6}$ (30°). Notice that choice (K), $-\dfrac{\pi}{6}$, is this angle in Quadrant IV, and is therefore the correct answer. $\dfrac{7\pi}{6}$, which is not given as an answer choice, is in Quadrant III and is also correct.

Note that the solutions you get from $\sin\theta = 1$ are $\dfrac{\pi}{2}$ plus integral multiples of 2π. None of these solutions is given as an answer choice.

> **TIP**
>
> Always try factoring when you solve an ACT quadratic equation. This goes for quadratic trig equations, too.

7. **(E)** If the triangle is labeled as shown, the required distance is b.

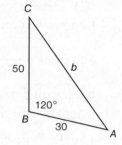

$$b^2 = a^2 + c^2 - 2ac \cos B$$
$$= 50^2 + 30^2 - 2(50)(30) \cos 120°$$
$$= 50^2 + 30^2 + 2(50)(30) \cos 60°$$
$$(\text{since } \cos 120° = -\cos 60°)$$

Since $\cos 60° = \dfrac{1}{2}$,

$$b^2 = 50^2 + 30^2 + 2(50)(30)\left(\dfrac{1}{2}\right)$$

$$= 50^2 + 30^2 + (50)(30)$$

$$\therefore b = \sqrt{50^2 + 30^2 + (50)(30)}$$

8. **(F)** Draw a picture. You are given that the angle is in Quadrant IV.

Since the tangent of an angle in Quadrant IV is negative, eliminate choices (J) and (K). If β is the reference angle,

$$\tan \alpha = -\tan \beta = -\frac{\text{opposite}}{\text{adjacent}} = -\frac{12}{5}$$

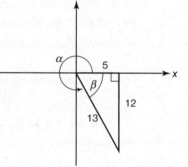

9. **(C)** $(\cot P)(\csc P) = \left(\dfrac{r}{p}\right)\left(\dfrac{q}{r}\right) = \dfrac{q}{p}$

10. **(F)** On the picture given, draw the right triangle with reference to angle β.

Remember, only the tangent and cotangent are positive in Quadrant III, and no other trig functions are. So you can eliminate choices (G), (H), and (J).

$$\sin \alpha = -\sin \beta = -\frac{\text{opposite}}{\text{hypotenuse}} = -\frac{3}{5}$$

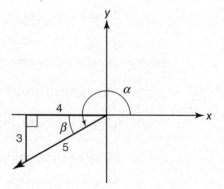

PART 2

THE SCIENCE SECTION

Overview of the Science Test

CHAPTER 8

> **CHAPTER GOALS**
>
> - What topics are on the test?
> - Data representation passages
> - Research summary passages
> - Conflicting viewpoints passages

Are you ready to tackle science? This chapter will take you on a brief tour.

WHAT TOPICS ARE ON THE TEST?

First, remember that the Science Test of the ACT follows a predictable (and therefore comforting) format. You will have:

- 35 minutes to answer 40 multiple-choice questions.
- Four choices for each question: A, B, C, D or F, G, H, J, in alternating questions.
- Seven subtests, each consisting of a passage describing something scientific, followed by 5–7 multiple-choice questions.

Second, what, exactly, is on the test? Well, you should know that the passages will span all of high school science—physics, chemistry, biology, astronomy, geology, meteorology, and environmental science. The small group of questions for each passage is typically—but not always—presented in increasing order of difficulty. Some of the questions will test your understanding of a given graph or table. Other questions will need some analysis. Sometimes you will be asked to make a prediction or generalization. Don't let this make you nervous. The format *never* varies. You can learn the test! Practicing the examples in this book is a great place to start.

Here is more good news: you will not need detailed or advanced knowledge of any topic. You will not be expected to produce Avogadro's number or to know the half-life of uranium. What you will need is to draw upon all of your high school science experience. What is the scientific method? How should you design or conduct an experiment? What is a control? A catalyst? A hypothesis? What can you predict from the results? Can you draw conclusions? Does extrapolating make sense? And so on. If you do not understand these terms now, you will after you have worked through the book.

If you have never had a course in a particular branch of science—environmental science, say—don't worry. You should be able to answer all questions on the ACT Test that deal with environmental science. This is because all the information that you need is presented in the passages and provided in the diagrams. Of course, your scientific knowledge can only enhance your understanding of the passages and subsequent questions. Mostly what you will need is the ability to focus—and some common sense.

No calculators will be allowed during the science part of the ACT. Stay calm. Nothing more than simple arithmetic calculations and estimation of quantities will be needed. Mostly, the questions will test your reasoning abilities.

Here is a final word of encouragement: the most complicated science passages on the ACT science test are often followed by easy questions. So if you persevere without being intimidated and follow the drills suggested in this book, you may strike gold.

The ACT science test is divided into three distinct passage types:

- Data representation (2–3 passages)
- Research summary (3–4 passages)
- Conflicting viewpoints (1 passage)

Here is a taste of each.

DATA REPRESENTATION PASSAGES

A passage with this format gives you at least one graph or diagram that displays data. The questions that follow test your ability to understand and analyze this data. Here is a sneak preview of the types of questions you will need to answer in data representation passages. Please note: This is *not* a complete sample of an ACT passage and question set.

Example

The process of photosynthesis begins when light is absorbed by pigments in a plant cell. The main pigment in green plants, chlorophyll, does not absorb light equally at all wavelengths. In fact, different forms of chlorophyll have their peak absorptions at different wavelengths. The graph below shows the relative absorption of light by chlorophyll 1 and chlorophyll 2. Wavelengths are given in nanometers (nm), and colors of the spectrum corresponding to different wavelengths are shown (violet, blue, green, yellow, orange, red).

TIP

Practicing sample ACT science passages ahead of time is your best strategy for learning the Science Test.

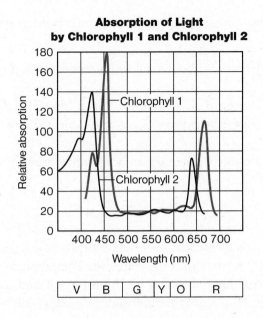

**Absorption of Light
by Chlorophyll 1 and Chlorophyll 2**

1. Which is a valid conclusion from the data shown in the table?

    A. Both forms of chlorophyll, chlorophyll 1 and chlorophyll 2, absorb red and blue light much more readily than they absorb green light.

    B. Neither form of chlorophyll absorbs any green, yellow, or orange light.

    C. Chlorophyll 1 absorbs green light, but chlorophyll 2 does not.

    D. Chlorophyll 1 and chlorophyll 2 reflect light mainly at wavelengths that are less than 475 nm or greater than 625 nm.

SOLUTION

(A) Try to tell yourself what the graph shows. Two lines are drawn, the gray line for chlorophyll 1 and the black line for chlorophyll 2. Each line gives you a way of comparing how much of that particular type of chlorophyll is absorbed at different wavelengths. The higher the vertical reading (relative absorption), the higher the absorption at the corresponding wavelength. The wavelengths are shown on the horizontal axis. Also shown on the horizontal axis is the range of wavelengths for each of the colors of the spectrum.

Notice that the peaks (highest values) for chlorophyll 1 and chlorophyll 2 occur in the red and blue parts of the light spectrum. This confirms that choice (A) is the correct answer. Each of the other choices is wrong:

Choice (B): Although the relative absorptions of green, yellow, and orange light are low, they are not zero.

Choice (C): The graph shows that chlorophyll 1 and chlorophyll 2 absorb about the same small amounts of green light.

Choice (D): Reflection is the opposite process of absorption. The graph shows that light is mainly absorbed, not reflected at the wavelengths given in choice (D).

2. Based on the graph, which is *not* a valid assessment of the relative absorptions shown?

   F. Chlorophyll 1 absorbs about nine times more blue light than yellow light.
   G. Chlorophyll 2 absorbs about twice as much blue light as red light.
   H. Chlorophyll 1 absorbs approximately the same amount of blue light as red light.
   J. Chlorophyll 1 absorbs approximately the same amount of green light as chlorophyll 2.

SOLUTION

(H) The vertical axis of the graph shows absorption of light for chlorophyll 1 and chlorophyll 2 relative to some standard. The graph therefore allows comparisons between light absorbed by chlorophyll 1 and chlorophyll 2 relative to each other. Notice that for chlorophyll 1, the ratio of blue to red absorption is approximately

$$\frac{180}{110} \approx 1.6$$

This is certainly not 1:1, which is what choice (H) asserts. The ratios in all of the other choices are correct.

Notice how for these questions you need very little knowledge of scientific facts. Even if you have never heard of chlorophyll before, you should be able to answer the questions by understanding the data displayed in the graph. Only in choice (D) of question 1 do you have to reason that if light is being absorbed, it is not simultaneously being reflected!

The most important benefit you will get from the science section of this workbook is practice in the techniques of extracting the important facts as you read and interpreting the diagrams that display data. These are skills that will serve you well, not only on the ACT but even when the ACT is a distant, pleasant memory.

RESEARCH SUMMARY PASSAGES

In these passages, you are given a description of experiments conducted by scientists or students. Typically, raw data will be provided in tables or graphs. You will be asked to evaluate the experimental design, analyze the experiment, and interpret the results. Here is a sneak preview of a research summary passage. Again, this is just a snippet to give you the flavor of this type of passage.

Example

A high school physics class performs an experiment to investigate the relationship between the volume and pressure of a gas at a constant temperature. Students use a 20 mL gas syringe attached to a gas pressure sensor to measure the pressure of an air sample at several different volumes.

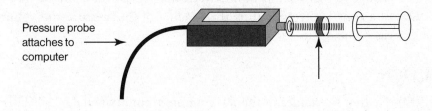

Pressure probe
attaches to
computer

The front edge of the inside black ring, indicated with an arrow in the diagram, shows the volume of air in the syringe. The corresponding air pressure will be read from a computer to which the pressure probe is attached.

To obtain the best data possible, students are instructed to add 0.8 mL to each syringe reading. This is because the scale on the syringe reports its own internal volume only. It does not account for air trapped in the small space inside the pressure sensor and associated tubing. Thus, for a volume of 5.0 mL read on the syringe, the students enter 5.8 mL as the volume.

For each reading of volume, the students read off the corresponding pressure in kPa (kilopascals).

One student produces the following results:

Volume (V)	Pressure (P)	PV
(mL)	(kPa)	(kPa · mL)
5.80	54.59	316.62
8.30	38.30	317.89
10.80	29.34	316.87
13.30	24.23	322.30
15.80	20.08	317.26

1. Based on the data shown, what could the student reasonably conclude?

    A. At a constant temperature, as the pressure of the gas increases, the volume increases.
    B. At a constant temperature, there is no discernible relationship between pressure and volume of a gas.
    C. A change in the temperature of the gas would produce little or no change in the relationship between the pressure and volume of a gas.
    D. At a constant temperature, the product of the pressure and volume of a gas is constant.

SOLUTION

(D) Each of the values in the *PV* column is approximately 317. This strongly suggests that choice (D) is valid. Choices (A) and (B) are contradicted by the numbers in the table. Choice (C) is incorrect because there is no information in the table about what happens when the temperature of the gas is changed. (You should be able to tell that this is wrong, independent of your knowledge of physics, which might tell you that when a gas is heated, it expands!)

2. What would a graph representing the pressure versus volume in this experiment look like?

    F. A hyperbola, indicating an inverse variation relationship between *P* and *V*
    G. A straight line, indicating a linear relationship between *P* and *V*
    H. An exponential curve, indicating an exponential relationship between *P* and *V*
    J. A parabola, indicating a quadratic relationship between *P* and *V*

SOLUTION

(F) When two variables are related by an equation of the form $PV = k$, where k is constant, the relationship is an inverse variation. Another way of saying this is if pressure decreases as volume increases, the relationship between pressure and volume is an inverse relationship. The graph is equivalent to $P = {}^{k}/v$, which is a hyperbola.

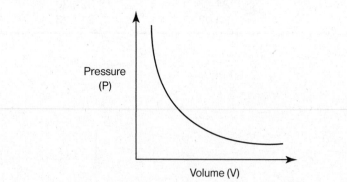

3. Which quantity in the students' experiment is not a control variable for this experiment?

    A. The air trapped in the tubing of the pressure probe.
    B. The temperature of the gas.
    C. The pressure of the gas.
    D. The circular cross-sectional area of the syringe.

SOLUTION

(C) Pressure is one of the quantities that is changed in the experiment and therefore cannot be a control. A control variable is a quantity that stays constant throughout the experiment, guaranteeing that this quantity is not responsible for any changes that are observed.

The relationship between the pressure and volume of a gas at constant temperature, namely, $PV = k$, is known as Boyle's law. Notice that even if you are unfamiliar with Boyle's law, you can still answer the questions in the passage by understanding the experiment and table of results.

A note about the experiment: In general, coming to a conclusion on the basis of a single experiment is not unreasonable. However, the conclusion is not necessarily true. If the experiment is repeated by different researchers with similar results, the degree of confidence in the conclusion increases. This is part of the scientific method, which will be discussed in detail in Chapter 12, "Conflicting Viewpoints."

Did you notice that the passage and questions assumed that you knew phrases like "control variable" and "inverse variation?" Never fear, vocabulary like this will become second nature to you as you work through these chapters.

CONFLICTING VIEWPOINTS PASSAGES

This type of passage describes an observable phenomenon and presents two conflicting viewpoints based on the phenomenon. Typically, the views will be held by two scientists who offer differing theories about the cause of the phenomenon or alternative ideas about what may result. If the phenomenon causes a problem, the scientists may suggest differing remedies.

What does the passage ask of you, the test taker? You will be expected to:

- Understand both the scenario and the points of disagreement.
- Interpret and analyze the viewpoints.

You will *not*, however, be asked to pass judgment.

Here is a sneak preview of a conflicting viewpoints passage.

Example

Red tide is the name commonly used for a type of algal bloom, a phenomenon in which marine algae multiply at an extremely rapid rate, swelling their populations to a density that can exceed tens of millions of cells per liter of seawater. These algae, called phytoplankton, are microscopic, single-celled organisms containing pigments that vary in color from green to brown to red. During a bloom they often discolor the water a rust-colored hue.

A red tide can be devastating to coastal communities, causing the deaths of thousands of marine and coastal fish, birds, and sea mammals.

Scientist 1

The cause of red tides is not definitively known. However, the frequency and increasing severity of algal blooms in many parts of the world are clearly linked to increased nutrient loading from human activities. The growth of phytoplankton is controlled by the availability of nitrates and phosphates, which are abundant in both agricultural and sewage system runoff. Humans have also contributed to coastal water pollution and rising seawater temperatures, two further factors that are implicated in red tides.

Scientist 2

Since red tides occur in some places where there are no obvious associated human activities, we can conclude that they are natural phenomena, independent of human activity. Some red tides on the Pacific coast have been linked to climatic oscillations like El Nino events. Iron-rich dust influxes from large desert areas, such as the Sahara Desert, probably play a major role in causing red tides. Red tides in the Gulf of Mexico have occurred since the time of early explorers like Cabeza de Vaca. One should ask whether the apparent increases in frequency and severity of red tides are really due to human pollution and global warming rather than merely a result of improved monitoring programs and species identification ability.

1. According to Scientist 1, which of the following is a cause of red tides?

    A. El Niño events
    B. Agricultural runoff
    C. Iron-rich dust influxes from the desert
    D. Increasing severity of algal blooms

SOLUTION

(**B**) Scientist 1 blames pollution by humans for contributing to nutrient loading in the oceans, which in turn leads to red tides. To quote Scientist 1, "agricultural and sewage system runoff" is a part of this pollution. The other choices are incorrect.

Choices (A), (C): These are natural phenomena, independent of humans. Notice that only Scientist 2 even mentions them.

Choice (D): The increasing severity of algal blooms is not a cause of red tides; it is a phenomenon observed when a red tide occurs.

2. Why does Scientist 2 probably mention Cabeza de Vaca?

    F. To emphasize that red tides could occur in unexplored regions of the world
    G. To draw attention to red tides in the Gulf of Mexico
    H. To bolster his case that red tides existed before global warming and large-scale human pollution
    J. To show that even in the days of early explorers, scientists were able to identify red tides

SOLUTION

(**H**) Scientist 2 holds the view that red tides are not caused by global warming or human pollution of the oceans. The scientist therefore mentions Cabeza de Vaca because he lived at a time when there was neither observed global warming nor human pollution, yet red tides had already been identified and recorded, perhaps by the explorer himself.

Did you know about red tides ahead of time? Did you notice that all you needed here was a focused reading of the passage?

The above examples give you a small preview of the types of questions you will need to answer on the ACT Science Test. They are neither complete passages nor complete sets of sample ACT questions. Many complete sample questions are in the chapters that follow.

As you practice your way through this workbook, you will become very good at tackling ACT science questions. Here is why:

- First, there is a certain sameness to the ACT science questions that make them easier and easier to understand the more you practice. I have experimented with this on my own students, and they have verified this!
- Second, you are a pretty brainy student. I say this confidently because you are planning to take the ACT Test, which means that you have been successful in school and are looking forward to college. You also have enough savvy to know that practicing before the ACT Test will boost your score! (You are working through this book, right?)

Please notice that the chapter does not end with a "good luck in this endeavor" message. Good luck is good management. The more you practice, the better your luck will get. Let's go!

General Strategies for Science

CHAPTER GOALS

- Tips for tackling ACT science
- How to read science passages
- Knowing the lingo
- ACT science vocabulary

As mentioned in the last chapter, you will have seven science passages, each with 5–7 multiple-choice questions: 40 multiple-choice questions in 35 minutes. Wow, not much time!

TIPS FOR TACKLING ACT SCIENCE

Here are some bits and pieces of advice that will help raise your science score. The tips are general and apply to all of the science formats. Think of this as a pep talk before you get into the really serious stuff.

Pace Yourself!

Just 35 minutes for seven passages means approximately 5 minutes per passage. Be sure to allot 1 or even 2 minutes to reading the passage. Understanding it is the key to answering the questions. So focus on the reading. You will then have between 30 and 40 seconds per question. If you cannot figure out the answer to a question, do not get hung up on it. Skip it and come back to it at the end. (Be sure to guess *some* answer if you run out of time!)

Practice the Tests

Practice the tests in this book under ACT Test conditions. This will give you a feel for the time pressures. Turn off the television and your cell phone, take off the headphones, and put away the calculator. (Calculators are not allowed for ACT Science!) Have a clock or watch visible. Then give yourself 35 minutes for a whole test or 5 minutes for one passage. You need to simulate *real* time constraints every time you practice. Doing this will help you be comfortable with the format on the Big Day.

Guess!

If you run out of time, you must guess, because there is no penalty for wrong answers. In other words, it pays for you to guess rather than to leave an answer blank. You *must* answer every question, whether you know the answer or not.

Estimate!

If a question calls for a numerical answer, do not waste time with a lengthy calculation. An estimate will usually work just as well.

Use the Passage

Base your answers on the passage. All of the information needed to answer an ACT science question is contained in the passage. Do not stray from the passage. If the question says, "Based on the graph, what can you say about the height of volcanoes?" do not pick the answer choice about the density of lava, especially if the passage doesn't mention lava. Also, beware of answer choices that are scientifically correct but wrong in the context of the passage. This is one test where your ability to read and comprehend a passage counts more than the A's you achieved in science classes.

No Peeking

Formulate answers without peeking (if possible). When a question is asked, come up with an answer *before* looking at the choices. Then find your answer among the choices. The advantage of this is that you avoid being suckered by the diabolical test writers who are magicians at composing alluring but wrong choices.

Do Not Be Intimidated

Formal scientific names should not intimidate you. When you see a weird-looking name, know that either a definition will soon follow in the passage or you will able to figure out the meaning from the context. For example, a certain passage talks about measuring the density of *Pterygophora californica* and *Laminaria farlowii* in a certain part of the ocean. Further reading confirms that these are fancy names for kelp, which is itself a high-class word for seaweed.

Use the Test Booklet

As you work through the test, don't forget that the booklet is yours. Mark it up as much as you want. Circle key words, and underline sentences in the passage. Jot down small summaries and trends—anything to help you focus as you read.

HOW TO READ SCIENCE PASSAGES

Here is something you can do long before the ACT Test to improve your science score: get in the habit of reading science. No, don't cringe. This does not mean you should haul out your high school textbooks and read a chapter a day. It means improve your scientific literacy by reading scientific articles in newspapers and magazines. Many newspapers have science sections. *The New York Times*, for example, has a special science section every Tuesday, which you can read online. Also, there are some wonderful science magazines like *Discover* and *Scientific American Reports*. Seek them out, and read about the latest discoveries and controversies.

Turn this into a serious exercise. Whenever you read a scientific article, give it all your concentration. Make it a point to understand each graph and table. This will be great training for the data representation passages on the ACT. Think of the impact of what you are reading when research is described. Be skeptical—do not believe what the scientist claims just because he or she says it is so. How about the design of the study—were there enough controls? Do the data support the claims? What about the size of the study—were there enough pieces of data to produce significant results? This type of thinking will help train you for the research summary passages of the ACT.

Journalists often present differing opinions of scientists in the same field. Read these with a critical eye and focus. What are the main arguments of each scientist? Who has the most convincing case? This is great preparation for the conflicting viewpoints passages on the ACT.

Reading newspaper and magazine articles about science is not only fun—it is also a great way of increasing your chances of scoring well on the ACT Science Test.

A good place to end is with a well-worn cliché: practice makes perfect. OK—let's just say that it can't hurt. The ACT science questions start to look familiar after a while. This means that the more of them that you do, the better you will become. Hone your skills by working through every passage in this workbook. However, do start your practice by reading about science in a non-ACT context.

KNOWING THE LINGO

Do you know the warm, fuzzy feeling of opening a science test and being familiar with all the terms in the first question? Although you do not need to memorize scientific content for the ACT Test, familiarity with what you are reading during the test can be a confidence booster. What follows is a list of common scientific terms that crop up often in different contexts on the ACT Science Test. Chances are good that you have heard of most of them. It can't hurt to bone up on these. Challenge yourself to come up with a definition of each word before you peek at how it is defined here. Alternatively, if you are not a definition type of person, skip ahead to the next chapter and use this section as a reference only.

ACT SCIENCE VOCABULARY

absolute zero: approximately –273°C, the lowest-possible temperature.

acid: a compound that releases hydrogen (H^+) ions when dissolved in water; has a pH less than 7.

algae: simple, one-celled plantlike organisms found in water or damp places; includes seaweeds, pond scum, and so on.

alloy: a substance composed of two or more metals.

atmosphere: the layer of air surrounding Earth.

atmospheric pressure: the pressure exerted by the atmosphere on every part of Earth's surface, approximately 10 newtons per square centimeter (10 N/cm^2).

atom: the smallest part of an element that is recognizable as that element.

barometer: an instrument that measures atmospheric pressure.

base: a compound that releases hydroxide ions (OH^-) in water; has a pH greater than 7; is sometimes called an *alkali*.

boiling point: the temperature at which additional thermal energy causes a substance to change from a liquid to a vapor.

calorie: a quantity of heat energy; the amount needed to raise the temperature of one gram (1 g) of water 1°C. The large Calorie, or "food calorie" is a kilocalorie (1000 calories).

carbohydrate: an organic compound like sugar or starch that contains carbon, hydrogen, and oxygen in the ratio 1:2:1; the human body's main source of energy.

carcinogen: a cancer-causing agent.

carnivore: a meat eater.

catalyst: a substance that speeds up a chemical reaction without being changed by the reaction.

cell: the lowest-level structure of any living organism that can perform all of the functions of life, including reproduction.

chlorophyll: the main pigment in plants that captures light energy during photosynthesis.

compound: a substance composed of two or more chemically bonded elements.

concentration: the exact amount of substance dissolved in a given amount of solvent; refers to a solution.

condensation: the process whereby a decrease in energy causes vapor particles to return to a liquid phase.

conductor: a material that allows heat or electricity to flow through it with minimal resistance.

control: a sample in which no variables are tested, thus serving as a basis for comparison.

control variable: a variable that stays constant in an experiment, allowing the effect of another variable to be measured.

convection: the circulation of fluid caused by warm fluid rising and cool fluid sinking.

density: in a physics sense, the amount of mass per unit volume; in a more general sense, the quantity per unit area or volume.

diffusion: the scattering of light; the spreading of a liquid or gas from areas of higher concentration to areas of lower concentration.

DNA: nucleic acid in the cells of an organism; contains the genes of the organism and transmits these to future generations.

ecological succession: a sequence of changes in the plant and/or animal life of a region over time.

electron: a negatively charged fundamental atomic particle.

element: a substance consisting of exactly one type of atom.

erosion: wearing away; typically the washing away of sand or rock by running water or wind.

evaporation: the changing of liquid into gas.

fossil: the preserved remains of a very old organism.

frequency: the number of cycles per unit time of a repeating phenomenon.

glucose: a simple sugar that is broken down to provide energy to an organism.

habitat: the part of an ecosystem where a plant or an animal naturally grows or lives.

herbivore: an animal that eats only plants.

hormone: a chemical substance secreted by a gland of the body that affects other parts of the body.

humidity: the amount of water vapor in the air.

hypothesis: a statement that is a proposed explanation of a scientific phenomenon.

infrared radiation: electromagnetic waves whose wavelength is longer than that of visible light.

insulator: a substance that blocks the flow of heat or electricity.

ion: a molecule or atom that has become charged by either gaining or losing an electron.

isotope: a variety of an element with the same number of protons per atom but a different number of neutrons.

kinetic energy: the energy of an object due to its motion.

melting point: the temperature at which additional thermal energy breaks the chemical bonds holding a substance together and causes the substance to change from the solid to the liquid state.

molecule: the smallest unit of a chemical compound.

neutron: a fundamental atomic particle that has no charge.

ore: a piece of rock from which metal can be profitably extracted.

osmosis: the movement of liquid through a membrane.

parasite: an organism that invades another organism (its host) and feeds off the host.

pH: a numerical scale from 1–14 representing the acidity or alkalinity of a solution; 1 is very acidic, 14 is very alkaline, and 7 is neutral.

photosynthesis: the process in which plants use the sun's energy to convert carbon dioxide and water into glucose.

pressure: force per unit area.

protein: a complex molecule composed of amino acids that carries out a variety of processes in cells.

proton: a positively charged fundamental atomic particle.

starch: a complex carbohydrate found in potatoes, rice, corn, and many other vegetables.

symbiosis: a close relationship between two organisms that is mutually beneficial.

ultraviolet radiation: electromagnetic waves with wavelength shorter than that of visible light.

vapor: the gaseous form of a liquid.

X ray: electromagnetic radiation with wavelength shorter than ultraviolet radiation.

Data Representation

CHAPTER 10

CHAPTER GOALS

- General strategies
- Reading simple graphs
- Reading more complicated graphs
- Reading tables
- Warm-up exercises
- Strategies for multiple figures in one passage
- Ace the ACT! Sample data representation passages

Of the seven mini-tests in the science section, two or three will be data representations. This format tests your ability to understand and analyze data that is presented in pictures, graphs, or tables.

The display of data can in fact be any graph, table, flowchart, layer diagram, or picture. The graph can be a line graph, bar graph, histogram, pictograph, pie chart, or scatter plot. The flowchart can be, for example, the life cycle of an organism, the stages in a chemical reaction, or the conversion of energy from one form into other forms. The layer diagram can, for example, show Earth's crust, Earth's atmosphere, or the ocean depths. It can be the cross section of a piece of apparatus. The picture can be a family tree, an evolution tree, or a distant galaxy. In other words, all visual representations of data are fair game on the ACT.

GENERAL STRATEGIES

Obviously, you need to use commonsense strategies to succeed on the ACT.

- Concentrate as you read. (You knew that!)
- Write as you go. Scribble on the figures. Jot down the main points of the passage. (If you are rolling your eyeballs at this one, stop right there. You must give it a try before you reject it. Never underestimate the power of the pencil.)
- Be aware of time, and use it wisely. Don't rush through in a way that scrambles your brain, but don't get hung up either. You can always skip a question and return to it later. Be sure to reserve a few minutes to return to skipped questions. Remember, you *must* answer all questions because there is no penalty for guessing incorrectly.

The real key to success in these data representation passages, however, is to approach each figure with the same automatic, disciplined four-step drill. Use this method always—whether you are looking at a table, a simple graph, or a complicated spider's web of a figure that gives you fits. See the figure, do the drill.

FOUR-STEP DRILL

1. Read and summarize
2. Variables
3. Units
4. Trends

We will return to this drill again and again, until it becomes second nature to you. You should practice this drill on the diagrams in this chapter. You should use the drill in the practice Science Test in the final chapter. You should nail down the drill every time you see a graph in a textbook at school. Do you read the newspaper at home? When you come to a graph, do the drill! This means that when you get to the actual ACT Test, you will be able to ace it. Seriously.

READING SIMPLE GRAPHS
The Topic

Focus on the sentence or two preceding the graph and on the graph's header. Now jot down what the graph shows.

What Are the Variables?

You will find them by reading the labels on the axes. The independent variable is the one being changed and manipulated. Typically, but not always, the independent variable is represented along the horizontal axis. The dependent variable changes as a result of manipulating the independent variable. These values are usually—but not always—shown along the vertical axis.

Check Out the Units

These units will always be mentioned somewhere in the given passage and will also appear as labels on the axes themselves. Units on the axes may be abbreviated. They may also be weird and unfamiliar. Fear not. You can always go back and read the preamble to the figure. There the units will be spelled out without their abbreviations.

Figure Out the Graph

By this stage, you should have a pretty good idea of what the graph is about. To check that you do, pick a single point and state precisely what it means. For example, "At an ocean depth of 20 meters, there are 100 critters per square meter." If you cannot do this, go back and reread the description of the graph.

What Does One Piece Mean?

A graph need not necessarily be a line graph. Whatever it is, though, you need to be able to state what a single component means. In a pie chart, what is one slice of the pie? In a bar graph, what is one bar? For a pictograph, what is one picture?

Find Trends

Once you understand the nuts and bolts of the scenario, you should look for trends in the numerical data. How are the quantities related? As x increases, does y increase, decrease, or stay the same? Are the points scattered, with no discernible pattern?

Example

The graph below shows the concentration of bacteria in a lake near an industrial meat-processing plant. An effluent pipe empties into the lake. The number of bacteria, in thousands per centiliter (cL), is plotted against distance, in meters (m), from the mouth of the pipe.

Concentration of Bacteria in Lake

Thousands of bacteria / cL

Distance from effluent pipe (m)

> **TIP**
>
> If you look at point A, say, you should be able to say: "At a distance of 20 m from the pipe, the concentration of bacteria is about 7,500 bacteria per cL."

Use the checklist to "read" this graph. Here is what you could jot down.

- **Read and summarize:** Graph shows number of bacteria plotted against distance from effluent pipe.
- **Variables:** Independent variable is distance from pipe (horizontal axis), and dependent variable is number of bacteria (vertical axis).
- **Units:** Distance in meters (m) and concentration of bacteria in thousands per centiliter (thousands / cL).
- **Trends:** Concentration increases with distance from pipe, until maximum concentration is reached at about 11 meters from pipe. Concentration falls off steeply after that.

Some Useful Facts About Graphs

Here are some odds and ends that you should know when it comes to interpreting graphs.

First, understand direct and inverse relationships between variables. If $y = kx$, where k is constant, the relationship between x and y is called a *direct variation* and the graph is a straight line. If $y = \dfrac{a}{x}$, where a is constant, the relationship between x and y is called an *indirect variation* and the graph is a hyperbola.

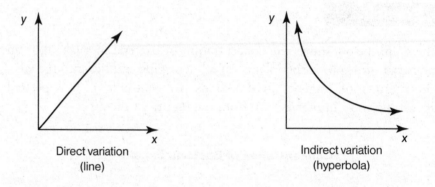

Direct variation
(line)

Indirect variation
(hyperbola)

If y increases as x increases, there is a *direct relationship* between x and y but not necessarily a linear relationship. Similarly, if y decreases as x increases, there is an *inverse relationship* between x and y, but the graph is not necessarily a hyperbola.

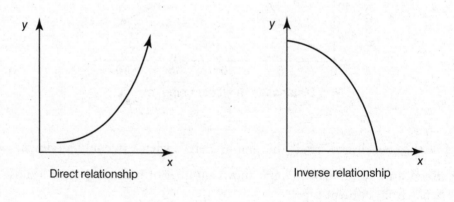

Direct relationship

Inverse relationship

Second, does it make sense to *interpolate* between two points on a graph? Interpolating means to connect the points and estimate a *y*-value that lies between two *x*-values. If the points are part of a scatter plot, draw the best-fit line, the line that comes closest to all of the points. Then find the *y*-value on the line that corresponds to the given *x*-value. Shown below is an example of a best-fit line in a scatter plot.

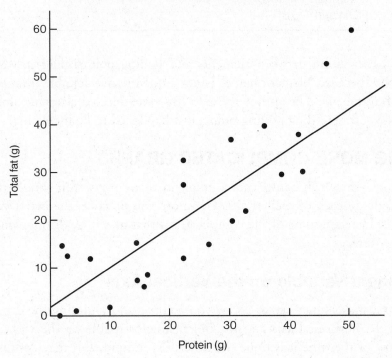

Total Fat versus Protein for Some Fast-Food Items

According to the graph, a person who wants to get 35 grams of protein from a fast food lunch can expect to consume about 31 grams of fat. This value was obtained by interpolating between 30 and 40 grams of protein.

Third, does it make sense to *extrapolate*? To extrapolate means to extend the graph beyond the values on the axes to find a *y*-value for an *x*-value that is out of the given range. If the graph is linear, just extend the line in your booklet. If the graph is a curve, extend it in a way that looks right to you and then estimate the required value.

Fourth, are there *correlations* between variables? Correlation measures the strength of the linear association between two numerical variables. For example, you could imagine that for children, age correlates with height: the older the child, the taller he or she is. You could reasonably expect to get a straight line or an upward curve with a positive slope when you plot age against height.

Look at the following partial table:

Element Name	Boiling Point (K)
Helium	4
Hydrogen	20
Neon	27
Nitrogen	77
Oxygen	90

Is there a correlation between elements and boiling points? The answer is an emphatic NO, because "element name" is not a quantitative variable (that is, measurable with numbers). The author chose to list some selected elements alphabetically, and the corresponding boiling points just happened to be increasing!

READING MORE COMPLICATED GRAPHS

Test question writers can complicate a graph in many ways. You simply need to break the code on each of their tricks. The more you practice, the better you will become at it. Here are some of the complications that may arise during your ACT science adventure.

Independent Variable on the Vertical Axis

The ACT test makers may try to throw you a curveball by placing the dependent variable on the horizontal axis and the independent variable on the vertical axis. Because most of the time it is done the other way around, this may confuse you. Don't let it! These graphs are easy to read as long as you read them from the point of view of the independent variable. Here is an example.

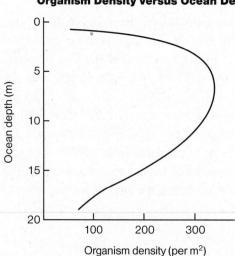

First, you must recognize that the quantity being measured at different depths, namely organism density, is the dependent variable. The variable being controlled by the scientist, namely the ocean depth, is the independent variable. Presumably the graph is plotted with the ocean depth vertical to let you visualize going deeper in the vertical direction. Can you picture the ocean? Turn the book sideways if you must, but here is what you should say to yourself, "As the ocean depth increases, the organism density increases. It reaches a peak density at a depth of about 6 meters and then decreases."

More Than One Line in a Line Graph

Be sure that you have the meaning of the different lines nailed down in your head. It may help to write on the actual graph which line stands for what. There is no excuse for getting a question wrong because you got the lines confused. Here is an example.

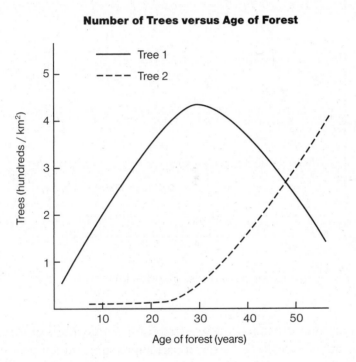

This is not a difficult graph to understand. Just be sure that you write "tree 1" on the solid line and "tree 2" on the dotted line. Then refer to the correct line when the questions ask you about the two types of trees!

More Than One Dependent Variable

Here is another little trick you may see on the ACT Science Test. The graph typically has one independent variable on one of the axes, usually the horizontal, and two dependent variables labeled on two vertical axes, one on the right and one on the left. The graph then consists of two lines, one of which refers to the right side and the other of which refers to the left side. You have to be able to tune out the second line and the wrong axis when you are looking at one of the lines! Here is a typical example:

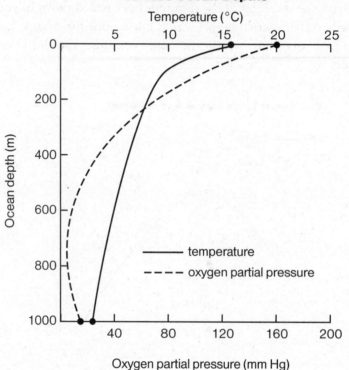

Water Temperature and Oxygen Partial Pressure at Various Ocean Depths

Notice, first of all, that the independent variable, ocean depth, is on the vertical axis. The two dependent variables are oxygen partial pressure and temperature. The graph key tells you that the solid line goes with temperature and the dotted line goes with oxygen partial pressure. You should take your pencil and write those words right on the relevant lines. For example, if you are asked what the temperature is at a depth of 800 m, you look at only the solid line and blot the dotted line from your consciousness. The answer is approximately 4°C.

Multiple Dependent Variables But Just One Line

The graph is set up in such a way that the axes for the dependent variables are differently scaled. As a result, for just one point in the graph, you can get multiple readings. This is the kind of figure that can make your hair stand on end at first glance. Still, it becomes quite easy to read when you see what is going on. Here's an example:

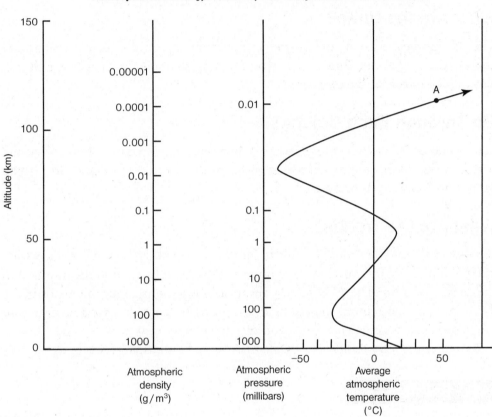

What this graph does is connect the four variables: altitude, atmospheric density, atmospheric pressure, and atmospheric temperature. When you get a reading for one of these, you can get corresponding readings for the other three. For example, look at point A on the graph. If you draw a horizontal line through A, you can see that point A occurs at an altitude of 110 km, where the atmospheric density is a little more than 0.0001 g/m^3, and the atmospheric pressure is approximately 0.01 millibars. These are readings at an average atmospheric temperature of 50°C. Notice that the labels on the vertical axes have been calibrated so that you can get correct simultaneous readings. Did you notice that those atmospheric density and pressure readings decrease as you go up the axis? That is just another diabolical little detail you need to be on the lookout for.

READING TABLES

Your approach to tables should be the same as your approach to graphs. Start by telling yourself what is shown in the table.

List the Variables

Typically, the header in the leftmost column will tell you the independent variable. The other column headers will tell you the dependent variables.

What Are the Units?

The column headers will contain this information. If you do not understand the abbreviations, read the sentence or two preceding the table in the passage. It will always spell out what the units are.

Go Through Each Column

You should be able to tell yourself what is shown in each separate column. Pick any row. You should be able to state what each number in that row stands for. If you cannot do this, reread the passage.

What Are the Trends?

For each column, you should be able to jot down a trend. Is the pressure increasing as the temperature increases? Is there no noticeable pattern at all to the numbers in the density column? The ACT almost always asks questions about the trends in the data. So if you have jotted something down for each dependent variable, this kind of question can become very quick and easy for you to answer.

As an example, try to analyze a table that contains multiple pieces of data.

Example

The following table represents the concentration of ions and dissolved gases in the sediment on the ocean floor. A depth of 10 centimeters (cm), for example, represents 10 cm from the top of the sediment. The concentrations are expressed in parts per million (ppm). The pH scale represents the acidity of a liquid. A pH of 1 is very acidic, a pH of 14 is very basic, and a pH of 7 is neutral.

Depth (cm)	Temperature (°C)	pH	Concentration in Sediment (ppm)					
			SO_4^{2-}	S^{2-}	CO_2	Fe^{3+}	Fe^{2+}	O_2
0	3	7.2	7.2	0.0	0.8	4.0	0.3	1.7
5	5	6.5	5.0	2.0	1.5	3.0	1.5	1.0
10	6	5.8	3.5	3.5	1.7	2.0	1.8	0.0
15	8	5.5	3.8	3.8	2.8	0.8	3.5	0.0
20	10	5.0	4.0	4.0	1.0	0.5	4.0	0.0

Here are some sample notes you may jot down.

- **Read and summarize:** *Table deals with concentrations of different ions and gases in sediments on ocean floor. Concentrations vary as depth from top of sediment changes. Temperature and pH at each depth are also given.*

- **Variables:** *Independent variable is depth from top of sediment. Dependent variables are temperature, pH, and concentrations of each of different ions and gases.*

- **Units:** *Depth in centimeters (cm) from top of sediment, temperature given in degrees Celsius (°C), pH is just a number, and each concentration is in parts per million (ppm).*

- **Trends:** *As depth increases, temperature increases and pH decreases (i.e., water becomes more acidic). Trends for concentrations: As depth increases, concentration of SO_4^{2-} decreases; concentration of S^{2-} increases; concentration of CO_2 increases, then decreases; concentration of Fe^{3+} decreases; concentration of Fe^{2+} increases; and, as depth increases, concentration of O_2 decreases at first, then stays constant at 0 from 10 cm on.*

> **TIP**
>
> Whether you make your notes on paper or only in your head, the checklist must become automatic.

A quick note about the notes: they do not need to be as detailed and beautiful as those shown. On the actual test, you will underline, circle, scribble, and abbreviate. The important thing is that you do the drill. If you have absorbed the information and jotted down a quick summary, you will be in good shape to answer questions about the table.

WARM-UP EXERCISES

You are now ready to try some warm-up exercises. For each passage, use the four-step drill to analyze the diagram before you try the questions. Answers, sample jottings, and explanations are at the end of each passage. Don't peek before you try!

Note that these are not sample ACT passages. They are the types of diagrams that you may need to analyze as part of an ACT passage. Think of these as practicing scales before you get to play sonatas.

Example 1

Comparison studies of international diets have investigated the relationship between the amount of fat in the diet and the risk of heart disease. The graph shows the results from three countries: Japan, which has a low-fat diet that contains much fish and rice; Eastern Finland, where saturated fats traditionally comprise much of the diet; and the island of Crete, which has a Mediterranean diet based on olive oil and monounsaturated fats. The graph shows the percent of calories from fat in each country's traditional diet, and the incidence of heart disease per 10,000 men over a period of ten years.

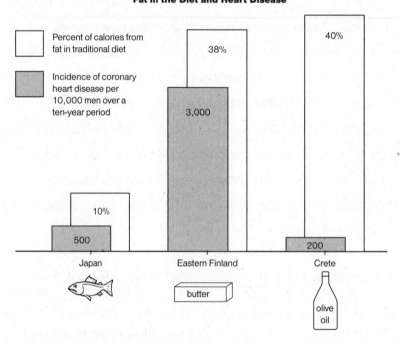

Adapted from "Fat and Heart Disease" in "Rebuilding the Food Pyramid" by Walter C. Willett et al., in *Scientific American Reports,* March 2007, p. 21.

1. According to the data shown:

   A. Over a ten-year period, a greater percentage of men contracted heart disease in Crete than in either Eastern Finland or Japan.

   B. Over a ten-year period, a greater proportion of men died in Eastern Finland than in either Japan or Crete.

   C. Over a ten-year period, a greater proportion of men in Eastern Finland had heart disease than in either Japan or Crete.

   D. Japanese men consume fewer calories than men in Eastern Finland or Crete.

2. According to the information provided in the figure, which statement is incorrect?

 F. Over a ten-year period, 1 in 20 men in Japan had heart disease.
 G. The ratio of percent of men with heart disease in Crete to percent of men with heart disease in Japan is 2:5.
 H. A typical man in Crete eats a diet that is 40 percent fat.
 J. A man chosen at random in Japan is less likely to have heart disease than a man randomly chosen in Crete.

3. Based on the data in the graph, which is a reasonable conclusion?

 A. A diet high in fat is likely to lead to heart disease.
 B. The type of fat consumed is a better predictor of heart disease than the total amount of fat.
 C. People who eat less are less likely to get heart disease.
 D. If a man moves from Eastern Finland to Crete, his risk of getting heart disease will be lowered.

- **Read and summarize:** *Japan: Lots of fish in diet. 10% of calories from fat. 500 in 10,000 men got heart disease in 10-year period. Eastern Finland: Lots of butter in diet. 38% of calories from fat. 3000 in men 10,000 got heart disease in 10-year period. Crete: Lots of olive oil in diet. 40% of calories from fat, and 200 in 10,000 men got heart disease in a 10-year period.*

- **Variables:** *Dominant food in diet (nonnumerical), percent of calories from fat, number of men per 10,000 who got heart disease in a ten-year period.*

- **Units:** *No units for calories—just percent. No units for number of men who got heart disease. (Number is how many in 10,000.)*

- **Trends:** *Japan's numbers low: only 10% of calories from fat, and only 500 in 10,000 got heart disease. Crete—largest percentage of calories from fat, 40%, yet lowest incidence of heart disease (200 in 10,000). Eastern Finland's incidence of heart disease by far the biggest: 3,000 in 10,000, yet percent of calories from fat was close to that of Crete, i.e., 38%.*

SOLUTIONS

1. **(C)**   2. **(J)**   3. **(B)**

1. **(C)** In the diagram, the shaded bar indicates the number of men per 10,000 in the population who had heart disease over a ten-year period. This number is largest in Eastern Finland. Each of the other choices is wrong:

    Choice (A): The percentages indicate calories from fat, not numbers of men with heart disease.

    Choice (B): This choice may sound plausible, but it is way off the mark. The study says nothing about death!

    Choice (D): The picture shows only the percentage of calories from fat, not total calories.

2. **(J)** Notice that in Japan, the incidence of heart disease is 500 in 10,000, or 1 in 20. In Crete, however, it is 200 in 10,000, or 1 in 50. Thus, a random man in Japan is more likely to have heart disease.

3. **(B)** Choice (B) is reasonable because the men whose fat intake was monounsaturated (in Crete) had the lowest incidence of heart disease. This occurred despite the fact that their diet is high in fat. None of the other conclusions is supported by the diagram.

    Choice (A): The data from Crete contradicts this choice. The men there had the highest percentage of calories from fat but the lowest incidence of heart disease.

    Choice (C): The data shown does not explore either the total number of calories or the calories from sources other than fat.

    Choice (D): The graph gives no indication that a man who changes location can be counted on to change his eating habits.

> **TIP**
>
> In a multibar graph, tell yourself precisely what each bar means.

Example 2

A position-time graph for linear motion of an object in one dimension shows the object's displacement d from some origin at any given time t. If the graph is linear, its slope m is given by

$$m = \frac{\text{rise}}{\text{run}} = \frac{\Delta d}{\Delta t} = \frac{d_1 - d_2}{t_1 - t_2} = \bar{v}$$

where $\bar{v}$ is the average velocity of the object. (t_1, d_1) and (t_2, d_2) are any two points on the line. The graph below is a position-time graph for a person who takes a walk from her house.

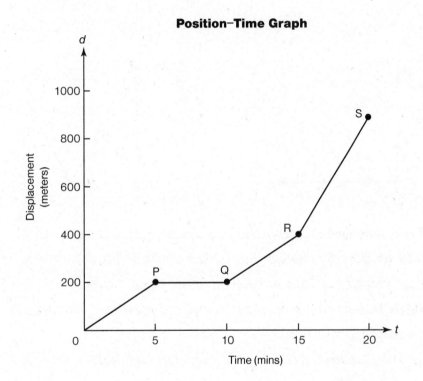

Position–Time Graph

1. Which of the following scenarios is consistent with the graph?

    A. After 20 minutes, the displacement of the person from her house is approximately 230 + 230 + 410 + 900 = 1770 m.
    B. The woman reverses direction every five minutes during her walk.
    C. After the first five minutes of her walk, the woman stops for five minutes. She then resumes walking.
    D. The woman stops walking briefly at t = 5, t = 10, and t = 15 minutes.

2. Which of the following graphs best describes the velocity of the woman on her walk?

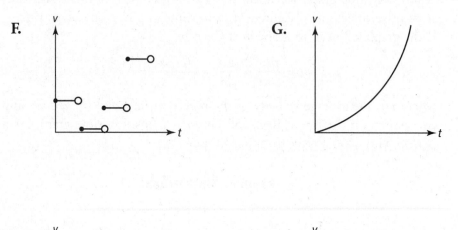

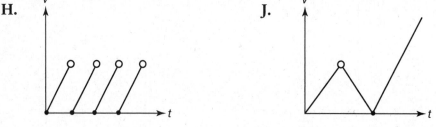

- **Read and summarize:** *Graph shows displacement vs. time as woman walks from house. For linear parts of graph, slope is average velocity of woman during that time frame.*
- **Variables:** *Independent variable is time. Dependent variable is displacement from house.*
- **Units:** *Time in minutes and displacement in meters.*
- **Trends:**

   Segment $\overline{OP}$: displacement increasing and velocity (slope) positive.

   Segment $\overline{PQ}$: displacement constant and velocity (slope) 0. So, for time equal to 5–10 min., woman is not moving.

   Segment $\overline{QR}$: displacement increasing and velocity (slope) positive.

   Segment $\overline{RS}$: displacement increasing and velocity (slope) positive. Slope of $\overline{RS}$ steeper than slope of $\overline{QR}$, so during the time interval 15–20 min., woman is walking faster than during interval 10–15 mins.

SOLUTIONS

1. **(C)**   2. **(F)**

1. **(C)** The horizontal segment in the graph, from $t = 5$ to $t = 10$, shows no change in displacement, indicating that the woman did not move during that time interval. Also, the slope of line segment $\overline{PQ}$ is 0; therefore the velocity during that time is 0. Each of the other choices is wrong:

Choice (A): Any point on the graph represents displacement from the origin at that time. The displacements are not cumulative.

Choice (B): Reversing direction would send the woman back to her house, causing the displacement to decrease, which is not the case.

Choice (D): If this scenario were true, there would be horizontal line segments starting at each of $t = 5$, $t = 10$, and $t = 15$.

2. **(F)** For each linear segment of the walk in the original position-time graph, the velocity is the slope $\dfrac{\Delta d}{\Delta t}$. The slope of a line is constant, which means that the graph representing the velocity is a horizontal segment for each part of the walk.

> **TIP**
>
> Don't forget—the slope of a line is constant.

Example 3

Rocks in Earth's crust are changed by heat and pressure over time. The diagram below shows the cycle of change.

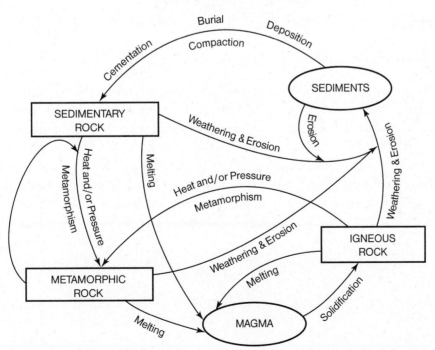

Rock Cycle in Earth's Crust

Based on *Earth Science Reference Tables*, 2001 Edition, The University of the State of New York, State Education Department.

1. Which of the following could *not* be inferred from the diagram?

   A. Igneous rock is formed when magma solidifies.
   B. Metamorphic rock is formed when igneous rock melts.
   C. Sediments are formed by the weathering of metamorphic rock or igneous rock.
   D. Metamorphic rocks can be formed from changes in igneous, sedimentary, or other metamorphic rocks.

2. Which conclusion is *not* supported by data in the diagram?

   F. Once heat and pressure reach a certain point, rocks melt and magma forms.
   G. Weathering and erosion of all rocks lead to sediments.
   H. When molten material deep inside Earth cools, it forms igneous rocks.
   J. Magma that reaches Earth's surface flows from volcanoes as lava.

- **Read and summarize:** *Flowchart shows changes in rocks in Earth's crust.*
- **Variables:** *No numerical variables. Just names of the types.*
- **Units:** *None.*
- **Trends:** *Melting rock becomes magma. Magma becomes igneous rock. Weathering and erosion lead to sediments. Heat and/or pressure lead to metamorphic rock.*

> **TIP**
>
> Follow the arrows to get answers in a flowchart.

SOLUTIONS

1. **(B)**   2. **(J)**

1. **(B)** When you follow the "melting" arrow from igneous rock, it leads to magma, not metamorphic rock. Each of the other answer choices have arrows that lead from the given rock(s) to those suggested in the choices.

2. **(J)** The conclusions in choices (F), (G), and (H) are all supported by evidence in the diagram. Choice (J), however, although it may be true, is not a valid conclusion because no information in the picture is about volcanoes or lava.

Example 4

During the process of photosynthesis, trees remove carbon dioxide from the air. Because of the longevity of trees, they can store carbon for decades. The table below shows estimates of biomass and carbon in above-ground wood plants in a large forested region of Earth. The table gives results of a recent study that used statistical sampling, with an estimate of error, and also results of five previous studies that did not. Each number in the table is obtained through both measurement and calculation based on assumptions described below. Biomass and carbon are both measured in kg/m^2 (columns 1 and 2). These are amounts per unit area of forest. Columns 4 and 5 represent the total biomass and carbon in the entire forested region in metric tons. Column 2 shows the above-ground biomass. Each number in this column assumes that 23 percent of all the biomass is in below-ground roots. Each number in column 4 assumes the same total area of forest. Columns 3 and 5 follow the scientifically accepted fact that carbon is 45 percent of total biomass.

Estimates of Above-ground Biomass in a Large Forested Region of Earth

Source	Biomass (kg/m^2)	Carbon (kg/m^2)	Total Biomass (10^9 metric tons)	Total Carbon (10^9 metric tons)
Recent study	4.2 ± 1.0	1.9 ± 0.4	22 ± 5	9.7 ± 2
Previous estimates				
1	17.5	7.9	90	40
2	15.4	6.9	79	35
3	14.8	6.7	76	34
4	12.4	5.6	64	29
5	5.9	2.7	30	13.8

1. Assuming that the statistical sampling technique for gathering data yields more accurate data than the methods used in previous studies, what does the information in the table suggest?

   A. Previous studies overestimated the amount of carbon stored in above-ground wood plants.

   B. The errors in previous studies were negligible and therefore not reported.

   C. The most recent study claims that the amount of carbon in the region of Earth investigated was in the range 1.9–2.3 kg/m^2.

   D. Study 5 is the least trustworthy because it differs from studies 1–4 by large amounts.

2. In order to provide a valid comparison of amounts of carbon stored for each of the six studies presented in the table, which of the following was not necessary as a control?

    F. Using above-ground wood plants only

    G. Using the same area of forested region

    H. Using the same percentage of biomass assumed to be carbon

    J. Using the same percentage of biomass assumed to be below-ground roots

3. It has been estimated that human activity, such as burning fossil fuels, contributes about 6×10^9 metric tons of carbon to the atmosphere every year, mainly in the form of carbon dioxide. What could an environmental policy maker, when presented with data like that shown in the table, reasonably conclude?

    A. Any study concerning the environment that does not use statistical sampling is a poor study.

    B. Removing carbon from the atmosphere will solve the problems of global warming.

    C. To compensate for human contributions of carbon to the atmosphere, planting trees in large numbers will significantly reduce the amount of carbon dioxide in the atmosphere.

    D. Any study concerning large areas of Earth that does not contain an estimate of error should not be used in environmental policy decisions.

- **Read and summarize:** *Table shows estimates of biomass and stored carbon in a large forest. Results shown for recent study that used statistical sampling with estimate of error in the numbers. Results shown for 5 previous studies that did not use sampling or give estimates of error in results.*

- **Variables:** *Amount of biomass per square meter, amount of stored carbon per square meter, total biomass in region, and total stored carbon in region.*

- **Units:** *For columns 2 and 3, kilograms per square meter (kg/m^2). For columns 4 and 5, total amount in metric tons.*

- **Trends:** *Numbers in the recent study are much lower than in studies 1–4. Numbers in study 5 are closer to those in recent study.*

SOLUTIONS

1. **(A)**   2. **(G)**   3. **(D)**

1. **(A)** The values in columns 3 and 5 for the previous studies are higher than the corresponding values for the most-recent study. None of the other choices is supported by the table.

    Choice (B): Just because errors were not reported does not mean that they did not occur.

    Choice (C): The minus sign in ± was ignored. The correct range is 1.5–2.3 kg/m^2.

    Choice (D): This choice uses faulty reasoning. If the most recent study is to be trusted, then study 5 is probably the *best* of the previous studies since its numbers are closest to those of the recent study.

> **TIP**
>
> In several studies that measure the same thing, a control is a quantity that is kept constant in each study.

2. **(G)** Since the biomass is measured per unit area, the total area measured in each study is irrelevant. The important thing is that a comparable region of Earth, with similar vegetation, is studied. Such a region should yield similar biomass numbers. It is essential that the items in choices (F), (H), and (J) are the same in all of the studies.

3. **(D)** The type of study described in this passage requires that the results be generalized to include areas not sampled. This comes with a degree of uncertainty. Therefore, in order for results to be meaningful, they must be accompanied with an estimate of error. There are problems with the conclusions in each of the other choices.

    Choice (A): This is too general. Many experiments do not need statistical sampling in order to be valid.

    Choice (B): The table does not even begin to suggest solutions to the problem of global warming.

    Choice (C): The amount of carbon stored is probably too small to have a significant effect on the amount of carbon dioxide in the atmosphere. Since human activity contributes about 6×10^9 metric tons of carbon a year, the recent study suggests that the forested region would need to be increased by two-thirds *every year* to compensate. This is not realistic.

> **TIP**
>
> In a table, internalize the meaning of each row and column.

Example 5

When an object is heated, it becomes incandescent and emits *thermal radiation*. The red glow of an electric hot plate and the white light of an electric lightbulb filament are examples of thermal radiation. The intensity of this radiation at a given wavelength depends on the temperature and composition of the object. For a given object, at each temperature, there is a wavelength at which the maximum amount of energy is emitted. If this peak intensity occurs at a wavelength in the visible part of the spectrum, the incandescent object will glow with the corresponding color.

The graph below is a plot of the intensity of radiation emitted at various wavelengths for an incandescent object. Results are shown for the same object at three temperatures: 4800K, 5800K, and 6800K. Wavelength is given in hundreds of nanometers (nm), while intensity is a normalized numerical value.

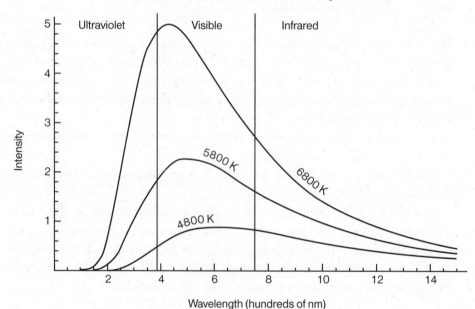

Radiation from an Incandescent Object

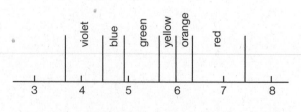

Colors in the Visible Part of the Spectrum

1. Based on the information in the figure, the incandescent object:

    A. will not glow at all when heated to 4800K.
    B. will emit ultraviolet radiation when heated to 6800K but will not have a visible glow.
    C. will emit an orange glow when heated to 5800K.
    D. will emit a blue glow when heated to 6800K.

2. According to the graph, which is true about thermal radiation for this object?

    F. As the temperature increases, the wavelength at which maximum energy is emitted decreases.
    G. As the temperature increases, the wavelength at which maximum energy is emitted increases.
    H. As the wavelength increases, the intensity of radiation emitted increases.
    J. As the wavelength increases, the intensity of radiation emitted decreases.

3. An arc light operates at a temperature of 6800K. The intensity of the radiation it emits is consistent with the graph shown above. The peak wavelength of its emitted radiation is between which values?

    A. 300 and 400 nm
    B. 400 and 500 nm
    C. 500 and 600 nm
    D. 600 and 700 nm

TIP
Before answering any questions, try to understand precisely what each line in a multiline graph means.

-   **Read and summarize:** *Graph shows intensity of radiation from incandescent object at different wavelengths. Three graphs—one for each of the temperatures 4800K, 5800K, and 6800K. Also shown—infrared, visible, and ultraviolet parts of spectrum. Wavelengths for colors in visible part of spectrum are shown below graph.*
-   **Variables:** *Independent variable, wavelength, on horizontal axis. Dependent variable, intensity, on vertical axis. Second independent variable implied in graph is temperature.*
-   **Units:** *For wavelength, hundreds of nanometers (nm). No units for intensity—it is just a number. Temperature in Kelvin (K).*
-   **Trends:** *For each curve (i.e., at each temperature), intensity increases with wavelength until peak intensity is reached. After that, intensity decreases with increasing wavelength.*

SOLUTIONS

1. **(D)**   2. **(F)**   3. **(B)**

1. **(D)** Notice that the curve for 6800K has its peak frequency in the blue part of the visible spectrum. Therefore, the body will glow blue. This makes choice (D) true but contradicts the second assertion in choice (B). Neither of the other choices is supported by the data in the graph.

   Choice (A): At 4800K, the peak intensity occurs for a wavelength in the visible part of the spectrum (about 600 nm). This means that when the object is heated to 4800K, it will glow yellowish orange.

   Choice (C): The 5800K curve has its peak at a wavelength of about 500 nm, which is in the bluish green part of the spectrum.

2. **(F)** To check statements (F) and (G), you need to look at peak wavelengths for each of the curves. 4800K has peak wavelength at approximately 600 nm. 5800K has peak wavelength at approximately 500 nm. 6800K has peak wavelength at approximately 425 nm.

   This shows that as temperature increases, the peak wavelength decreases. Thus, choice (F) is correct and (G) is wrong. Choices (H) and (J) are also wrong. As the wavelengths increase for each curve, the intensities initially increase. After the wavelength for peak intensity is reached, as the wavelengths increase, the intensities *decrease*.

3. **(B)** To get this answer, simply look at the 6800K curve. The wavelength of the peak intensity is a little over 400 nm.

Ace the Act!
Sample Data Representation Passages

You are now ready to graduate to sample ACT data representation questions. On the ACT, these passages usually contain multiple data representations, sometimes as many as four graphs and tables as part of one passage. You have seen strategies for reading individual graphs and tables. What follows now is an array of strategies for dealing with ACT questions that have multiple figures.

- Read carefully, jotting down or underlining key points of the passage as you find them.
- For each figure in the passage, treat it as a separate diagram and use the four-step drill: read and summarize, variables, units, trends. If you do this, you should have a decent grasp of the passage when you are ready to tackle the questions. Note that you do not need to write an essay about each figure. Just jot down the main features. It really is worth the effort!
- Many of the data representation questions tell you which figure to use for a particular question. This means that you can tune out the other figures and focus on this one figure; it will contain the answer.
- If you are not told which figure to use, let the key words in the question guide you to the correct graph or table. If the key words span two diagrams, you will

need to find a piece of information from one diagram and use it in the other diagram to come up with the answer.

- You will often be asked about trends in the data. If you have already jotted down trends for each figure, this type of question will be a piece of cake.
- When there are multiple components in a graph or a table, try to look at one component at a time and understand what it means.
- Some final words of encouragement: Often a tricky picture is followed by straightforward, easy questions. Also, if you do not really understand everything in the diagram, sometimes common sense alone will lead you to a correct answer. Don't give up! Remember, the more you practice ahead of time, the better you will do!

For the sample ACT passages that follow, you will find answers, sample jottings, and complete explanations at the end of this chapter. Please do not forget the checklist as you work your way through the passages. There will occasionally be small reminders in the margin, whispered words of encouragement. Imagine having a personal trainer at your side, egging you on.

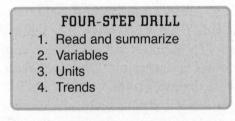

FOUR-STEP DRILL
1. Read and summarize
2. Variables
3. Units
4. Trends

PASSAGE I

Sea otters feed on sea urchins, which in turn feed on kelp. Kelp are large brown algae that form undersea forests and provide a habitat for many species. Sea urchins graze along the bottom of the kelp beds, feeding on the stems (called *stipes*) that anchor the kelp to the bottom of the ocean. When these stipes are broken, the kelp floats free and dies.

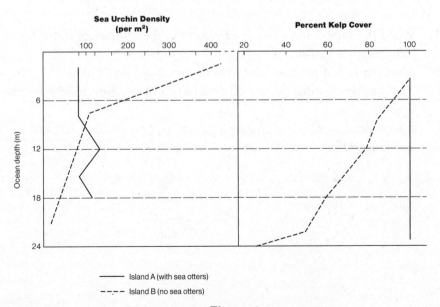

Figure 1

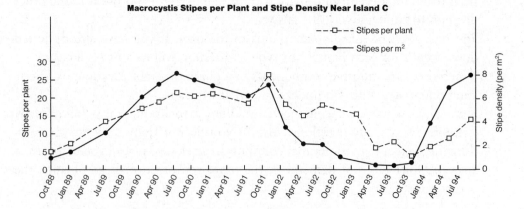

Macrocystis Stipes per Plant and Stipe Density Near Island C

Reprinted with permission. © 1997 Inter-Research. "Large-scale, low-frequency oceanographic effects on kelp forest succession: a tale of two cohorts" by M.J. Tegner et al., in *Marine Ecology Progress Series*, Vol. 146.

Figure 2

Figure 1 shows the effect of sea otters on the ocean environment surrounding two islands, Island *A* and Island *B*. Sea otters are abundant on Island *A*, whereas Island *B* has no sea otters. The figure shows the density of sea urchins (per m^2) at various ocean depths (m) surrounding the two islands. It also indicates the percent of kelp cover observed in the ocean at different depths for the two islands.

Macrocystis pyrifera is a dominant, competitive species of kelp. Figure 2 shows the density of *Macrocystis pyrifera* stipes (in m^2) and the average number of stipes per kelp plant, taken at an ocean depth of 18 m off the coast of Island *C*. The data was collected from October 1988 through July 1994. Each point represents the average measurement in each 3-month period.

1. According to the graph in Figure 2, what assertion can be made about stipe density of *Macrocystis pyrifera* kelp in the ocean surrounding Island *C*?

   A. When the stipe density was at a maximum, the number of stipes per plant was at a maximum.
   B. More than 25 stipes per plant were observed in July 1990.
   C. The number of stipes per m^2 observed in April and July 1993 was close to zero.
   D. A stipe density of approximately 5 per m^2 was observed in January 1992 and July 1992.

2. On the basis of the data presented in Figure 1, which of the following situations is true at an ocean depth of approximately 9 m?

   F. The amount of kelp bed cover is approximately the same for Islands *A* and B.

   G. The density of sea urchins is approximately the same for Islands *A* and *B*.

   H. The population of sea otters is approximately the same for Islands *A* and *B*.

   J. The percent of kelp cover in the ocean surrounding Island *B* is greater than the percent of kelp cover in the ocean surrounding Island *A*.

3. According to Figure 1, which best describes the sea urchin populations in the ocean areas surrounding Islands *A* and *B*?

   A. For Island *A*, as the depth increases, the sea urchin population increases.

   B. For Island *B*, as the depth increases, the sea urchin population increases.

   C. For Island *A*, as the depth increases, the sea urchin population decreases.

   D. For Island *B*, as the depth increases, the sea urchin population decreases.

4. Given the information in Figure 1, which of the following conclusions concerning the effect of sea otters on kelp cover is most plausible?

   F. The presence of sea otters has little or no effect on the density of kelp.

   G. When there are no sea otters, kelp beds thrive.

   H. The greater the population of sea otters, the lower is the density of kelp.

   J. The lower the population of sea otters, the lower is the density of kelp.

5. A marine biologist investigated the density of sea urchins off the coast of Island *C* from April 1989 until July 1994. Which finding would be consistent with the information in this passage?

   A. Sea urchin density was at its highest in April 1993.

   B. Sea urchin density was at its lowest in April 1993.

   C. Sea urchin density was approximately constant from April 1989 until July 1994.

   D. Sea urchin density increased from April 1989 until July 1994.

PASSAGE II

When the brakes are applied in a moving car, the car does not come to an immediate stop. In fact, it can travel some distance before it stops. The distance that a car travels from the time that a driver applies the brakes until the car stops is called the *braking distance*. The distance that a car travels from the time that the driver decides to stop to the time he or she applies the brakes is called the *reaction distance*. (The car is assumed to be traveling at a constant speed before braking.) The *total stopping distance* is the sum of the reaction and braking distances.

The table below shows the various distances for different speeds. The table is one that may be shown in a driving manual. Metric units are shown, along with their English equivalents.

REMEMBER

Are you jotting as you go? An active pencil equals an active mind.

Reaction and Braking Distances Versus Speed

Original Speed		Reaction Distance		Braking Distance		Total Distance	
m/s	mph	m	ft	m	ft	m	ft
11	25	8	27	10	34	18	61
16	35	12	38	20	67	32	105
20	45	15	49	34	110	49	159
25	55	18	60	50	165	68	225
29	65	22	71	70	231	92	302

The relationship between speed and the various stopping distances is shown in the graph below.

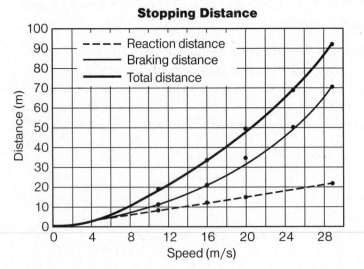

1. Which observation is consistent with the data shown?

    A. For every 5 m/s increase in speed, the braking distance increases 10 m.
    B. For every 10 mph increase in speed, the total stopping distance increases by approximately 44 ft.
    C. For every 4–5 m/s increase in speed, the reaction distance increases 3–4 m.
    D. At all speeds, the braking distance is greater than the reaction distance.

2. Suppose a person in a car slams on the brakes when a deer runs into the road in front of the car. Let t be the reaction time, in seconds, from the time the driver decides to stop the car to the time the driver actually hits the brakes. Based on the information shown, which is true about t?

    F. $0 < t \le 0.5$
    G. $0.5 < t \le 1.0$
    H. $1.0 < t \le 1.5$
    J. There is insufficient information to find the range of t.

3. Based on the information in the table and the graph, what is the breaking distance of a car whose speed is 75 mph?

    A. Less than 264 ft.
    B. Between 264 and 280 ft.
    C. Between 280 and 300 ft.
    D. Greater than 300 ft.

4. Suppose a dog runs into a busy street in front of an approaching car. Let the speed of the car be x mph. Assume that the dog is 205 ft. in front of the car at the instant the driver sees the dog and tries to stop the car. Assuming that the car cannot swerve (due to another car and/or a concrete wall being in the way) and that the dog remains stationary in the road, which of the following is closest to the largest value of x that will allow the driver to stop without hitting the dog?

    F. 40 mph
    G. 45 mph
    H. 50 mph
    J. 55 mph

5. What should a student driver, studying the table in a driving manual, conclude from the table?

    A. She should never drive faster than 55 mph.
    B. She should practice braking to improve her reaction time.
    C. She should not drive too near to the car in front of her.
    D. She should use the brakes sparingly.

PASSAGE III

The pH of a solution is a measure of its hydrogen ion (H^+) concentration. A pH of 1 is very acidic and corresponds to a high concentration of H^+ ions. A pH of 14 is very basic and corresponds to a low concentration of H^+ ions. The pH of a neutral solution is 7.

Table 1 shows the pH and H^+ ion concentration of some common aqueous solutions. The leftmost column shows the number of moles of H^+ ions in 1 mole of liquid.

Table 1: The pH and Hydrogen Ion (H+) Concentration of Some Solutions

H^+ Concentration (moles)	pH	Solution
10^{-1}	1	
10^{-2}	2	Gastric (stomach) juice, cola, lemon juice
10^{-3}	3	Vinegar, beer, wine
10^{-4}	4	Tomato juice
10^{-5}	5	Black coffee, rain water
10^{-6}	6	Urine
10^{-7}	7	Pure water
10^{-8}	8	Sea water
10^{-9}	9	Baking soda
10^{-10}	10	
10^{-11}	11	Milk of magnesia
10^{-12}	12	Household bleach
10^{-13}	13	Oven cleaner
10^{-14}	14	

An enzyme is a protein that acts as a catalyst in speeding up the chemical reactions involved in metabolism. Two environmental factors that influence the activity of an enzyme are temperature and pH. Graph 1 below shows the optimal temperature for typical human enzymes and typical enzymes of thermophilic (heat-loving) bacteria.

Optimal Temperature for Two Enzymes

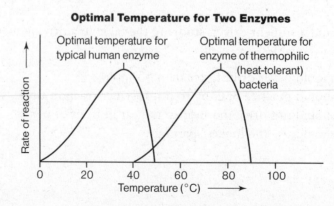

Graph 2 shows the optimal pH for pepsin and trypsin, two typical human enzymes. Pepsin is found in the stomach and aids in the digestion of proteins. Trypsin is an enzyme that is secreted into the small intestine by the pancreas. It, too, aids in the digestion of proteins.

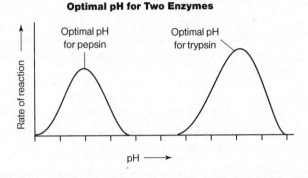

Optimal pH for Two Enzymes

An experiment was performed to measure the effects of antacids on pepsin's ability to digest proteins. An antacid tries to neutralize the normal stomach acid (HCl) causing the pH to rise and therefore approach a neutral value close to 7. Various known brands of over-the-counter antacids were used in the experiment. For each antacid, one dose was dissolved in 100 mL of 0.8 percent HCl, and 5 mL of the solution was added to 5 mL of a 1 percent pepsin solution. Additionally, a small sliver of protein in the form of egg white was added to each of the test tubes. The pH of each solution was recorded after 48 hours. The reaction effect of each solution on the egg white was recorded after 48 hours as follows: a score of 0–3 was given, where 0 = no change in egg white and 3 = total disappearance of egg white. The results of the experiment are recorded in Table 2 below. Note that the antacids are in test tubes 7–11 only.

> **REMEMBER**
>
> What does "average reaction" mean? Be sure you understand obscure table headers before moving on.

Table 2: Pepsin and Antacid Results (Averages of Collected Data After 30 Trials)

Tube Number	Contents	Average pH	Average Reaction
1	H_2O	6.16	0.35
2	H_2O + pepsin	4.37	1.30
3	$NaHCO_3$ + H_2O	7.88	0.55
4	HCl + H_2O	1.94	0.60
5	$NaHCO_3$ + pepsin	7.55	1.42
6	HCl + pepsin	1.68	2.57
7	Rolaids + pepsin + HCl	5.44	1.50
8	Tums + pepsin + HCl	5.46	1.44
9	Mylanta + pepsin + HCl	5.00	1.50
10	Pepto-Bismol + pepsin + HCl	4.86	1.57
11	Maalox + pepsin + HCl	5.50	0.50
12	Tylenol + HCl	1.00	2.50
13	Aspirin + HCl	2.00	3.00
14	Powdered ginger + HCl	1.33	2.33

1. According to Table 1, which is a correct assertion about the H⁺ ion concentration in liquids?

   A. A urine sample can be expected to have twice as many H⁺ ions as an equal volume of vinegar.
   B. A beaker of vinegar can be expected to have 1000 times as many H⁺ ions as an equal volume of urine.
   C. A neutral solution of pure water contains no H⁺ ions.
   D. Each pH unit represents a hundredfold difference in H⁺ ion concentration.

2. Pepsin, an enzyme in the human stomach, combines with gastric juice to digest food. Based on Graphs 1 and 2, which would represent ideal conditions in the stomach for fastest digestion?

   F. A temperature of approximately and pH of approximately 8.
   G. A temperature of approximately and pH of approximately 8.
   H. A temperature of approximately and pH of approximately 2.
   J. A temperature of approximately and pH of approximately 2.

3. Suppose a liquid was combined with a solution of trypsin and maintained in a water bath at 40°C. According to the data shown, the trypsin is likely to be most active if the liquid is:

   A. lemon juice.
   B. black coffee.
   C. oven cleaner.
   D. seawater.

4. Based on the data collected in Table 2, which of the following substances is the least effective in neutralizing acid in a solution?

   F. Powdered ginger
   G. Maalox
   H. Pepto-Bismol
   J. Sodium bicarbonate ($NaHCO_3$)

5. Which conclusion seems to be confirmed by the data in Table 2?

   A. In an acidic environment, antacids decrease the ability of pepsin to aid in the digestion of egg white.
   B. In an acidic environment, antacids increase the ability of pepsin to aid in the digestion of egg white.
   C. The more acidic the environment, the lower is the digestion of egg white.
   D. Without pepsin, digestion of egg white cannot occur.

6. A water molecule can separate into a hydrogen ion, H^+, and a hydroxide ion, OH^-, as follows: $H_2O \rightarrow H^+ + OH^-$. In any solution, the product of H^+ ion concentration and OH^- ion concentration is constant at 10^{-14}. This statement can be written as $[H^+][OH^-] = 10^{-14}$. Thus, when $[H^+]$, the concentration of H^+ ions, increases, $[OH^-]$, the concentration of OH^- ions, decreases. Based on the information in Table 1, which is a true statement about the concentration of hydroxide (OH^-) ions?

   F. Lemon juice has a higher concentration of OH^- ions than milk of magnesia.
   G. The concentration of H^+ ions in pure water equals the concentration of OH^- ions.
   H. A pH of 1 implies that the solution contains no OH^- ions.
   J. As pH increases, the concentration of OH^- ions decreases.

7. For any enzymatic reaction, the rate of reaction initially increases with increasing temperature. Beyond an optimum temperature, however, the thermal agitation of the enzyme molecule disrupts some of the molecule's chemical bonds, causing the enzyme to denature (come apart). Consider an experiment in which trypsin is maintained in a water bath at 65°C for 1 minute. It is then mixed with protein suspended in a liquid of pH 8 at a temperature of 40°C. The length of time taken to change the protein is measured. The procedure is repeated, exposing the same quantity of trypsin to different periods of time at 65°C, such as 3 minutes, 5 minutes, 10 minutes, and 20 minutes before mixing it with the same quantity of the protein. Which of the following is a reasonable graph to expect when time of exposure to 65°C is plotted against rate of reaction with protein?

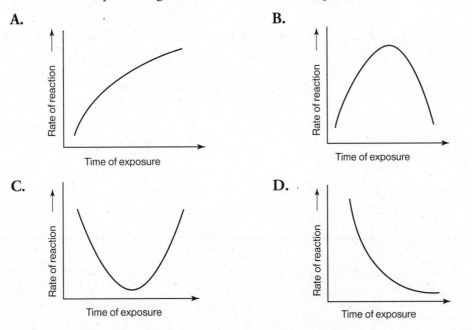

PASSAGE IV

In an electrical circuit, the resistance R is defined by the equation $R = \dfrac{V}{I}$, where the electrical current I is in amperes (A), and the potential difference V is in volts (V). R is measured in ohms (Ω).

Ohm's law states that for certain conductors the resistance R is constant. Any resistance device or conductor for which R is constant is said to obey Ohm's law. Not all devices obey this law.

Students performed two experiments. In Experiment 1, they investigated the resistance of a small resistor device. In Experiment 2, they investigated the resistance of a small lightbulb. In Experiment 1, the students measured current through the resistor at various voltage values between 0 and 20 V. In Experiment 2, the students measured current through the lightbulb at about 10 voltage values between 0 and 20 V. Figures 1 and 2 show the symbolic circuit diagrams for Experiments 1 and 2, respectively. The lines connecting the various devices represent wires whose resistance is negligible. Note that for any given voltage, the current is the same at all points in the circuit.

REMEMBER

Take note of the equation. There is a high probability that you will need to use it in the questions.

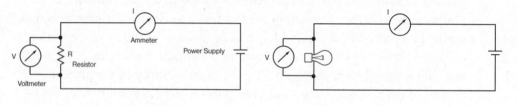

| Figure 1 | Figure 2 |

Figure 3 shows the results of Experiment 1. Current I in milliamps (mA) is plotted against potential V in volts (V).

THINK

Where is the resistance R in these graphs?

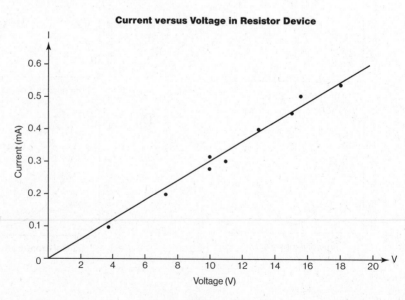

Current versus Voltage in Resistor Device

Figure 3

Figure 4 shows the results of Experiment 2. Current *I* in amps (A) is plotted against potential *V* in volts (V).

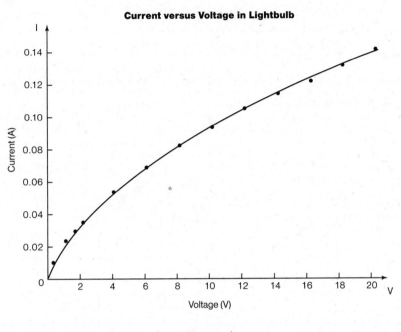

Figure 4

1. Based on the graphs in Figures 3 and 4, what could the students reasonably conclude?

   A. The resistor device and the lightbulb both obeyed Ohm's law.
   B. Neither the resistor device nor the lightbulb obeyed Ohm's law.
   C. The lightbulb obeyed Ohm's law, but the resistor device did not.
   D. The resistor device obeyed Ohm's law, but the lightbulb did not.

2. According to the results obtained in the experiments, which statement about the resistance of the devices is *false*?

   F. The resistance of the resistor device is approximately equal to $\dfrac{0.00025}{8}\,\Omega.$

   G. The resistance of the resistor device is approximately equal to $\dfrac{15}{0.00045}\,\Omega.$

   H. The resistance of the lightbulb at 2 V is approximately equal to $\dfrac{2.0}{0.035}\,\Omega.$

   J. The resistance of the lightbulb at 15 V is approximately equal to $\dfrac{15}{0.119}\,\Omega.$

3. Based on the data in the graph for Experiment 2 (Figure 4), which describes the relationship between voltage through the lightbulb and resistance?

   A. There is no pattern in the relationship between voltage and resistance.
   B. As voltage increases, resistance increases.
   C. As voltage increases, resistance decreases.
   D. As voltage increases, resistance stays constant.

4. Which of the following circuit diagrams is equivalent to Figure 1, namely the circuit used for Experiment 1?

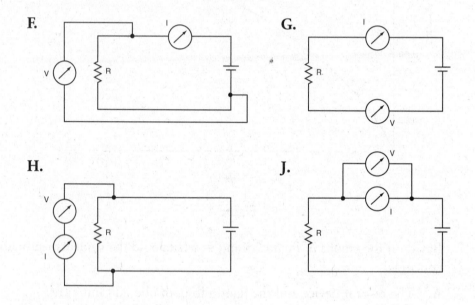

5. The power rating of a lightbulb is the rate at which energy is used, namely converted to heat and light energy. Power in a resistor is given by $P = IV$, where P is in watts (W), I is current in amps, and V is electrical potential in volts. Suppose that household lightbulbs are designed to operate at a constant voltage of 110 V. If you were to compare a 60 W lightbulb with a 75 W lightbulb, what could you conclude?

   A. The resistance in the 60 W bulb is less than the resistance in the 75 W bulb.
   B. The resistance in the 60 W bulb is greater than the resistance in the 75 W bulb.
   C. The resistance in the two lightbulbs is the same.
   D. There is insufficient information to compare the resistance of the two lightbulbs.

PASSAGE V

As glaciers retreat, they leave behind rocky terrains called moraines. Ecological succession of moraines at Glacier Bay, Alaska, has been studied extensively. Ecological succession is the progression of changes over time in the plant and/or animal life of a region. Figure 1 below shows the ordered appearance of plants during moraine succession at Glacier Bay.

TIP

Ecological succession is a popular topic on ACT Science Tests.

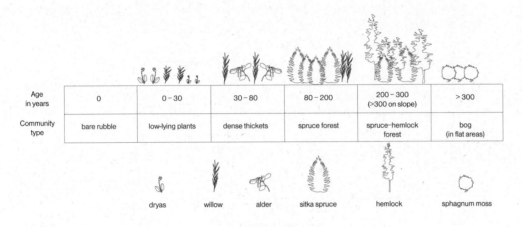

Figure 1

The final stage of ecological succession is called the *climax community*. In Glacier Bay, if the terrain is a well-drained slope, the climax community is a spruce-hemlock forest. If the terrain is flat and the drainage is poor, the forest is eventually replaced by a bog of sphagnum moss.

Figure 2 depicts the gradual change from spruce forest to spruce-hemlock forest in a climax community of spruce-hemlock forest. The base density of each species, which is a measure of the area covered by the species per unit area, is given in square meters per hectare (m^2/ha).

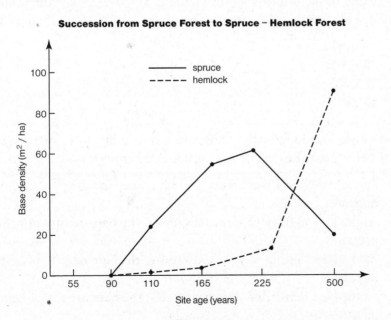

Figure 2

The soil concentrations of mineral nutrients change during succession. Figure 3, for example, shows the change in soil nitrogen levels during moraine succession in Glacier Bay.

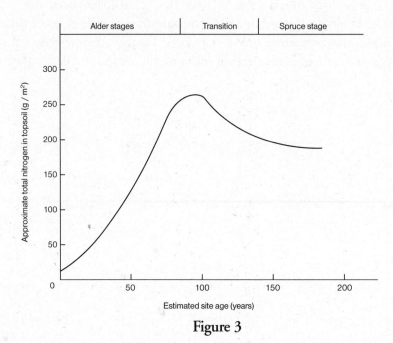

Figure 3

1. Based on the data in Figure 1, approximately 100 years after glacial retreat, the moraine would contain:

   A. sitka spruce only
   B. alder, willow, and sitka spruce
   C. sitka spruce and hemlock only
   D. alder and willow only

2. According to the information in Figure 2, a 225-year-old climax community would contain sitka spruce with a base density of approximately:

   F. 12 m²/ha
   G. 20 m²/ha
   H. 40 m²/ha
   J. 58 m²/ha

3. The spruce forest gradually changes to a spruce-hemlock forest. Which statement about the densities of spruce and hemlock after 225 years is true?

   A. As the base density of spruce increases, the base density of hemlock decreases.
   B. As the base density of spruce decreases, the base density of hemlock decreases.
   C. As the base density of spruce decreases, the base density of hemlock increases.
   D. As the base density of spruce increases, the base density of hemlock increases.

4. Based on the data in this passage, which is a reasonable conclusion?

    F. One of the characteristic features of bare soil after glacial retreat is its high nitrogen content.
    G. Dryas plants thrive in soil with low nitrogen concentration.
    H. Soil nitrogen decreases rapidly during the alder stage of succession.
    J. The presence of spruce raises the concentration of nitrogen in the soil.

5. Based on the data in Figure 1, which conclusion is most correct concerning moraine succession in Glacier Bay?

    A. Moraine succession begins on a bare glacier.
    B. After 300 years, conditions exist in parts of the terrain that cause the spruce-hemlock forests to die.
    C. The height of the plants decreases as succession progresses from the early (pioneer) stage to the climax stage.
    D. The rate of change of plant species increases as succession approaches the climax stage.

Solutions and Explanations

PASSAGE I (SEA OTTERS)

There are two different figures in this passage. Apply your checklist to each figure in turn.

Figure 1

This is a complex picture, with two graphs in one. To add to your troubles, each graph deals with Island *A* and Island *B*. You need to keep a cool head and analyze each side separately. Make a note or write on the graph that the solid line refers to Island *A* while the dotted line means Island *B*. Jot down what you know, and then analyze the graphs.

- **Read and summarize:** *Sea otters eat sea urchins that eat kelp. Island A has sea otters, Island B does not. Left side of Figure 1 shows sea urchin density at different depths for both islands. Right side shows percent of kelp cover at different depths for both islands.*

- **Variables:** *Independent variable for each side of figure is ocean depth (on vertical axis!). Dependent variables: sea urchin density on left and percent kelp cover on right (on horizontal axes!).*

> **TIP**
> When several lines are on a graph, jot down *on each line* what each one shows.

TIP

Because of the somewhat strange way that Figure 1 is presented, with the independent variable (depth) on the vertical axes, you need to run your eyes vertically down the graphs, describing to yourself what happens as the ocean depth increases.

- **Units:** *Ocean depth in meters (m). Sea urchin density is a number per m^2. Kelp cover is a percent.*
- **Trends:** *Left side graph: For Island A (with otters), sea urchin density is constant, then increases slightly, then decreases slightly, then increases again. Never gets above 130 per m^2. For Island B (no otters!) sea urchin density starts out large (above 400 per m^2) and decreases gradually. At depth of about 8 m it falls off steeply. Right side graph: For Island A (with otters), kelp cover is 100% at all depths. For Island B (no otters), kelp cover decreases with depth.*

Figure 2

CAUTION

Don't be put off by the fancy name. *Macrocystis* is simply the name of a common species of kelp!

- **Read and summarize:** *For Island C, shows kelp stipe density and number of stipes per plant from October 1988–July 1994.*
- **Variables:** *Independent variable (on horizontal axis) is a time frame, i.e., an actual time. For both graphs, solid and dotted, labels on axis are selected months from April 1989–July 1994. Dependent variables: stipes per kelp plant on left vertical axis (for dotted line only). Stipe density on right vertical axis (for solid line only).*
- **Units:** *Stipes per plant—a number; stipe density—number per m^2.*

TIP

Take the time to do the quick four-step drill for each figure in the passage.

- **Trends:** *From October 1988–October 1990, both stipes per plant and stipe density increase. Both decrease until July 1991, then increase through October 1991. Then steep decline down to almost 0 in 1993. After 1993, both variables increase.*

SOLUTIONS

1. **(C)**   2. **(G)**   3. **(D)**   4. **(J)**   5. **(A)**

1. **(C)** Stipe density is shown by the solid line, which dips to 0 in April and July 1993. The other choices are false.

    Choice (A): Stipe density is at a maximum in July 1990. Notice, however, that the number of stipes per plant reached a maximum in October 1991.

    Choice (B): Do not confuse the two lines. For stipes per plant, refer to the dotted line and the left side vertical axis. You will see that the value corresponding to July 1990 is a little more than 20.

    Choice (D): In January 1992 and July 1992, about 18 stipes per plant were observed. (See the dotted line, and use the axis on the left.) The stipe density (on the solid line and using the axis on the right) was about 4 in January 1992 and 2 in July 1992.

2. **(G)** Refer to the left side graph of Figure 1. The solid line represents Island *A* and the dotted line Island *B*. Those lines cross at a depth of about 9 m, which means that the sea urchin density is approximately the same at that depth. The other choices are wrong:

    Choices (F) and (J): For kelp cover, refer to the right side graph of Figure 1. At 9 m, the kelp cover for Island *A* is 100% while for Island *B* it is a little more than 80%.

    Choice (H): You are told early on in the passage that Island *B* has no sea otters!

3. **(D)** Refer to the left side graph of Figure 1. You must be sure to start at the top of the graph and move down for increasing ocean depth. The dotted line represents the sea urchin density for Island *B*. Notice that the values for density decrease as you move down to greater depths. Therefore, choice (D) is correct, while choice (B) is wrong.

    Island A is represented by the solid line. As you move down the line, increasing the ocean depth, notice that the corresponding values stay constant for a while, then increase, then decrease, and then increase again. This behavior contradicts both choices (A) and (C).

4. **(J)** From Figure 1, notice that kelp density is lower on the island without sea otters. Also, when the sea urchin density is small, the kelp density is high. Since sea otters eat sea urchins, their presence on the island reduces the number of sea urchins and therefore contributes to greater kelp density. When there are no otters, the sea urchin population is unchecked. The sea urchins will eat much of the kelp, reducing its density. Thus, a low population of otters means a low density of kelp, choice (J). Each of the other choices contradicts this reasoning.

TIP

When two lines on a graph refer to different axes, write something on each line that makes it crystal clear which axis goes with which line.

5. **(A)** Not much is known about Island *C*, other than the kelp stipes density and number of stipes per plant over a certain time period. Based on the information in this passage, a low kelp density corresponds to a high population of sea urchins. Since April 1993 had the lowest measurements for kelp, it is reasonable to assume that one of the factors reducing the kelp was a high population of sea urchins and that when kelp was at its lowest, sea urchin population was at its highest. Each of the other findings would be surprising.

Choice (B): When kelp is at its lowest density, the biologist could expect a big population of sea urchins eating the kelp. Thus, sea urchin density would surely not be at its lowest.

Choice (C): If sea urchin density was constant, what caused the destruction of the kelp? It is possible that there were other factors. However, the information in the passage suggests that sea urchins contributed to the kelp's demise.

Choice (D): It is very unlikely that sea urchin density increased the entire time. Notice that kelp started recovering after October 1993, for example. This is not consistent with an increasing sea urchin population.

PASSAGE II (BRAKING DISTANCE)

Graph

- **Read and summarize:** *Shows relationship between speed of car and distance in which car can stop. Three distances shown, each on separate line: reaction (dotted line), braking (gray line), and sum of these (black line).*

- **Variables:** *Independent variable: speed (on horizontal axis). Dependent variables: reaction distance, braking distance, total stopping distance.*

- **Units:** *Speed in meters per second (m/s), distance in meters (m). Table shows approximate equivalents in mph (miles per hour) and ft. (feet) for speed and distance.*

- **Trends:** *As speed increases, stopping distances increase. Reaction stopping distance is approximately linear, while braking distance looks to be quadratic.*

TIP

Did you notice that the graphs for braking distance and total stopping distance look like parts of parabolas?

Table

- **Read and summarize:** *Shows relationship between speed of car and distance in which car can stop. The 3 distances are shown in separate columns.*
- **Variables:** *Original speed, reaction distance, braking distance, and total stopping distance.*
- **Units:** *Speed is given in meters per second (m/s) and also approximate equivalents in miles per hour (mph), while distance is given in meters (m) and approximate equivalents in feet (ft.).*
- **Trends:** *As speed increases, stopping distances increase.*

> **TIP**
>
> When more than one unit is used for a given variable, you need to summon an extra level of concentration.

SOLUTIONS

1. **(C)**　2. **(G)**　3. **(D)**　4. **(H)**　5. **(C)**

1. **(C)** In the table, the values for speed are given in increments of 5 m/s: 11, 16, 20, . . . Notice that the corresponding reaction distances in meters are 8, 12, 15, 18, . . . These are increments of 3 or 4 m. The other choices are false.

    Choice (A): The braking distances corresponding to 11, 16, 20, . . . m/s are 10, 20, 34, 50, . . . m, respectively. These represent increments of 10, 14, 16, . . . m.

    Choice (B): The total stopping distances corresponding to 25, 35, 45, . . . mph are 61, 105, 159, 225, . . . ft. These represent increments of 44, 54, 66, . . . ft.

    Choice (D): From the graph you should be able to see that at very low speeds (less than 9 m/s), the reaction and braking distances are approximately equal. Note that this conclusion requires you to extrapolate from the table as shown on the graph, which goes all the way down to 0.

2. **(G)** During the reaction time, the driver has not yet applied the brakes and is therefore traveling at a constant speed. Thus, $t = \dfrac{d}{s}$. For any point on the "Reaction Distance" graph, the quantity $\dfrac{\text{distance}}{\text{speed}}$ is in the range 0.5 to 1.0.

    For example, when s is 20, $t \approx \dfrac{15}{20} = 0.75$.

3. **(D)** In this question, you must extrapolate slightly beyond the given values. From the first column of the table, you can deduce that an original speed of 75 mph corresponds to a speed of 33 m/s. (Every 4 m/s translates approximately into 10 mph.) If you extend the horizontal axis of the graph to include a speed of 33 m/s and then extend the graph for braking distance, maintaining the upward parabolic arc, you should see that the distance that corresponds to 33 m/s extends to at least 100 m, possibly beyond. From the "Braking Distance" column, you can see that if 10 m is approximately 34 ft., 100 m is beyond 300 ft., which makes choice (D) the correct answer.

4. **(H)** You need to look at the values in the "Total Distance" column to find the answer. Start with choice (J) and work backward since you are asked for the *largest* value that allows the car to stop within 205 ft. A speed of 55 mph has a total stopping distance of 225 ft. So this speed is too high. A speed of 45 mph would allow the driver to stop in 159 ft. So now you must check whether 50 mph allows the driver to stop in time. 50 mph is approximately equal to 22.5 m/s. Go to the graph and find the *total* stopping time corresponding to a speed of 22.5 m/s. This is no more than 60 m, which is approximately 200 ft. This means that the driver can stop in time if the car's original speed is 50 mph.

5. **(C)** The student should see from the numbers that if she needs to brake suddenly, and is too near to the car in front of her, she may not be able to avoid hitting that car. The other conclusions are spurious:

   Choice (A): In many places, it is legal to drive faster than 55 mph. The information in this passage does not address the issue of whether it is wise to do so!

   Choice (B): Reaction distances are small compared with braking distances at high speeds. It is also not clear what "practice braking" means or that any kind of practice could improve reaction times.

   Choice (D): Nothing in the data suggests that the student driver should not use the brakes!

PASSAGE III (ENZYMES)

There are four different figures in this passage. Apply your checklist to each figure in turn.

Table 1

- **Read and summarize:** *Table shows H^+ ion concentration at each pH value. Examples of everyday liquids are given for some pH values.*
- **Variables:** *H^+ ion concentration at different pH values.*
- **Units:** *Moles of H^+ ions in 1 mole of liquid.*
- **Trends:** *As H^+ ion concentration decreases pH increases. Acid = low pH = high H^+ ion concentration. Base = high pH = low H^+ ion concentration.*

> **TIP**
> This is not really a trend. It is a scientific fact about how the pH of various liquids is calibrated.

Graph 1

- **Read and summarize:** *Graph shows reaction rates at different temperatures for typical human enzyme and enzyme of thermophilic (i.e., heat-loving) bacteria. Human enzyme works best at about 35°C, while thermophilic bacteria enzyme works best at about 78°C.*
- **Variables:** *Independent variable is temperature, on horizontal axis. Dependent variable, on vertical axis, is rate of reaction.*
- **Units:** *Temperature in degrees C. No unit given for reaction rate.*
- **Trends:** *For human enzyme, reaction rate goes up as temperature increases until optimum temperature reached (approximately 35°C.). Beyond this temperature, reaction rate decreases.*

Graph 2

- **Summarize:** *Graph shows reaction rates at different pH values for two human enzymes, pepsin and trypsin. Pepsin works best at pH = 2 (i.e., acidic environment). Trypsin works best at pH = 8 (i.e., basic environment).*

- **Variables:**

  Independent variable is pH, on horizontal axis.

  Dependent variable is rate of reaction, on vertical axis.

- **Units:** *pH is just a number. No unit given for reaction rate.*

- **Trends:** *For both pepsin and trypsin, reaction rate goes up as pH increases until optimum pH is reached (2 for pepsin and 8 for trypsin). Beyond optimum pH, reaction rate falls off rapidly.*

Table 2

- **Summarize:** *There are 14 solutions, some with pepsin, acid, and/or antacid. Ability to digest protein and pH measured for each solution. Ability to digest protein measured on scale of 0 to 3. Score of 0 means no protein digested, and score of 3 means all protein digested.*

- **Variables:** *Independent variables for table are different components of test tube mixtures. 2 dependent variables: average pH and average reaction with protein (egg white).*

- **Units:** *pH is just a number. Average reaction is number from 0 to 3.*

- **Trends:** *In acidic environments with pepsin, average reaction with egg white was at least 2. All antacids raised pH to about 5 and showed low digestion of egg white.*

> **TIP**
>
> Notice that in a table, the variables are found in the column headings.

SOLUTIONS

   1. **(B)**   2. **(H)**   3. **(D)**   4. **(F)**   5. **(A)**   6. **(G)**   7. **(D)**

1. **(B)** Notice that vinegar has pH 3 and urine has pH 6. As pH increases, H^+ ion concentration decreases by a factor of 10 for each pH unit. Thus, to go from pH 3 to pH 4, divide the H^+ ion concentration by 10. To go from pH 4 to pH 5, divide the H^+ ion concentration by 10 again. To go from pH 5 to pH 6, divide the H^+ ion concentration by 10 yet again. Thus, a solution of pH 3 has a thousand times as many H^+ ions as a solution of pH 6. Here is how we could correct each of the other (incorrect) statements:

    Choice (A): A urine sample can be expected to have 1000 times fewer H^+ ions than an equal volume of vinegar.

    Choice (C): A neutral solution of pure water contains 10^{-7} moles of H^+ ions per mole of water.

    Choice (D): Each pH unit represents a tenfold difference in H^+ ion concentration.

2. **(H)** For optimum temperature, use the graph for a typical human enzyme (Graph 1). Notice that the rate of reaction peaks at approximately 35°C. The graph for optimal pH of pepsin peaks at about 2. All other choices misread the graph or use the wrong graph.

3. **(D)** The pH graph for trypsin suggests that the optimal pH is about 8. Since seawater has a pH of approximately 8, it seems reasonable—in the absence of other information—to predict that trypsin would have its greatest activity in seawater. All of the liquids in the other choices are at the wrong pH.

4. **(F)** The average pH of the powdered ginger solution was 1.33, which is very acidic. You can therefore conclude that the ginger solution was not effective in neutralizing acid. The other choices were incorrect.

    Choices (G) and (H): Each of these was somewhat effective at lowering the acidity by raising the pH to about 5.

    Choice (J): Sodium bicarbonate ($NaHCO_3$) is a base. Adding it to an acidic solution would lower the acidity.

5. **(A)** In all of the solutions containing antacid, the average reaction was lower than 2. The acidic solution with pepsin had an average reaction of 2.57, almost perfect digestion of the egg white. Thus choice (B) is clearly wrong. Choices (C) and (D) are wrong because they are contradicted by the results for test tubes 12–14. There was significant digestion of egg white even though no pepsin was added to those solutions.

6. **(G)** Since the product of the concentrations of H^+ ions and OH^- ions is constant at 10^{-14} and $[H^+]$ in pure water is 10^{-7} moles, $[H^+]$ and $[OH^-]$ both equal 10^{-7}. This comes from the equation $(10^{-7})(10^{-7}) = 10^{-14}$. Each of the other statements is false.

   Choice (F): Lemon juice is very acidic (pH = 2), and milk of magnesia is quite basic (pH = 11). An acidic liquid has a lower concentration of OH^- ions than a basic one.

   Choice (H): Since $[H^+][OH^-] = 10^{-14}$, and $[H^+]$ for a solution with pH 1 is 10^{-1}, $[OH^-]$ must equal 10^{-13}, which is small but not 0.

   Choice (J): As pH increases, the solution becomes more basic. This means that $[H^+]$ decreases as $[OH^-]$ *increases*.

7. **(D)** Note that for trypsin, 65°C is 25° higher than the optimal temperature shown in Graph 1. One could therefore reasonably expect the trypsin molecules to denature at this temperature. Further, as the period of exposure to a high temperature is increased, it is reasonable to expect the amount of denaturation to be increased. This, in turn, will lower the rate of reaction since less stable enzyme will be present in the mixture. Choice (D) corresponds to a decreasing rate of reaction as time exposure increases. None of the other graphs conform to this analysis.

   Choice (A): This shows an increasing rate of reaction with time. This is not very likely if the amount of stable enzyme is decreasing!

   Choice (B): Here the rate decreases to a minimum point and then, for no apparent reason, starts increasing again. This is not likely to happen if fresh enzyme is not added.

   Choice (C): Again, this graph makes no sense. In the first half of the graph, the rate of reaction will surely not increase as more of the enzyme becomes denatured.

PASSAGE IV (OHM'S LAW)

- **Read and summarize:** *Resistance in electrical circuit given by $R = \frac{V}{I}$. When R constant, resistor obeys Ohm's law. Not all resistors obey Ohm's law. Two experiments, one with resistor and one with lightbulb, where current is measured at different voltages. Resistance in each circuit calculated from results. Figure 1 is circuit diagram for resistor experiment, and Figure 2 is circuit diagram when lightbulb is used.*

- **Variables:** *Voltage V, current I, and resistance R. Voltage is independent variable on horizontal axis of each graph, current is dependent variable on vertical axis of each graph, while resistance is dependent variable not shown on graphs but calculated with formula $R = \frac{V}{I}$ (reciprocal of slopes of graphs!).*

- **Units:** *For Figure 3, resistor experiment, horizontal axis values in volts V. Vertical axis gives current in milliamps, mA. For Figure 4, lightbulb experiment, horizontal axis values in volts V while vertical axis currents in amps A.*

- **Trends:** *In both experiments, current increases with voltage. In Experiment 1, for resistor, linear relationship, suggesting $R = \frac{V}{I}$ is constant. Nonlinear relationship in Experiment 2 means $R = \frac{V}{I}$ not constant.*

> **CAUTION**
>
> Were you alert here? Did you notice the amps and *milli*amps?

SOLUTIONS

1. **(D)**   2. **(F)**   3. **(B)**   4. **(F)**   5. **(B)**

1. **(D)** The relationship in the graph for Experiment 1 (Figure 3) is approximately linear. This means that its slope $\frac{I}{V}$ is constant, which means that $\frac{V}{I} = R$ is constant. Therefore, the resistor device obeys Ohm's law. The nonlinear relationship between V and I in Experiment 2 (Figure 4) suggests that $\frac{V}{I}$ calculated at different points will yield different values for resistance. This means that R is not constant and that the lightbulb does not obey Ohm's Law.

> **TIP**
>
> When a formula is given in the passage, write it down as part of your summary. You will need to use it in the questions.

2. **(F)** Resistance $R = \frac{V}{I}$, where V is in volts and I is in amps. From the graph in Figure 3, when voltage V is 8, $I = 0.25$ mA $= 0.00025$ A. Therefore, $R = \frac{8}{0.00025}\ \Omega$.

   The error in choice (F) is that $\frac{1}{R}$ is given, not R. All of the other choices correctly give $R = \frac{V}{I}$ for the points selected.

> **TIP**
>
> Don't waste time on difficult calculations when an observation of a trend or a quick estimate will work just as well.

3. **(B)** At voltage = 2 V, $R = \dfrac{V}{I} = \dfrac{2.0}{0.035} \approx \dfrac{200}{4} \approx 50\Omega$

   At voltage = 15 V, $R = \dfrac{15}{0.119} \approx 150\Omega$

   If you estimate R at a few points, the pattern is that R increases as V increases. Alternatively: The slope of the graph decreases as V increases. Since slope equals $\dfrac{1}{R}$, as $\dfrac{1}{R}$ decreases, R increases.

4. **(F)** Since current is constant in the circuit, whether the voltmeter's connections are near the resistor or far from it does not matter. The important thing is that its connections surround the resistor. Since the wires in the circuit have negligible resistance, there is no potential difference between two uninterrupted points along the wire. ($V = IR$ with R approaching 0.) Therefore, connecting the voltmeter as in choice (F) is equivalent to Figure 1. None of the other choices is equivalent to the experiment's setup.

   Choices (G) and (H): The voltmeter will read 0 since there is no resistance between its terminals.

   Choice (J): Placing the voltmeter as shown will give a reading that corresponds to the resistance of the ammeter! (Which, ideally, is 0.)

5. **(B)** In household use, the voltage is kept constant. In the equation $P = VI$, if V is constant, I increases as P increases. This means that for $P = 75$ W, the current I is larger than for $P = 60$ W. Now look at the equation linking resistance to current: $V = IR$. Since V is constant, the larger I is, the smaller R must be. Thus, since current is larger in a 75 W bulb, the resistance is lower than it is in a 60 W bulb.

PASSAGE V (GLACIERS)

There are three different figures in this passage. Apply your checklist to each figure in turn.

Figure 1:

- **Summarize:** *Picture shows various plant communities at different stages of moraine succession. Range of years given for each stage of succession. A picture key for each plant type is shown.*
- **Variables:** *Independent variable is age of site, in years, while dependent variable is type of plant(s).*
- **Units:** *Years.*
- **Trends:** *As years proceed, plant life changes. Eventually, type of vegetation stabilizes, either as spruce-hemlock forest (on well-drained slopes) or bog (in flat areas).*

Figure 2

- **Summarize:** *Graph is for climax community of spruce-hemlock forest. Shows base densities of spruce (solid line) and hemlock (dotted line) during years of succession. Lets you compare relative numbers of spruce and hemlock at any given age of site.*
- **Variables:** *Independent variable, on horizontal axis, is site age. Dependent variable, on vertical axis, is base density per area.*
- **Units:** *Age of site given in years. Base density in square meters per hectare (m^2/ha).*
- **Trends:** *Incidence of spruce first appears at site age = 90, and it increases in base density until site age is approximately 200 years. Then density decreases. Hemlock also first appears at about year 90. Increases gradually until just past year 225. Then increases sharply, overtaking the density of spruce.*

Figure 3

- **Summarize:** *Graph shows total nitrogen in topsoil of moraine during succession.*
- **Variables:** *Independent variable is estimated age of site (horizontal axis). Dependent variable (on vertical axis) is number of grams of nitrogen per square meter of topsoil.*
- **Units:** *Site age in years. Concentration of nitrogen in topsoil is in grams per square meter (g/m^2).*
- **Trends:** *Density of nitrogen starts close to 0 and increases until close to year 100. Drops off slightly and flattens out at about year 125.*

SOLUTIONS

1. **(B)**   2. **(J)**   3. **(C)**   4. **(G)**   5. **(B)**

1. **(B)** After 100 years, the dense thickets of alder and willow are invaded by sitka spruce. To find the answer to this question, look in the range 80–200 years, labeled "spruce forest." Notice that there are three pictures: alder, willow, and sitka spruce.

TIP

Don't forget—when you are told which figure to use in a question, you can find the answer in that figure alone.

2. **(J)** Be sure to use the solid graph for spruce. An age of 225 years corresponds to a value close to 60. Thus 58, choice (J), is the correct answer.

3. **(C)** The key words "spruce forest" and "spruce-hemlock forest" give you the clue that Figure 2 is the place to search for the answer to this question. Look at the piece of the graph in Figure 2 that is to the right of the "225 years" label. Notice that as the solid graph representing spruce decreases, the dashed line representing hemlock increases.

4. **(G)** According to Figure 3, in early succession (0–30 years), the nitrogen concentration is low. During this time, one of the dominant species is dryas. This suggests that dryas does well in soil with low nitrogen content. None of the other choices is supported by the data.

   Choice (F): The graph in Figure 3 shows that immediately after glacial retreat, the nitrogen concentration in soil is close to 0. Also, Figure 1 shows that bare rubble is present for less than a year.

   Choice (H): The graph in Figure 3 shows the nitrogen concentration *increasing* during the alder stage (0–80 years), not decreasing.

   Choice (J): During the spruce stage, the nitrogen concentration decreases. This suggests that the presence of spruce *lowers*, not raises, the concentration of nitrogen in the soil.

TIP

Let key words in the question guide you to the relevant figure that contains the answer.

5. **(B)** The final stage of succession in Figure 1 shows that the spruce-hemlock forest has been replaced by a bog of sphagnum moss in flat areas. From this, one could reasonably conclude that environmental conditions caused the spruce and hemlock to die. Each of the other conclusions contradicts the information in the figure.

   Choice (A): Succession begins on bare rubble after the glacier has retreated, not on the glacier itself.

   Choice (C): The plant height increases. Notice that in years 0–30 the terrain contains "low-lying plants." The plants that succeed these are thickets and trees, both of which are taller.

   Choice (D): If you look at the numbers in the range of years for each stage, you will notice that in the early stages, the changes happen quickly compared with in the later stages. The spruce forest and spruce-hemlock forest stages take place over much longer periods of time, with fewer changes. This contradicts the assertion in choice (D).

Research Summary

CHAPTER GOALS

- The scientific method
- Strategies for reading about an experiment
- Warm-up exercises
- Strategies for research summary passages
- Ace the ACT! Sample research summary passages

Recall that three or four of the ACT science passages are research summaries. Most of these passages start out with a brief description of a scientific principle or unifying theme for the entire passage. Then two or more related experiments are described, with results provided in tables and / or graphs.

This format tests a lot of skills. You will be expected to:

- Understand the details of an experiment.
- Absorb the ins and outs of an apparatus.
- Comment on the design of the experiment.
- Identify independent variables, dependent variables, and control variables of the experiment.
- Interpret the results in the graphs and tables.
- Evaluate the effects when new variables are added to the mix.
- Formulate hypotheses about related experiments.
- Assess the impact of these experiments in a broader sense.

Whew! This seems like a tall order. The good news is that you will not be expected to know in-depth course content. What you *will* be expected to do is bring along your common sense and focus.

THE SCIENTIFIC METHOD

Now that you are feeling comfortable because you have been assured that you do not need to know all of high school science, here is a reality check. You do need to know how scientists work. The process by which experiments are devised falls under a loose umbrella called *the scientific method*. Here is a brief summary of the steps in the method:

1. Based on some earlier observations, come up with a proposed explanation of some aspect of these observations. This is called a *hypothesis*.
2. Carry out a controlled experiment to test that hypothesis.
3. Collect data and organize it in tables and graphs.
4. Analyze the data, and draw conclusions about it.
5. Compare the conclusions with the hypothesis and see whether the hypothesis is disproved or supported.
6. If the hypothesis is supported, devise additional experiments to test it further.
7. If the hypothesis is disproved, make further observations and construct a new hypothesis.

> **REMEMBER**
>
> You *can* prove that a hypothesis is false. You *cannot* prove that it is always true, just that it is probably true.

Did you notice that the scientific method is organized common sense? Well, that is how the ACT treats it. Here is a simple example of the scientific method.

Observation: The car does not start.
Hypothesis: The battery is dead.
Experiment: Turn the key and try again.
Results: The starter motor works, but the car does not turn over or "catch."
Analysis: The battery is fine. Something else is wrong.
Conclusion: The battery is OK. (Hypothesis disproved.)
New hypothesis: The car is out of gas.

And so on . . . .

Here is a more complex example of the scientific method.

Observation: Maple leaves change color in the fall.
Hypothesis: The colder temperatures in the fall cause the leaves to change color.
Controlled experiment: You need two identical setups. Find two small maple trees of the same age, size, and physical condition. Plant them in two pots of the same size with the same potting soil. Water both trees at the same time with the same amounts of water. Enclose the trees in two identical chambers, one of which is kept at normal summer temperatures and the other at cooler fall temperatures. During one month, record the number of green leaves on each tree every other day.

In this experiment, the tree at summer temperatures is the *controlled* setup, while the tree at fall temperatures is the *experimental* setup. Notice that age of tree, size of tree, physical condition of tree, size of pot, type of potting soil, and amount of water are all *independent variables* that are also *control variables*. This means that they are identical in both setups. Control variables do not change. The *experimental variable*, which is the thing being tested, is also an *independent variable*. For this experiment, the experimental variable is the temperature in the enclosed chambers. Notice that the temperature is the only quantity that is different in the two setups. This means that if there is a change or difference in only the experimental tree, we can be pretty sure that it was caused by the temperature.

Results: During the month, most of the leaves stayed green in *both* setups!

Conclusion: The hypothesis is disproved. Colder temperatures alone do not cause the leaves of a tree to change color in the fall.

New hypothesis: Colder temperatures combined with a change in the number of hours of daylight cause the leaves of a maple tree to change color in the fall.

1. The new hypothesis needs to be tested with a new controlled experiment.

2. A hypothesis can be disproved with a single experiment that shows it is false. A hypothesis cannot, however, be proved, even if it turns out to be supported by an experiment. If many different scientists can verify the hypothesis with many different experiments, it then becomes part of an accepted scientific theory.

SCIENCE FACT ALERT!

A scientific theory is an explanation of some aspect of nature that is supported by a large body of evidence. Newton's theory of gravity explains everything from the falling of apples to the orbit of the moon. This is very different from the everyday meaning of the word "theory."

STRATEGIES FOR READING ABOUT AN EXPERIMENT

In the research summary format, you will need to read the descriptions of multiple experiments in a given passage. This means that you must understand each individual experiment as you go. As is true for the data representation passages, you should try to develop an automatic checklist for each experiment that you read about, a four-step drill.

FOUR-STEP DRILL

1. Read and summarize
2. Apparatus
3. Variables CDE (control, dependent, experimental)
4. Results

Read and Summarize

Jot down what each experiment is investigating. Try to state the hypothesis, or what the experiment is trying to measure. For example, "Find boiling points of liquids under a given fixed pressure."

Apparatus

To understand an experiment, you need to understand the apparatus. On the ACT Science Test, several questions ask about the apparatus and possible modifications. So part of your focus in reading and summarizing an experiment should be to take note of the apparatus.

Variables CDE

Remember, control variables are independent variables that stay constant. Dependent variables are those whose values are being measured—the results of the experiment. Experimental variables are the variables whose effects are being investigated.

For the maple tree experiment described above, the control variables are the size of pot, the size of chamber, the size of tree, the amount of water each day, the type of potting soil, and so on. The dependent variable is the number of green leaves on each tree. The experimental variable is the temperature. For the experiment that finds boiling points of liquids under fixed pressure, a control variable would be the pressure. A dependent variable would be boiling point temperature. The experimental variable would be the different liquids used.

Results

This is the table or graph that shows the values of the experimental variables and the corresponding dependent variables. The control variables are unlikely to appear in the results. When you study the results, you should jot down any trends or conclusions that you see.

Be on the lookout for any limitations of the experiment. Suppose a passage investigates removing pollutants from the smokestack of a factory by bubbling emissions through a concentrated chemical solution. In the description of the experiment, nothing indicates that the size of the smokestack is being taken into account in the experiment. For a question that asks "What is the effect of doubling the size of the smokestack?" you must pick the answer choice that says "Cannot be determined from the given information." Do not even waste your time reading the other choices, most of which will sound reasonable.

One of the things that you *can* do is make suggestions for further investigations. This is one of the commonsense aspects of the ACT Science Test. What you *cannot* do is reach conclusions not supported by the data.

TIP

Do not be led astray by answer choices that cite "facts" that are not in the passage.

WARM-UP EXERCISES

Are you ready to try some warm-up exercises? As you read the passages, you will see some coaching tips. Think of these as words of wisdom whispered in your ear by your personal ACT trainer. For each minipassage below, use the four-step drill to analyze the experiment before you try the questions.

Answers and explanations are at the end of each passage. Also included are examples of what your jottings may look like. Tailor these to your own style. If you do not like making quick notes, then underline parts of the passage when you read and summarize. Be sure to study and internalize the apparatus. Circle the variables. Highlight the results. However you do it, just be sure to hit all four steps as you focus on the passage.

Be aware that these warm-up exercises are not sample ACT passages. They are the types of experiments that you may need to analyze as part of an ACT research summary passage. Think of them as a gentle dip your toes in the water introduction to research summaries.

TIP

- Read and summarize
- Apparatus
- Variables CDE
- Results

Example 1

A student studied the changes in gas volume caused by temperature changes at constant pressure. He performed an experiment to investigate what happens to a gas under normal air pressure.

The apparatus at his disposal was a plastic syringe graduated in milliliters (mL), ice, hot plates, beakers, thermometers, and water. The syringe was set to contain a certain volume of air at room temperature. The syringe was exposed to several different temperatures. For each temperature, the new volume in the syringe was measured. For example, to get the volume of the air in the syringe at 0°C, the syringe was submerged for a while in a beaker of ice and then the volume of air was recorded.

To find the volume at a temperature above room temperature, the syringe was totally immersed in water, whose temperature in degrees Celsius (°C) was recorded. After coming to equilibrium, the new volume of air in the syringe was read. All temperatures were converted to Kelvin. The results are shown in Table 1.

CAUTION

Do not be distracted by the details. Focus on what is being changed and what is being measured.

Table 1		
Temperature (°C)	**Temperature (K)**	**Volume (mL)**
0	273	4.5
7	280	4.8
22	295	5.5
70	343	6.2
90	363	6.6

1. For the experiment described, what, in order, is the independent (experimental) variable, a control variable, and the dependent variable?

    A. Temperature of air, volume of air, air pressure
    B. Air pressure, temperature of air, volume of air
    C. Temperature of air, air pressure, volume of air
    D. Volume of air, air pressure, temperature of air

2. Suppose the volume of air had been recorded at 100°C. Based on the results, which of the following is the most reasonable prediction for the corresponding volume?

    F. 12.0 mL
    G. 7.0 mL
    H. 6.5 mL
    J. 3.2 mL

3. Which of the following is *not* likely to be a source of error in the experiment?

    A. Maintaining the surrounding air pressure at a constant value
    B. Reading the temperature of the heated water
    C. Reading the volume of air in the syringe
    D. The friction of the plunger in the syringe

4. French chemists Jacques Charles and Joseph Gay Lussac were also hot-air balloonists. Charles was the first person to fill a balloon with hydrogen gas and make a solo balloon flight. His calculations were based on his law describing the relationship between temperature and volume of a gas under constant pressure. The law states that under constant pressure, the volume of a sample amount of gas varies directly with its temperature in Kelvin. Given that a hot-air balloon is open on the bottom, which of the following could contribute to causing a balloon to rise?

    F. The air pressure in the balloon decreases when the air in the balloon is heated.
    G. The air pressure outside the balloon increases when the air in the balloon is heated.
    H. The air in the balloon contracts when it is heated.
    J. The air in the balloon expands when it is heated

- **Read and summarize:** *Change in air volume measured at different temperatures at constant pressure.*
- **Apparatus:** *Air contained in syringe, which is immersed in liquid whose temperature is recorded in degrees Celsius (°C). The plunger can move up or down as the air expands or contracts.*
- **Variables:**

  Control: air pressure (kept constant).

  Dependent: volume of air (being recorded).

  Experimental: air temperature (being manipulated).
- **Results:** *Table shows that as temperature rises, volume of air rises, i.e., air expands when heated.*

SOLUTIONS

   1. **(C)**   2. **(G)**   3. **(A)**   4. **(J)**

1. **(C)** If you have sorted out the variables in your summary, you should get the answer to this question at a glance. The experimental, control, and dependent variables are the temperature of the air, the air pressure, and the volume of air, respectively.

2. **(G)** The trend in the data shows that as the temperature rises, so does the volume. Therefore, the volume at 100°C is unlikely to be less than the volume at 90°C. This means that choices (F) and (G) are the only two choices that you should consider. From the table, notice that a change in temperature of 10°C will produce a change in volume closer to 0.4 mL than to 5.4 mL.

   If you know about Charles's law, you could use a different line of reasoning to get to choice (G) as the answer. The temperature in K divided by the volume is a constant, in this case somewhere between 53 and 61 for each pair of readings. A temperature of 100°C = 373 K. When you divide 373 by 12, you get approximately 31. When you divide 373 by 7, you get approximately 53, which looks reasonable for this set of data.

> **TIP**
>
> Learn about the different types of variables *before* you take the ACT Science Test.

SCIENCE FACT ALERT!

Charles's law states that the volume of a gas at constant pressure is proportional to its kelvin temperature. Therefore temperature in K divided by volume at that temperature is constant.

3. **(A)** The experiment is simple and the apparatus fairly primitive. Keeping the air pressure constant is unlikely to be a problem since the plunger can move freely and the air pressure is simply the air pressure in the lab. Each of the other choices is potentially a problem if the student is not careful.

Choice (B): The student must wait a few minutes for the thermometer to come to equilibrium before reading the temperature of the water. An immediate reading will not be accurate.

Choices (C) and (D): Friction of the plunger in the syringe may prevent an accurate reading of the volume. This will happen if the student is impatient and does not allow the syringe to reach equilibrium before the volume is recorded.

4. **(J)** Remember, your answer to the question must be based on the information in the passage, namely the fact that air expands when it is heated (Charles's law). This is one of the factors that make the balloon buoyant. The other choices do not make sense and/or contradict the information in the passage.

Choice (F): Since the air in the balloon is not confined, the air pressure stays the same when the air is heated.

Choice (G): It is not possible to change the atmospheric pressure!

Choice (H): The air in the balloon *expands* when heated. Saying that it contracts contradicts the principle illustrated in the experiment.

Example 2

Consider the following three-day experiment in which a chemist produced silver by setting up a chemical reaction between copper (Cu) and silver nitrate ($AgNO_3$).

Day 1
30 milliliters (mL) of $AgNO_3$ solution were placed into a beaker. A 20 centimeter (cm) length of copper wire was bent into a spring shape and weighed to the nearest 0.01 grams (g). The wire was then placed into the solution and left overnight.

Day 2
The chemist observed that the previously shiny, smooth copper wire had become rough and was covered with some spindly silver fibers. The initially clear silver nitrate solution had become bluish, and it contained some silver-gray crystals. The chemist gently dislodged the silver from the copper wire, removed the wire from the solution, and set it aside to dry on a paper towel. He then weighed a piece of filter paper to the nearest 0.01 g and set it up in a conical funnel. He next poured off the experimental solution into another beaker, leaving the remaining silver solid behind. He repeatedly washed the remaining solid and poured off the liquid. The solid was then transferred to the filter paper cone, and excess liquid was drained away. Finally, the filter paper plus solid were removed and left to dry overnight.

Day 3
The chemist weighed each of the following: the remaining wire, the dry filter paper, and the solid silver.

The results of the experiment are shown in Tables 1 and 2. Table 1 shows the weights in grams of copper wire and filter paper at various stages of the experiment. Table 2 shows the weights in grams of copper used and silver produced as well as the corresponding number of moles for each element.

> **TIP**
>
> Did you underline the first sentence? It looks like a summary of the passage.

> **NOTICE**
>
> Filter paper is crucial to this experiment. Think about how it is being used.

Table 1

Material	Weight (g)
Copper wire before reaction	0.52
Copper wire after reaction	0.42
Dry filter paper	0.86
Filter paper plus silver	1.17

Table 2

	Weight (g)	Moles
Amount of copper (Cu) used in reaction	0.10	0.0016
Amount of silver (Ag) produced	0.31	0.0029

1. What was the purpose of the filter paper in this experiment?

   A. To act as a control variable for the copper used and the silver produced
   B. To isolate the silver from the solution in which it was formed
   C. To isolate the copper from the silver
   D. To allow the silver nitrate solution to be weighed separately

2. The results in Table 2 suggest that the chemical equation for the reaction is:

   F. $Cu + AgNO_3 \rightarrow CuNO_3 + Ag$
   G. $2Cu + AgNO_3 \rightarrow 2CuNO_3 + Ag$
   H. $Cu + 2AgNO_3 \rightarrow Cu(NO_3)_2 + 2Ag$
   J. $2Cu + 2AgNO_3 \rightarrow Cu(NO_3)_2 + 2Ag$

3. The chemist calculated that if all of the copper had been used up in the reaction, 1.7 g of silver would have been produced. In the actual experiment, what was the approximate percentage yield of silver?

   A. 10
   B. 18
   C. 25
   D. 33

Notice that this experiment is completely different than the previous example. Here the scientist uses a known scientific fact—namely that copper reacts with silver nitrate to produce silver—and performs an experiment that uses this fact. In Example 1, where volumes of air at different temperatures are measured, an investigation is done to discover or verify a fact. The previous experiment was a controlled experiment, whereas the copper/silver experiment was not controlled. There were no experimental variables whose effects were being tested.

Remember to use the checklist.

- **Read and summarize:** *Silver is produced from a chemical reaction between copper and silver nitrate.*
- **Apparatus:** *Copper wire and silver nitrate in a beaker. Filter paper funnel used to separate silver from solution.*
- **Variables:** *Dependent variables only: the weights of copper used and silver produced.*
- **Results:** *Ratio of silver produced to copper used ≈ 2:1 in moles (not weight!).*

SOLUTIONS

1. **(B)**   2. **(H)**   3. **(B)**

1. **(B)** Since the weight of the silver solid needed to be calculated, the liquid needed to be drained away, thus isolating the silver. One of the main uses of filter paper is to isolate solids from the liquids in which they are suspended. The other uses are all incorrect.

   Choice (A): This statement does not make sense. The experiment is not a controlled experiment.

   Choice (C): The copper *did* need to be isolated from the silver, but the filter paper did not do the job. The chemist gently dislodged the silver from the wire.

   Choice (D): The silver nitrate solution was never weighed in the experiment.

2. **(H)** Notice from Table 2 that you need 1 mole of Cu to produce 2 moles of Ag. The ratio of silver produced to copper used is about 2:1 (0.0029 moles:0.0016 moles). The equation in choice (H) has 1 Cu and 2 Ag, which is consistent with the experimental result.

   Here is something you should know about chemical equations: the number of atoms of a given element on the left side must equal the number of atoms of that element on the right side. Choice (J) has 2 atoms of copper (Cu) on the left and only 1 on the right. Choice (G) has, for example, 3 atoms of oxygen (O) on the left and 6 atoms of oxygen on the right. So the real choice of answers is between (F) and (H), both of which balance correctly.

> **TIP**
>
> To balance a chemical equation, the number of atoms on the left side must equal the number of atoms on the right side for any given element.

> **SCIENCE FACT ALERT!**
> An equal number of moles of two elements means an equal number of atoms of each element. But equal masses of each element does not mean an equal number of atoms, since atoms of different elements have different masses.

3. **(B)** You are told that 1.7 g of silver was the maximum amount of silver that could have been produced. However, only 0.31 g was produced. Thus,

   percentage yield $= \dfrac{0.31}{1.7} \cdot 100 = \dfrac{31}{1.7} \approx \dfrac{32}{2} = 16$. This is closest to

   18 percent, choice (B).

> **TIP**
>
> Don't waste time performing accurate calculations when a quick estimate will do the trick.

Example 3

A class performed an experiment on carrot disks to observe the effect of osmosis on plant cells. Osmosis is the movement of water molecules from a less concentrated, *hypotonic*, solution to a more concentrated, *hypertonic*, solution through a partially permeable membrane.

When a plant cell is surrounded by a hypotonic solution—for example, bathed by rainwater—the plant cell swells as water enters the cell by osmosis. The cell becomes turgid (firm) as the cell wall exerts a back pressure opposing too much water intake. This is a healthy state for the plant. If the plant cell is in an isotonic environment, namely one of equal concentration of solutes, there is no water transport. The cell becomes flaccid (limp), causing the plant to wilt. If the plant cell is immersed in a hypertonic environment, it will lose water to its surroundings and shrink, causing the wall of the cell to pull away from the membrane. This phenomenon is called *plasmolysis* and is usually lethal for the plant.

TIP

Quick! Jot down or underline these words and their meanings: osmosis, hypotonic, hypertonic, isotonic, and plasmolysis.

Each student in the class that performed the experiment received six thin disks of carrot, each 2–3 millimeters (mm) thick; two Petri dishes, one used for weighing only; a beaker labeled *A, B, C, D, E,* or *F*, where each designation was a different concentration of sodium chloride (NaCl); and access to a balance. Mary started by weighing the six carrot disks in a Petri dish and recorded the weight under "Starting Mass." She then placed the carrots into a second dish, spread them out, and covered them with enough of the NaCl solution to immerse them completely.

TIP

You need to think about what it means for the start to end ratio to be less than 1, equal to 1, or greater than 1.

The dishes were left in a safe place for as long as possible. Toward the end of the lab period, each student drained the liquid and blotted the carrots with a paper towel. Mary reweighed the carrot disks and recorded the result under "Mass at End." She then calculated the ratio of the starting mass to the mass at end. Students with the same concentration of NaCl pooled their results and found the mean of the start to end ratio for their concentration of NaCl. Average results for the class are shown in Table 1.

Table 1

Solution	A	B	C	D	E	F
Concentration of NaCl	0% (pure water)	15%	30%	45%	60%	75%
Starting mass (g)	15.1	18.1	23.3	19.2	22.7	13.9
Mass at end (g)	15.5	18.2	22.8	18.0	21.1	12.7
Start to end ratio	0.97	0.99	1.02	1.07	1.08	1.09
Mean value of start to end ratio including other students' data	0.94	0.99	1.02	1.06	1.06	1.08

*Passage based on "Pupils' Experiments with Osmosis in Carrot Tissue" from the *Bio Topics* web site, *www.biotopics.co.uk/index.html*

1. According to the results in Table 1, what was the concentration of solutes in the carrot cells at the start of the experiment?

    A. Between 0 and 15 percent
    B. Between 15 and 30 percent
    C. Between 30 and 45 percent
    D. Between 60 and 75 percent

2. For the experiment described, what would a start to end ratio of 1.00 indicate?

    F. The carrot cells were immersed in pure tap water.
    G. The carrot cells were immersed in pure distilled water.
    H. No water entered or left the carrot cells.
    J. The carrot cells gained weight at the start of the experiment and then lost an equal amount of weight during the time of immersion.

3. Which of the following solutions represents the most hypertonic environment for the carrot cells?

    A. Solution *A*
    B. Solution *B*
    C. Solution *C*
    D. Solution *D*

4. At the end of the experiment, the carrots were examined. Based on the results for Solution *A* in Table 1, what characteristics would you expect the carrots that were immersed in Solution *A* to show?

    F. Crisp and not flexible
    G. Swollen with water
    H. Colorless and odorless
    J. Flabby and easily bent

5. Assuming that houseplant cells behave similarly to carrot cells, which of the following actions is likely to cause plasmolysis in a houseplant?

    A. Watering it with tap water
    B. Watering it with distilled water
    C. Watering it with seawater
    D. Not watering it for a week

6. The density of a substance is defined as mass per unit volume. If the density of water is 1.00 g/mL, what volume of water was lost by the carrots immersed in Solution *D*? Base your answer on the results in Table 1.

    F. 0.45 mL
    G. 1.06 mL
    H. 1.07 mL
    J. 1.2 mL

Notice that each student's experiment is a control for all of the other students' experiments. The experiments are performed identically, except for the variations in solution concentration.

TIP

When you read the passage, jot down unfamiliar scientific terms.

- **Read and summarize:** *Experiment examines effect of osmosis on carrot cells. Six solutions with different NaCl concentrations are used. Ratio of initial to final weight recorded.*

  Osmosis: Water passes through membrane. Less concentrated → more concentrated.

  Hypotonic = less concentrated, hypertonic = more concentrated, isotonic = same concentrations.

  Plasmolysis: Plant cell in hypertonic environment. Cell loses water and dies.

- **Apparatus:** *Six pieces of carrot in Petri dish; NaCl solution (six different strengths, A, B, C, D, E, or F). Each student gets one of six solutions. Scale for weighing.*

- **Variables:**

  Control: Number of carrot disks; length of time of immersion in NaCl solution; temperature and pressure in room; and so on.

  Dependent: Final weight of carrot disks.

  Experimental: Concentration of liquid.

- **Results:** *For liquid A, the carrot cells absorbed water (final weight greater than initial weight). For liquids B and C, start to end ratio was close enough to 1; so carrots neither absorbed nor lost very much water. For liquids D, E, and F, carrots lost water (initial weight greater than final weight).*

SOLUTIONS

1. **(B)**   2. **(H)**   3. **(D)**   4. **(F)**   5. **(C)**   6. **(J)**

1. **(B)** Notice from Table 1 that Solutions *B* and *C* have a start to end ratio of approximately 1.00. This means that the concentration of solutes inside the carrot cell was approximately equal to that of the immersing solution, namely somewhere between 15 and 30 percent. Each of the other choices represents a concentration for which the carrots either lost or gained water.

   Choice (A): When the carrots were in pure water, they absorbed water, resulting in a start to end ratio of less than 1.00.

   Choices (C) and (D): These concentrations were more concentrated than the carrot cells, causing water to flow out of the carrot cells. Thus, the carrots lost weight, giving a start to end ratio greater than 1.00.

2. **(H)** A start to end ratio of 1.00 means that there was no net gain or loss of weight for the carrot cells. This can happen only if no water entered or left the carrot cells. The other choices are false.

   Choices (F) and (G): Water without solutes in it is less concentrated than the carrot cells. So water will flow into the cells, causing an increase of weight. Thus, the start to end ratio will be less than 1.00.

   Choice (J): This is a nonsensical choice that you should reject immediately. Carrots cannot spontaneously gain weight at the start of the experiment!

3. **(D)** "Most hypertonic" means most concentrated, as compared to the cell. Note that solutions *D*, *E*, and *F* are all hypertonic with respect to the cell, with *F* being the most concentrated. The correct answer from the choices given is (D). The other choices are incorrect.

   Choice (A): Solution *A*, pure water, is less concentrated than the cell, i.e., is hypotonic.

   Choices (B) and (C): Each of Solutions *B* and *C* is approximately isotonic, which means they are the same concentration as the carrot cells.

4. **(F)** Since Solution *A* is hypotonic (less concentrated) compared with the carrot cells, the cells will absorb water. This causes a back pressure in the cells, leading to a crisp, rigid texture. The other choices are wrong.

   Choice (G): When water is absorbed by plant cells, a back pressure prevents the cells from becoming swollen with water. Although the cells do gain weight because they are absorbing water, the plant does not become swollen.

   Choice (H): No information in the passage deals with color or odor. You should immediately peg this as a wrong answer.

   Choice (J): Flabby and easily bent is what happens when the cells are in a hypertonic solution that causes loss of water. This is not the case for Solution *A*.

5. **(C)** Refer to the passage to remind yourself that plasmolysis occurs when plant cells lose water because they are in a hypertonic environment (too concentrated). Seawater is very salty and will cause this effect.

   Choices (A) and (B): Using pure water is always a good choice when watering plants!

   Choice (D): Not watering a plant may cause the plant to wilt, but it will not cause the destruction that occurs during plasmolysis.

6. **(J)** Look only at the Solution *D* column to find the weight loss: 19.2 − 18.0 = 1.2 g. Since the density of water is 1.00 g/mL, a loss of 1.2 g of water means a loss of 1.2 mL of water.

STRATEGIES FOR RESEARCH SUMMARY PASSAGES

Are you ready to try some sample ACT° research summary passages? On the ACT, these passages usually contain several experiments in one passage. You have learned quite a bit about the scientific method and how to approach individual experiments. What follows now are strategies for dealing with ACT passages that have multiple experiments or studies. Several of the strategies mirror those given for data representation passages.

- Read the passage carefully, jotting down key points as you read.
- Treat each experiment as a separate entity using the same four-step drill: read and summarize, apparatus, variables CDE, results.
- After reading the entire passage, take a moment to tell yourself what links all the experiments in the passage. Ask yourself what distinguishes them from each other. For example, the passage may have three experiments testing different ways of reducing pollution. Reducing pollution is the common thread. What are the differences between experiments? You may jot down:
  Exp. 1: Electrified plates to remove dust.
  Exp. 2: Several filters with different pore sizes.
  Exp. 3: Emissions bubbled through solutions of concentrated alkali.
- Be aware that sometimes the experiments are only loosely linked.
- Know your basic scientific vocabulary! Every now and then, a question is asked that requires you to understand words like "insulator," "conductor," "diffusion," and so on. Be prepared. Review the scientific terms on pages 244–246 in Chapter 9.
- Pay special attention to the setup of an experiment. Several easy questions on the ACT check your understanding of how the apparatus was assembled. More often than not, understanding the apparatus is key to understanding the experiment.
- Many of the questions that follow the passage tell you which experiment to use for that question. For example, "The results of Experiment 1 suggest that . . . ." This means you should tune out the other experiments and focus on just this one. It alone will contain the answer.
- If you are not explicitly told which experiment to refer to, let the key words guide you to the relevant graph or table. If the key words span two experiments, you will need to get information from one of them and then use it to extract information from the other. Focus well—these are the hardest types of questions.
- You will be asked about results of experiments. If you have already jotted down results and conclusions for each experiment, this type of question will be relatively easy.
- Persevere, even if the passage seems difficult. Often, tough passages are followed by easy questions.
- Make sure that your deductions are based on the facts displayed. When you are asked a question along the lines of, "Based on the results of Experiment 1, what can you conclude about . . . ?" reject any answer choice that provides a fact about a quantity not dealt with in that experiment—even if the fact sounds reasonable!

Ace the ACT!
Sample Research Summary Passages

Don't forget your checklist!

> **FOUR-STEP DRILL**
> 1. Read and summarize
> 2. Apparatus
> 3. Variables CDE (control, dependent, experimental)
> 4. Results

PASSAGE I

The mechanical energy of a pendulum was investigated by examining its properties at different locations in the pendulum's trajectory.

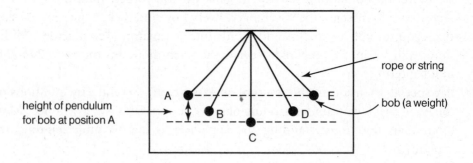

The mechanical energy M of a pendulum is constant. At any position M is the sum of its kinetic energy K and potential energy P.

$$M = K + P$$

K is the energy of motion. P is the energy of position, namely the stored energy, waiting to be released.

Experiment 1

The mass of the bob was set to 1 kilogram (kg) and the string length to 2.5 meters (m). The air resistance was assumed to be 0. At each of the positions A–E in the diagram, the height in meters and speed of the pendulum in meters per second (m/s) were recorded.

The results are in Table 1. The kinetic energy K in joules (J) was calculated using the formula $K = \frac{1}{2}mv^2$, where m is the mass and v is the velocity of the bob. The potential energy P in joules was calculated with the formula $P = mgh$, where m = mass and h = height of the bob, and g is the gravitational constant 9.8 m/s^2.

Table 1

Location	Height (m)	Speed (m/s)	Potential Energy (J)	Kinetic Energy (J)
A	0.5	0	4.90	0
B	0.25	2.23	2.45	2.49
C	0	3.13	0	4.89
D	0.25	2.23	2.45	2.49
E	0.5	0	4.90	0

Experiment 2

In this experiment, the effect of mass on the speed of the bob was studied. The mass of the bob was set at values from 1 to 5 kg, and the speed of the pendulum at only point C was recorded. The results are in Table 2.

Table 2

Mass (kg)	Speed at Position C (m/s)
1	4.43
2	3.11
3	2.52
4	2.20
5	1.98

Experiment 3

Students made a pendulum with a string 1 m long and a bob of mass 1 kg by attaching the string to a table. The setup is shown in Figure 2. A wooden block with dimensions approximately 5 × 5 × 5 cm was placed at the lowest point of the pendulum's arc, 2.5 cm above the ground, as shown in Figure 2. The pendulum bob was pulled back to a height of 30 cm and released. After impact with the wooden block, the distance that the block moved was recorded. Three trials were performed.

The block was then raised by placing bricks under its supporting plank and moved closer to the bob's initial position. This is shown in Figure 3. The experiment was repeated, and results are shown in Table 3.

> **NOTICE**
>
> Did you understand the purpose of the bricks?

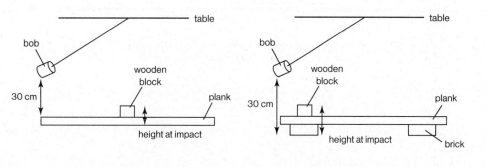

Figure 2   Figure 3

Table 3

Height of Bob at Impact (cm)	Distance Block moved along plank (cm)			
	Trial 1	Trial 2	Trial 3	Average
2.5	40	38.1	37.3	38.5
5	30.2	28.3	27.1	28.5
7.5	13.6	14.2	13.8	13.9

1. As a pendulum swings from its highest to its lowest position along an arc, what happens to its kinetic and potential energy?

   A. Both potential and kinetic energy decrease.
   B. The potential energy decreases while the kinetic energy increases.
   C. The kinetic energy decreases while the potential energy increases.
   D. Both potential and kinetic energy increase.

2. Which of the following bar graphs correctly represents the relationship between kinetic energy K, potential energy P, and mechanical energy M for the pendulum bob in position E in Figure 1?

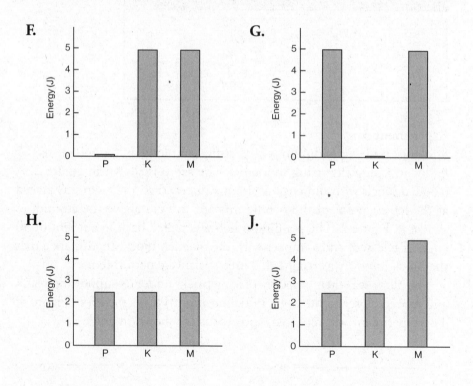

3. Which of the following statements about the energy of the pendulum bob is *false*?

   A. The mechanical energy of the bob is the same at each of points *A, B, C, D,* and *E* along its trajectory.
   B. If air resistance is 0, the potential energy of the bob at point *A* is equal to its potential energy at point *E.*
   C. The kinetic energy of the bob at point *C* is equal to the potential energy of the bob at point *A.*
   D. The potential energy of the bob is at a maximum when the bob's velocity is at a maximum.

4. In Experiment 2, which was a control variable for the experiment?

   F. The position of the bob
   G. The mass of the bob
   H. The velocity of the bob
   J. The kinetic energy of the bob

5. Suppose Experiment 3 were repeated with the wooden block placed even closer to the pendulum bob's initial position, such that the height of the bob at impact was 10 cm. Based on Table 3, the greatest kinetic energy will be imparted to the block when the height of the bob at impact is:

   A. 2.5 cm
   B. 5 cm
   C. 7.5 cm
   D. 10 cm

6. Suppose another location, *X*, in the pendulum's trajectory is added to Table 1. If the potential energy at *X* is found to be 1.00 J, which of the following is closest to the corresponding kinetic energy?

   F. 1.00 J
   G. 2.90 J
   H. 3.90 J
   J. 4.90 J

PASSAGE II

Several studies have been done to investigate whether population differences in size and age of sexual maturity of guppies (*Poecilia reticulata*) are closely associated with differences in the predators that the guppies are exposed to.

In some pools, where the killifish (*Rivulus hartii*) is the only potential guppy predator, the guppies produce relatively large offspring and are older at sexual maturity. The killifish eat predominantly small, juvenile guppies. At other pools, where guppies coexist with the pike cichlid (*Crenicichla alta*) that prey selectively on large, mature guppies, the guppies seem to produce relatively small offspring and generally reproduce at a younger age.

The pools are completely separate. Certain landscape features prevent the migration of populations between pools even though the populations live in the same geographical area.

CAUTION

Don't be confused by the fancy scientific names. Just ignore them.

Study 1

Scientists studied two populations of guppies. One group consisted of guppies that coexisted with pike cichlids in a pike-cichlid pool. Denote these as pc-guppies. For the second group, guppies were removed from only pike-cichlid sites and added to an environment that contained killifish and no other guppies. Denote these transplanted guppies as k-guppies. Over a period of 11 years, the scientists compared the age and weight at maturity of the k-guppies with the age and weight of the pc-guppies. The results, recorded 30 to 60 generations after the start of the study, are shown in Table 1.

TIP

Did you distinguish between the control group and the experimental group?

Table 1

	Average Weight at Maturity (mg)	Average Age at Maturity (days)
Male pc-guppies	67.5	48.5
Male k-guppies	76.1	58.2
Female pc-guppies	161.5	85.7
Female k-guppies	185.6	92.3

Study 2

The responses of guppies from two different populations exposed to a simulated aerial predator, one population upstream and one downstream to an aquatic predator, were studied.

Since large fish are unable to colonize areas above waterfalls, upstream guppies meet few predators. In contrast, downstream guppies often encounter a variety of predators.

Matching groups of upstream and downstream guppies were exposed one at a time, alone in a tank, to a realistic fake bird, a kingfisher, moving across the top of a tank. After a period of time to recover, each guppy was also exposed to an aquatic predator, a hungry sea bass placed into the tank. The following behaviors were observed: swim, freeze, hide (the tank had a small area of cover), drop (fast vertical move to the tank's bottom), dash (unusually rapid swimming), and inspect (approach and face the predator). For each guppy in the experiment, the length of time exposure to each predator was the same.

Graph 1 shows the mean duration that downstream (high predation) and upstream (low predation) guppies spent swimming during the 3-minute periods before and after the predators were introduced. Graph 2 shows the fraction of nonswimming guppies (of both types) that exhibited various antipredator behaviors.

> **CAUTION**
>
> Did you notice the different time scales on the vertical axes of each graph?

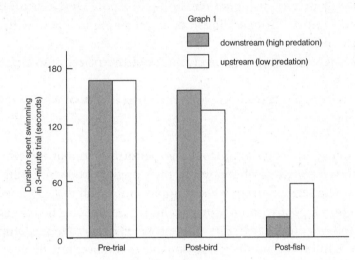

Graph 1

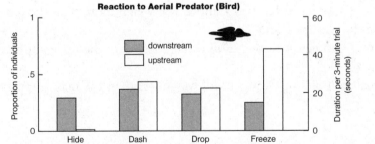

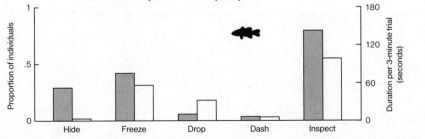

Graph 2

Christopher N. Templeton and Walter M. Shriner, "Multiple selection pressures influence Trinidadian guppy (*Poecilia reticulata*) antipredator behavior." *Behavioral Ecology* 2004, Vol. 15 #4, pp. 673–678, by permission of the International Society for Behavioral Ecology.

1. What conclusion is supported by the results in Table 1?

   A. The pc-guppies in the pike-cichlid pools developed characteristics during the course of the experiment to help them survive the pike-cichlid predators.
   B. The transplanted k-guppies developed characteristics during the course of the experiment to help them survive the killifish predators.
   C. The transplanted k-guppies eventually lived longer than the pc-guppies.
   D. The pc-guppies in the pike-cichlid pools evolved to become sexually mature adults at a later age than the k-guppies.

2. Which of the following accurately describes the control group for Study 1?

   F. Guppies from a killifish pool remaining in a pool with killifish only
   G. Guppies removed from a killifish pool remaining in a pool with pike cichlids only
   H. Guppies removed from a pike-cichlid pool and placed into a pool with killifish only
   J. Guppies from a pike-cichlid pool remaining in a pool with pike cichlids only

3. Suppose a follow-up study to Study 1 was performed so that the two groups observed consisted of guppies in their original pool with killifish (Group 1) and a second group where guppies from a killifish pool were introduced into a pool with only pike cichlids (Group 2). The two groups were then followed for many years through several generations of guppies. Which of the following results is a reasonable prediction for the new study?

   A. The female guppies in Group 2 will reproduce at an age greater than that for the female guppies in Group 1.
   B. The male guppies in Groups 1 and 2 will weigh more than the female guppies in Groups 1 and 2.
   C. The male guppies in Group 2 will weigh less than the male guppies in Group 1.
   D. The male guppies in Group 1 will weigh less than the male guppies in Group 2.

4. According to Graphs 1 and 2, which would *not* be a reasonable statement about guppy behavior in the presence of predators?

  F. After the aquatic predator stimulus, guppies from both populations significantly decreased the amount of swimming.

  G. Downstream guppies sometimes hid when the aerial predator was presented, whereas upstream guppies never hid.

  H. In the presence of both predators, upstream guppies froze on the bottom of the aquarium significantly longer than did downstream guppies.

  J. After introduction of the aquatic predator, upstream guppies swam for a longer time than those from downstream.

5. Which of the following is a design flaw in Study 2?

  A. No control stimulus was used for the fake kingfisher. It is possible that guppies were reacting to a novel overhead object rather than to the threat of a predator.

  B. Upstream guppies were taken from a stream with little vegetation. They therefore did not have the concept of hiding from predators.

  C. Each guppy was alone in the tank for the duration of the experiment. Guppies may behave differently when they are in groups.

  D. The researchers' definitions of guppy behavior—dropping, hiding, freezing, and so on—were arbitrary and therefore not applicable to the real world.

6. Which of the following would reasonably account for the fact that in Study 2, many more downstream guppies than upstream guppies inspected the aquatic predator before taking further action?

  F. Upstream guppies come from an environment where aquatic predators are nonexistent. They are not aware of danger.

  G. Downstream guppies come from a multipredator environment. They have therefore developed the ability to tailor the evasive action taken to the specific predator.

  H. The downstream guppies have a stronger survival instinct than the upstream guppies and hence more interest in predators.

  J. Upstream guppies have evolved to be less aware of other fish in their environment than have downstream guppies.

PASSAGE III

Metallic switches are often used to control electrical devices. The switch should be designed so that as it is opened or closed, good metal-to-metal contact is created. Often the contacts are placed in an enclosed environment, where sparking creates ozone that can react with the contacts, oxidizing the metal.

Scientists conducted three experiments to establish the effects of ozone on metallic switch performance.

Thin rectangular pieces of metal called coupons were used in the experiments. Contact resistance data were collected using a computerized gold-tipped probe, which could be brought into contact with a coupon with a varying amount of force, thereby closing a switch and setting up an electric circuit. The contact resistance in this circuit provided a measure of the effectiveness of the metal when used in a switch. (Note that if the force applied by the probe was too small, however, the contact would be poor, causing an unnaturally high contact resistance.) An ozone chamber was designed in which ozone was generated by an ultraviolet light source and maintained at a constant level.

Four material systems commonly used in switches were tested: 85 percent silver (Ag) with 15 percent nickel (Ni); 90 percent silver with 10 percent nickel; fine-grain silver (produced by adding a minute amount of nickel to fine silver); and fine silver (0.999 pure).

Experiment 1

Two coupons of each of the four material systems were cleaned and polished. One coupon of each material system was placed into the ozone chamber at 7.0 ppm (parts per million) ozone. Each matching coupon was placed in clean laboratory air. After nine days, 25 resistance readings for each coupon were collected with the computerized probe at 60 g (grams) normal force. Table 1 contains the contact resistance averages obtained.

TIP
Underline the second paragraph. It summarizes the passage.

Table 1: Average Contact Resistance Values at 7 ppm Ozone After 9 Days at 60 g Normal Force

Material	Contact Resistance (milliohms)	
	Clean Air	7 ppm Ozone
85% Ag 15% Ni	1.333	50.56
90% Ag 10% Ni	0.996	74.62
Fine-grain Ag	0.546	22.61
Fine Ag	0.477	9.923

Reprinted with permission. © 1999 IEEE. "The Effect of Ozone on Silver, Silver Alloys and Gold Plated Silver" by Neil R. Aukland, et al., in *Electrical Contacts, 1999 Proceedings of the 45th IEEE Holm Conference.*

Experiment 2

A second series of identical experiments was conducted on the silver and silver alloys at 20.0 ppm ozone. Table 2 contains the average resistance values obtained.

THINK

What does it mean if the contact resistance is high?

Table 2: Average Contact Resistance Values at 20 ppm Ozone After 9 Days at 60 g Normal Force

Material	Contact Resistance (milliohms)	
	Clean Air	20 ppm Ozone
85% Ag 15% Ni	1.48	259.02
90% Ag 10% Ni	1.15	40.31
Fine-grain Ag	0.65	37.21
Fine Ag	0.44	2.98

Reprinted with permission. © 1999 IEEE. "The Effect of Ozone on Silver, Silver Alloys and Gold Plated Silver" by Neil R. Aukland, et al., in *Electrical Contacts, 1999 Proceedings of the 45th IEEE Holm Conference.*

Experiment 3

After Experiments 1 and 2, a set of contact resistance data was collected on two of the silver metal systems that were electroplated with soft gold (Au). Coupons of fine silver and coupons of 85 percent silver with 15 percent nickel were each plated with 10 microinch-thick gold and with 60 microinch-thick gold. The data for these four coupons were collected after nine days at an ozone level of 7 ppm. Table 3 contains the average contact resistance values from 25 different data points. The data points were collected at random locations on each coupon.

Table 3: Average Contact Resistance Values at 7 ppm Ozone After 9 Days at 60 g Normal Force

Material System	Average Contact Resistance (milliohms)
10 μ inches* Au over 85% Ag 15% Ni	1.514
10 μ inches Au over Fine Ag	1.269
60 μ inches Au over 85% Ag 15% Ni	0.767
60 μ inches Au over Fine Ag	0.804

Reprinted with permission. © 1999 IEEE. "The Effect of Ozone on Silver, Silver Alloys and Gold Plated Silver" by Neil R. Aukland, et al., in *Electrical Contacts, 1999 Proceedings of the 45th IEEE Holm Conference.*

*Note that μ inch is an abbreviated form of microinch.

1. If a switch is used in an electrical device, which of the following material systems for the switch is likely to produce the best contact performance in the presence of 7.0 ppm of ozone?

   A. Fine silver plated with 10 µ inches of gold
   B. 85 percent silver with 15 percent nickel plated with 60 µ inches of gold
   C. 90 percent silver with 10 percent nickel
   D. Fine silver

2. According to the results of the experiments, which is a reasonable conclusion about the metals used in switches? In high concentrations of ozone:

   F. the higher the nickel content is, the higher the contact resistance.
   G. gold plating the metal has little or no effect on contact resistance.
   H. the higher the concentration of ozone is, the higher the contact resistance.
   J. the thicker the metal is, the lower the contact resistance.

3. Ozone (O_3) is a highly reactive form of oxygen, commonly produced as a result of electrical discharges in the air. Ozone degrades metal by direct oxidation. Which of the following is a reasonable decomposition reaction for ozone?

   A. $O_3 \leftrightarrow \frac{3}{2} O_2$

   B. $O_3 \leftrightarrow \frac{2}{3} O_2$

   C. $O_3 \leftrightarrow \frac{2}{3} O_3 + O_2$

   D. $O_3 \leftrightarrow \frac{3}{2} O_3 + O_2$

4. In Experiments 1 and 2, what was the main purpose of measuring contact resistance for a set of coupons placed in clean laboratory air?

   F. To calculate the amount of ozone that occurs naturally in the atmosphere
   G. To investigate the feasibility of creating switches that operate with no ozone present
   H. To establish an initial baseline reading for all of the material systems using the contact resistance probe
   J. To show that the increased contact resistance was primarily due to the presence of ozone

5. Suppose that for Experiment 3 the researchers had also used fine-grain silver. Which result could they confidently expect?

   A. The contact resistance with 10 μ inches of gold plating would be lower than the contact resistance with 60 μ inches of gold plating.
   B. The contact resistance with 10 μ inches of gold plating would be higher than the contact resistance with 60 μ inches of gold plating.
   C. The contact resistance with 10 μ inches of gold plating for the fine-grain silver would be higher than the contact resistance for the pure silver with 60 μ inches of gold plating.
   D. The contact resistance with 10 μ inches of gold plating for the fine-grain silver would be lower than the contact resistance for the pure silver with 60 μ inches of gold plating.

6. In an earlier experiment, the scientists collected contact resistance data on test coupons in the ozone chamber with 0.1 ppm ozone and also on a set of coupons exposed to clean laboratory air. The data was collected using discrete increments between 20 and 60 grams of force to make contact. Based on the information in the passage, which of the following graphs represents a reasonable expectation of results obtained for the fine-grain silver coupons only? In each graph, the solid line represents the coupons in the ozone chamber. The dotted lines are for the coupons in clean laboratory air.

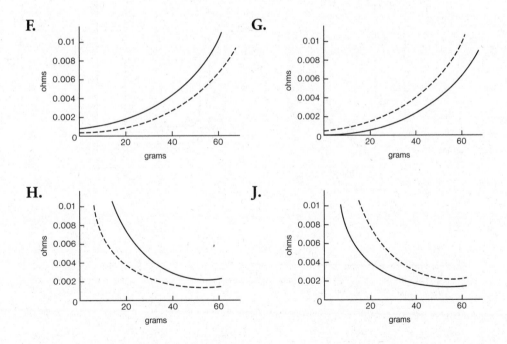

PASSAGE IV

Experiments have shown that a scanning tunneling microscope can be used to deposit single nanoscopic silver structures onto a graphite basal plane surface. The silver is obtained during electrolysis, a process that uses electricity to induce a chemical reaction in a solution.

Experiment 1

Some preliminary electrochemical measurements were made using a glass one-compartment electrolytic cell consisting of a freshly polished platinum electrode and a silver electrode both immersed in a 0.5 millimolar (mM) silver fluoride solution. An electrical bias (potential) of 20 millivolts (mV) was applied, and the current generated at the platinum electrode was recorded against time in seconds (s). The electrical charge associated with this current, in microcoulombs (μC), was calculated for platinum disk electrodes having four different areas. The results are shown in Graph 1. Note that the negative current values in the graph imply that the current direction is opposite to that of the applied voltage.

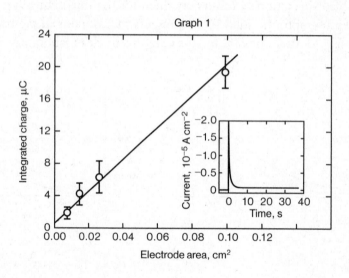

Graph 1

Reprinted with permission. © 1996 Am. Chem Soc. "Mechanistic Study of Silver Nanoparticle Deposition Directed with the Tip of a Scanning Tunneling Microscope in an Electrolytic Environment" by W. Li et al. *J. Phys. Chem* 1996, Vol. 100 #51.

Experiment 2

A scanning tunneling microscope (STM) was used to deposit nanoscopic clumps of silver onto a graphite basal plane surface. To do this, a platinum microelectrode was used in the tip of the microscope. The electrode was inserted into an aqueous silver solution in the STM. The STM tip described behaves as a microelectrode in aqueous solution, very similar to the platinum electrode described in Experiment 1.

A tunneling junction was established with the graphite plane surface, and a 20 mV bias was applied at this junction. With the STM tip at a defect-free region of the surface, two bias pulses were applied in quick succession. The first pulse caused a shallow circular pit in the graphite surface to appear. The second pulse caused silver, formed at the platinum STM tip, to migrate and be deposited in the pit. This process occurred within the next 50 microseconds (μs).

The pulses were repeated, and silver was deposited at regular intervals in different pits formed on the graphite surface. The quantities of silver deposited decreased with each new pit formed until, eventually, the STM tip was stripped of silver. Several minutes were needed for regeneration. Graph 2 shows the average heights, in angstroms (Å), of several sets of 6 silver nanostructures that were formed, plotted in order of deposition. The error bars indicate the range of heights measured for each structure in corresponding order of deposition.

Scientists varied the voltage of the first bias pulse. Based on observation, they calculated the probability that a silver deposit would occur at each voltage. The results are shown in Graph 3.

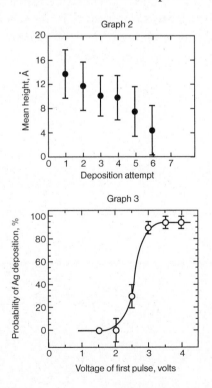

Reprinted with permission. © 1996 Am. Chem Soc. "Mechanistic Study of Silver Nanoparticle Deposition Directed with the Tip of a Scanning Tunneling Microscope in an Electrolytic Environment" by W. Li et al. *J. Phys. Chem* 1996, Vol. 100 #51.

1. In Experiment 1, after the 20 mV bias was applied, which of the following times corresponded to the highest observed current in the electrolytic solution?

   A. 2 seconds
   B. 5 seconds
   C. 10 seconds
   D. 30 seconds

2. Based on the information shown in Graph 1, when the platinum disk electrode had an area of 0.10 cm^2, what was the approximate integrated charge associated with the chemical reaction?

   F. Greater than 22 µC
   G. Between 16 and 22 µC
   H. Between 5 and 16 µC
   J. Less than 5 µC

3. In Experiment 2, the average heights of silver nanostructures deposited in the graphite basal plane pits was recorded. Which of the following is the least likely height to have been recorded for the third silver deposit?

   A. 7 Å
   B. 10 Å
   C. 12 Å
   D. 15 Å

4. In Experiment 2, the scientists observed that not every bias pulse resulted in a silver-filled pit in the graphite surface. Which voltage for the bias pulse was most likely to result in a silver-filled pit?

   F. 1 V
   G. 2 V
   H. 3 V
   J. 4 V

5. The silver deposits described in Experiment 2 are formed as a result of an electrolytic chemical reaction in an aqueous silver solution. The silver (Ag) is reduced. Namely, it gains electrons. At the same time, water (H_2O) is oxidized. Namely, it loses electrons. Which equation correctly represents this reaction?

   A. $4\,Ag^- + 2\,H_2O \rightarrow 4\,Ag + O_2 + 4\,H^+$
   B. $4\,Ag + O_2 + 4\,H^+ \rightarrow 4\,Ag^- + 2\,H_2O$
   C. $4\,Ag^+ + 2\,H_2O \rightarrow 4\,Ag + O_2 + 4\,H^+$
   D. $4\,Ag + O_2 + 4\,H^+ \rightarrow 4\,Ag^+ + 2\,H_2O$

6. The goal of Experiment 2 was to use a scanning tunneling microscope to deposit minute clumps of silver into tiny craters on a graphite surface and to obtain precise measurements for these clumps. Which of the following would *not* have helped the scientists achieve their goal?

   F. Instruments that could take measurements within a precision of 1 mm
   G. A defect-free, atomically smooth surface
   H. A chemically unreactive surface
   J. A surface to which silver particles would strongly adhere

7. Which is a true statement about Experiment 2?

   A. Whenever a pit is formed in the graphite basal plane surface, a nanoscopic clump of silver will be formed in the pit.
   B. Electrochemical deposits of silver will occur only if the voltage of the bias pulses is large enough to drive an oxidation reaction at the STM tip anode.
   C. The platinum microelectrode used in the STM tip can be immersed into any aqueous solution in the STM to produce silver deposits on the graphite surface.
   D. Formation of silver is due to an electrochemical reaction between the platinum in the STM tip and the graphite of the basal plane.

PASSAGE V*

Sorghum is one of the staple cereals in several regions in India. Experiments were conducted at two farms in India to investigate the feasibility of using sorghum in poultry feed, in combination with maize and commercial noncereal concentrate.

Experiment 1

Three groups, each containing 156 egg-laying hens (layers), were fed a diet in which cereal comprised 45 percent of the total diet. Each group of hens was fed one of the following diets:

- 45 percent maize
- 45 percent sorghum
- 15 percent sorghum plus 30 percent maize

The sorghum grains, which came in two varieties, were obtained from a local market. Maize was obtained commercially. Five different feed mixes were used. The quantity of feed consumed and the number of eggs laid were recorded for 21 days. The results are given in Table 1.

Table 1: Feed Consumption and Egg Production in Egg-Layer Feed Containing Maize and Sorghum

Cereal Component of Feed[1]	Feed Consumed (grams/bird/day)	Egg Production (percent of total eggs laid)
45% maize	117	95
15% white sorghum + 30% maize	118	94
45% white sorghum	116	94
15% yellow sorghum + 30% maize	118	96
45% yellow sorghum	116	94

[1] Feed contained 55 percent noncereal concentrate and 45 percent cereal.

Experiment 2

Three groups of 160 broiler birds (broilers), each 37 days old, of mixed sex were fed a diet in which cereal comprised 60 percent of the total diet. Each group of birds was fed one of the following diets:

- 60 percent maize
- 15 percent sorghum plus 45 percent maize
- 45 percent sorghum plus 15 percent maize

Again, five different feed mixes were used. The feed consumed and the weight of birds were recorded for 21 days. Results are shown in Table 2. (Weight gain is in grams per bird per day. Bird weight is in kilograms (kg) per bird.)

*Data taken from "Sorghum grain for poultry feed" by Subramanian V. et al., in *Technical and institutional options for sorghum grain mold management: proceedings of an international consultation*, ICRISAT 2000.

Table 2: Broiler Weight Gain, Final Bird Weight, and Feed Efficiency Ratio with Maize and Sorghum Feed

Cereal Component of Feed[1]	Weight Gain (grams/bird/day)	Bird Weight (kg/bird)	Feed Efficiency Ratio
60% maize	42.4	1.12	3.30
15% white sorghum + 45% maize	42.3	1.18	3.22
45% white sorghum + 15% maize	41.2	1.15	3.35
15% yellow sorghum + 45% maize	39.5	1.11	3.87
45% yellow sorghum + 15% maize	44.4	1.24	3.18

[1] Feed contained 40 percent noncereal concentrate and 60 percent cereal.

Experiment 3

An improved variety of maize (Deccan 103) and scientifically developed sorghum (ICSV 112) were fed to groups of layers and broilers. The layers were fed one of the following diets:

• 50 percent maize (Deccan 103)
• 50 percent sorghum (ICSV 112)
• 25 percent maize (Deccan 103) plus 25 percent sorghum (ICSV 112)
• Farmers' feed, purchased commercially

The broiler birds were fed one of the following diets:

• 60 percent maize (Deccan 103)
• 60 percent sorghum (ICSV 112)
• 30 percent maize (Deccan 103) plus 30 percent sorghum (ICSV 112)
• Farmers' feed, purchased commercially

Table 3 shows the chemical composition of the improved varieties of maize and sorghum.

TIP

The experiments are similar. Are you keeping track?

Table 3: Comparison of Constituents in Maize and Sorghum Grains

Constituent	Maize (Deccan 103)	Sorghum (ICSV 112)
Protein (%)	9.8	8.9
Starch (%)	71.7	72.3
Sugars (%)	1.4	1.2
Fat (%)	5.2	3.7
Crude fiber (%)	1.4	1.2
Ash (%)	1.3	1.7
Gross energy (cal/100g)	414	412

Table 4 shows data collected for Experiment 3.

Table 4: Comparison of Sorghum and Maize for Poultry Feed

Cereal Component of Feed[1]	Layer Feed Consumed (grams/bird/day)	Layer Egg Production (%)	Broiler weight[2] (kg/bird)	Broiler Taste Panel Score for Chicken[3]
Maize (Deccan 103)	102	83	1.63	3.9
Sorghum (ICSV 112)	99	82	1.53	3.8
ICSV 112 + maize (1:1)	102	84	1.60	3.5
Farmers' feed	97	81	1.62	3.4

[1]For layers, feed contains 50 percent concentrate and 50 percent cereal. For broilers, feed contains 40 percent concentrate and 60 percent cereal.
[2]Mean of four-week-old birds.
[3]Score: 1 = poor; 5 = excellent (mean of 16 panelists).

1. Which of the following was a constant in all three experiments?

   A. The type of sorghum in the feed
   B. The type of maize in the feed
   C. The composition of the noncereal portion of the feed
   D. The percentage of maize plus sorghum in the feed

2. Based on Experiment 2, which is an invalid statement about broilers that had sorghum in their feed?

   F. The final bird weight did not vary much among birds that had different levels of maize and of white and yellow sorghum in their feed.
   G. The feed efficiency ratio did not seem to vary much among feeds that had different levels of maize and of white and yellow sorghum.
   H. Sorghum can replace up to 60 percent of maize grain without having an adverse effect on broilers.
   J. Broiler birds receiving 60 percent maize and broiler birds receiving sorghum at the 15 or 45 percent level had similar growth rates.

3. In the experiments described, which diet for layer hens appears to lead to the greatest percentage of eggs laid?

   A. 30 percent Deccan 103 plus 30 percent ISCV 112
   B. 45 percent local yellow sorghum
   C. 15 percent local yellow sorghum plus 30 percent commercial maize
   D. 45 percent local yellow sorghum plus 15 percent commercial maize

4. Which hypothesis appears to be contradicted by the data in the passage?

   F. Sorghum has significantly less energy than maize grain.

   G. The nutritional compositions of maize and sorghum are similar.

   H. Using sorghum in poultry feed will not adversely affect the taste of chicken.

   J. The growth rates of broiler birds reared on feeds with and without sorghum in the cereal component are comparable.

5. Table 2 shows a feed efficiency ratio for each of the diets used for broiler birds in Experiment 2. Which of the following is a reasonable definition for this quantity?

   A. The feed efficiency ratio is the ratio of total weight gain per bird to total final average weight of all the birds.

   B. The feed efficiency ratio is the ratio of total final average weight of birds to total weight gain.

   C. The feed efficiency ratio is the ratio of average weight gain of birds to average weight of feed consumed.

   D. The feed efficiency ratio is the ratio of average weight of feed consumed to average weight gain of birds.

6. Based on the passage, which of the following would be a reasonable assumption for poultry farmers to make?

   F. The greater the percentage of sorghum in the feed, the greater the weight gain of broiler birds.

   G. The greater the percentage of sorghum in the feed, the higher the number of eggs laid by layer hens.

   H. The greater the percentage of sorghum in the feed, the better the taste of the broiler hens.

   J. Adding sorghum to poultry feed does not significantly affect the amount of feed consumed by the birds.

Solutions and Explanations

PASSAGE I (PENDULUM)

Three different experiments are in this passage. Apply your checklist to each one.

Experiment 1

- **Read and summarize:** *Pendulum is shown at different positions. For each position, height of bob above lowest point is recorded. Speed is measured, and potential energy and kinetic energy are calculated. Mechanical energy stays constant.*
  Mechanical energy = Kinetic energy + Potential energy.
- **Apparatus:** *Just a pendulum.*
- **Variables:**
  Control variables: mass of bob (kept constant at 1 kg); length of pendulum string (2.5 m).
  Dependent variable is speed of bob. Variables calculated from this are potential energy and kinetic energy.
  Experimental variable is height of bob above lowest point.
- **Results:** *Energy relationship: M = K + P. (Mechanical energy is constant.) At highest points of swing (A and E), potential energy at maximum and kinetic energy at minimum (= 0). At lowest point of swing (C), kinetic energy is maximum and potential energy minimum (= 0).*

Experiment 2:

- **Read and summarize:** *Mass of bob is varied, and speed measured at only point C (lowest point of swing) for each weight.*
- **Apparatus:** *Just a pendulum with different weights.*
- **Variables:**
  Control: length of string and position where measurement is taken.
  Dependent: velocity of pendulum bob.
  Experimental: mass of pendulum bob.

TIP

When summarizing an experiment, keep your jottings to a minimum. Try to capture the essence of the experiment in a few words.

- **Results:** *Inverse relationship between mass and speed of bob: As mass increases, velocity decreases.*

Experiment 3

- **Read and summarize:** *Pendulum set up to hit wooden block on plank at three different points of its arc. Distance moved by block is measured for these different points.*
- **Apparatus:** *Plank with small block of wood is placed so bob will hit the wood. Bricks are used to raise the plank and thus the height of bob at impact. In Figure 2, wood is placed so bob will hit it at lowest point of swing.*
- **Variables:**
  Control: length of string and initial height of pendulum bob. Also, same plank and wooden block used for each trial.
  Dependent: distance moved by block.
  Experimental: height of bob at impact.
- **Results:** *The lower the height at impact, the farther the block moves (see Table 3). Block goes farthest when bob hits it at lowest point in its swing (maximum possible kinetic energy imparted to block). The more kinetic energy the block gets from the bob, the farther it moves.*

> **NOTE**
>
> You should understand that the "real" experimental variable here is the position in the pendulum's arc.

SOLUTIONS

1. **(B)**   2. **(G)**   3. **(D)**   4. **(F)**   5. **(A)**   6. **(H)**

1. **(B)** This is a question about understanding the relationship between M, P, and K. In order for M to stay constant, P must decrease as K increases, and K must decrease as P increases.

   To get the correct answer, you must notice that the question is restricting the bob to the first part of its swing, namely going from position A to position C. At A, the potential energy P is at a maximum, while the kinetic energy K equals 0. At C, the potential energy P is 0, and the kinetic energy K is at a maximum. Thus, potential energy decreases as kinetic energy increases.

2. **(G)** At position E, the bob is at its maximum height and is momentarily not moving, so its kinetic energy equals 0. Its potential energy (from Table 1) is approximately 4.90 J. The mechanical energy equals the sum of kinetic and potential energies. It equals 4.90 J. Graph (G) is the only graph that shows these values.

3. **(D)** For the pendulum, the kinetic energy or energy of motion is 0 at the highest points (A and E) because the bob is not moving. The potential energy at these points is at a maximum. The mechanical energy, which is the sum of kinetic energy and potential energy, is a constant. Choice (D) is therefore the incorrect statement and the correct answer. Notice that choice (D) could reasonably be corrected in two ways. First, the kinetic energy of the bob is at a maximum when its velocity is at a maximum. Second, the potential energy of the bob is at a minimum when its velocity is at a maximum. Each of the other choices is *true*, which is a *wrong* answer for this question!

   Choice (A): True, because mechanical energy is constant for every position of the bob's swing.

   Choice (B): True, because you are told that air resistance is assumed to be 0. At points A and E, when the bob is not moving, the potential energy is at a maximum, and therefore equal at those positions.

   Choice (C): True, because mechanical energy is the same at all positions. At point C, kinetic energy is at a maximum and potential energy is 0; therefore, mechanical energy equals kinetic energy. At point A, kinetic energy is 0 and potential energy is at a maximum; therefore mechanical energy equals potential energy. Thus, kinetic energy at C equals potential energy at A.

4. **(F)** Remember, a control for an experiment is a variable that stays the same in every run of the experiment. Since point *C* in the trajectory is used in every run, the same position of the bob is used in every run. Thus, position of the bob is a control. Note that the variables in all the other choices are changing.

   Choice (G): The mass of the bob is the experimental variable and, by definition, cannot be the control!

   Choice (H): The velocity of the bob is the dependent variable being measured, so it cannot be a control.

   Choice (J): The kinetic energy depends on velocity, a quantity that is changing. It is also being calculated *after* the experiment, so it cannot be a control.

TIP

Questions about variable types are easy if you have studied the scientific method.

5. **(A)** To answer this question, you need to understand that the greater the kinetic energy of the bob, the greater the resulting kinetic energy of the wooden block and the farther it will move. Based on Table 3, you can infer that for the 10 cm height, the wooden block will move even less than it does for the 7.5 cm height. Greatest kinetic energy occurs when the block moves the farthest. This happens when the pendulum bob strikes the block at the bottom of its swing, namely, when the height of the block at impact is 2.5 cm.

6. **(H)** From Table 1, you can determine:

$$M = P + K \Rightarrow P + K = 4.90$$

Thus, if $P = 1.00$ J, $K = 4.90 - 1 = 3.90$ J.

PASSAGE II (GUPPIES)

The two studies are loosely connected: Each involves guppies and their predators.

Study 1

- **Read and summarize:** *Two sets of guppies used. (Note: These two groups existed before experiment.)*

  1) Small guppies that reproduce early. Predator = pike cichlid, eats bigger guppies.

  2) Big guppies that reproduce late. Predator = killifish, eats smaller guppies.

  Scientists made two groups for experiment:

  1) Control group: Pike-cichlid pool left as is. Called pc-guppies.

  2) Experimental group: pc-guppies transplanted to killifish pool. No other guppies in this pool.

  Both groups observed through several generations. After 11 years, age of maturity (in days) and weight (in milligrams) of males and females from each group recorded.

- **Apparatus:** *Natural habitat provided for each group. Same conditions and same geographical location.*

- **Variables:**

  Control: All conditions of place, habitat, and temperature (same for both groups).

  Dependent: Age and weight at maturity.

  Experimental: Type of predator and group type of guppy (not numerical).

- **Results:** *Both male and female k-guppies (experimental group) had higher weights and age of maturity than pc-guppies (control group). Conclusion? Over several generations, the k-guppies evolved to survive the new type of predator (killifish), which eats smaller guppies.*

Study 2

- **Read and summarize:** *Two groups of guppies studied:*

  1) Downstream. Many aquatic predators.

  2) Upstream. No aquatic predators.

  Each group was exposed to an aquatic predator (bass) and aerial predator (fake kingfisher). Various guppy responses were recorded: swim normally, dash, drop, hide, freeze, inspect.

- **Apparatus:** *Aquarium tank with small place to hide. One guppy in tank. Exposed to fake kingfisher bird passed across top of tank. Guppy is given time to recover. Then, aquatic predator, bass, placed into tank with guppy.*

- **Variables:**

  Control: Tank conditions; one-guppy setup; identical predator exposure; time before next exposure; duration of predator exposure; and so on.

  Dependent: duration spent swimming during 3-minute trial; duration spent for each type of reaction behavior; proportion of individual guppies that exhibited each type of reaction behavior.

  Experimental: guppy type and predator type (nonnumerical).

- **Results:**

  From Graph 1:

  Both guppy types swam normally in the 3-minute period before introduction of predator. After aerial predator (postbird), both downstream and upstream guppies spent less time swimming normally. More pronounced for upstream guppies.

  After aquatic predator (postfish) both groups stopped swimming normally for most of postfish period (especially pronounced for downstream guppies).

From Graph 2:

Hide: upstream guppies never hid; a little more than $\frac{1}{4}$ of the downstream guppies hid an average of 20 s for the bird (aerial predator) and an average of 60 s for the bass (aquatic predator).

Dash: A little less than $\frac{1}{2}$ of both guppy types dashed for about 30 s after introduction of bird. Neither guppy type dashed when fish placed into the tank.

Drop: A little less than half of each guppy type dropped for about 25 s after appearance of bird. After introduction of fish, hardly any downstream guppies dropped. About $\frac{1}{4}$ of upstream guppies dropped for about 30 s.

Freeze: Postbird, about $\frac{3}{4}$ of upstream guppies froze for about 45 s, while just $\frac{1}{4}$ of downstream guppies froze for about 15 s. After fish, a little less than $\frac{1}{2}$ of each group froze for about 90 s (more pronounced for downstream guppies).

Inspect: Results given for fish predator only. The downstream guppies were more prone to inspect fish before taking action: about $\frac{3}{4}$ inspected the fish for about 150 s, almost the full 3 minutes postfish. A little more than half the upstream guppies inspected the fish about 100 s before acting.

TIP

When more than one graph is presented for one experiment, you really need to concentrate.

SOLUTIONS

1. **(B)**   2. **(J)**   3. **(C)**   4. **(H)**   5. **(A)**   6. **(G)**

1. **(B)** Before the study, the transplanted k-guppies had coexisted with pike-cichlid predators that ate larger guppies. These guppies were relatively small and reproduced at a younger age. During the study, these transplanted guppies were placed into a pool with a different predator—killifish—that ate smaller guppies. The results of the experiment showed that the experimental group of k-guppies, after many generations, gained in weight compared with the control group of pc-guppies and also reproduced at a later age than the pc-guppies. This suggests that the transplanted k-guppies developed characteristics that would help them survive the killifish. Each of the other choices is wrong.

    Choice (A): The pc-guppies in the pike-cichlid pools were the control group and did not change over time. Nothing in their circumstances changed.

    Choice (C): Nothing in the results gives information about the comparative life expectancies of k-guppies and pc-guppies.

    Choice (D): The pc-guppies were the control group and did not change their age of sexual maturity.

2. **(J)** The control group was the group of guppies whose habitat and predator type were unchanged: namely guppies in the pool with pike-cichlid predators (the pc-guppies) who remained in a pool with pike cichlids.

3. **(C)** One might reasonably expect the experimental group of guppies, Group 2, to develop characteristics over time that would help them survive pike-cichlid predators that eat bigger guppies. Thus, it is not unreasonable to expect that these experimental guppies will eventually get smaller and also mature sexually at a younger age. In particular, the male guppies in Group 2 can be expected to weigh less than those in Group 1. None of the other predictions makes sense.

    Choice (A): The expectation is that the female guppies in the experimental group will reproduce at an *earlier* age than the females in Group 1, the control group.

    Choice (B): Nothing in Study 1 suggests that male guppies will weigh more than the female guppies.

    Choice (D): The expectation is that the male guppies in the control group, Group 1, will weigh *more* than the male guppies in the experimental group, Group 2.

4. **(H)** This is a fairly tricky question because you must consult both bar graphs in Graph 2 to get the correct answer. It may be true that upstream guppies froze significantly longer than downstream guppies when the bird was introduced.

However, when the fish was introduced, downstream guppies froze slightly longer than upstream guppies, so the statement in choice (H) is false. Every other choice is a *true* statement and therefore a *wrong* choice.

Choice (F): Notice that in Graph 1, the height of the second pair of bars (postfish) is considerably shorter than the first pair, representing a significant decrease in the amount of swimming.

Choice (G): Note that the hide behavior in both sections of Graph 2 contains no bar for the upstream guppies, confirming that upstream guppies never hid. About $\frac{1}{4}$ of the downstream guppies hid for some of the time.

Choice (J): The second pair of bars in Graph 1 represents time swimming postfish. The white bar for upstream guppies is higher than the black bar for downstream guppies.

5. **(A)** No evidence in this study suggests that if a tennis ball had been passed over the tanks rather than a fake kingfisher, the guppies would not have reacted in the same way. The assumption in the experiment is that because the fake aerial predator looks like an actual kingfisher, the guppies are responding as they would to an actual predator. Since no control was included, this is not a valid assumption. None of the other choices represent flaws in the experiment.

Choice (B): This is a true statement, not a design flaw. The results of the study *confirmed* the statement: the upstream guppies never hid.

Choice (C): Although guppies may behave differently in groups, the point of the study was to examine a guppy's reaction in the presence of two types of predators. As long as all guppies in the experiment were treated in the same way—in this case individually—the results were valid.

Choice (D): As long as the same definitions were applied to all of the guppies in the study, the researchers could define behaviors they were looking for.

6. **(G)** In a multipredator environment, predators may lurk on the river floor, for example, making it dangerous for a drop or dash action that may send the guppies into the jaws of another predator. Downstream guppies have probably evolved to take different evasive actions depending on the type of predator. To do this successfully will require more time to assess the predator, hence the longer inspection time. None of the other choices is a reasonable explanation for the longer inspection time of the downstream guppies.

Choice (F): It is not reasonable to say that upstream guppies are not aware of danger. One could argue that the reason for the shorter inspection time is that the stranger in the tank made them run away faster!

Choice (H): The survival instinct of any guppy depends on the specific dangers in the specific habitat. Notice that in the presence of the aerial predator, many more of the upstream guppies froze. This does not necessarily show a stronger survival instinct. What is does suggest is that freezing in the shallow riffles of an upstream tributary may be the most effective evasive behavior against an aerial predator because it makes the guppies harder to see.

Choice (J): The studies in this passage show that all guppies are aware of other fish that normally threaten their survival.

PASSAGE III (METALLIC SWITCHES)

Experiments 1 and 2

- **Read and summarize:** *Effect of ozone on metals used for switches was tested. Experiments 1 and 2 identical except for concentration of ozone. In Experiment 1, it was 7.0 ppm; in Experiment 2, it was 20 ppm. Four different metals were tested, both in ozone and in laboratory air:*
  85% silver with 15% nickel
  90% silver with 10% nickel
  fine-grain silver
  0.999 pure silver
  Contact resistance was measured after nine days. Several readings taken and average results recorded. Experimental group: set of coupons in ozone chamber. Control group: set in laboratory air.
- **Apparatus:** *Contact resistance data collected with computer-controlled gold-tipped probe at a given force. Ozone generated by ultraviolet light source in electronically controlled chamber.*
- **Variables:**
  Control: Force applied to metal (kept constant). Same probe used throughout. Concentration of ozone was kept constant during each run of the experiment.
  Dependent: Contact resistance.
  Experimental: Composition of the metal. Also, the concentration of ozone. While constant during each run, concentration of ozone was varied in the different runs of the experiment. So, within one experiment, ozone concentration was a control (constant for all metals tested). When Experiments 1 and 2 are looked at together, ozone concentration is an experimental variable.

- **Results:** *In both experiments, all coupons in ozone chamber had higher contact resistance values than coupons in clean lab air, i.e., presence of ozone increased contact resistance. Conclusion? Metal damaged by ozone. Same trends seen in both tables, but much more pronounced in Experiment 2, where concentration of ozone was much higher. Additionally, metals that contained nickel had higher contact resistance than the pure silver, both in ozone and clean air.*

Experiment 3

- **Read and summarize:** *Effects of gold plating looked at for two types of metal: fine silver, and 85% silver with 15% nickel. Two different gold-plating setups tested: 10 μ inch thick gold and also 60 μ inch thick gold. Contact resistance data collected at ozone concentration of 7.0 ppm only.*
- **Apparatus:** *Same as for Experiments 1 and 2 (computerized probe, ozone chamber).*
- **Variables:**

  Control: Concentration of ozone, kept constant at 7.0 ppm.
  Dependent: Contact resistance, as before.
  Experimental: Composition of metal; thickness of gold plating.
- **Results:** *Contact resistance averages for 10 microinch gold plating were higher than contact resistance averages for 60 microinch gold plating. Conclusion? Gold protects surface from oxidation effects of ozone, and thicker is better. (Data also suggests that gold has very low resistance.)*

TIP

Jotting down a conclusion that comes to mind will save time when you answer the questions.

SOLUTIONS

1. **(B)**   2. **(H)**   3. **(A)**   4. **(J)**   5. **(B)**   6. **(H)**

1. **(B)** Tables 1 and 3 deal with contact performance in 7.0 ppm ozone. Ignore Table 2 when answering this question. You are looking for the material with the best contact, namely the *lowest* contact resistance. Notice that when the metal is coated with gold, the resistance is dramatically lowered. And, the thicker the gold, the better. The metal alloy with 85 percent silver and 15 percent nickel that is coated with 60 microinches of gold gives the lowest contact resistance and is therefore the answer.

2. **(H)** From Tables 1 and 2, notice that the contact resistance for a given metal is higher in ozone than in clean air. These results are especially pronounced in 20 ppm ozone. Each of the other statements is unreasonable, based on the data shown.

   Choice (F): In Table 1, in 7 ppm ozone, the coupon with 15 percent nickel has a *lower* contact resistance than the coupon with 10 percent nickel. This example contradicts the statement.

   Choice (G): From Table 3, you can see that gold plating has a dramatic effect in lowering the contact resistance of the metals.

   Choice (J): The passage says nothing about the thickness of the metal and its effect on contact resistance. Also, the thickness is unlikely to influence results since resistance is measured at the point of contact only.

> **TIP**
> Just a single counterexample makes a statement false.

3. **(A)** In a chemical equation, the number of "parts" for each element on the left side must equal the number of "parts" for that element on the right. Each of the equations in choices (B), (C), and (D) violates this rule.

   Choice (B): 3 atoms of O on the left and $\frac{4}{3}$ atoms of O on the right.

   Choice (C): 3 atoms of O on the left and 4 atoms of O on the right.

   Choice (D): 3 atoms of O on the left and $6\frac{1}{2}$ atoms of O on the right.

4. **(J)** To find the effect that ozone has on the contact resistance of metals, a set of identical metals must be measured in normal air (control setup) and in ozone (experimental setup). Without the measurements in normal air, the experiment has no control and its results become meaningless. The other choices are wrong.

   Choice (F): Nothing in the experiments calculates the percentage of ozone in the atmosphere.

   Choice (G): You should realize that this answer is way off base. You are told early on in the passage that switches are often in a closed environment, which in itself creates ozone and leads to oxidation of the metal.

   Choice (H): If there is such a thing, this choice is the "best" wrong answer! This is because the metals in the control group *were* used to get a baseline reading with the probe for all the metals. The main purpose of the set of metals in normal air, however, was to be a control for the identical metals that were also exposed to ozone. The effect of the ozone cannot be calibrated if there is no data for the metals in normal air.

5. **(B)** The dramatic results in Experiment 3 are that gold plating significantly lowers the contact resistance of any of the metals and that the thicker the gold, the more pronounced the effect. Thus, the contact resistance of fine-grain silver plus 60 microinches of gold plating will give a better result than fine-grain silver plus 10 microinches of gold plating. The researchers cannot be confident about any of the other choices.

Choice (A): The result in this answer choice would be unexpected. Table 3 shows that thicker gold is better.

Choices (C) and (D): Notice (again, from Table 3) that the two contact resistance readings given for a metal coated with 60 microinches of gold are very close: 0.767 and 0.804 milliohms. From these values, it is not clear that a confident prediction can be made about where fine-grain silver will fall with the 60-microinch coating.

6. **(H)** The first thing you must realize is that within a certain range of forces, the greater the force applied at the point of contact, the better that contact will be (and hence the lower the contact resistance.) In the passage, you are told that if the force applied is too low, the contact resistance will be unnaturally high. So the answer is going to be either choice (H) or (J). All of the results in the passage suggest that in the presence of ozone, the contact is worse, namely contact resistance is higher. You should therefore expect the graph for 0.01 ppm ozone to be above the graph for clean air. Thus, choice (H) is the answer.

PASSAGE IV (SILVER DEPOSITS)

Experiment 1

- **Read and summarize:** *Measurements taken in electrolytic cell with silver fluoride solution and two electrodes, platinum and silver. A 20 mV potential was applied.*
  Two different plots:

  1. Current versus time
  2. Integrated charge versus platinum electrode area

- **Apparatus:** *Container with silver fluoride solution and two electrodes, platinum and silver.*

- **Variables:**
  Control: 20 mV potential to get reaction going; silver fluoride solution, used throughout.
  Dependent: current; integrated charge.
  Experimental: time, platinum electrode area.

- **Results:**
  In Current versus Time: Initial pulse causes the biggest current (time < 5 s). Then current tails off with time.
  In Charge versus Electrode area: Just 4 measurements. As area increased, charge increased. Error of about ±2 μC in each measurement.

Experiment 2

- **Read and summarize:**

  1. The scanning tunneling microscope (STM) tip is a platinum microelectrode dipped in aqueous silver solution.
  2. Tip is put on graphite basal plane surface.
  3. Two bias pulses:

     First causes pit in graphite.

     Second causes silver to form and get deposited in pit.
  4. Reaction at STM tip does not always produce silver. Time needed for tip to regenerate.
  5. Two graphs:

     Mean height of silver clump versus each attempt to get silver deposited.

     Probability of silver being deposited versus voltage of first bias pulse.

- **Apparatus:** A graphite basal plane surface and scanning tunneling microscope. The STM tip is a platinum microelectrode in silver solution. Electrolytic chemical reaction set in motion by 2 electrical pulses. Voltage causes pit in surface followed by silver deposit in the pit.

- **Variables:**

  Control: Same STM tip and apparatus for electrolytic reaction. Same graphite plane.

  Dependent: Height of silver clump (Graph 2); probability of getting silver (Graph 3).

  Experimental: The attempt number (Graph 2); voltage of the first pulse.

- **Results:** Height of silver deposit decreased with each attempt. Errors in height measured were ±3.5 Å. Silver not formed at 7th attempt, so no measurement recorded.

SOLUTIONS

1. **(A)**   2. **(G)**   3. **(D)**   4. **(J)**   5. **(C)**   6. **(F)**   7. **(B)**

TIP

Let key words in the question guide you to the place in the passage where the answer is lurking.

1. **(A)** "Experiment 1" means "Look at Graph 1." The key words "time" and "current" mean "Look at the inset graph." The highest observed current corresponds to the highest part of the graph, namely, when time is less than 5 s. Therefore, of the available answer choices, 2 seconds after the pulse gives the highest current. Do not be thrown by the negative current values: Remember, those imply that the current direction is opposite that of the applied voltage. This question is about the *magnitude* of the current, not the direction.

2. **(G)** Here the key words "electrode," "area," and "integrated charge" tell you to find the answer in the main plot of Graph 1. The point on the line when electrode area is 0.10 cm^2 corresponds to a charge of about 20 μC. There is also an error bar of ± 2.5 μC, which means that the actual value is somewhere between approximately 17.5 and 22.5 μC.

3. **(D)** In Graph 2, the height that corresponds to the third attempt to deposit silver was 10 Å. The magnitude of the error is approximate. Thus, most of the values obtained lie between 6 and 14 Å. This eliminates 15 Å as a possibility.

REMEMBER

No measurement is exact.

4. **(J)** The words "Experiment 2" and "voltage" should steer you to Graph 3. In this graph, the higher the voltage, the closer the probability of silver deposits gets to 100 percent. You should therefore select 4 V as the answer.

5. **(C)** You do not need to know a lot about chemistry to find a logical path to the correct answer. The question asks you to recognize which equation leads to silver deposits (Ag) formed in a water (H$_2$O) solution. If you understand this much, eliminate choices (B) and (D), both of which produce silver ions (Ag$^+$ and Ag$^-$) instead of pure silver (just plain Ag). You are told that the silver in solution gains electrons. Since electrons are negatively charged (yes, you *do* need to know that!), if Ag$^-$ ions gain electrons, they will become even *more* negatively charged. This should suggest that choice (A) is wrong. Notice that in the correct answer, (C), positively charged ions (Ag$^+$) gain electrons, which neutralize the charge, causing pure silver, Ag, to form.

6. **(F)** From Graph 2, notice that the measurement for the height of the silver is in angstroms, which is an atomic scale. 1 Å = 10^{-10} m, whereas 1 mm = 10^{-3} m. This means that a precision of 1 mm is insufficient and will not be of use in taking measurements in these experiments. Each of the other requirements *will* help the scientists and is crucial for success.

Choice (G): A defect-free, atomically smooth surface is necessary because the depth of the craters formed is tiny; the depth is measured on an atomic scale. The scientists need to be sure that the craters are due to the scanning tunneling microscope, not a preexisting defect in the surface.

Choice (H): A chemically nonreactive surface is necessary because the scientists are testing whether silver deposits are due to an electrolytic reaction independent of the surface.

Choice (J): Having a surface that the silver adheres to is necessary. Without this anchoring effect, the forces applied to the silver by the STM tip might dislodge the silver during the experiment.

7. **(B)** From Graph 3, the probability of getting silver deposits depends on the initial voltage applied. If the bias pulses are not big enough, no silver is formed. Each of the other statements is incorrect.

Choice (A): Not every pit formed is accompanied by silver production. You are told this in the passage and shown this in Graph 2. Deposition attempt #7 has no height of silver recorded. This means that there was no silver.

Choice (C): If the aqueous solution does not contain silver ions, silver cannot be formed.

Choice (D): The electrochemical reaction occurs at the STM tip. The plane itself is nonreactive.

PASSAGE V (CHICKEN FEED)

This passage contains three different experiments. Apply your checklist to each one.

Experiment 1

- **Read and summarize:** *3 groups of layers (i.e., hens that laid eggs) and 3 types of poultry feed (5 combinations in table).*

  1. 45% maize

  2. 45% sorghum

  3. 15% sorghum plus 30 % maize

  Each group got different feed type. The feed consumed (grams/bird/day) and percentage egg production were recorded.
- **Apparatus:** *Irrelevant in this passage.*
- **Variables:**

  Control: Same 55% noncereal concentrate in the feed.

  Dependent: Weight of feed consumed per day; percentage egg production.

  Experimental: Different types of feed. In particular, the percentage of sorghum in feed was varied.
- **Results:** *No significant difference in feed consumed or percentage egg production.*

Experiment 2

- **Read and summarize:** *3 groups of broilers and 3 types of poultry feed (5 combinations in table).*

  1. 60% maize

  2. 15% sorghum plus 45% maize

  3. 45% sorghum plus 15% maize

  Each group got different feed type. The weight gain (grams/bird/day) and final bird weight (kg/bird) were recorded. Also feed efficiency ratio was recorded (not defined in passage).

- **Apparatus:** *Irrelevant.*

- **Variables:**

  Control: Same 40% noncereal concentrate in the feed.
  Dependent: Weight gain; final weight; feed efficiency ratio.
  Experimental: Different types of feed. In particular, percentage of sorghum in feed was varied.

- **Results:** *No significant difference in average weight gain or final weight for broilers. Lowest values recorded for feed that contained 15 percent yellow sorghum and 45 percent maize. Highest values for feed that contained 45 percent yellow sorghum and 15 percent maize. Highest feed efficiency ratio was recorded for feed that contained 15 percent yellow sorghum and 45 percent maize (but numbers comparable).*

Experiment 3

- **Read and summarize:** *Improved varieties of maize (Deccan 103) and sorghum (ICSV 112) were fed to layers and broilers.*
  4 groups of layers, fed one of the following types of poultry feed:

  1. 50% maize (Deccan 103)

  2. 50% sorghum (ICSV 112)

  3. 25% maize (Deccan 103) plus 25% sorghum (ICSV 112)

  4. Commercial farmers' feed

4 groups of broilers, fed one of the following types of poultry feed:

1. 60% maize (Deccan 103)

2. 60% sorghum (ICSV 112)

3. 30% maize (Deccan 103) plus 30% sorghum (ICSV 112)

4. Commercial farmers' feed

Each group got different feed type. Feed consumed (grams/bird/day), percentage egg production, and broiler weight (kg/bird) recorded. Broiler taste test conducted.

- **Apparatus:** *None.*

- **Variables:**

  Control: Same 50% noncereal concentrate in the feed for layers and same 40% noncereal concentrate in feed for broilers

  Dependent: Layer feed eaten (g/bird/day); percentage egg production; mean broiler bird final weight (kg/bird); taste score for chicken.

  Experimental: Different types of feed but especially percentage of sorghum in feed.

- **Results:**

  Egg production comparable but biggest for 1:1 ratio of maize to sorghum.

  Sorghum-only diet produced bird weight lower than that for other feeds. Weights for other diets were comparable.

  Taste of broiler birds comparable. Chickens fed either all-maize or all-sorghum diets had highest scores.

  Table 3 shows that for Experiment 3, maize (Deccan 103) and sorghum (ICSV 112) very similar in nutritional composition and in energy (calories).

SOLUTIONS

1. **(C)**   2. **(H)**   3. **(C)**   4. **(F)**   5. **(D)**   6. **(J)**

1. **(C)** The same noncereal concentrate was used in all three experiments, which means it was a constant in the experiments. The other choices all represent variables in the experiments.

   Choices (A) and (B): For Experiment 3, new types of maize and sorghum were used.

   Choice (D): The percentage of maize and sorghum was the experimental variable (varied in the different experiments) and therefore could not have been constant.

2. **(H)** Choice (H) may well be true, but you cannot deduce it from Experiment 2. None of the diets included a percentage of sorghum greater than 45 percent. Each of the other choices can be confirmed by the results in Table 2.

3. **(C)** The key words "percentage of eggs" should lead you to Tables 1 and 4 since these are the only places in the passage that have results for egg production. All of the numbers in Table 1 are greater than all of the numbers in Table 4, so you should select your answer from Table 1. Notice that 96 percent is the highest number. This corresponds with a diet of 15 percent yellow sorghum and 30 percent maize. Each of the other choices has lower numbers for egg production.

> **TIP**
>
> Let key words in the question guide you to the relevant tables that contain the answer.

4. **(F)** Table 3 contradicts the assertion that sorghum has significantly lower energy than maize grain. Sorghum has 412 calories per 100 grams, while maize has 414 calories per 100 grams. The difference between these numbers is too small to be significant. If you are not sure of this answer, notice that each of the other statements is verified by the data.

   Choice (G): The numbers for protein, starch, sugars, and so on in Table 3 are comparable.

   Choice (H): Taste scores in Table 4 were similar for all diets.

   Choice (J): Weight gain numbers in Table 2 were comparable.

5. **(D)** The phrase "feed efficiency" should be a measure of how much feed led to weight gain. For example, if 1 gram of feed led to 1 gram of weight gain, the feed efficiency would be 1:1, or just 1. If 3 grams of feed led to 1 gram of weight gain, the ratio would be 3:1, or just 3. Since feed efficiency should involve amount of feed consumed, you should quickly eliminate choices (A) and (B). The reason to eliminate choice (C) is that the numbers given in the table are all greater than 1. Since average weight gain is unlikely to exceed the amount of feed consumed, the ratio will not be weight gain to amount of feed.

6. **(J)** The question is asking "Which of the following is true?" Only choice (J) is true. Table 1 explicitly shows that feed consumed was more or less the same for all of the feeds. Table 2 shows comparable feed efficiency ratios for high maize and also high sorghum percentages. Table 3 shows that about the same amount of feed was consumed by layer birds for the 50 percent maize feed and for the 1:1 maize to sorghum feeds, confirming the conclusion that adding sorghum to the feed did not significantly affect the amount of feed consumed. Each of the other choices is contradicted by the data.

Choice (F): In Table 2, notice that the 60 percent maize (where there is *no* sorghum) shows a higher weight gain than both the 15 percent white sorghum plus 45 percent maize and the 15 percent yellow sorghum plus 45 percent maize.

Choice (G): The egg production percentages show very little variation for different diets.

Choice (H): In Table 4, the broiler taste panel scores for chicken show little variation for the different diets. The fact that the maize-only diet had the highest taste score directly contradicts the assertion in choice (H).

Conflicting Viewpoints

CHAPTER **12**

CHAPTER GOALS

- Strategies for conflicting viewpoints passages
- Further advice
- Ace the ACT! Sample conflicting viewpoints passages

Of the seven minitests in the science section, just one will be on conflicting viewpoints. This means that of the 40 multiple-choice questions, *exactly 7* will refer to the conflicting viewpoints passage.

In a typical passage, a scientific phenomenon is described in some detail. Then two or more theories are presented, either to explain the phenomenon or illuminate some aspect of it. Often conflicting viewpoints are simply different interpretations of, or conclusions made from, the same data.

You can recognize a conflicting viewpoints passage from headings like "Scientist 1," "Scientist 2;" or "Student 1," "Student 2," "Student 3;" or "Theory 1," "Theory 2;" or "Blurf Theory," "Blank Theory", where "Blurf" and "Blank" are names of theories. For example, an actual ACT conflicting viewpoints passage offered two different theories to explain combustion and the headings were "Phlogiston Theory" and "Oxygen Theory."

The topics for these passages can range from formation of dew to cell division to gammaray bursts in the galaxy. As is true for all ACT science questions, you will not need to have in-depth knowledge of scientific content. What you *will* need is to be able to

- Understand the phenomenon as explained in the passage.
- Distinguish the different viewpoints presented.
- Determine the main points of disagreement.
- Cite data *in the passage* that supports or refutes each argument.

You will *not* need to state who is right! Some of the theories may be off the wall, but you will not be asked to judge them. Your job is to understand the points of each argument.

STRATEGIES FOR CONFLICTING VIEWPOINTS PASSAGES

To succeed on the conflicting viewpoints portion of the science test, you must follow the following seven strategies.

Work Quickly

Spend no more than 5 or 6 minutes on this passage. Remember, you have only 35 minutes for *all* of the science questions, and this portion is just 1/7 of the test.

Answer All the Questions!

Remember, you will not be penalized for choosing the wrong answer. So if you do not know the answer or are unsure, just make an educated guess.

Be Focused

On your initial reading of the passage, underline the main points. Be especially focused while reading the preamble before the different viewpoints.

Be particularly tuned in to the opening sentence of each viewpoint. It often summarizes that person's theory. For example, the viewpoint for Environmentalist 1 might begin, "The formation of red tides is due to natural phenomena like wind patterns and ocean tides." In contrast, the viewpoint for Environmentalist 2 might begin, "Human activities, like dumping of industrial wastes and allowing agricultural runoff, have led to the formation of red tides." These two arguments clearly contradict each other and provide the core of the differences. Everything else is an expansion of these opinions.

Highlight the Disagreement

Jot down very briefly what the main point of disagreement is between the different viewpoints. Also jot down what they agree on (if anything).

Restate the Viewpoints

Concisely restate the viewpoint of each scientist (or student, or theory) in side-by-side columns. Use one column for each viewpoint. List specific differences side by side, each in their correct column. If there are similarities, list these too. Your plan is to contrast the theories at a glance. For example, if Theory 1 says that oxygen is necessary for some process to happen while Theory 2 says that nitrogen is needed, jot down "needs oxygen" in Theory 1's column and "needs nitrogen" in Theory 2's column, side by side.

List Supporting Data

Jot down supporting data that is cited in each viewpoint. List this data in the correct column.

A MOMENT OF REFLECTION . . .

It may seem to you that you are being encouraged to jot down this and jot down that, an awful lot of jotting that takes valuable time away from question answering. What you should realize is that organizing the information in this way is part of answering the questions. If your notes are terse and clear, a glance at them during question-answering time will give you quick (and correct!) answers to the questions. On the other hand, if you do not quickly and easily take notes in column format, be sure that you instead underline the main points of the passage and follow the checklist in your mind.

> **IMPORTANT STEPS**
> - Read and underline
> - Identify points of agreement and disagreement
> - Make one column for each viewpoint
> - Summarize viewpoints
> - Highlight supporting data for each theory

FURTHER ADVICE

Here are some bits and pieces to help you answer the questions in these passages.

- Keep the two viewpoints straight. If a question explicitly says, "According to Scientist 1," make sure that you look only at Scientist 1's argument. Do not fall into a trap when data to support Scientist 2 is cited as an argument to support Scientist 1's theory. These question writers can be diabolical!
- Beware of extraneous information, namely extra stuff that does not have much to do with the passage but is introduced into the questions. Your answers must be based on the given passage only.
- Beware of any answer choice that begins, "It is generally known that . . . ." This type of vague, blanket statement is not part of scientific discourse, and the answer choice usually sounds good but is invariably wrong.
- Here is something that is a bit tricky that you may be questioned on: What flaws would Scientist 1 find in the argument of Scientist 2 (and vice versa)? If you have concisely nailed down the arguments of each scientist, you should be able to deduce the correct answer choice from your summary.

Are you ready to try some sample conflicting viewpoints passages? There are no warm-ups here. We will go straight to the real deal.

Ace the Act!
Sample Conflicting
Viewpoints Passages

PASSAGE I

THINK

Before reading further, do you have the roles of wasp and caterpillar straight?

A common wasp, *Copidosoma floridanum*, is a parasite. The female wasp lays one or two eggs inside the egg of the cabbage looper moth. As the host egg develops into a 2- to 3-inch-long caterpillar, each wasp egg develops into wasp embryos. A single wasp egg can produce more than 3000 genetically identical siblings, each about one-fifth of an inch long. Most of the larvae are maggotlike creatures that drink the caterpillar's blood. However, up to one-fourth of them grow into a different form, called soldiers. These soldiers develop slender, snakelike bodies and rasping jaws. Instead of drinking the blood of their hosts, they attack other wasp larvae and kill them.

The bloodsuckers that are not killed by the soldiers eventually begin to devour the organs of their host, become pupae, develop into adults, and fly away. The soldiers themselves cannot escape and die with the eviscerated husk of the caterpillar.

Two biologists discuss the purpose of the soldiers in the host.

Biologist 1:

Much evidence suggests that soldiers exist to destroy the competition. Recall that thousands of wasps are all struggling for food inside a single host. A cabbage looper often plays host to larvae from several wasp mothers. It may even carry larvae from other species of wasps. Soldiers kill off unrelated wasps, thus allowing their siblings to have more food.

The soldiers themselves cannot reproduce. Yet by killing off competitors, they increase the odds that their genetically identical (nonsoldier) siblings will survive and have offspring.

It has been found that soldiers can tell the difference between their siblings and unrelated wasps. In one experiment, unrelated *Copidosoma* wasp eggs were injected into a cabbage looper that was already host to developed larvae. The intruders were almost always eliminated by the resident soldiers.

Biologist 2:

The main purpose of the soldiers is to ensure that their sisters succeed. To this end, they kill off many of their brothers. When *Copidosoma* mothers lay two eggs in a host, one egg produces thousands of males and the other, thousands of females. The female soldiers will kill many of their brothers. This fratricide appears to be driven by evolution.

Although the female soldiers are genetically identical to their sisters, they share only some of their genes with the males, which come from a separate egg. Thus, these soldiers get a bigger evolutionary benefit from the success of their sisters than from that of their brothers. A few males are more than enough to fertilize thousands of female wasps. Any extra males in the host are just unwanted competition for food.

It has been shown experimentally that female eggs produce more soldiers than male eggs do, which leads to the culling of more male wasps.

> **THINK**
>
> What, exactly, do the two biologists disagree about?

1. Based on the information in the passage, which of the following is an *incorrect* statement about the development of *Copidosoma* wasps?

   A. As the moth egg develops into a caterpillar, the wasp egg develops into thousands of wasp larvae, most of which drink the caterpillar's blood.

   B. Up to one-fourth of the wasp larvae become soldiers, whose job is to attack rival larvae.

   C. The bloodsucking wasp larvae that are not killed by the soldiers are in danger of being killed by rival bloodsucking larvae from other species.

   D. Wasps eventually fly away from the caterpillar, leaving the soldiers trapped inside to die.

2. According to the passage, what do wasp soldiers tend to do?

   F. Attack other soldiers

   G. Eat the organs of the host caterpillar

   H. Suck the blood of the host caterpillar

   J. Attack bloodsucking larvae

3. According to Biologist 2:

   A. female wasp soldiers are responsible for killing male wasp soldiers.

   B. female wasp soldiers are responsible for killing female wasp soldiers.

   C. female wasp soldiers are responsible for killing female bloodsuckers.

   D. female wasp soldiers are responsible for killing male bloodsuckers.

4. Biologists 1 and 2 would agree that:

   F. the main purpose of the wasp soldiers is to eliminate wasps from other families.

   G. the main purpose of the wasp soldiers is to provide an evolutionary benefit for their species.

   H. the *Copidosoma* wasp and cabbage looper moth are mutually beneficial in each other's development.

   J. the male and female wasp soldiers compete with each other for food.

5. According to Biologist 1, Biologist 2 is wrong because he has overlooked which fact?

   A. Female soldiers are unable to reproduce.
   B. It has been shown that male soldiers do not attack other wasps.
   C. It has been experimentally established that soldiers kill off wasps from other species.
   D. It has been experimentally established that when a wasp lays two eggs in a host, more female eggs develop into soldiers than male eggs.

6. Suppose a subsequent experiment shows that wasp soldiers come in two different forms. Soldiers that develop early tend to attack their own families. Late-developing soldiers are more likely to attack other species of wasps. Whose theory would this experiment tend to confirm?

   F. Biologist 1 only.
   G. Biologist 2 only.
   H. Biologist 1 and Biologist 2.
   J. Neither Biologist 1 nor Biologist 2.

7. Which of the following studies would be likely to resolve the difference of opinion of the two biologists?

   A. Study the development of several generations of a different wasp species that also uses soldiers.
   B. Study mixed colonies of *Copidosoma* wasps and other wasp species. Document the development of *Copidosoma* wasps for several generations.
   C. Create a colony of only *Copidosoma* wasps and document their development for several generations.
   D. Study the development of several generations of at least two other species that depend on parasites for their development.

PASSAGE II

Sounds are caused by vibrations—for example, a vibrating string on a violin or a vibrating membrane on a drum. The collision between solids and liquids also produces sounds, as when an explosion or splash is heard. What all these sound sources have in common is the fact that air is set in motion. If all air is removed from a vessel in which an electric bell is suspended, no sound is heard when the current is turned on.

Every elastic body (like a tuning fork or a violin string) has a particular frequency, called its *natural frequency*, at which it will vibrate if disturbed. When a periodic force is applied to an elastic body at this frequency, the body absorbs energy and the amplitude of its vibration increases. This vibration of a body at its natural frequency caused by the action of a vibrating source with the same frequency is called *resonance*.

For example, a tuning fork that is not vibrating and that has a natural frequency of 512 Hz (hertz, where 1 hertz = 1 cycle per second) will resonate when a vibrating tuning fork with a natural frequency of 512 Hz is brought near it. However, if a vibrating fork with a different natural frequency is brought near, there will be no audible response.

Two students studied the phenomenon of resonance and attempted to explain its effects with two tuning forks of the same frequency. Although they agreed that the nonvibrating fork began to vibrate soon after the nearby fork was struck, they disagreed on the nature of the air propagating between the two forks. Two models were presented.

Student 1

When the prongs of the first tuning fork are struck, the resulting vibration sets up a wave that is an alternating sequence of compressions (high-pressure regions) and rarefactions (low-pressure regions) of the air immediately in contact with the vibrating fork. This alternating sequence, which varies smoothly from high to low to high pressure, travels outward from the source and strikes the second fork, which is alternately pushed and pulled at the same frequency as the source fork. The second fork then starts to vibrate at its natural frequency. If this natural frequency is the same as the frequency of the first fork, the pushing and pulling will be in phase with the vibrations. The amplitude of the sound wave will increase. If the frequencies of the two forks are different, the pushing and pulling will be out of phase. The amplitude of the vibrations of the second fork will be very small.

REMEMBER

The devil is in the details. Try to extract the main points.

THINK

Do you understand the disagreement? If the answer is "no," try again.

Student 2

When the prongs of the first fork are struck, a region of compression (high pressure) is formed in the immediate vicinity of this fork. The air behaves like a rigid cylinder, so pushing on one end of the air column immediately pushes on the second tuning fork, causing a similar compression at the second fork. When the first fork moves back as it vibrates, a region of rarefaction (low pressure) at the first fork causes the air column to move backward toward the first fork, setting the second tuning fork into vibration. This back-and-forth motion of the rigid air column causes both forks to vibrate in unison.

The vibrations of the second turning fork will be amplified if they get into a pattern such that a compression at one fork is simultaneously matched by compression at the other fork, and vice versa.

1. Based on the information in the passage, which of the following would not produce sound vibrations?

   A. Striking a piano key in a room with no other people
   B. Setting off an electric buzzer in a jar whose air has been removed
   C. Plucking a guitar string in an empty concert hall
   D. Throwing a stone into a pond that has no fish

2. What is the main point of disagreement between Student 1 and Student 2?

   F. The definitions of compression and rarefaction
   G. The definition of resonance
   H. The way air moves during resonance
   J. The natural frequencies of tuning forks

3. Both students would most likely agree that during resonance:

   A. a column of air moves back and forth between two vibrating bodies.
   B. a sound wave travels from one elastic body to another.
   C. a rigid column of air moves from one elastic body and strikes a second.
   D. the vibrations of an elastic body are amplified.

4. Which of the following descriptions is most consistent with Student 1's model of resonance between two tuning forks?

   F. The air vibrates in unison with the two forks.
   G. The air between the two forks surges back and forth like a piston rod fixed between two prongs.
   H. The air between the two forks is like a column of water forced backward and forward through a tube.
   J. The air between the two forks acts like a vacuum, pulling the prongs of the tuning forks inward.

5. Consider an experiment designed to understand the nature of sound propagation. A whistle is blown in one end of a tube with two arms leading to the ear.

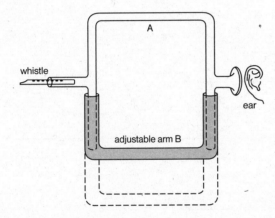

   Suppose the length of arm *B* can be altered by sliding the tube. Which of the following observations would tend to bolster Student 2's model of air propagation?

   A. The sound of the whistle is heard at the same volume irrespective of the length of arm *B*.
   B. The sound of the whistle is not heard when the length of arm *A* equals the length of arm *B*.
   C. The sound of the whistle is heard only when the length of arm *A* equals the length of arm *B*.
   D. The sound of the whistle alternately increases to a maximum and is silenced as the length of arm *B* is gradually diminished or increased.

6. Suppose that the air pressure between the two tuning forks is measured when the first fork is struck. Which of the following graphs showing the relationship between time and air pressure is consistent with Student 1's assertion about air propagation? Note that the origin of the time coordinate is the moment the first tuning fork is struck.

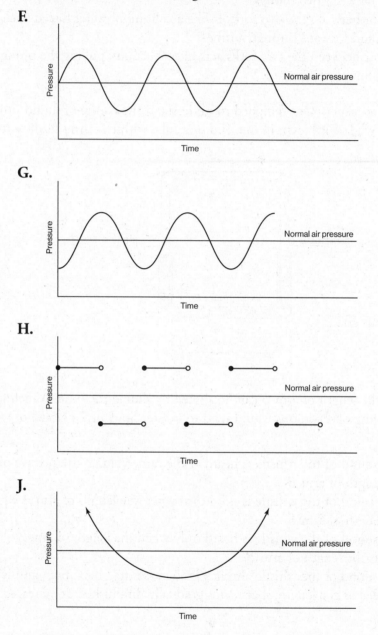

F.

G.

H.

J.

7. Which of the following actions does *not* illustrate resonance?

    A. Pushing a child on a swing
    B. Jumping on a trampoline
    C. Striking a tennis ball with a racket
    D. Singing a high note that causes a glass to shatter

PASSAGE III

Dinosaurs lived on Earth for 150 million years from the Triassic to Cretaceous periods. About 65 million years ago, they became extinct. Two scientists present conflicting theories to explain their disappearance. Both theories rely, in part, on interpreting the fossil record. Different layers of rock can be dated as to when they were laid down, with more recent layers above older layers. Fossils found in various layers thus provide approximate dates for when the animals lived.

Scientist 1

About 65 million years ago, a meteorite about 10 km (kilometers) across and traveling at 30–60 km/sec struck Earth. The impact released energy equivalent to 100 million megatons of TNT. At the moment of impact, the kinetic energy of the meteorite turned to heat energy, sending out a shock wave in all directions into Earth, vaporizing, melting, or pulverizing matter in its wake. A shock wave traveling back through the meteorite instantly vaporized it, too. An enormous crater, perhaps 40 km deep, was created on Earth. The waters of an adjacent sea, disturbed by a 1 km high tsunami (undersea earthquake) came crashing down to fill the crater.

The effect of the impact was to fill Earth's atmosphere with soot. Life on the ocean's surface died either from the heat or the lack of light for photosynthesis. The temperature of Earth at first fell to below freezing. Then, when the sky cleared, the planet overheated due to huge carbon dioxide emissions. All land animals larger than about 20 kg (kilograms), including the dinosaurs, died of hunger during the blackout and became extinct.

Evidence for this "catastrophic" theory can be found in the fossil record of rocks formed during the major extinction about 65 million years ago. These rocks mark the boundary between the Cretaceous and Tertiary periods, called the KT boundary. The Cretaceous limestone beneath the KT boundary is rich in fossils. Directly above the limestone is a layer of clay with practically no fossils. This "barren" layer represents when the dinosaurs became extinct. Directly above this layer, and right at the KT boundary, an unusually large amount of iridium was discovered, which is consistent with the meteorite theory. Meteorites are rich in iridium. The impact raised an immense cloud of dust that mixed with the dust of the disintegrating meteorite. This spike in iridium concentration at the KT boundary has been found at over 100 sites throughout the world, at the same level in the rock at which the extinction took place. This cannot be due to chance alone.

BE ALERT

This is a long passage. Are you still awake? Keep yourself alert by identifying and underlining the main points as you go.

Scientist 2

Dinosaurs became extinct as a result of the gradual evolution of geological phenomena such as volcanic activity and marine regression (retreat of the sea).

The early Cretaceous period was a time of marine transgression, the spread of sea over land areas accompanied by the appearance of new fauna. The belt of shallow water adjoining the seacoast up to a depth of about 120 m (meters) is known as the neritic regions. These regions have deep penetration of sunlight and are rich in microflora and fauna.

In the middle Cretaceous period, neritic regions covered most of Europe. By the late Cretaceous, however, retreat of the sea reduced these regions dramatically. Lack of space led to competition for food between marine mammals and a corresponding reduction of fauna. Many marine invertebrates that fed on this fauna disappeared completely. Others were not wiped out but were strongly affected. The sea retreated slowly over a period of 15 million years. Extinction of various zoological groups took place gradually, as did that of the dinosaurs.

Another phenomenon contributing to dinosaur extinction was volcanic activity. About 65–68 million years ago, there was a major volcanic eruption in India known as the Deccan Traps. This resulted in enormous areas (about 200,000 square miles) being covered in lava over a period of 3 million years. It also released large quantities of soot into the air, darkening the skies. The resulting global climate change led to reduced survival of plants, algae, and plankton, which in turn contributed to the extinction of many species, including the dinosaurs.

The fossil record supports this "gradualist" theory because it points to a gradual decline of dinosaurs over a period of 5–10 million years. This is consistent with plate tectonic forces and massive volcanic activity. Studies of specific fossils show dwindling populations and possible extinction well before the end of the Cretaceous period. For example, there is a radical decline of dinosaur teeth in early layers preceding the KT boundary. There is also a dramatic decline in the diversity of dinosaur species. Furthermore, a layer of rock directly below the high-iridium layer at the KT boundary is practically devoid of dinosaur bones, suggesting extinction well before the end of the Cretaceous period.

Finally, the simultaneous occurrence of marine regressions and mass extinctions cannot be due to chance—there is surely a causal relationship.

THINK

What wiped out the dinosaurs?

1. Which of the following discoveries could be used to bolster Scientist 2's theory of dinosaur extinction?

   A. A deep crater on Earth
   B. Evidence of a tsunami about 65 million years ago
   C. Layers of iridium-rich rock formed about 65 million years ago
   D. Evidence of massive volcanic activity about 65 million years ago

2. Which of the following phenomena is used to support Scientist 2's gradualist theory of dinosaur extinction?

   F. Marine regression
   G. Shock waves
   H. Kinetic energy
   J. Concentration of iridium

3. Based on the passage, which of the following is consistent with both theories of dinosaur extinction?

   A. Large quantities of iridium in Earth's atmosphere caused the death of marine life.
   B. Large quantities of soot in Earth's atmosphere prevented photosynthesis from occurring.
   C. Reduction in the ocean's surface area led to global warming.
   D. A sudden reduction of the food chain led to the reduction of all land mammals.

4. Which of the following characteristics of the geologic and fossil record is most consistent with Scientist 1's theory?

   F. Evidence of dwindling populations of dinosaurs well before the end of the Cretaceous period
   G. Decline of dinosaur teeth in layers below the iridium layer of the KT boundary
   H. Discovery of a high-iridium layer at multiple sites at the level of rock at which extinction took place
   J. The layer of clay beneath the high-iridium layer that contains practically no fossils

5. Which of the following discoveries in the clay of the KT boundary is *not* likely to be used as evidence of Scientist 1's catastrophic theory of dinosaur extinction?

   A. Tiny glasslike spheres formed when molten rock hardens in flight
   B. Fossil records showing that 90 percent of Earth's ocean species became extinct at the time of dinosaur extinction
   C. Quartz crystals with fracture planes seen previously only at sites of nuclear explosion
   D. Microscopic diamonds formed under only conditions of great temperature and pressure

6. Studies of rock formations beneath the iridium-rich layer at the KT boundary show that there is a 2–3-meter barren zone with practically no evidence of dinosaur remains. A scientist recently performed several experiments to test the hypothesis that the absence of bone in the barren zone is due to acid leaching and erosion. If confirmed, this hypothesis would support:

   F. Scientist 1's catastrophic theory, because it would open the possibility that dinosaurs were reproducing at a fairly constant rate until they were suddenly wiped out.

   G. Scientist 1's catastrophic theory, because acid rain occurred as a result of the meteorite collision with Earth.

   H. Scientist 2's gradualist theory, because it would show that the dinosaur population had dwindled sufficiently by the time of the gap that small effects like acid leaching and erosion could essentially eliminate all remaining bones.

   J. Scientist 2's gradualist theory, because the presence of dinosaur remains close to the boundary of this layer shows that the rock sediments beneath the KT boundary have the capacity to preserve bone.

7. Each of the following graphs represents a distribution of dinosaur remains with respect to the KT boundary. Which distribution is consistent with Scientist 2's theory of dinosaur extinction?

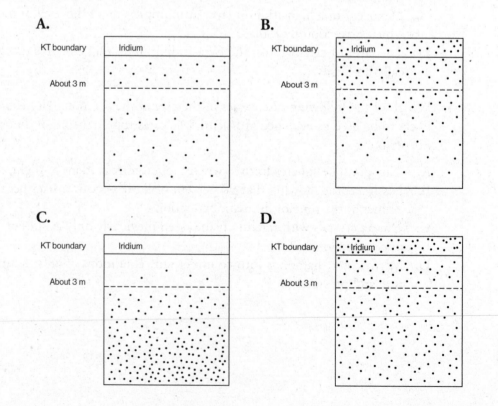

PASSAGE IV

About once a day, a burst of gamma rays appears from a random direction in the sky. The gamma rays are detected by special astronomical satellites in orbit above Earth's atmosphere. These gamma-ray bursts vary in duration from about 30 milliseconds to 1000 seconds.

The gamma-ray detectors can localize the position of a burst in the sky to within a few degrees. It has been found that the directions of the bursts are uniformly distributed in the sky. Up until the 1990s, searches with large optical telescopes in the region of a burst had not shown any unusual objects that might be the source of the burst. During this period, there was debate among astronomers concerning the origins of gamma-ray bursts and the distances to the sources of these bursts.

Local Hypothesis

The sources of gamma-ray bursts are high-velocity neutron stars that are "local." They originate in our own galaxy, the Milky Way. Recall that the directions of gamma-ray bursts are uniformly distributed in the sky. This uniform distribution occurs because many neutron stars in our galaxy have velocities high enough to let them escape the disk of the Milky Way and form a roughly spherical halo around our galaxy. If these neutron stars are indeed the sources of gamma-ray bursts, formation of this galactic halo would explain this observed uniform distribution of the directions of gamma-ray bursts in the sky.

A piece of evidence that supports the local neutron star theory is that a handful of gamma-ray bursts have been detected from so-called soft gamma-ray repeaters. These are known to be produced by high-velocity neutron stars in the galactic halo. (A soft gamma-ray repeater is a sequence of gamma-ray bursts that come from the same direction in the sky.)

Further evidence for the local hypothesis is that the spectra of some gamma-ray bursts show spectral lines similar to those in the spectra of some neutron stars. The local hypothesis also explains why gamma-ray bursts cannot be seen through optical telescopes. Neutron stars have small surface areas and would be undetectable at the distances of the galactic halo.

Cosmological Hypothesis

Gamma-ray bursts are produced by rapidly exploding stars at distances that are "cosmological." They are associated with distant galaxies beyond the Milky Way.

The main evidence for this hypothesis is that the uniform distribution of directions of gamma-ray bursts in the sky is consistent with the distribution of all other objects that are known to be at cosmological distances, like galaxies and quasars. However, this uniform distribution is inconsistent with the distribution of any objects known to be in our galaxy, like stars and globular clusters. It is known that the distribution of stars in our

REMEMBER

This is fairly complicated. Did you underline the main points so far?

TIP

Perk up when you see the word "evidence." You will be asked about supporting data.

galaxy is a flattened disk, whose directions are not uniformly distributed but, instead, cluster in the sky along the narrow band of the Milky Way.

The soft gamma-ray repeaters that have been observed are a fraction of a percent of all gamma-ray bursts and show characteristics that are different from gamma-ray bursts in general. For one thing, the bursts that comprise one soft gamma-ray repeater all come from the same direction in the sky. Furthermore, most observed gamma-ray bursts have properties that differ from those of soft gamma-ray repeaters. Therefore, one has to postulate that the soft gamma-ray repeater mechanism is modified in some arbitrary way to explain the similarity to all gamma-ray bursts.

The lack of optical evidence for gamma-ray bursts can be explained by the cosmological hypothesis. By the time an optical search is mounted, the source has faded into the background.

1. Based on the information presented:

   A. a gamma-ray burst is a flash of light that can be seen in the sky.
   B. the distribution of directions of gamma-ray bursts in the sky is a flattened disk.
   C. at the time of the debate about gamma-ray bursts, the distances to the sources of gamma-ray bursts were unknown.
   D. at the time of the debate about gamma-ray bursts, the sources of the gamma-ray bursts were known to be high-velocity neutron stars.

2. Which of the following observations strongly supports the cosmological hypothesis?

   F. Galaxies and quasars are uniformly distributed in the sky.
   G. The spectral lines for some gamma-ray bursts are similar to those observed for neutron stars.
   H. Sources of some soft gamma-ray repeaters are high-velocity neutron stars in the galactic halo.
   J. Gamma-ray bursts have similar durations to pulsars observed in the Milky Way.

3. The local and cosmological hypotheses disagree on:

   A. the distances to the sources of gamma-ray bursts.
   B. the distribution of velocities of neutron stars.
   C. the distribution of stars and globular clusters in the Milky Way.
   D. the distances to galaxies outside of the Milky Way.

4. An astronomer who supports the cosmological hypothesis might point out which of the following as a weakness in the evidence put forward to support the local hypothesis?

   F. Neutron stars cannot be observed through a telescope.
   G. Gamma-ray repeaters are just a tiny fraction of gamma-ray bursts.
   H. Spectral lines of some gamma-ray bursts resemble those in magnetic neutron stars.
   J. The galactic halo is composed of stars, including neutron stars from our galaxy.

5. In the early 2000s it was discovered that gamma-ray bursts lasting over 2 seconds were from massive star explosions in distant galaxies. It was also found that the gamma rays formed when the core of a star imploded to create a black hole. These discoveries:

   A. support the local hypothesis because black holes are not visible and could be part of the galactic halo.
   B. support the cosmological hypothesis because black holes are uniformly distributed beyond the Milky Way.
   C. support the cosmological hypothesis because they show that the sources of gamma-ray bursts are in galaxies beyond the Milky Way
   D. support the local hypothesis because it is generally known that black holes and neutron stars are formed by the collapse of massive stars.

6. Which is false about soft gamma-ray repeaters?

   F. Their source is known to be high-velocity neutron stars in the galactic halo.
   G. Bursts from a soft gamma-ray repeater are uniformly distributed on the sky.
   H. They are just a small subset of gamma-ray bursts.
   J. To make the case that all gamma-ray bursts can be explained by soft gamma-ray repeaters, simplifying assumptions must be made about the soft gamma-ray repeater mechanism.

7. Which of the following discoveries would bolster the local hypothesis?

   A. Gamma-ray bursts originating in galactic objects, such as globular clusters, stars, and planetary nebulae, found in galaxies beyond the Milky Way
   B. A very-high-velocity neutron star that repeatedly emitted gamma-ray bursts
   C. Gamma-ray bursts detected in galaxies beyond the galactic halo
   D. X-ray bursts whose sources are in our galaxy, the Milky Way

PASSAGE V

The chromosomes that determine the sex of a human being are called the X and Y chromosomes. Females have two X chromosomes, XX, while males have an X and a Y, XY. The X chromosome carries hundreds of genes that are responsible for many traits unrelated to sex, for example, a dominant gene that causes blood to clot properly. A recessive mutation of this gene can lead to hemophilia, a condition in which blood does not clot.

During reproduction, an egg from the mother, containing one X chromosome, unites with a sperm cell containing either an X chromosome or a Y chromosome. The diagrams below show how a trait like hemophilia can be passed on to children from their parents. In the diagram, the bottom half shows the possibilities at conception.

Let X^A represent a dominant gene with normal blood-clotting factor, and let X^b represent a recessive gene that causes hemophilia. ♀ is the symbol for female, while ♂ is the symbol for male. Let white boxes represent children unaffected by the mutant gene, shaded boxes represent carriers of hemophilia who do not have the illness, and framed boxes represent children who will be afflicted with the disease. In the example shown below, the father does not have the mutant gene, while the mother is a carrier. In other words, she is *heterozygous*, with one normal X chromosome (dominant) and one mutant X chromosome (recessive).

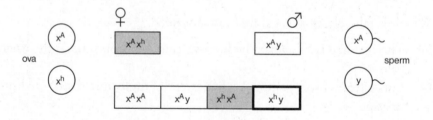

There are four possibilities. Roughly half the sons and half the daughters will inherit the defective gene. Sons with the mutation will have hemophilia. Daughters with the mutation will be carriers, but will not have the disease because they have a normal X chromosome that is dominant.

In the next example, the father is a hemophiliac (has the disease), while the mother is a carrier.

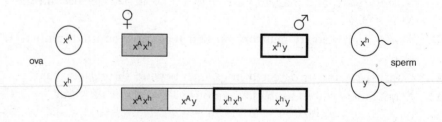

REMEMBER

These diagrams are key to the whole passage. Don't gloss over them!

Again, there are four possibilities. Three out of four children, on average, will inherit the defective gene. Daughters will either be carriers or have the disease. Sons will either have the disease or be normal, without the trait. Notice that daughters with the disease are *homozygous*, with both X chromosomes having the same form of the gene (in this case, the mutant gene).

In a fertilized egg, human females have two X chromosomes, whereas males only inherit one X chromosome. This means that females have two copies of every gene on the X, while males have only one. During embryonic development, however, one X chromosome in each female cell becomes inactivated and condenses into a compact object called a Barr body. As a result, balance is restored and the cells of females and males each have just one active copy of genes on the X chromosome.

The mechanism for X chromosome inactivation is thought to involve two RNA molecules, XIST and Tsix, produced by genes on the X chromosome. These two RNA molecules appear to be in opposition to each other. On the X chromosome that is becoming inactivated, Tsix is lost while XIST increases. Multiple copies of XIST attach to this future Barr body, which becomes completely "painted" with it. On the other X chromosome, the one that will stay active, Tsix levels are maintained and XIST drops off.

After an X chromosome is inactivated in a particular cell, all descendants through mitotic cell division have the same inactive X. By contrast, during reproduction, all X chromosomes in the ova and sperm cells are active.

Three students studied the formation of Barr bodies in female embryonic cells. They disagreed about which X chromosome is selected to become a Barr body.

NOTE
So far, there are no disagreements . . . .

Student 1
The selection of which of the two X chromosomes will form the Barr body is random and independent in each of the embryonic cells present at the time of X inactivation. As a result, females have a mosaic of two types of cells, those with the active X derived from the father and those with the active X derived from the mother.

Student 2
The father's X chromosome is always inactivated to form a Barr body. As a result, females have a single type of cell, with an active X derived from the mother.

Student 3
The mother's X chromosome is always inactivated to form a Barr body. As a result, females have a single type of cell, with an active X derived from the father.

1. Color blindness is inherited as a sex-linked trait. The gene for color blindness is recessive, whereas normal color perception is dominant. Based on the information in the passage, which of the following situations *must* be true if a mother is color-blind and the father has normal color perception?

    A. All daughters will be color-blind, and all sons will have normal color perception.

    B. All daughters will be carriers of color blindness without being color-blind, and all sons will be color-blind.

    C. All daughters will either be carriers of color blindness or be color-blind, while all sons will have normal color perception.

    D. All sons and daughters will be color-blind.

2. In humans, the term *sex-linked* refers to genes on the X chromosome. Alternate versions of a given gene are called *alleles*, where one allele is dominant and one recessive. Which of the following is a *false* statement about sex-linked alleles?

    F. Fathers pass sex-linked alleles to all of their daughters but to none of their sons.

    G. Mothers can pass sex-linked alleles to both sons and daughters.

    H. Fathers can pass sex-linked alleles to both sons and daughters.

    J. If a sex-linked trait is due to a recessive allele, a female will exhibit the trait only if she is homozygous, namely both of her X chromosomes have the same allele.

3. Suppose a female cat has two sex-linked alleles for fur color: an allele for black fur from her father and an allele for orange fur from her mother. The cat is a calico cat with a coat of mottled orange and black patches of fur. The cat's coat color supports which student's theory of Barr body formation?

    A. Student 1

    B. Student 2

    C. Student 3

    D. None of the students

4. Hemophilia is caused by a mutant gene on the X chromosome encoding the clotting factor VIII. Denote it X^b. The mutant gene prevents production of factor VIII. The normal allele, X^A, allows production of factor VIII. A girl who inherits the normal allele from her father and the mutant allele from her mother will become a carrier of hemophilia but will not have the disease. Which of the following students' claims (about why the girl does not have the disease despite being a carrier) is correct?

    F. Student 3 claims that her viewpoint is supported because X^b is always inactivated, leaving all the cells with X^A activated.

    G. Student 2 claims that her viewpoint is supported because X^A is always inactivated, leaving all the cells with X^b activated.

    H. Student 1 claims that her viewpoint is supported because no Barr bodies are formed if the girl is heterozygous (that is, has both the X^A and the X^b alleles).

    J. Student 1 claims that her viewpoint is supported because there is a 50 percent chance that a Barr body will form in any given cell.

5. The three students would most likely *not* agree about which of the following?

   A. The reason that one of two X chromosomes in females is inactivated is to balance the number of genes provided on male and female X chromosomes.

   B. After an embryonic cell "decides" which X chromosome will become inactivated, all descendant cells that arise from this cell due to mitotic cell division will inherit that "decision."

   C. The "decision" of which of the two X chromosomes is inactivated is made in the early stages of female development.

   D. Heterozygous females with alleles X^A and X^B will have some cells in which X^A is active and other cells in which X^B is active.

6. When mature (nondividing) cells are treated with stains that bind to chromosomes, Barr bodies show up as dark stains visible in the nuclei of the cells. The stains reveal no further information about the X chromosomes in the cells. A reasonable application of this staining feature of Barr bodies is:

   F. in medical diagnoses, to determine whether a patient has an illness like hemophilia.

   G. in genetic counseling, to determine whether a person is a carrier of a disease like hemophilia.

   H. in medical forensics, to determine and legally define the sex of an individual.

   J. in biological research, to determine which X chromosome is selected for inactivation.

7. Suppose a geneticist examined embryonic cells of a female kangaroo and discovered high levels of Tsix RNA in all of the maternal X chromosomes. Based on the information in the passage, this finding would most likely strengthen the viewpoint(s) of which student(s)?

   A. Student 1 only

   B. Student 2 only

   C. Student 3 only

   D. Students 2 and 3 only

Solutions and Explanations

PASSAGE I (WASPS)

- **Read and summarize:**

  Wasp lays 1 or 2 eggs in a moth egg.
  1 wasp egg can produce 3000 siblings.
  2 types of larvae: bloodsucking and soldiers.
  Soldiers kill bloodsuckers.
  Surviving bloodsuckers eat caterpillar's organs.
  Bloodsuckers fly away when ready, soldiers die in caterpillar.

- **Disagree:**

  Which bloodsuckers, exactly, do soldier wasps kill?

- **Agree:**

  About $\frac{1}{4}$ of the wasp larvae are soldiers.

  Soldiers are not bloodsuckers.
  Soldiers kill bloodsucker wasp larvae for evolutionary gain;
  i.e., increased survival rate of genetically similar individuals.

Now make two columns, one for each biologist.

	Biologist 1	Biologist 2
Viewpoint summary (purpose of soldiers)	Kill larvae from other mothers so that their family can get more food. (Goal: survival of their own family.)	Female soldiers kill their blood-sucking brothers—gives genetic advantage for sisters to survive. (Goal: survival of sisters vs brothers.)
Data	Observed: killing of other species.	Observed: 1) Number of female soldiers greater than number of male soldiers. 2) Fratricide: males more likely to be killed.

SOLUTIONS

1. **(C)**   2. **(J)**   3. **(D)**   4. **(G)**   5. **(C)**   6. **(H)**   7. **(B)**

1. **(C)** All of the statements are confirmed in the passage except for choice (C). The bloodsucking larvae do not kill other larvae. Only the soldiers kill.

2. **(J)** The soldiers attack only bloodsucking wasp larvae. Each of the other choices is wrong.
   Choice (F): Soldiers are not attacked. They do not compete for food as there is a large supply of bloodsuckers for them to eat.
   Choice (G): Only the bloodsuckers eventually eat the organs of the host.
   Choice (H): The soldiers eat other (bloodsucking) larvae. They do not compete with the bloodsuckers for food (host blood).

3. **(D)** According to Biologist 2, the female soldiers kill their bloodsucking brothers. Every other choice is incorrect.
   Choices (A) and (B): Soldiers do not kill other soldiers.
   Choice (C): The female wasp soldiers help their sisters by killing off their bloodsucking brothers.

> **TIP**
>
> Get the answer immediately by glancing at the correct column when the question begins with "According to . . . ."

4. **(G)** In each of the theories, the actions of the soldiers tend to provide an advantage for the wasps within their own gene pool. According to Biologist 1, this advantage is provided when the soldiers attack larvae from other species and other mothers. According to Biologist 2, the advantage comes when sister soldiers, who are genetically identical to sister bloodsuckers, kill off their brothers with whom they are genetically different. The other choices may be downright incorrect, or they may be correct but not in the viewpoint of one of the biologists.
   Choice (F): Biologist 2 would disagree, saying that the purpose of the soldiers is to eliminate male bloodsuckers from their own family.
   Choice (H): This is wrong: The caterpillar derives no benefit from the wasps, which eventually cause its (the caterpillar's) death.
   Choice (J): This is wrong because the soldiers do not compete for food—more than enough larvae are available for them to eat.

5. **(C)** Biologist 2 does not mention the fact that soldiers have been observed to kill larvae from other species. The other choices may be factually correct but not necessarily flaws in Biologist 2's theory.
   Choice (A): The fact that soldiers do not reproduce is not a factor in either theory.
   Choice (B): This fact is not mentioned in the passage. Even if it were true, it would not be consistent with either theory.
   Choice (D): The fact that the female egg produces more soldiers than the male egg would tend to *bolster* Biologist 2's theory.

6. **(H)** An experiment that showed that soldiers attack both other species and their own siblings would support both biologists' points of view. The purpose of the soldiers is the crux of their disagreement.

7. **(B)** In order to resolve questions about *Copidosoma* wasps, studies must be done *of these wasps*. Also, to confirm the viewpoint of Biologist 1, other species need to be included in this experiment. Thus, choice (B) is correct and choice (C) is wrong.

Choice (A): Studying different wasp species may lend support for either theory but would not be satisfactory in resolving the differences between Biologist 1 and Biologist 2 for *Copidosoma* wasps.

Choice (D): This study would not be useful. The *Copidosoma* wasps do not depend on parasites for development. They themselves are the parasites! Note that this is an answer choice that you should eliminate immediately; no species depends on parasites to aid in their development. Parasites cause only harm.

PASSAGE II (RESONANCE)

- **Read and summarize:**

Sounds are vibrations of the air.

No air, no sound.

Elastic body has natural frequency.

Resonance: a periodic force applied to body, causes amplification of vibrations in body whose natural frequency = frequency of applied force.

- **Disagree:**

What happens to air after tuning fork is struck, causing second fork to vibrate?

- **Agree:**

If tuning fork struck, air movement from first fork causes second with same frequency to vibrate.

	Student 1	Student 2
Viewpoint summary	Air travels as wave.	Air travels as rigid column.
	Wave consists of sequence of alternating regions of compression and rarefaction.	Region of compression at fork 1 causes region of compression at fork 2. Backward movement of either fork causes region of rarefaction at that fork.
	Fork 2 vibrates if sound wave in phase with vibrations.	Fork 2 vibrates if compression at one fork is matched by compression at other fork.

SOLUTIONS

1. **(B)**   2. **(H)**   3. **(D)**   4. **(F)**   5. **(A)**   6. **(F)**   7. **(C)**

1. **(B)** A sound vibration is produced when air is caused to vibrate. Therefore, no sound can be produced in an environment whose air has been removed. All of the other answer choices imply that air is present that can vibrate and cause sound.

2. **(H)** The only point of disagreement is how air moves to the second tuning fork. The students are in agreement about each of the other choices.
    Choice (F): Compression is high pressure, while rarefaction is low pressure. These terms are not in dispute.
    Choice (G): Both students agree that resonance is the phenomenon that causes tuning fork 2 to vibrate when tuning fork 1 is struck because fork 2 has the same natural frequency as fork 1.
    Choice (J): The natural frequency of the tuning forks is not at issue here.

> **TIP**
>
> The main point of disagreement is easy to spot if you have jotted it down in your summary.

3. **(D)** Both viewpoints accept that the second tuning fork vibrates. The students would disagree with each other in each of the other choices.
    Choice (A): Only Student 2 believes that a column of air moves back and forth. Student 1's model has air moving in just one direction, outward from the first tuning fork.
    Choice (B): Student 2's model does not include a sound wave.
    Choice (C): Student 1's model does not consider air to move in a rigid column.

4. **(F)** In Student 1's model, the vibration of the second fork is set up by air vibrating in unison with the two forks. Choices (G) and (H) are consistent with Student 2's model of air movement. Choice (J) is not consistent with either model. It is a contradiction of terms to say that "air . . . acts like a vacuum."

5. **(A)** In the apparatus shown, the whistle is the only vibrator. If, consistent with Student 2's model, air surges to and fro as a single column in each of the arms leading to the ear, altering the length of one arm would not prevent the air column in it from keeping in step with the air column in the other arm. This means that the whistle would be heard, independent of the relative lengths of the air columns.
    Suppose Student 1's model is correct. When the lengths of arms *A* and *B* are the same, then corresponding regions of compression (or rarefaction) from each arm reach the ear at the same time. The sound of the whistle will be loudest. If the arm lengths are different such that a region of compression from arm *A* reaches the ear at the same time that a region of rarefaction from arm *B* reaches the ear, these regions will cancel each other out. No sound will be heard. In certain positions of arm *B*, the sound will be intensified and in others, diminished. Thus, choice (D) is consistent with Student 1's model, while choices (B) and (C) are consistent with *neither* model.

6. **(F)** Student 1's model describes alternating regions of compression (high pressure) and rarefaction (low pressure). Also, the air pressure "varies smoothly from high to low to high." This implies that the pressure reaches normal in between. Assuming that air pressure is normal before the first tuning fork is struck, graph (F) represents the alternating sequences of high and low pressure.

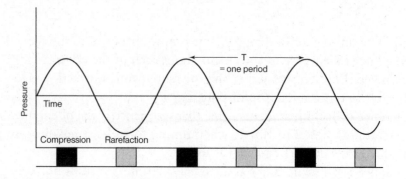

Here is what is wrong with the other choices.

Choice (G): This graph starts out with a jump to a region of rarefaction (low pressure). This is not consistent with Student 1's model, which starts out at normal pressure.

Choice (H): Air cannot go through patches of high and low pressure without becoming normal in between. This means that the graph of pressure versus time must be continuous.

Choice (J): This graph shows air pressure as starting off very high, gradually attaining a minimum value, and then becoming high again. This does not represent the sequence of alternating high- and low-pressure regions suggested by Student 1's model.

7. **(C)** In resonance, a repeating vibration must get larger and larger as a force is applied at regular intervals with the same frequency of the vibration. This effect is seen when pushing a child on a swing or jumping on a trampoline (choices (A) and (B)). Resonance would also be the cause in choice (D). If the singer's note has the same frequency as the natural frequency of the glass and the glass is placed in the right place, the glass will start vibrating at the same frequency of the high note. If the amplification of the vibrations is high enough, the glass will crack or even shatter.

Choice (C) is the only choice in which no periodic force is applied. The tennis ball is given a one-time smack that propels it forward. Although the physical laws of force and motion come into play here, this is not an example of resonance.

PASSAGE III (DINOSAURS)

- **Read and summarize:** *Dinosaurs became extinct about 65 million years ago, at end of Cretaceous period.*

- **Disagree:**

  What caused dinosaurs to become extinct?

- **Agree:**

  Soot in Earth's atmosphere.

  No photosynthesis.

  Global cooling, then global warming.

  Disruption of food chain due to death of ocean creatures.

  Large mammals, including dinosaurs, became extinct.

	Scientist 1	Scientist 2
Viewpoint summary	Catastrophic, sudden event, i.e., a meteorite collision with Earth, caused sudden extinction.	Natural events, like marine regression and volcanic activity, caused gradual extinction.
Data	High-concentration iridium layer at KT boundary consistent with high iridium content of meteorites.	Periods of marine regression long before end of Cretaceous period correspond to dates of large dinosaur extinctions.
	Iridium layers found at over 100 sites around world, corresponding to date of dinosaur extinction.	Major volcano in India about 65 million years ago corresponds to time of large dinosaur extinctions.
	Barren layer beneath KT boundary shows sudden event led to extinction.	Barren layer suggests dinosaurs already extinct.
	Layers beneath barren layer rich in dinosaur fossils. Suggests normal distribution until sudden extinction.	Fossil record shows gradual decline of dinosaurs over 5–10 million years.
		Specific fossils show population decline well before end of Cretaceous period.
		Dramatic decline of diversity of dinosaur species during Cretaceous period.
		Decline of dinosaur teeth in early layers preceding KT boundary.

SOLUTIONS

1. **(D)**   2. **(F)**   3. **(B)**   4. **(H)**   5. **(B)**   6. **(F)**   7. **(C)**

1. **(D)** Massive volcanic activity is a natural phenomenon used as part of Scientist 2's theory of gradual dinosaur extinction. Volcanic eruptions would not necessarily be set off by a meteorite collision with Earth. Each of choices (A), (B), and (C) could be considered a result of the meteorite impact described in Scientist 1's theory.

   Choices (A) and (B): A huge crater or massive earthquake would both be direct consequences.

   Choice (C): Finding large amounts of iridium is consistent with the disintegration of a meteorite.

2. **(F)** Marine regression (retreat of the sea) is a natural geological phenomenon that occurred over a long period of time, leading to gradual extinction. The other choices are all used to explain Scientist 1's catastrophic theory.

   Choice (G): Shock waves were caused by the meteorite striking Earth.

   Choice (H): Kinetic energy of the meteorite turned to heat energy.

   Choice (J): A high concentration of iridium was due to the high concentration of iridium in the meteorite.

TIP

"Consistent with both theories . . ." is synonymous with "They agree . . . ."

3. **(B)** According to Scientist 1, after the meteorite struck Earth, the planet's atmosphere was filled with soot, which then blocked out the light needed for photosynthesis. According to Scientist 2, volcanic activity released large amounts of soot into the atmosphere. Thus, both scientists agree that soot in Earth's atmosphere prevented photosynthesis. The other statements are not in agreement with *both* Scientist 1's and Scientist 2's theories.

   Choice (A): Neither scientist claims that iridium in the atmosphere caused the death of marine creatures. Scientist 1 simply gives an explanation of the spike in iridium in the rocks at the KT boundary.

   Choice (C): Neither scientist claims that retreat of the oceans led to global warming. Scientist 2 presents it as one of the causes of the extinction of the dinosaurs since it led to the reduction of marine life.

   Choice (D): Only Scientist 1 believes that a sudden event led to extinction. Scientist 2 would say that the disruption of the food chain was gradual.

TIP

A summary with notes jotted on it is really helpful, especially when the passages are long.

4. **(H)** The high iridium layer supports Scientist 1's meteorite theory since meteorite dust, which is rich in iridium, mingled with dust caused by the impact. The other choices are all consistent with Scientist 2's theory of gradual extinction.

   Choice (F): Evidence suggests that populations of dinosaurs were dwindling long before the end of the Cretaceous period.

   Choice (G): Dinosaur teeth beneath the iridium layer of the KT boundary were in decreased numbers.

   Choice (J): Beneath the high-iridium layer is a barren layer of clay.

5. **(B)** A finding that 90 percent of Earth's ocean species became extinct at the time of dinosaur extinction suggests that whatever caused the dinosaurs to become extinct also caused the ocean creatures to become extinct. The finding does not support one theory over the other. Each of the other discoveries is likely to be used as evidence of Scientist 1's catastrophic theory.

   Choice (A): Flying pieces of molten rock are consistent with the theory that the shock wave from the meteorite melted matter in its wake.

   Choice (C): Fracture planes seen only at sites of nuclear explosion suggest that an equally violent event—like a massive impact of a meteorite with Earth—caused these planes.

   Choice (D): A meteorite's impact with Earth would cause extreme conditions of temperature and pressure; thus, finding such diamonds bolsters the catastrophic theory.

6. **(F)** The catastrophic theory of Scientist 1 depends on a constant distribution of dinosaurs until a catastrophic event caused their extinction. Any evidence that suggests that there could have been dinosaur remains right up until the KT boundary bolsters this theory. The acid-leaching/erosion hypothesis suggests that the bones could have been there but were destroyed by acid or erosion. None of the other choices is correct.

   Choice (G): First, nothing in the passage suggests that acid rain is produced as a result of the meteorite collision. More importantly, *where* the acid comes from that dissolves the bones is irrelevant. The fact that the bones might have been there right up until the extinction supports the catastrophic theory.

   Choice (H): You cannot assume that acid leaching and erosion are small effects and would not have eliminated a large number of bones.

   Choice (J): The presence of dinosaur remains close to the boundary of the barren layer does nothing to support either theory.

7. **(C)** Graph (C) shows a barren gap suggesting that dinosaurs gradually became extinct before the KT boundary. At the time of the high-concentration iridium layer, the dinosaurs were already extinct. Each of the other graphs is inconsistent with Scientist 2's gradualist theory.

   Choice (A): This shows a constant distribution up until the iridium layer. This supports Scientist 1's catastrophic theory.

   Choices (B) and (D): These graphs support neither theory. At the KT boundary, i.e., in the iridium layer, the dinosaurs were already extinct. Therefore, there should not be any dinosaur remains.

PASSAGE IV (GAMMA-RAY BURSTS)

- **Read and summarize:**

  Gamma-ray bursts:

  > *30 ms – 1000 s duration.*
  > *Uniform distribution of directions in sky.*
  > *Can't be seen with telescope.*
  > *Detected with gamma-ray detectors.*

- **Debate:**

  Where do gamma-ray bursts originate? (Distance to source?)
  What causes gamma-ray bursts? (What is source?)

- **Agree:**

  Distribution of stars in our galaxy is a flattened disk.
  gamma-ray bursts not distributed like stars.

	Local Hypothesis	Cosmological Hypothesis
Viewpoint summary	Gamma-ray bursts (grb's) caused by high-velocity neutron stars that originate in the Milky Way.	Grb's caused by rapid explosive events outside Milky Way.
Data	Some neutron stars have enough velocity to escape Milky Way to galactic halo.	Uniform distribution of directions of Grb's in sky.
	Soft gamma-ray repeaters produced by neutron stars.	Soft gamma-ray repeaters are tiny fraction of Grb's. Also, all come from same direction in sky, and show different properties from Grb's.
	Spectral lines similar in Grb's and some neutron stars.	
	Grb's not visible—explained by small surface area of neutron stars.	Grb's not visible—explained by rapid fading of source.

SOLUTIONS

1. **(C)**   2. **(F)**   3. **(A)**   4. **(G)**   5. **(C)**   6. **(G)**   7. **(B)**

1. **(C)** The crux of the debate was that neither the source of gamma-ray bursts nor the distance to their source was known. The other choices are incorrect.

   Choice (A): Gamma-ray bursts cannot be seen in the conventional sense—they are not in the visible spectrum. They are detected with gamma-ray detectors.

   Choice (B): The directions of gamma-ray bursts are uniformly distributed in the sky.

   Choice (D): At the time of the debate, the sources of gamma-ray bursts were unknown.

2. **(F)** Since galaxies and quasars are at cosmological distances from the Milky Way, their uniform distribution in the sky suggests that the source of gamma-ray bursts is outside the Milky Way. None of the other choices supports the cosmological hypothesis:

   Choice (G): Spectral lines being similar to those observed for neutron stars would support the local hypothesis, which postulates that neutron stars are the sources of gamma-ray bursts.

   Choice (H): If the soft gamma-ray repeaters are known to be neutron stars and are the source of gamma-ray bursts, this would bolster the local hypothesis.

   Choice (J): Any object detected as being the source of gamma-ray bursts in the Milky Way would contradict, not support, the cosmological hypothesis.

> **TIP**
>
> Supporting data for a theory should be listed in its correct column.

3. **(A)** One of the points of debate is the distance to the sources of gamma-ray bursts. Each of the other choices is a point of agreement in the hypotheses.

4. **(G)** If a tiny percent of gamma-ray bursts are gamma-ray repeaters whose origin is the Milky Way, one cannot extrapolate and say all gamma-ray bursts originate in the Milky Way. Therefore, the gamma-ray repeaters argument for the local hypothesis is a weak one. Although the other choices may be true, they are not necessarily facts that weaken the local hypothesis.

   Choice (F): Whether neutron stars can be observed through a telescope or not is irrelevant to the debate. Gamma-ray bursts cannot be observed through a telescope either.

   Choice (H): The fact that spectral lines of some gamma-ray bursts resemble those in some neutron stars would appear to strengthen, rather than weaken, the local hypothesis. Remember—the local hypothesis postulates that neutron stars are the source of gamma-ray bursts.

   Choice (J): A galactic halo that includes neutron stars would strengthen, not weaken, the local hypothesis. The galactic-halo theory is one of the cornerstones of the local hypothesis.

> **TIP**
>
> Points of disagreement should be in your summary.

5. **(C)** Any experiment that confirms that the source is outside our galaxy would support the cosmological hypothesis. Each of the other choices is false.

    Choice (A): The gamma-ray bursts were found to originate from distant stars. Whether black holes exist both in distant galaxies and in the galactic halo is irrelevant.

    Choice (B): There is no information about the distribution of black holes beyond the Milky Way.

    Choice (D): The formation of black holes and neutron stars is beside the point. The key to this question is where the source was detected, namely beyond our galaxy.

6. **(G)** A soft gamma-ray repeater is a sequence of gamma-ray bursts that come from the same direction in the sky. This contradicts choice (G). Each of the other assertions is true and can be verified in the passage.

7. **(B)** Finding high-velocity neutron stars that are the source of gamma-ray bursts would help confirm the local hypothesis. Each of the other choices is wrong.

    Choices (A) and (C): Gamma-ray bursts from galactic objects beyond our galaxy would strongly suggest that gamma-ray bursts could originate anywhere, including in a distant galaxy. This bolsters the cosmological hypothesis, not the local hypothesis.

    Choice (D): Any discovery about X-ray bursts would allow conclusions about X-ray bursts, not gamma-ray bursts, which are in a different part of the spectrum.

PASSAGE V (CHROMOSOMES)

Don't forget to summarize the main points of the passage before attempting the questions.

- **Read and summarize:**

    Female chromosomes are XX; male chromosomes XY.

    Sex-linked traits are carried on the X chromosome.

    Homozygous female has the same gene for a given trait on each X.

    Heterozygous female has the dominant gene for a given trait on one X and the recessive gene for the same trait on other X.

    At conception, child gets one X chromosome from mother and either an X or a Y from father.

    During embryonic development, one X in female becomes inactivated (a Barr body).

    Barr body high in XIST, low in Tsix. Activated X high in Tsix.

- **Agree:**

  All female cells have one inactivated X called a Barr body.
  Descendant cells for any cell have same X inactivated.

- **Disagree:**

  Which X chromosome is selected to become a Barr body?

	Student 1	Student 2	Student 3
Viewpoint summary	Random X chosen to be Barr body. Results in two types of cells in female.	Father's X always chosen to be Barr body.	Mother's X always chosen to be Barr body.

SOLUTIONS

1. **(B)**   2. **(H)**   3. **(A)**   4. **(F)**   5. **(D)**   6. **(H)**   7. **(B)**

1. **(B)** Let X^A represent a dominant gene for normal color perception and X^c represent a recessive gene that causes color blindness. You are given that the mother is color-blind, which means that both of her X chromosomes carry the recessive gene, X^c. (If the mother were heterozygous, $X^A X^c$, she would not be color-blind, since X^A is dominant.) The father has normal color perception, which means that his X chromosome carries X^A. (If his X chromosome were X^c, then he would be color-blind.) Here, then are the possibilities at conception:

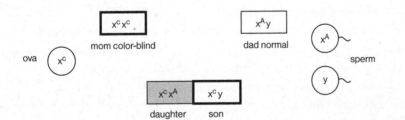

Notice that all daughters will be carriers. By receiving the dominant gene, X^A, from the father, they will not be color-blind. The sons, however, will inherit the color blindness trait, since their X chromosome must contain X^c.

2. **(H)** Choice (H) is false because sex-linked alleles are on only the X chromosomes. Fathers pass their Y chromosome to their sons. Each of the other choices is true.

Choice (F): Fathers must pass their single X chromosome to their daughters. (The daughter is XX, where one X comes from the mother and one from the father.)

Choice (G): Each child gets an X chromosome from the mother, irrespective of the sex of the child. The chromosome from the father determines the sex of the child: X produces a girl, Y produces a boy.

Choice (J): In order to have a trait due to a recessive gene, both of the girl's X chromosomes must have the recessive gene. If just one X chromosome has the dominant gene, the girl will be a carrier of the trait but will not exhibit the trait.

3. **(A)** The mosaic of colors on the cat's coat suggests that about half of the cat's cells express the gene for black fur, X^B, and about half express the gene for orange fur, X^O. This means that if the cat embryo cells were $X^B X^O$, in about half the cells X^B became a Barr body (inactivated). In the other half, X^O became a Barr body. This is consistent with Student 1's viewpoint. The other choices are incorrect.

Choice (B): If Student 2 were correct, namely, the father's X chromosome always became a Barr body, all cells would have an active X^O and the cat would have all-orange fur.

Choice (C): If Student 3 were correct, namely, the mother's X chromosome always became a Barr body, all cells would have an active X^B and the cat would have all-black fur.

Choice (D): This is incorrect because Student 1's viewpoint is supported.

4. **(F)** Since the girl does not have hemophilia, it does suggest that the X chromosome with the mutant gene, X^b, became inactive in all the cells. Each of the other student claims is incorrect.

Choice (G): This choice does not make sense. If every "normal" X chromosome (from the father) became inactive, then every cell will have an active mutant gene, which suggests that the girl will be sick with hemophilia.

Choice (H): *Heterozygous* means that the girl embryo will be $X^A X^b$. The reason given is wrong. One of a girl's X chromosomes will always become a Barr body (inactivated).

Choice (J): As in choice H, the wrong reason is given. Since each cell contains two X chromosomes, there is a 100 percent chance that a Barr body will form.

Note that in both choices (H) and (J), the reason provided invalidates Student 1's claim. Therefore, you cannot pick these choices. Suppose one of the choices had been as follows; "Student 1 claims her viewpoint is supported because in about half the cells, the normal (nonmutated) copy of the gene will provide enough factor VIII to prevent the disease." This answer would have been a correct choice. However, from the choices given, only choice (F) is logically consistent with both the passage and the viewpoint of the given student.

5. **(D)** Choices (A), (B), and (C) are each consistent with the description of Barr body formation in the passage. None of these choices describes how the decision is made concerning which X chromosome becomes inactivated. Choice (D) implies that in some cells, X^B became inactivated while in others, X^A became inactivated. Students 2 and 3 would disagree with this view.

6. **(H)** Barr bodies occur only in female cells. If a Barr body shows up in a cell, then the cell had to come from a female. This feature can therefore be used to identify the sex of an individual. None of the other choices is correct.

   Choices (F) and (G): The presence of a Barr body does not provide further information about the person's genetic makeup. It therefore cannot be used to diagnose illness, nor can it be used to determine whether a person is a carrier of illness.

   Choice (J): The staining indicates the presence of a Barr body. It gives no information about which X chromosome got targeted for inactivation.

7. **(B)** According to the passage, high levels of Tsix are found in the X chromosome that stays active. The geneticist's results suggest that all maternal X chromosomes stay active, which means that the paternal X chromosomes become Barr bodies. This is consistent only with Student 2's viewpoint.

   Choice (A): To strengthen the viewpoint of Student 1, the experiment would need to find high levels of Tsix RNA in some of the maternal X chromosomes and some of the paternal X chromosomes. This is consistent with the hypothesis that the inactivated chromosome is randomly selected.

   Choice (C): To strengthen the viewpoint of Student 3, the experiment would need to find high levels of Tsix RNA in all of the paternal X chromosomes. This would suggest that all of the paternal X chromosomes stay active. In other words, all the maternal X chromosomes become inactivated.

   Choice (D): This choice is wrong because the finding strengthens the viewpoint of Student 2 only.

TIP

Beware of questions with *not* in them. They are harder to process and need extra care.

PART 3

MODEL ACT TESTS

Model ACT Tests

What follows is one complete practice Math Test and one complete practice Science Test. These will help you assess your math and science skills as you study for the ACT.

Try to take the tests under test conditions:

- Set yourself up in a quiet room where you will not be disturbed. Let your family know that you are doing this so that they do not inadvertently disturb you.
- Be sure to allot yourself the exact same amount of time that you will have on the real ACT Tests. Learning to pace yourself is an essential ingredient of success, one that you need to acquire before the actual test.
- Use the answer sheet provided on the next page. You should tear it out of the book.
- Use a pencil with a good eraser, and make sure that you darken just one oval per question. Beware of stray marks. If you have a change of heart on any given question, be sure to erase the old answer completely before bubbling in the new one.

When you have completed the tests, check your answers against the answer keys provided at the end of this chapter. For the wrong answers, be sure to check out the explanations—you want to avoid repeating your mistakes!

Are you ready to go?

Answer Sheet
PRACTICE MATHEMATICS TEST

1 Ⓐ Ⓑ Ⓒ Ⓓ Ⓔ   16 Ⓕ Ⓖ Ⓗ Ⓙ Ⓚ   31 Ⓐ Ⓑ Ⓒ Ⓓ Ⓔ   46 Ⓕ Ⓖ Ⓗ Ⓙ Ⓚ

2 Ⓕ Ⓖ Ⓗ Ⓙ Ⓚ   17 Ⓐ Ⓑ Ⓒ Ⓓ Ⓔ   32 Ⓕ Ⓖ Ⓗ Ⓙ Ⓚ   47 Ⓐ Ⓑ Ⓒ Ⓓ Ⓔ

3 Ⓐ Ⓑ Ⓒ Ⓓ Ⓔ   18 Ⓕ Ⓖ Ⓗ Ⓙ Ⓚ   33 Ⓐ Ⓑ Ⓒ Ⓓ Ⓔ   48 Ⓕ Ⓖ Ⓗ Ⓙ Ⓚ

4 Ⓕ Ⓖ Ⓗ Ⓙ Ⓚ   19 Ⓐ Ⓑ Ⓒ Ⓓ Ⓔ   34 Ⓕ Ⓖ Ⓗ Ⓙ Ⓚ   49 Ⓐ Ⓑ Ⓒ Ⓓ Ⓔ

5 Ⓐ Ⓑ Ⓒ Ⓓ Ⓔ   20 Ⓕ Ⓖ Ⓗ Ⓙ Ⓚ   35 Ⓐ Ⓑ Ⓒ Ⓓ Ⓔ   50 Ⓕ Ⓖ Ⓗ Ⓙ Ⓚ

6 Ⓕ Ⓖ Ⓗ Ⓙ Ⓚ   21 Ⓐ Ⓑ Ⓒ Ⓓ Ⓔ   36 Ⓕ Ⓖ Ⓗ Ⓙ Ⓚ   51 Ⓐ Ⓑ Ⓒ Ⓓ Ⓔ

7 Ⓐ Ⓑ Ⓒ Ⓓ Ⓔ   22 Ⓕ Ⓖ Ⓗ Ⓙ Ⓚ   37 Ⓐ Ⓑ Ⓒ Ⓓ Ⓔ   52 Ⓕ Ⓖ Ⓗ Ⓙ Ⓚ

8 Ⓕ Ⓖ Ⓗ Ⓙ Ⓚ   23 Ⓐ Ⓑ Ⓒ Ⓓ Ⓔ   38 Ⓕ Ⓖ Ⓗ Ⓙ Ⓚ   53 Ⓐ Ⓑ Ⓒ Ⓓ Ⓔ

9 Ⓐ Ⓑ Ⓒ Ⓓ Ⓔ   24 Ⓕ Ⓖ Ⓗ Ⓙ Ⓚ   39 Ⓐ Ⓑ Ⓒ Ⓓ Ⓔ   54 Ⓕ Ⓖ Ⓗ Ⓙ Ⓚ

10 Ⓕ Ⓖ Ⓗ Ⓙ Ⓚ   25 Ⓐ Ⓑ Ⓒ Ⓓ Ⓔ   40 Ⓕ Ⓖ Ⓗ Ⓙ Ⓚ   55 Ⓐ Ⓑ Ⓒ Ⓓ Ⓔ

11 Ⓐ Ⓑ Ⓒ Ⓓ Ⓔ   26 Ⓕ Ⓖ Ⓗ Ⓙ Ⓚ   41 Ⓐ Ⓑ Ⓒ Ⓓ Ⓔ   56 Ⓕ Ⓖ Ⓗ Ⓙ Ⓚ

12 Ⓕ Ⓖ Ⓗ Ⓙ Ⓚ   27 Ⓐ Ⓑ Ⓒ Ⓓ Ⓔ   42 Ⓕ Ⓖ Ⓗ Ⓙ Ⓚ   57 Ⓐ Ⓑ Ⓒ Ⓓ Ⓔ

13 Ⓐ Ⓑ Ⓒ Ⓓ Ⓔ   28 Ⓕ Ⓖ Ⓗ Ⓙ Ⓚ   43 Ⓐ Ⓑ Ⓒ Ⓓ Ⓔ   58 Ⓕ Ⓖ Ⓗ Ⓙ Ⓚ

14 Ⓕ Ⓖ Ⓗ Ⓙ Ⓚ   29 Ⓐ Ⓑ Ⓒ Ⓓ Ⓔ   44 Ⓕ Ⓖ Ⓗ Ⓙ Ⓚ   59 Ⓐ Ⓑ Ⓒ Ⓓ Ⓔ

15 Ⓐ Ⓑ Ⓒ Ⓓ Ⓔ   30 Ⓕ Ⓖ Ⓗ Ⓙ Ⓚ   45 Ⓐ Ⓑ Ⓒ Ⓓ Ⓔ   60 Ⓕ Ⓖ Ⓗ Ⓙ Ⓚ

Practice Mathematics Test

60 MINUTES—60 QUESTIONS

Directions

1. After you have solved each problem, choose your answer and fill in the corresponding oval on your answer sheet.
2. Do not spend too much time on any given problem. Note the problems that you find difficult and come back to them after you have answered all that you can.
3. You are allowed to use a calculator.
4. Note that you may make each of the following assumptions unless specifically stated otherwise:

   - Figures are not necessarily drawn to scale.
   - Geometric figures lie in one plane.
   - The word *line* in a problem means "straight line."
   - The word *average* in a problem means "arithmetic mean."

1. $3x \cdot (2x)^3 = ?$

   A. $24x^4$
   B. $6x^4$
   C. $18x^4$
   D. $24x^3$
   E. $18x^3$

2. In the figure below, $\overline{AB}$ is congruent to $\overline{AC}$ and D is on $\overrightarrow{BC}$. What is the measure of $\angle ACD$?

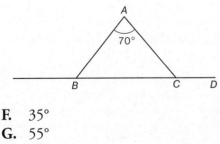

   F. $35°$
   G. $55°$
   H. $70°$
   J. $110°$
   K. $125°$

3. Dasom earns $10.75 an hour in a summer job. She is saving to buy a television set that costs $599.00. What is the least number of hours she must work, to the nearest hour, in order to save up enough to buy the television set?

   A. 54
   B. 55
   C. 56
   D. 57
   E. 60

4. If $2 + \sqrt{x-3} = 5$, then $x = ?$

   F. 4
   G. 6
   H. 10
   J. 12
   K. 52

5. A ladder leans against a wall as shown. If the height of the wall to the top of the ladder is 10 meters and the distance from the foot of the ladder to the wall is 7 meters, which of the following equations could be used to find θ, the angle that the ladder makes with the ground?

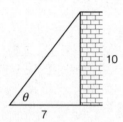

A. $\tan \theta = \dfrac{10}{7}$

B. $\sec \theta = \dfrac{10}{7}$

C. $\cot \theta = \dfrac{10}{7}$

D. $\sin \theta = \dfrac{7}{10}$

E. $\cos \theta = \dfrac{7}{10}$

6. What is the slope of a line parallel to the line $2y - 6x = 3$?

F. 3

G. 2

H. $\dfrac{3}{2}$

J. $-\dfrac{1}{3}$

K. −6

7. A box of cereal contains 510 grams of cereal. If one serving is $1\dfrac{1}{4}$ cups and 1 cup of cereal weighs 26.4 grams, what is the maximum number of complete servings contained in the box?

A. 408

B. 26

C. 19

D. 16

E. 15

8. In the figure below, $\overleftrightarrow{AB} \parallel \overleftrightarrow{CD}$, and $\overleftrightarrow{EF} \parallel \overleftrightarrow{GH}$.

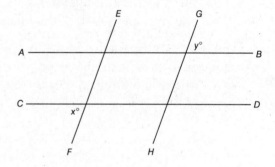

Which of the following is true?

F. $x = y$

G. $x > y$

H. $x < y$

J. $x = 2y$

K. There is insufficient information to determine the relationship between x and y.

Questions 9 and 10 refer to the following chart:

Math Test Scores for Five Students

Student	Score on Math Test 1	Score on Math Test 2
1	60	80
2	85	95
3	100	65
4	98	75
5	90	92

9. Which student had the highest average (mean) score?

   A. 1
   B. 2
   C. 3
   D. 4
   E. 5

10. Which is true about the scores shown?

   F. The median score for Math Test 1 is 100.
   G. The median score for Math Test 2 is 65.
   H. The median of all the scores (for both tests) is 87.5.
   J. The median score for Math Test 2 is greater than the median score for Math Test 1.
   K. The median score for Math Test 2 is greater than the mean score for Math Test 2.

11. A scale drawing of a new building has $\frac{1}{2}$ inch representing 40 feet. If a conference room has a floor length of 60 feet, what is the floor length, in inches, on the scale drawing?

   A. $\frac{3}{4}$

   B. $\frac{7}{8}$

   C. 1

   D. $1\frac{1}{2}$

   E. $1\frac{3}{4}$

12. A circle in the standard (x, y) coordinate plane has the equation $(x - 3)^2 + (y + 5)^2 = 25$. What is the distance from the center of the circle to the point $(-9, -5)$?

   F. 6

   G. 12

   H. $12\sqrt{2}$

   J. $2\sqrt{34}$

   K. $2\sqrt{61}$

13. Joan watched a movie on television from 2 P.M. until 5 P.M. From 2 P.M. until 3 P.M., there were 20 minutes of commercials. From 3 P.M. until 4 P.M., there were 15 minutes of commercials. From 4 P.M. until 5 P.M., there were 10 minutes of commercials. What percent of the movie-viewing time was taken up by commercials?

   A. 20%
   B. 25%
   C. 30%
   D. 45%
   E. 81%

14. An urn contains 3 red marbles and 4 white marbles. Two marbles are randomly removed. What is the probability that these two are both white?

F. $\dfrac{1}{42}$

G. $\dfrac{2}{7}$

H. $\dfrac{16}{49}$

J. $\dfrac{4}{7}$

K. $\dfrac{1}{2}$

15. The circle shown below has center O. Points Q, O, and R divide line segment $\overline{PS}$ into four equal segments, and each of the curved regions is a semicircle.

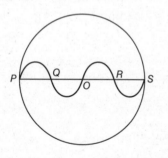

Given that the circumference of the large circle is 24π, what is the length of the curved path from P to S through Q, O, and R?

A. 6π
B. 9π
C. 12π
D. 15π
E. 24π

16. John spent $\dfrac{1}{5}$ of his allowance on notebooks, $\dfrac{1}{4}$ of what was left on candy, $\dfrac{1}{3}$ of what was left (after the notebook and candy purchases) on bus tickets, and $\dfrac{1}{2}$ of what was finally left on a snack. He then had $6.00 left over. What was his allowance?

F. $60
G. $50
H. $40
J. $30
K. $20

17. Which of the following represents an equation for which the sum of its roots is -3 and the product of its roots is 4?

A. $x^2 + 4x - 3 = 0$
B. $x^2 + 3x + 4 = 0$
C. $x^2 - 3x + 2 = 0$
D. $2x^2 + 6x - 3 = 0$
E. $x^2 - 3x + 4 = 0$

18. $\begin{bmatrix} 1 & 6 & 3 \\ 5 & 0 & 4 \end{bmatrix} \begin{bmatrix} 2 & 1 \\ -3 & 4 \\ 1 & -2 \end{bmatrix} = ?$

F. Undefined for the given matrices.

G. $\begin{bmatrix} 14 & -3 \\ -13 & 19 \end{bmatrix}$

H. $\begin{bmatrix} -13 & 19 \\ 14 & -3 \end{bmatrix}$

J. $\begin{bmatrix} 2 & 12 & 3 \\ 5 & 0 & -8 \end{bmatrix}$

K. $\begin{bmatrix} 5 & 0 & -8 \\ 2 & 12 & 3 \end{bmatrix}$

19. Which of the following represents the complete solution set for the inequality $x^2 - 2x > 15$?

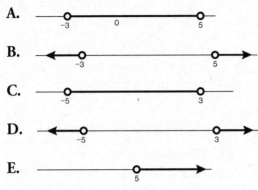

A.

B.

C.

D.

E.

20. If a particle travels 4×10^{-3} feet per second, how many feet will it travel in 3×10^5 seconds?

F. 1.2×10^{-2} feet
G. 1.2×10^{-3} feet
H. 1.2×10^{-15} feet
J. 1.2×10^2 feet
K. 1.2×10^3 feet

21. For all x for which the expression is defined,

$$\frac{2x^2 - 6x - 20}{2x^2 - 50} \text{ simplifies to:}$$

A. $\dfrac{2}{5}$

B. 1

C. $\dfrac{x-2}{x-5}$

D. $\dfrac{x+2}{x+5}$

E. $\dfrac{2(x+2)}{x+5}$

22. In the figure below, the circle with center P is inscribed in $\triangle ABC$. The length of $\overline{AB}$ is 10, the length of $\overline{BD}$ is 4, and the length of $\overline{DC}$ is 5. What is the length of $\overline{ED}$?

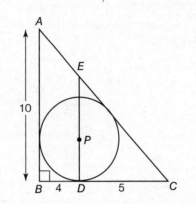

F.   9

G. $5\dfrac{5}{9}$

H. $5\dfrac{3}{5}$

J. $4\dfrac{1}{2}$

K. $3\dfrac{3}{5}$

23. Consider the following system of inequalities:

    $x + y > 3$
    $x - 2y > -1$

    Which region in the graph shown below indicates the solution set of the system of inequalities?

    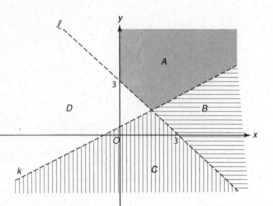

    A. Region *A*
    B. Region *B*
    C. Region *C*
    D. Region *D*
    E. The empty set (no region on the graph)

24. A freight-moving company charges $25 per ton for the first 10 tons of freight, $20 per ton for the next 15 tons, and $15 per ton for any tons over 25 tons. What will the company charge for a shipment weighing 55 tons?

    F. $900
    G. $925
    H. $1000
    J. $1100
    K. $1150

25. *ABCD* is a parallelogram, and the angles are as marked.

    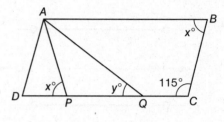

    Which conclusion(s) is/are valid?

    I. $AP = BC$
    II. $x > y$
    III. $x + y = 180$

    A. I only
    B. II only
    C. I and II only
    D. II and III only
    E. I, II, and III

26. What is the minimum value of the expression $4 \cos 3\theta$?

    F. -4
    G. -3
    H. -1
    J. 3
    K. 4

27. If $2x + y = 16$, $x + 2z = 14$, and $2y + z = 12$, then what is the arithmetic mean of x, y, and z?

    A. $\dfrac{14}{3}$

    B. $\dfrac{16}{3}$

    C. 14
    D. 12
    E. 4

28. In the diagram below, $l \| m$. What is the value of y?

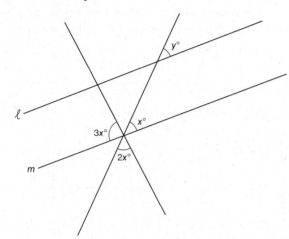

F. It cannot be determined from the given information.
G. 150
H. 60
J. 40
K. 30

29. John earns 6 percent commission on monthly receipts. Washing machines have a list price of $600. In one month, when washing machines were selling at a 10 percent discount, John sold 4 washing machines. What was his commission for these sales, to the nearest dollar?

A. $384
B. $360
C. $130
D. $120
E. $60

30. Consider points A, B, C, and D as shown on line segment $\overline{AD}$ below.

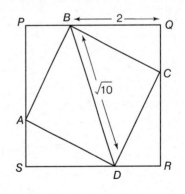

AB, BC, and CD are all positive integer lengths, and the length of $\overline{AD}$ is 18. If the ratio of AB to BC is 3:1, which of the following is *not* a possible length of $\overline{CD}$?

F. 2
G. 6
H. 10
J. 14
K. 18

31. In the complex numbers where $i^2 = -1$,

$$\frac{i-1}{i} = ?$$

A. -1
B. $-1 - i$
C. $1 - i$
D. $1 + i$
E. $-1 + i$

32. In the figure below, $ABCD$ and $PQRS$ are both squares. What is the area of $PQRS$?

F. 36
G. 25
H. 16
J. 9
K. 5

33. In parallelogram *ABCD* shown below, $\overline{DB}$ is a diagonal and *F* is on $\overrightarrow{DB}$. Point *E* is on line $\overleftrightarrow{DC}$. If ∠*BCE* measures 70° and ∠*DBC* measures 32°, find the measure of ∠*FBA*.

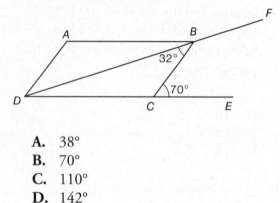

- **A.** 38°
- **B.** 70°
- **C.** 110°
- **D.** 142°
- **E.** 148°

34. If $x - 3y$ is 60% of $9y$, what is the value of $\frac{x}{y}$?

- **F.** 60
- **G.** 18
- **H.** $\frac{42}{5}$
- **J.** $\frac{18}{5}$
- **K.** $\frac{3}{5}$

35. The number of cars parked in the lot of a large office complex on a typical weekday is a function of the time of day. In the graph below, a given *x*-value is the number of hours after 7 A.M.

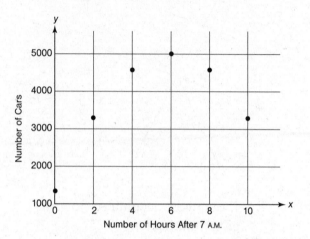

The equation of the function is given by $y = -100(x - 6)^2 + 5000$. According to this function, how many cars could one expect to find in the lot at 4 P.M. on a typical weekday?

- **A.** 3,400
- **B.** 4,100
- **C.** 4,600
- **D.** 4,900
- **E.** 5,000

36. The graph below shows the price of tea from 1990 to 2005.

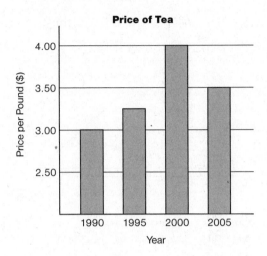

According to the graph, what was the percent decrease in the price of tea from 2000 to 2005?

F. 12.5
G. 20
H. 25
J. 50
K. 87.5

37. For which of the following functions is $f(x) = f(-x)$?

A. $f(x) = x - 3$
B. $f(x) = x^3$
C. $f(x) = -x$
D. $f(x) = x^2 - x + 2$
E. $f(x) = -x^2 + 4$

38. If a is a real number such that $0 < a < 1$, which of the following numbers has the largest value?

F. a

G. $\dfrac{1}{a}$

H. a^2

J. $\dfrac{1}{a^2}$

K. $-a^2$

39. Thomas and Jay are each rolling a wheel along a pavement. The diameter of Jay's wheel is double the diameter of Thomas's wheel. How many revolutions does Thomas's wheel make for each revolution of Jay's wheel?

A. 10
B. 8
C. 4
D. 2
E. $\dfrac{1}{2}$

40. The total surface area of a cylindrical can equals the sum of the lateral surface area and the areas of the base and lid. The lateral surface area is given by the equation $L = 2\pi rh$, where r is the radius of the base and h is the altitude. In square inches, what is the total surface area of the can pictured below?

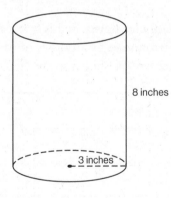

8 inches

3 inches

F. 48π
G. 54π
H. 57π
J. 60π
K. 66π

41. A certain linear function $f(x)$ is such that $f(0) = 4$, $f(2) = p$, and $f(-1) = q$. What is the value of $p + 2q$?

  A. 10
  B. 12
  C. −4
  D. −10
  E. −12

42. The formula $S = 20\sqrt{t + 273}$ gives the speed of sound S in meters per second near Earth's surface, where t is the surface temperature in degrees Celsius. At a point near Earth's surface, if the speed of sound is 348 meters/second, what is the corresponding temperature in degrees Celsius?

  F. 3
  G. 30
  H. 100
  J. 200
  K. 300

43. A rectangular flower bed is 8×10 feet. It is surrounded by a border of uniform width x feet, as shown in the figure below.

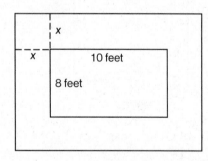

If the area of the bordering region alone is 40 square feet, what is the value of x?

  A. 1
  B. 2
  C. 3
  D. 10
  E. 11

44. The area of a trapezoid with parallel bases b_1 and b_2 and altitude h is given by $A = \frac{1}{2}h(b_1 + b_2)$. What is the area of the trapezoid shown below?

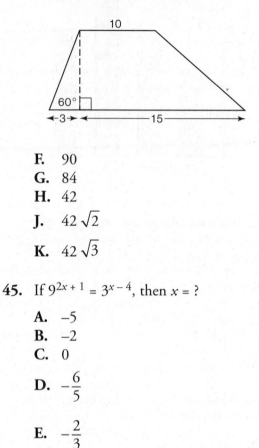

  F. 90
  G. 84
  H. 42
  J. $42\sqrt{2}$
  K. $42\sqrt{3}$

45. If $9^{2x + 1} = 3^{x - 4}$, then $x = ?$

  A. −5
  B. −2
  C. 0
  D. $-\dfrac{6}{5}$
  E. $-\dfrac{2}{3}$

46. A rectangular pyramid, shown below, with base area B and height h has volume V, where $V = \dfrac{1}{3}Bh$. In terms of V, what is the volume of a rectangular pyramid with base area B and altitude $4h$?

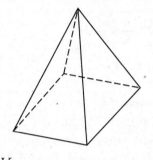

   F. $2V$
   G. $4V$
   H. $16V$
   J. $36V$
   K. $V + 4$

47. If the value, to the nearest thousandth, of $\tan \theta$ is -2.747, which of the following could be true about θ?
Note: You may use the following table of values:

θ	$\tan \theta$
$\dfrac{\pi}{6}$	$\dfrac{\sqrt{3}}{3}$
$\dfrac{\pi}{3}$	$\sqrt{3}$

   A. $0 < \theta < \dfrac{\pi}{4}$

   B. $\dfrac{\pi}{4} < \theta < \dfrac{\pi}{2}$

   C. $\dfrac{\pi}{2} < \theta < \dfrac{3\pi}{4}$

   D. $\dfrac{3\pi}{4} < \theta < \pi$

   E. $\pi < \theta < \dfrac{5\pi}{4}$

48. A jug containing 4 pints of milk was passed in turn to 4 boys. Each drank $\dfrac{1}{4}$ of the milk that was in the jug when he received it. How many pints of milk were left in the jug at the time it reached the last boy?

   F. $\dfrac{27}{64}$

   G. 1

   H. $1\dfrac{17}{64}$

   J. $1\dfrac{11}{16}$

   K. $2\dfrac{1}{4}$

49. Which is a point of intersection of the graphs of the following equations?
$$y = -x^2 + 5$$
$$y = -0.5x^2 + 3$$

   A. $(3, 5)$
   B. $(0, 5)$
   C. $(2, -1)$
   D. $(-2, 1)$
   E. $(0, 3)$

50. A high school club is trying to raise money for its annual trip to Washington by selling specialty T-shirts. The table below shows the profit it can make by selling the shirts at different prices.

x	Price of 1 T-shirt in dollars	0	5	10	15	20
P	Profit in dollars	−50	−7.5	30	62.5	90

Which of the following equations fits the data?

F. $P = 12.5x - 50$
G. $P = 2^x - 48$
H. $P = 2^x - 50$
J. $P = 0.1x^2 + 9x - 50$
K. $P = -0.1x^2 + 9x - 50$

51. A circle with center (2, 1) has a tangent to the circle at (3, 6). What is the equation of the tangent?

A. $y - 5x = -9$
B. $5y - x = 27$
C. $y + 5x = 21$
D. $x + 5y = 21$
E. $5y + x = 33$

52. The area of a rhombus is 20 square centimeters, and one diagonal is twice the length of the other. What is the length of a side of the rhombus?

F. 5
G. 10
H. $\sqrt{5}$
J. $\sqrt{10}$
K. $\sqrt{30}$

53. If $12 + 6n$ is 20 percent bigger than k, what is k?

A. $\dfrac{12 + 6n}{5}$
B. $10 + 5n$
C. $2 + n$
D. $\dfrac{6(12 + 6n)}{5}$
E. $20 + 10n$

54. Jeremy wants to put out snacks for unexpected guests, and he notices that he has 2 opened cans of mixed nuts. The capacity of the larger can is 3 times the capacity of the smaller can. Jeremy estimates that the smaller can is about $\dfrac{3}{4}$ full of nuts and the larger can is about half full. He pours all the nuts from the smaller can into the larger can. After he does this, about how full is the larger can?

F. $\dfrac{3}{4}$

G. $\dfrac{5}{6}$

H. $\dfrac{17}{18}$

J. Completely full
K. Overflowing

55. Which of the following is the graph of $y = \dfrac{2x^2 + x - 6}{x + 2}$?

A.

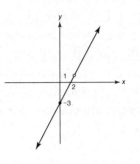

B.

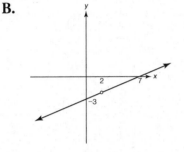

C.

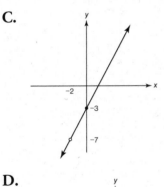

D.

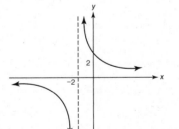

E.

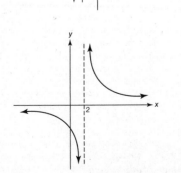

56. In $\triangle ABC$ shown below, interior triangles are formed by joining trisection points of two sides and repeating the process.

Thus, $AD = \dfrac{1}{3}AB$, $AE = \dfrac{1}{3}AC$, $AP = \dfrac{1}{3}AD$,

and $AQ = \dfrac{1}{3}AE$.

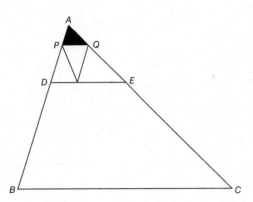

A point is picked at random in $\triangle ABC$. What is the probability that it lands in the shaded area?

F. $\dfrac{1}{243}$

G. $\dfrac{1}{81}$

H. $\dfrac{1}{27}$

J. $\dfrac{1}{9}$

K. $\dfrac{1}{3}$

57. $\triangle PQR$ is reflected across the y-axis in the standard (x, y) coordinate plane. Its image is $\triangle P'Q'R'$, where P reflects to P'. If the coordinates of point P are (a, b), what are the coordinates of P'?

A. (b, a)
B. $(-b, a)$
C. $(-a, -b)$
D. $(-a, b)$
E. $(a, -b)$

58. In the standard (x, y) coordinate plane shown below, A is the point $(0, 8)$, B is the point $(6, 0)$, and the circle is inscribed in $\triangle ABO$. Point P is on $\overline{AB}$ and is a point of tangency for the circle. If $AP = 6$, what is the equation of the circle?

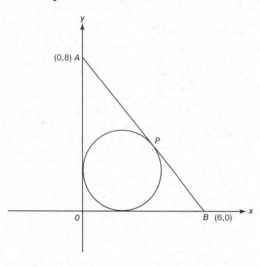

F. $(x - 2)^2 + (y - 2)^2 = 16$
G. $(x - 1)^2 + (y - 1)^2 = 4$
H. $(x - 2)^2 + (y - 2)^2 = 4$
J. $(x - 3)^2 + (y - 3)^2 = 4$
K. $(x - 3)^2 + (y - 3)^2 = 9$

59. The area of an equilateral triangle is given by the formula $A = \dfrac{s^2 \sqrt{3}}{4}$, where s is the length of a side. If an equilateral triangle has an area of $64\sqrt{3}$ square inches, what is the length, in inches, of a side of the triangle?

A. $2\sqrt{2}$

B. $4\sqrt{2}$

C. $16\sqrt{3}$

D. 4

E. 16

60. The center of the circle shown below is point O. Points A, B, C, and D are on the circle. $\angle BOC$, $\angle BOD$, and $\angle BOA$ are angles in standard position. They have measures of α, β, and θ, respectively, measured in the directions of the arrows shown. Both α and β are positive. The length of arc DC equals the length of arc AB. What is θ, the measure of $\angle BOA$, measured in the direction of the arrow shown?

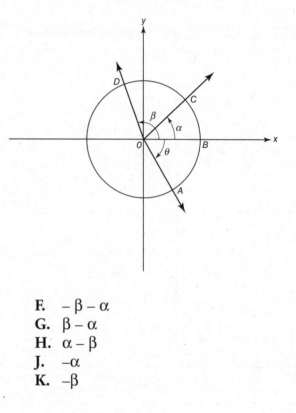

F. $-\beta - \alpha$
G. $\beta - \alpha$
H. $\alpha - \beta$
J. $-\alpha$
K. $-\beta$

Answer Key
PRACTICE MATHEMATICS TEST

Answer	Difficulty	Answer	Difficulty	Answer	Difficulty
1. (A)	E	21. (D)	M	41. (B)	H
2. (K)	E	22. (G)	M	42. (G)	M
3. (C)	E	23. (B)	M	43. (A)	M
4. (J)	E	24. (H)	M	44. (K)	M
5. (A)	E	25. (C)	H	45. (B)	M
6. (F)	E	26. (F)	M	46. (G)	M
7. (E)	M	27. (A)	H	47. (C)	H
8. (F)	E	28. (K)	M	48. (J)	H
9. (E)	E	29. (C)	M	49. (D)	M
10. (H)	M	30. (K)	H	50. (K)	H
11. (A)	E	31. (D)	M	51. (E)	M
12. (G)	E	32. (J)	M	52. (F)	H
13. (B)	E	33. (D)	M	53. (B)	H
14. (G)	E	34. (H)	H	54. (F)	H
15. (C)	M	35. (B)	H	55. (C)	H
16. (J)	M	36. (F)	M	56. (G)	H
17. (B)	M	37. (E)	M	57. (D)	M
18. (H)	M	38. (J)	M	58. (H)	H
19. (B)	M	39. (D)	M	59. (E)	M
20. (K)	M	40. (K)	M	60. (H)	H

(E = easy; M = medium; H = hard)

Math Answers and Explanations

1. **(A)** Don't forget to cube every factor in parentheses:

$$(2x)^3 = 2^3 x^3 = 8x^3$$
$$\therefore 3x \cdot (2x)^3 = (3x)(8x^3) = 24x^4$$

2. **(K)** Since $\triangle ABC$ is isosceles, its base angles are congruent. You can fill in the angles as shown:

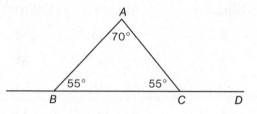

Remember, the sum of angles in a triangle is $180°$. The required angle, $\angle ACD$, is supplementary to $\angle ACB$ since they are adjacent angles on a line.

Therefore, the measure of $\angle ACD = 180° - 55° = 125°$

3. **(C)** The question is asking how many times $10.75 will go into $599. The answer will give you the number of hours needed:

$$\frac{599}{10.75} = 55.7 \ldots$$

This means that 55 hours will not be enough. Therefore, Dasom needs to work at least 56 hours.

4. **(J)**
Method 1: Plug in
Try all the answer choices and see which one works. Choice (J), 12, does.

$$2 + \sqrt{12 - 3} \overset{?}{=} 5$$

$$\Rightarrow 2 + \sqrt{9} \overset{?}{=} 5$$

$$\Rightarrow 2 + 3 \overset{?}{=} 5 \quad \text{Yes!}$$

Method 2: Solve
When you solve equations with radicals, start by getting all the radicals together on one side and the numbers on the other side.

$$2 + \sqrt{x - 3} = 5$$

$$\Rightarrow \sqrt{x - 3} = 3$$

$$\Rightarrow x - 3 = 9 \text{ (squaring both sides)}$$

$$\Rightarrow x = 12$$

5. **(A)** For $\angle\theta$ you are given the opposite side (10) and the adjacent side (7).

$$\tan\theta = \frac{\text{opposite}}{\text{adjacent}} = \frac{10}{7}$$

Note that you can eliminate choices (B), (D), and (E) immediately since $\sin\theta$, $\cos\theta$, and $\sec\theta$ all use the hypotenuse in their ratios. The only real choice is between $\tan\theta$ and $\cot\theta$. Eliminate $\cot\theta$, choice (C), because $\cot\theta = \dfrac{\text{adjacent}}{\text{opposite}} = \dfrac{7}{10}$.

6. **(F)** Get the line $2y - 6x = 3$ into slope-intercept form:

$$2y - 6x = 3 \Rightarrow 2y = 6x + 3$$

$$\Rightarrow y = 3x + \frac{3}{2}$$

The slope of the line is 3, the coefficient of x. Parallel lines have the same slope; therefore the slope of the required line is also 3.

7. **(E)** Since 1 cup of cereal weighs 26.4 grams, there are $\dfrac{510}{26.4}$ cups in the box.

$$\frac{510}{26.4} = 19.3181\ldots$$

You now want to find how many times $1\frac{1}{4}$ cups will go into $19.3181\ldots$ cups.

Use your calculator to find $\dfrac{19.3181\ldots}{1.25}$. The answer is $15.4545\ldots$, which means 15 full servings.

8. **(F)** Label the figure as shown, with intersection points P, Q, R, and S and with angles 1 and 2.

Notice that $m\angle 1 = x$ (vertical angles).

Similarly, $m\angle 2 = y$.

However, $PQRS$ is a parallelogram since its opposite sides are parallel.

$\therefore \angle 1 \cong \angle 2$ (opposite angles of parallelogram are congruent)

$\therefore x = y$

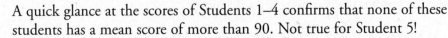

9. **(E)** The mean score $= \dfrac{\text{sum of scores}}{2}$.

A quick glance at the scores of Students 1–4 confirms that none of these students has a mean score of more than 90. Not true for Student 5!

Mean score for Student 5 $= \dfrac{90 + 92}{2} = 91$.

10. **(H)** To answer questions about median scores, you should list the scores in order. The median is the middle score.

Math Test 1: 60 85 $\boxed{90}$ 98 100

Math Test 2: 65 75 $\boxed{80}$ 92 95

All the scores: 60 65 75 80 $\boxed{85\ \ 90}$ 92 95 98 100

There are 10 scores altogether for both tests. Therefore, the median score is

the mean of the two middle scores: $\dfrac{85+90}{2} = 87.5$

The other choices are wrong:

Choice (F): The median score for Math Test 1 is 90.

Choice (G): The median score for Math Test 2 is 80.

Choice (J): Notice that 80, the median score for Math Test 2, is less than 90, the median score for Math Test 1.

Choice (K): The mean for Math Test 2 will be greater than 80 since 65 and 70 are at least 10 points less than 80, while 92 and 95 are at least 12 points greater than 80. Therefore the mean will be slightly more than 80. This is a quick, intuitive way to see the answer. Alternatively, you could of course just find the mean of the scores for Math Test 2:

$\dfrac{65+75+80+92+95}{5} \approx 81$

11. **(A)** If $\dfrac{1}{2}$ inch represents 40 feet, 1 inch represents 80 feet.

$\dfrac{80}{1} = \dfrac{60}{x} \Rightarrow x = \dfrac{60}{80} = \dfrac{3}{4}$

12. **(G)** The center of the circle is (3, –5).

The distance between (3, –5) and (–9, –5) is the length of the horizontal segment shown in the diagram.

Length = $|-9 - 3| = 12$

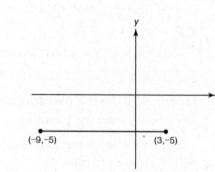

13. **(B)** Total length of movie = 3 hours = 180 mins.

Total minutes for commercials = 45 mins.

As a percent: $\dfrac{45}{180} \times \dfrac{100}{1} = 25\%$

14. **(G)** For the first marble, $P(\text{white}) = \dfrac{4}{7}$.

For the second marble, $P(\text{white}) = \dfrac{3}{6} = \dfrac{1}{2}$.

Both events must happen:

$P(\text{white, white}) = \dfrac{4}{7} \cdot \dfrac{1}{2} = \dfrac{2}{7}$

15. **(C)** Since the circumference of the big circle is 24π, you can find the diameter d:

$\pi d = 24\pi \Rightarrow d = 24$

Therefore each semicircle has diameter 6.

The required path is the circumference of two little circles with diameter 6.

$\therefore$ length of path $= (2)(6\pi) = 12\pi$

16. **(J)** Work backward from the answer choices, and see which one leaves John with $6. Choice (F), $60, leaves John with $12, double what you want. This suggests that choice (J), $30, may work. Try it next.

$\dfrac{1}{5}$ of $30 = $6, which leaves $24.

$\dfrac{1}{4}$ of $24 = $6, which leaves $18.

$\dfrac{1}{3}$ of $18 = $6, which leaves $12.

$\dfrac{1}{2}$ of $12 = $6, which leaves $6, which was required.

17. **(B)** Sum of roots $= -3$ means $-\dfrac{b}{a} = -3 \Rightarrow b = 3a$

Product of roots $= 4$ means $\dfrac{c}{a} = 4 \Rightarrow c = 4a$

Notice that these relationships are true only in choice (B), where $a = 1$, $b = 3$, and $c = 4$.

18. **(H)** A 2×3 matrix multiplied by a 3×2 matrix gives a 2×2 matrix as the result.

To get the first-row, first-column value of the answer, multiply the first row of the first matrix by the first column of the second matrix.

To get the first-row, second-column value of the answer, multiply the first row of the first matrix by the second column of the second matrix, and so on.

For the given matrices:

$$\begin{bmatrix} 1 & 6 & 3 \\ 5 & 0 & 4 \end{bmatrix} \begin{bmatrix} 2 & 1 \\ -3 & 4 \\ 1 & -2 \end{bmatrix}$$

$$= \begin{bmatrix} (1)(2)+(6)(-3)+(3)(1) & (1)(1)+(6)(4)+(3)(-2) \\ (5)(2)+(0)(-3)+(4)(1) & (5)(1)+(0)(4)+(4)(-2) \end{bmatrix}$$

$$= \begin{bmatrix} -13 & 19 \\ 14 & -3 \end{bmatrix}$$

19. **(B)** This is a quadratic inequality. Therefore, you should get it into standard form $ax^2 + bx + c > 0$, and then factor the left side to find the roots.

$x^2 - 2x > 15$
$\Rightarrow x^2 - 2x - 15 > 0$
$\Rightarrow (x - 5)(x + 3) > 0$

Roots are 5 and −3.

For $y = x^2 - 2x - 15$, y is positive outside of the roots.

Therefore, the solution is $x < -3$ or $x > 5$, the two separate regions represented in choice (B).

20. **(K)** Use the fact that distance = speed × time.

The particle will travel $(4 \times 10^{-3})(3 \times 10^5)$ feet.

$$\begin{aligned} (4 \times 10^{-3})(3 \times 10^5) &= (4 \times 3)(10^{-3} \times 10^5) \\ &= 12 \times 10^2 \text{ (add exponents)} \\ &= (1.2 \times 10^1) \times 10^2 \\ &= 1.2 \times 10^3 \end{aligned}$$

21. **(D)** Factor and cancel:

$$\frac{2x^2 - 6x - 20}{2x^2 - 50} = \frac{2(x^2 - 3x - 10)}{2(x^2 - 25)} = \frac{2(x-5)(x+2)}{2(x-5)(x+5)} = \frac{x+2}{x+5}$$

22. **(G)** The circle is inscribed,

$\therefore \overline{BDC}$ is tangent to the circle at D.

$\therefore \angle EDC$ is a right angle (tangent-radius theorem).

Also, $\angle B$ is a right angle (given).

Both triangles ABC and EDC contain $\angle C$.

$\therefore \triangle ABC$ is similar to $\triangle EDC$ (angle-angle similarity)

$$\therefore \frac{AB}{BC} = \frac{ED}{DC}$$

$$\therefore \frac{10}{9} = \frac{ED}{5}$$

$$\Rightarrow ED = \frac{50}{9} = 5\frac{5}{9}$$

23. **(B)** First write the inequalities in standard form: $y < mx + b$ or $y > mx + b$.

$x + y > 3$
$\Rightarrow y > -x + 3$

This region is above the line l.

$x - 2y > -1$
$\Rightarrow -2y > -x - 1$

$\Rightarrow y < \frac{1}{2}x + \frac{1}{2}$

This region is below the line k. The solution to the system of inequalities is in the overlapping regions for the two inequalities, namely region (B).

Notice that in writing the second inequality in standard form, the inequality sign switches when dividing both sides by a negative number.

24. **(H)** For the first 10 tons: $(10)(25)=\$250$.

For the next 15 tons: $(15)(20)=\$300$.

For the remaining 30 tons: $(30)(15)=\$450$.

Total = \$1,000.

25. **(C)** Refer to the diagram, with additional labels w and z.

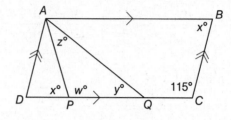

Conclusion I is valid. Since *ABCD* is a parallelogram,

$\angle B \cong \angle D$ (opposite angles congruent)

$\therefore \text{m} \angle D = x$

$\therefore \triangle ADP$ is isosceles (base angles congruent)

$\therefore AD = AP$

However, $AD = BC$ (opposite sides of parallelogram congruent)

$\therefore AP = BC$

Conclusion II is valid. $\angle APD$ and $\angle APQ$ are adjacent angles on a straight line.

$\therefore x = 180 - w$ degrees.

Also, since three angles of $\triangle APQ$ add up to 180°, $y = 180 - (z + w)$ degrees.

Since $z > 0$, $x > y$, Conclusion III is invalid. In $\triangle ADQ$, $\text{m} \angle D = x$.

$x + y = 180 - \text{m} \angle DAQ$ since 3 angles in a triangle add up to 180 degrees.

This statement shows that $x + y \neq 180$.

26. **(F)** For any angle α, the range of $\cos \alpha$ is $-1 \leq \cos \alpha \leq 1$.

When you multiply by 4, the inequality becomes $-4 \leq 4 \cos \alpha \leq 4$.

Notice that the size of α does not matter—whether it is 3θ, or 6θ, or 10θ. The minimum value of the expression is -4.

27. **(A)** You are given:

$2x + y = 16$

$x + 2z = 14$

$2y + z = 12$

The arithmetic mean of x, y, and z equals $\dfrac{x + y + z}{3}$. So a good place to start might be to add the three equations and see where that takes you.

Adding the left sides and setting that equal to the sum of the right sides leaves you with: $3x + 3y + 3z = 42$ Dividing by 3 gives you the sum of x, y, and z that you want: $x + y + z = 14$. Thus, the average of the three numbers is $\dfrac{14}{3}$.

28. **(K)** Suppose the figure is labeled as shown:

    $m\angle 1 = 2x$ since vertical angles are congruent.

    On line m, $3x + 2x + x = 180$.

    $\therefore x = 30$

    Since $l \| m$, using transversal k,

    $x = y$ since corresponding angles are congruent.

    $\therefore y = 30$

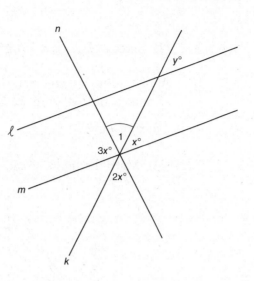

29. **(C)** Since 10% of 600 = 60, the discounted price for each machine is $540.

    6% commission for each machine sold means that commission on one machine is

    $(540)(0.06) = \$32.40$

    Thus, commission on 4 machines is

    $(32.40)(4) = 129.60$

    To the nearest dollar, commission = $130.

30. **(K)** Let $BC = x$. Then $AB = 3x$. You are given that $AB + BC + CD = 18$.

    $\therefore 3x + x + CD = 18$, which implies that $CD = 18 - 4x$.

    Notice that if $CD = 18$, $x = BC = 0$, which is not consistent with the information given in the problem. (The lengths must be positive.) Therefore, CD cannot be 18. All of the other values of CD allow corresponding values of BC and AB that satisfy the conditions of the problem:

    If $x = 1$, $CD = 14$, $BC = 1$, and $AB = 3$.
    If $x = 2$, $CD = 10$, $BC = 2$, and $AB = 6$.
    If $x = 3$, $CD = 6$, $BC = 3$, and $AB = 9$.
    If $x = 4$, $CD = 2$, $BC = 4$, and $AB = 12$.

31. **(D)** You need to eliminate the i in the denominator by multiplying the given fraction by $\frac{i}{i}$:

    $$\frac{i-1}{i} = \frac{i-1}{i} \cdot \frac{i}{i} = \frac{i^2 - i}{i^2} = \frac{-1-i}{-1} = 1 + i$$

32. **(J)** Since $\triangle BCD$ is a 45°-45°-90° special triangle, $BC = \dfrac{\sqrt{10}}{\sqrt{2}} = \sqrt{5}$.

Applying the Pythagorean theorem to $\triangle BQC$ gives $QC = 1$. From the symmetry of the figure, each side of $PQRS = 2 + 1 = 3$.

$\therefore$ area of $PQRS = 9$.

33. **(D)** Mark the figure as shown.

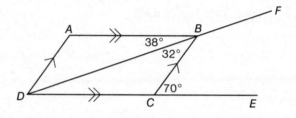

$m\angle ABC = 70°$ (alternate interior angles, $\overline{AB} \parallel \overline{DE}$ cut by $\overline{BC}$)
$\therefore m\angle ABD = 70° - 32° = 38°$

Notice that $\angle ABD$ and $\angle FBA$ are adjacent supplementary angles on line $\overrightarrow{DBF}$.

$\therefore m\angle FBA = 180° - 38° = 142°$

34. **(H)**

$$\frac{x - 3y}{9y} = \frac{60}{100} = \frac{3}{5}$$
$$\Rightarrow 5x - 15y = 27y$$
$$\Rightarrow 5x = 42y$$
$$\Rightarrow \frac{x}{y} = \frac{42}{5}$$

35. **(B)** 4 P.M. corresponds to $x = 9$ hours after 7 A.M. When x is 9, y is 4,100. A quick way to get this is on your graphing calculator. Graph the equation, and then use the **value** feature of the $\boxed{\text{CALC}}$ menu to find the value of y when $x = 9$.

36. **(F)** The price difference from 2000 to 2005 = 50¢ = actual decrease.

$$\therefore \% \text{ decrease} = \frac{\text{actual decrease}}{\text{price in 2000}} \times 100 = \frac{50}{400} \times 100 = 12.5\%$$

The above solution uses cents. Make sure that you use the same units for the numerator and denominator. The calculation using dollars would be:

$$\therefore \% \text{ decrease} = \frac{\text{actual decrease}}{\text{price in 2000}} \times 100 = \frac{0.5}{4} \times 100 = 12.5\%$$

37. **(E)** $f(x) = f(-x)$ for any function whose powers of x are all even. A quick glance at the answer choices shows that choice (E) is the only function with this feature. If you did not figure this out, you can get the answer by substituting simple numerical values into the functions given. For example, try $x = 1$. The function in choice (E) is the only one in which $f(1) = f(-1)$:

$$f(1) = -1 + 4 = 3$$
$$f(-1) = -(-1)^2 + 4 = -1 + 4 = 3$$

38. **(J)** Use the pick-a-number strategy. Pick a number that lies between 0 and 1, for example $\frac{1}{3}$. Comparing values is now very easy:

Choice (F): $a = \dfrac{1}{3}$

Choice (G): $\dfrac{1}{a} = 3$

Choice (H): $a^2 = \dfrac{1}{9}$

Choice (J): $\dfrac{1}{a^2} = 9$

Choice (K): $-a^2 = -\dfrac{1}{9}$

Of these, 9 is the biggest. Therefore, $\dfrac{1}{a^2}$ has the largest value.

39. **(D)** Here is what this question boils down to:

The ratio $\dfrac{\text{Jay's circle diameter}}{\text{Thomas's circle diameter}} = \dfrac{2}{1}$.

Find the ratio $\dfrac{\text{circumference of Jay's circle}}{\text{circumference of Thomas's circle}}$.

Jay   Thomas

Recall these facts: For two circles, if the ratio of their radii is $\dfrac{r_1}{r_2}$, then the ratio of their diameters is $\dfrac{r_1}{r_2}$, the ratio of their circumferences is $\dfrac{r_1}{r_2}$, and the ratio of their areas is $\left(\dfrac{r_1}{r_2}\right)^2$.

$\therefore \dfrac{C_1}{C_2} = \dfrac{r_1}{r_2} = \dfrac{2}{1}$. This means that the smaller wheel makes 2 revolutions for every revolution of the larger wheel.

40. **(K)** Total surface area = 2(area of circle) + lateral surface area.

    $$= 2\pi r^2 + 2\pi rh$$
    $$= 2\pi r(r + h)$$
    $$= 6\pi(3 + 8)$$
    $$= 66\pi$$

41. **(B)** Since $f(0) = 4$, the equation is $f(x) = mx + 4$, where m is the slope and 4 is the y-intercept.

    Since $f(-1) = q$, $q = -m + 4 \Rightarrow m = 4 - q$

    Since $f(2) = p$, $p = 2m + 4 = 2(4 - q) + 4$

    $\therefore p = 8 - 2q + 4$

    $\therefore p + 2q = 12$

42. **(G)**

    Method 1: Plug in

    You want to find the value of t such that $348 = 20\sqrt{t + 273}$ or, more simply, $17.4 = \sqrt{t + 273}$.

    You should be able to get the answer quickly by plugging in the answer choices and estimating which value of t gives the answer closest to 17.4.

    If $t = 3$, $\sqrt{276} \approx 16.56$ (too small)

    If $t = 30$, $\sqrt{303} \approx 17.4$ (looks good). Therefore t is 30.

    Notice that $t = 100$ gives an answer that is too high.

    Method 2: Solve the equation

    This is a problem where the given equation is easy enough for you and your calculator to find a quick solution!

    $348 = 20\sqrt{t + 273}$

    $\Rightarrow 17.4 = \sqrt{t + 273}$

    $\Rightarrow 302.76 = t + 273$ (squaring both sides)

    $\Rightarrow t = 29.76$

    $\Rightarrow t \approx 30$

43. **(A) Method 1:** Algebra

    The total area $= 80 + 40 = 120$.

    $(2x + 10)(2x + 8) = 120$
    $\Rightarrow 4x^2 + 36x + 80 = 120$
    $\Rightarrow 4x^2 + 36x - 40 = 0$
    $\Rightarrow x^2 + 9x - 10 = 0$
    $\Rightarrow (x + 10)(x - 1) = 0$
    $\Rightarrow x = 1$ (Reject the negative value -10)

Method 2: Plug in

If $x = 1$, total length $= 10 + 2$ and total width $= 8 + 2$.

$\therefore$ area $= (12)(10) = 120$, which is consistent with what is given.
Thus, $x = 1$ is the answer.

44. **(K)**

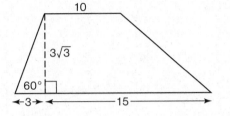

The area of a trapezoid $= \dfrac{1}{2}h(b_1 + b_2)$ where h is height and b_1 and b_2 are

the bases. You need to find the value of the altitude. Notice that it is in a special 30°-60°-90° triangle. In the triangle, the side adjacent to 60° is 3; and the altitude, which is opposite the 60° angle, is $3\sqrt{3}$.

Area $= \dfrac{1}{2}(3\sqrt{3})(10 + 18) = 42\sqrt{3}$

45. **(B)**
Method 1: Solve algebraically

$9^{2x + 1} = 3^{x - 4}$
$\Rightarrow 3^{2(2x + 1)} = 3^{x - 4}$
$\Rightarrow 3^{4x + 2} = 3^{x - 4}$
$\Rightarrow 4x + 2 = x - 4$
$\Rightarrow 3x = -6$
$x = -2$

Method 2: Plug in
You may want to try plugging in the fairly easy numbers, 0 and −2. First try 0:

$9^{2(0) + 1} \overset{?}{=} 3^{0 - 4}$
$\Rightarrow 9^{1} \overset{?}{=} 3^{-4}$ No!

Now try −2:

$9^{2(-2) + 1} \overset{?}{=} 3^{-2 - 4}$
$\Rightarrow 9^{-3} \overset{?}{=} 3^{-6}$
$\Rightarrow (3^2)^{-3} \overset{?}{=} 3^{-6}$ Yes!

46. **(G)** The volume of a pyramid $= \dfrac{1}{3}$ (area of base)(height).

$\therefore V = \dfrac{1}{3}Bh$

If the altitude is $4h$, the volume $= \dfrac{1}{3}B(4h) = 4(\dfrac{1}{3}Bh) = 4V$.

47. **(C)**

Method 1: Logical reasoning

Because the value of tan θ is negative, θ cannot be in either Quadrant I or III. Therefore, you should eliminate choices (A), (B), and (E). The only possibilities are choices (C) and (D), both of which place θ in Quadrant II. Will the picture of θ in standard position look like Figure 1, choice (C), or Figure 2, choice (D)?

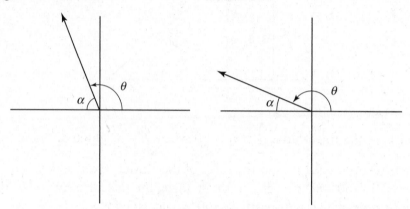

Since $y = \tan x$ is an increasing function, $\tan \frac{\pi}{3} > \tan \frac{\pi}{6}$. (You can also see this from the given table.) Therefore, you will get a bigger answer numerically if α, the reference angle, is closer to $\frac{\pi}{2}$, as in Figure 1, than to 0, as in Figure 2. This suggests choice (C), where θ is between $\frac{\pi}{2}$ (90°) and $\frac{3\pi}{4}$ (135°).

Method 2: Graphing calculator.

Use the inverse tan function, $\tan^{-1}$, to find an angle whose tan is 2.747. The calculator will give you a reference angle close to 70°. This tells you that the angle, θ, is approximately 110° and lies between $\frac{\pi}{2}$ (90°) and $\frac{3\pi}{4}$ (135°).

48. **(J)** The amount of milk left at each stage is $\frac{3}{4}$ of the previous amount.

The numbers representing how much milk is left are shown in the following sequence:

after boy 1, after boy 2, after boy 3, . . .

$$4\left(\frac{3}{4}\right), \qquad 4\left(\frac{3}{4}\right)^2, \qquad 4\left(\frac{3}{4}\right)^3, \qquad \cdots$$

The amount left after boy 3 is what is required.

$$4\left(\frac{3}{4}\right)^3 = \frac{3^3}{4^2} = \frac{27}{16} = 1\frac{11}{16} \text{ pints left}$$

49. **(D)** Use the plug-in technique. Remember, the ordered pair that works must satisfy *both* equations. Choices (A), (B), (C), and (E) are very easy to eliminate:

Choice (A): Plug (3, 5) into the first equation—it does not work.
Choice (B): (0, 5) does not work in the second equation.
Choice (C): (2, –1) does not work in the first equation.
Choice (E): (0, 3) does not work in the first equation.
Choice (D), however, works in both:

$$1 = -(-2)^2 + 5$$
$$1 = -\frac{1}{2}(-2)^2 + 3$$

50. **(K)** All of the ordered pairs must satisfy the equation that is the correct answer. If you can find just one ordered pair that does not work for a given equation, then you can eliminate that choice. Using a process of elimination is your best strategy here. Notice that when $x = 0$, $P = -50$. This ordered pair does not work for either choices (G) or (H), so eliminate them.

Choice (G):
$-50 \overset{?}{=} 2^0 - 48$
$\Rightarrow -50 \overset{?}{=} 1 - 48$ No!

Choice (H):
$-50 \overset{?}{=} 2^0 - 50$
$\Rightarrow -50 \overset{?}{=} 1 - 50$ No!

The choice is between (F), (J), and (K).

Try the ordered pair (10, 30) since 10 is an easy number to substitute.

Choice (F):
$30 \overset{?}{=} 12.5(10) - 50$
$\Rightarrow 30 \overset{?}{=} 125 - 50$ No!

Eliminate choice (F).

Choice (J):
$30 \overset{?}{=} 0.1(10)^2 + 9(10) - 50$
$\Rightarrow 30 \overset{?}{=} 10 + 90 - 50$ No!

Eliminate choice (J).

By process of elimination, choice (K) is the answer. Notice that (10, 30) does satisfy the equation in choice (K):

Choice (K):
$30 \overset{?}{=} 0 - 1(10)^2 + 9(10) - 50$
$\Rightarrow 30 \overset{?}{=} -10 + 90 - 50$ Yes!

All of the ordered pairs should work in choice (K). On the ACT test, you should not waste your time checking!

51. **(E)**

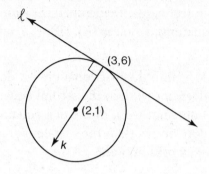

Let lines l and k be as marked.

Notice that $l \perp k$, since l is tangent at (3, 6) (tangent-radius theorem).

Slope of $k = \dfrac{6-1}{3-2} = 5$.

Since $l \perp k$, slope of $l = -\dfrac{1}{5}$ (negative reciprocal of 5).

The problem now boils down to finding the equation of a line with slope $-\dfrac{1}{5}$ and containing point (3, 6). Here is the point-slope form of the equation:

$$y - 6 = -\frac{1}{5}(x - 3)$$

$$\Rightarrow 5y - 30 = -x + 3$$
$$\Rightarrow 5y + x = 33$$

52. **(F)** Suppose the diagonals are d and $2d$. Recall that the area of a rhombus is half the product of the diagonals.

$$\therefore \text{area} = \frac{1}{2}(d)(2d) = 20$$

$$\Rightarrow d^2 = 20$$
$$\Rightarrow d = \sqrt{20}$$

You are required to find a side of the rhombus. Label a side $\overline{AB}$, as shown. Since the diagonals of a rhombus intersect at right angles, use the Pythagorean theorem in $\triangle AOB$.

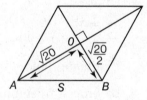

$$s^2 = (\sqrt{20})^2 + \left(\frac{\sqrt{20}}{2}\right)^2$$

$$= 20 + 5$$
$$= 25$$
$$\therefore s = 5$$

53. **(B)** $12 + 6n$ is 20% bigger than k

$$\Rightarrow 12 + 6n = \left(k + \frac{1}{5}k\right) = \frac{6}{5}k.$$

$$\Rightarrow k = \frac{5(12 + 6n)}{6}$$

$$= 10 + 5n$$

54. **(F)** Let x be the capacity of the larger can.

Then $\frac{x}{3}$ is the capacity of the smaller can.

Before pouring, the smaller can is $\frac{3}{4}$ full $\Rightarrow \left(\frac{3}{4}\right)\left(\frac{x}{3}\right) = \frac{x}{4}$ is $\frac{1}{4}$ the capacity

of the larger can.

(This means that the nuts currently in the smaller can would take up $\frac{1}{4}$ of the capacity of the larger can.)

The larger can is $\frac{1}{2}$ full.

After pouring, the total used capacity of the larger can equals $\frac{x}{2} + \frac{x}{4} = \frac{3}{4}x$

Therefore, the larger can is now $\frac{3}{4}$ full.

55. **(C)** First simplify $y = \frac{2x^2 + x - 6}{x + 2}$.

Then, remember that the graph is undefined at $x = -2$.

$$y = \frac{2x^2 + x - 6}{x + 2}$$

$$= \frac{(2x - 3)(x + 2)}{(x + 2)}$$

$$\Rightarrow y = 2x - 3$$

This is a straight line with slope 2, y-intercept -3, and a "hole" at the point where $x = -2$, namely $(-2, -7)$. The only graph with these features is choice (C).

56. **(G)** Since D and E are both trisection points, $\overline{DE} \parallel \overline{BC}$. Similarly, $\overline{PQ} \parallel \overline{DE}$.

$\therefore \triangle APQ$ is similar to $\triangle ABC$.

$$\frac{AP}{AB} = \frac{1}{9}$$

Recall that for two similar triangles, if the ratio of sides is $\frac{1}{k}$, then the ratio of areas is $\frac{1}{k^2}$.

$$\therefore \frac{\text{area of } \triangle APQ}{\text{area of } \triangle ABC} = \frac{1}{81} = \text{the probability that a point lands in the shaded area.}$$

57. **(D)** Make a sketch with actual numbers as coordinates.

From this, you can see that (3, 1) reflects to (–3, 1). In general, when a point is reflected across the *y*-axis, the image keeps the same *y*-coordinate but the *x*-coordinate changes sign.

58. **(H)** Fill in what you can on the diagram:

Label the radius *r*, and points *Q*, *R*, and *S* as shown.

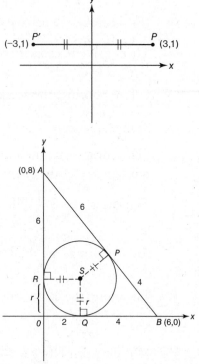

Using the Pythagorean theorem in $\triangle AOB$ gives $AB = 10$.

$\therefore PB = 10 - 6 = 4$

$\therefore QB = PB = 4$ (equal tangent segments to circle from same outside point)

$\therefore OQ = 6 - QB = 6 - 4 = r = 2$

Since $\overline{SR} \perp \overline{AO}$ (tangent-radius theorem), $SR = SQ$.

Since $ORSQ$ is a square, $SR = SQ = OQ = OR = r = 2$.

Therefore, the radius of the circle is 2 and the center is (2, 2).

The equation of the circle is $(x - 2)^2 + (y - 2)^2 = 2^2 = 4$

59. **(E)**

$$A = \frac{s^2\sqrt{3}}{4}$$

$$\therefore 64\sqrt{3} = \frac{s^2\sqrt{3}}{4}$$

$$\Rightarrow s^2 = \frac{(4)64\sqrt{3}}{\sqrt{3}}$$

$$\Rightarrow s^2 = (4)(64)$$
$$\Rightarrow s = (2)(8) = 16$$

60. **(H)** Since arc length DC = arc length AB, $m\angle COD = m\angle BOA$.

From the picture, note that $m\angle COD = \beta - \alpha$.

$\therefore m\angle BOA = -(\beta - \alpha) = \alpha - \beta$

Note: θ is negative because it is measured clockwise.

Answer Sheet

PRACTICE SCIENCE TEST

1 Ⓐ Ⓑ Ⓒ Ⓓ   11 Ⓐ Ⓑ Ⓒ Ⓓ   21 Ⓐ Ⓑ Ⓒ Ⓓ   31 Ⓐ Ⓑ Ⓒ Ⓓ

2 Ⓕ Ⓖ Ⓗ Ⓙ   12 Ⓕ Ⓖ Ⓗ Ⓙ   22 Ⓕ Ⓖ Ⓗ Ⓙ   32 Ⓕ Ⓖ Ⓗ Ⓙ

3 Ⓐ Ⓑ Ⓒ Ⓓ   13 Ⓐ Ⓑ Ⓒ Ⓓ   23 Ⓐ Ⓑ Ⓒ Ⓓ   33 Ⓐ Ⓑ Ⓒ Ⓓ

4 Ⓕ Ⓖ Ⓗ Ⓙ   14 Ⓕ Ⓖ Ⓗ Ⓙ   24 Ⓕ Ⓖ Ⓗ Ⓙ   34 Ⓕ Ⓖ Ⓗ Ⓙ

5 Ⓐ Ⓑ Ⓒ Ⓓ   15 Ⓐ Ⓑ Ⓒ Ⓓ   25 Ⓐ Ⓑ Ⓒ Ⓓ   35 Ⓐ Ⓑ Ⓒ Ⓓ

6 Ⓕ Ⓖ Ⓗ Ⓙ   16 Ⓕ Ⓖ Ⓗ Ⓙ   26 Ⓕ Ⓖ Ⓗ Ⓙ   36 Ⓕ Ⓖ Ⓗ Ⓙ

7 Ⓐ Ⓑ Ⓒ Ⓓ   17 Ⓐ Ⓑ Ⓒ Ⓓ   27 Ⓐ Ⓑ Ⓒ Ⓓ   37 Ⓐ Ⓑ Ⓒ Ⓓ

8 Ⓕ Ⓖ Ⓗ Ⓙ   18 Ⓕ Ⓖ Ⓗ Ⓙ   28 Ⓕ Ⓖ Ⓗ Ⓙ   38 Ⓕ Ⓖ Ⓗ Ⓙ

9 Ⓐ Ⓑ Ⓒ Ⓓ   19 Ⓐ Ⓑ Ⓒ Ⓓ   29 Ⓐ Ⓑ Ⓒ Ⓓ   39 Ⓐ Ⓑ Ⓒ Ⓓ

10 Ⓕ Ⓖ Ⓗ Ⓙ   20 Ⓕ Ⓖ Ⓗ Ⓙ   30 Ⓕ Ⓖ Ⓗ Ⓙ   40 Ⓕ Ⓖ Ⓗ Ⓙ

Practice Science Test

35 MINUTES—40 QUESTIONS

Directions
1. There are seven passages in the science test.
2. Each passage is followed by 5–7 questions.
3. Choose the best answer to each question, and fill in the corresponding oval on your answer sheet.
4. During the test, you may refer to any passage on the test as often as you need to.
5. You may not use a calculator on this test.

PASSAGE I

The *solubility* of a substance is a measure of how much of the substance (solute) will dissolve in a liquid (solvent). A solution is a homogeneous mixture of substances in the same physical state. If a substance has low solubility in water, it is likely to precipitate from the aqueous solution. If it has high solubility in water, no precipitate will form.

Table 1 below shows the maximum solubility of five different solids, in grams per 100 milliliters of water (g/100 mL), observed at different temperatures. The solids are sodium chloride (NaCl), cerium sulfate ($Ce_2(SO_4)_3$), potassium chloride (KCl), potassium chlorate ($KClO_3$), and mercuric chloride ($HgCl_2$).

Table 1
Maximum Solubility (g/100 mL)

Temperature (°C)	NaCl	$Ce_2(SO_4)_3$	KCl	$KClO_3$	$HgCl_2$
10	34	10	27	5	6
20	34	8	30	6	7
30	35	5	32	8	8
40	36	4	34	10	9
50	36	3	38	17	12
60	37	2	40	21	16
70	38	2	44	28	20
80	38	2	48	33	24
90	38	1	52	43	31

It is also possible for gases to dissolve in liquids. Graph 1 shows solubility curves for four gases dissolved in water—carbon dioxide (CO_2), xenon (Xe), nitrogen (N_2), and oxygen (O_2).

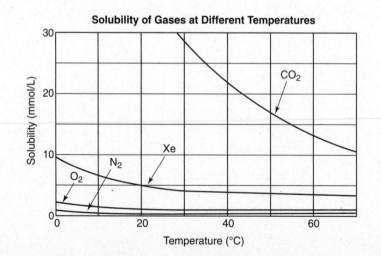

Solubility of Gases at Different Temperatures

An experiment at a lake on the west coast of the United States investi-gated amounts of dissolved oxygen (O_2) in milligrams per liter (mg L^{-1}) and amounts of sulfide (HS^-) and ammonia (NH_3) in millimoles per liter (mmol L^{-1}) at different depths. Temperature was also recorded at differ-ent depths. Graph 2 below shows the results.

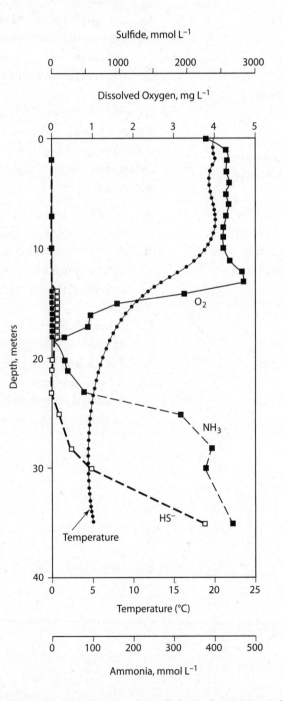

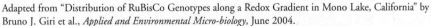

Adapted from "Distribution of RuBisCo Genotypes along a Redox Gradient in Mono Lake, California" by Bruno J. Giri et al., *Applied and Environmental Micro-biology*, June 2004.

1. Based on the information in the passage, as temperature increases:

   A. the solubility of gases increases.
   B. the solubility of gases decreases.
   C. the solubility of solids increases.
   D. the solubility of solids decreases.

2. According to the data in Table 1, what would happen if 38 grams of sodium chloride were added to 50 milliliters of water at 90°C?

   F. It would all dissolve.
   G. Approximately half of it would dissolve.
   H. Approximately one-fourth of it would dissolve.
   J. None of it would dissolve.

3. Which graph best represents the relationship between the temperature of water and the solubility of sodium chloride?

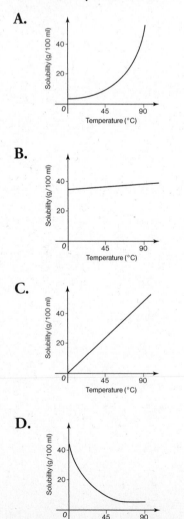

   A.

   B.

   C.

   D.

4. Based on the information in Graph 2, one can conclude that as the depth of the lake increases:

   F. the quantity of dissolved oxygen decreases.
   G. the quantity of sulfide decreases.
   H. the quantity of ammonia stays constant.
   J. the temperature increases.

5. Aquatic life depends on dissolved oxygen for its survival. Suppose a power station discharges purified hot water into a lake. What effect is this likely to have on aquatic life in the lake?

   A. No effect since the water is pure and the lake will cool the water
   B. A harmful effect because there will be an overabundance of dissolved oxygen, upsetting the balance of aquatic organisms
   C. A harmful effect because the amount of dissolved oxygen will be decreased due to higher temperatures
   D. A helpful effect since the amount of dissolved oxygen will be increased due to higher temperatures

PASSAGE II*

Scientists at an experimental poultry farm carried out three experiments. Two evaluated the feasibility of producing live termites and fly larvae locally. A third tested the use of termites and fly larvae as protein supplements for chickens raised on the farm.

Experiment 1: Production of Termites

Method 1
Shallow holes surrounding termite mounds and under shady trees were filled with bundles of bagasse (residue of processed plants) and dry wood of silk cotton trees. These were covered with jute sacks and sprinkled with water to keep the holes dark and humid. The termites were harvested after 3 weeks.

Method 2
Cartons were filled with bagasse and wood from silk cotton trees. Termite nests containing whole families were collected from different sites and placed into the cartons. Each carton was tightly closed to keep the inside dark and humid. Termites were harvested after 3 to 4 weeks.

Experiment 2: Production of Fly Larvae

Method 1
Small holes were dug and filled with damp rice straw and fresh cow manure in alternating 15-centimeter-thick layers. These were covered with thin layers of rice gruel. About 1 kilogram of spoiled fish was added. To maintain high humidity, 2 to 3 liters of water were poured over the holes when the eggs had been laid. Growing larvae were harvested 5 days after the first observation of larvae.

Method 2
Open rectangular wooden boxes were placed under trees. The boxes were lined with rice straw and then filled with fresh pig manure; 3 to 4 liters of wastewater from a fish shop were sprinkled over the boxes. Fly larvae were harvested 5 days after the first observation of larvae.

Table 1 on the next page shows the yield, in grams per hole or box (g/setup), for termite and fly larvae production.

*Data based on "Production and evaluation of Black Soldier fly larvae and termites as protein supplements for chickens," by Bui Xuan Men, et al. 2005.

Table 1

	Termite Yield (g/setup)	Fly Larvae Yield (g/setup)
Method 1	97	negligible
Method 2	133	210

Experiment 3: Termites and Fly Larvae as Protein in Chicken Feed

Sixty 10-day-old chicks were brooded in wire cages under the same conditions of temperature, humidity, lighting, feeding times, and feeding containers. During the brooding stage, before the 10th day, all chicks were fed commercial crumbs, as much food as they wanted.

When they were 10 days old, the chicks were randomly assigned to one of three groups. Each group was then fed one of three diets:

- The control group was fed a commercial diet consisting of approximately 51.6% maize meal, 13% rice bran, 21.3% roasted soybean, 14.2% fish meal, and 0.25% vitamin-mineral premix.
- The "termite" group was fed freshly harvested termites twice daily, in the morning and afternoon. Additionally, they were offered maize meal at all times of day.
- The "fly larvae" group was fed freshly harvested fly larvae that had been cleaned, drained, and weighed before feeding, also in the morning and afternoon. This group, too, was offered maize meal at all times of day.

All of the feeds were analyzed for their nutrient composition as a percentage of the dry matter (DM) they contained. Table 2 shows the chemical composition of the feed ingredients used in the experiment, including crude protein (CP), ether extract (EE), nitrogen-free extract (NFE), crude fiber (CF), and ash. The metabolizable energy (ME) was calculated based on a chemical analysis and is given in megajoules per kilogram (MJ/kg).

Table 2
Chemical Composition of Feed Ingredients

	% of DM						
	DM, %	CP	EE	NFE	CF	Ash	ME (MJ/kg)
Maize meal	85.9	8.2	4.5	82.7	2.4	1.9	16.0
Rice bran	90.0	13.5	12.7	58.5	7.6	7.7	12.6
Soy bean	91.0	43.1	15.4	32.6	4.1	4.8	16.3
Fish meal	81.3	29.7	4.4	18.1	6.0	41.7	8.5
Fresh termites	21.0	70.1	7.0	1.2	13.5	8.3	14.1
Fresh larvae	26.5	59.0	23.0	2.6	8.7	6.6	17.5

Table 3 below shows the daily intakes, in grams (g), of maize, termites or larvae, dry matter (DM), and crude protein (CP). Metabolizable energy (ME) is shown in megajoules (MJ).

Table 3
Daily Intakes of Ingredients by Chicks

	Control Group	Termite Group	Fly Larvae Group
Maize intake (g)	28.7	26.0	26.2
Termite or larvae intake (g)	0	1.9	2.1
Total DM intake (g)	28.7	27.9	28.3
ME intake (MJ)	0.42	0.44	0.46
CP intake (g)	5.6	3.5	3.4
CP/ME (g/MJ)	13.3	8.0	7.4

Table 4 shows the weight gain data of chicks under the three treatments.

Table 4
Daily Weight Gain and Feed Conversion Ratios of Chicks

	Control Group	Termite Group	Fly Larvae Group
Average daily weight gain (g)	9.1	9.0	10.9
Feed conversion ratio (kg feed/kg gain)	3.2	3.1	2.6
Crude protein per kg gain (g)	615	388	312
Metabolizable energy per kg gain (MJ/kg)	46.1	48.9	42.2

6. Based on the information in the passage, which of the following was necessary to produce fly larvae successfully?

   F. Pig manure
   G. Cattle manure
   H. Bagasse
   J. Silk cotton tree wood

7. According to the information in the passage, which of the following statements is true about termite or fly larvae production?

   A. Spoiled fish is an essential ingredient in the production of fly larvae.
   B. Cattle manure alternating with layers of spoiled fish is an effective method of fly larvae production.
   C. It was not possible to harvest termites if the colonies were not housed in cartons.
   D. Placing termites into cartons was a more effective method of termite production than cultivating termites in holes in the ground.

8. Scientists speculated as to why Method 2 yielded more termites than Method 1. Which of the following is a plausible explanation?

   F. The bagasse and silk cotton tree wood rotted in the holes but were preserved in the cartons.
   G. Termite reproduction was lowered by sunlight. The interiors of the cartons were dark.
   H. The termites in the holes were exposed to attack by other insects, like ants and small centipedes. Those in the cartons were protected from other insects.
   J. Termites in the holes, exposed to rain, sun, and wind, were less likely to reproduce than those in the cartons, which were protected from the elements.

9. When researchers analyzed the dry matter in the feed of the chicks, what did they find?

   A. The amount of ash in the termite and larvae dry matter was lower than that in the fish meal.
   B. The crude protein content of the dry matter of soybean meal and fish meal was higher than that of the termite and fly larvae dry matter.
   C. The metabolizable energy content of the larvae was lower than that of soybean meal.
   D. The fiber content of fresh termites and larvae was comparable to that in the maize, soybean, and fish meal.

10. Which of the following is *not* borne out by the data in the passage? The consumption of metabolizable energy was:

   F. dependent on the quantities of maize meal consumed by the chicks in the three groups.

   G. independent of the crude protein consumption of the three groups of chicks.

   H. independent of the concentration of metabolizable energy of the feed of the three groups of chicks.

   J. relatively constant for the three groups of chicks.

11. Let the three groups of chicks be represented as follows:

Control Group: CG
Termite Group: TG
Fly Larvae Group: FLG

Which of the following statements is best supported by the information provided in Tables 3 and 4?

   A. The rates of weight gain were comparable for the CG, TG, and FLG diets.

   B. Crude protein intake per kilogram of weight gain for FLG was lower than that of CG, but daily weight gains for FLG were higher.

   C. The dry matter feed conversion ratio was best for the CG diet.

   D. The chicks in FLG consumed more metabolizable energy per kilogram of weight gain than those in the other two groups.

PASSAGE III

Mumps is a contagious viral infection spread by direct contact with respiratory droplets from infected persons. Figure 1 shows the course of mumps from the time of exposure through 28 days. The common symptoms of the disease are indicated on the figure, as is the period that the person with mumps is infectious. The lighter color of a "symptom bar" represents a lessening of the severity of that symptom.

During the course of the disease, the infected person develops antibodies that lead to future immunity from mumps. Figure 1 also indicates the antibody level.

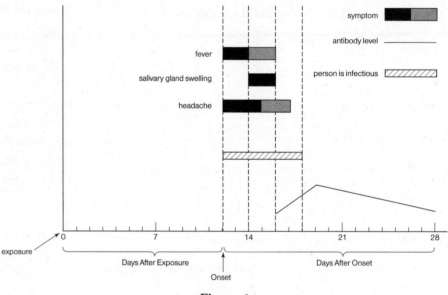

Figure 1

During 2005, 47 cases of mumps were reported in California, of which 21% were reported in Los Angeles County. Figure 2 below shows the cases in 2005 in Los Angeles County as well as the previous 5-year average for Los Angeles County.

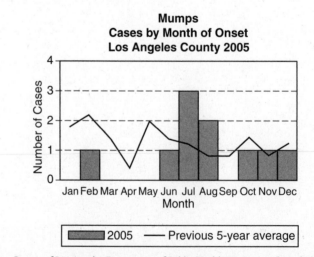

Taken from County of Los Angeles Department of Public Health 2005 Annual Morbidity Report.

Figure 2

12. On day 11 after exposure to mumps, a person could be expected to have which symptoms? ·

    F. Fever and headache only

    G. Fever and salivary gland swelling only

    H. Fever, headache, and salivary gland swelling

    J. No symptoms

13. A person with mumps is infectious:

    A. from days 1 through 12 after exposure.

    B. from days 1 through 18 after exposure.

    C. from days 12 through 18 after exposure.

    D. from days 16 through 28 after exposure.

14. Based on Figure 2, you could assert which of the following about mumps cases reported in Los Angeles County?

    F. From 2000–2004, there were no cases of mumps with onset in April.

    G. During 2005, there were no cases of mumps with onset in April.

    H. The number of cases of mumps with onset in July 2005 was greater than the national average for July.

    J. The number of cases reported with onset in November 2005 equaled the average number of cases reported in November for the years 2000–2004.

15. Based on the information in the passage, what was the number of cases of mumps reported in Los Angeles County in 2005?

    A. 3

    B. 9

    C. 10

    D. 47

16. Based on Figure 1, when can one conclude that antibody levels first start to rise?

    F. When the person's fever disappears

    G. When the person no longer has a headache

    H. When the person is no longer infectious

    J. When the person first has symptoms of illness

Practice Science Test

PASSAGE IV

Nuclei of atoms consist of protons and neutrons. Most naturally occurring nuclei are stable. The stability of a given nucleus is determined by its ratio of neutrons to protons, the *N/P* ratio. Graph 1 is a plot of all stable nuclei. Each dot on the graph represents a stable nucleus with the given values of *N* and *P*, from which the *N/P* ratio can be deduced.

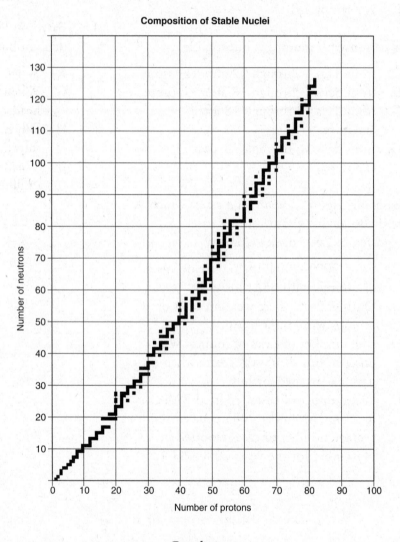

Composition of Stable Nuclei

Graph 1

Radioactive decay is a process whereby an unstable nucleus spontaneously breaks down to become more stable. When an unstable nucleus decays, it emits radiation in the form of alpha particles, beta particles, or gamma radiation. Alpha and beta decay are described on the following page.

Alpha Decay

An alpha particle is a helium nucleus, composed of two protons and two neutrons, and is represented as $_2^4\text{He}$. In this notation, the upper number, 4, is the *mass number* of the nucleus, namely the sum of the numbers of neutrons and protons. The lower number, 2, is the *atomic number*, or the number of protons. The following nuclear reaction is an example of alpha decay:

$$_{92}^{238}\text{U} \rightarrow {}_{90}^{234}\text{Th} + {}_2^4\text{He}$$

The uranium-238 nucleus (parent nucleus) breaks down to produce a thorium-234 nucleus (daughter nucleus) and a helium-4 nucleus (alpha particle). Whenever alpha decay occurs, the atomic number of the daughter nucleus is 2 less than its parent's and the mass number is decreased by 4.

In all nuclear reactions, the total number of particles stays the same. Therefore, the sum of superscripts on the right side of the equation must equal the sum of superscripts on the left side. Electric charge is also conserved. Since protons carry one unit of charge, the sum of subscripts on the right side of the equation must equal the sum of subscripts on the left side.

Beta Decay

A beta particle is an electron, denoted β^-. A *positron* is identical to an electron except that it has a positive charge. A positron is denoted β^+. In β^- decay, the reaction produces an electron. Here is an example:

$$_{82}^{214}\text{Pb} \rightarrow {}_{83}^{214}\text{Bi} + {}_{-1}^{0}\text{e}$$

The atomic number of the daughter is increased by 1, while the mass number remains unchanged. Note that the electron produced, $_{-1}^{0}\text{e}$, can also be represented as β^-.

In β^+ decay, the reaction produces a positron. Here is an example:

$$_{10}^{19}\text{N} \rightarrow {}_{9}^{19}\text{F} + {}_{+1}^{0}\text{e}$$

Notice that in positron decay, the atomic number of the daughter nucleus is decreased by 1, while its mass number remains unchanged. The positron produced, $_{+1}^{0}\text{e}$, can also be denoted β^+.

An unstable nucleus that decays may produce an unstable daughter nucleus, which will also eventually decay, and so on. The sequence of related nuclei is called a radioactive decay series. An example is shown in Graph 2, where the parent nucleus is uranium-235, $_{92}^{235}\text{U}$, and the final, stable nucleus of the series is lead-207, $_{82}^{207}\text{Pb}$. The graph shows that several intermediate nuclei in the series can decay in two ways, by either alpha decay or beta decay.

Practice Science Test

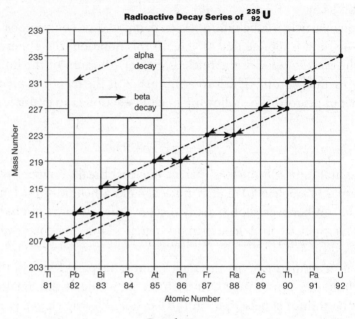

Graph 2

A radioactive isotope is one with an unstable nucleus. The time required for half of any given quantity to decay is known as the isotope's *half-life*. Thus, if the half-life of an isotope is 1,000 years, a 20-gram sample will decay to 10 grams of isotope after 1,000 years. After another 1,000 years, 5 grams will be left, and so on.

The decay rate, or number of decays per second, of a radioactive substance is called its *activity*. The activity of a particular sample is also reduced by half in one half-life. For example, if the activity of a certain sample with a half-life of 6 days is 8×10^4 decays per second, then 6 days later its activity will be 4×10^4 decays per second. After 6 more days, its activity will be 2×10^4 decays per second.

Graph 3 shows the activity of an unstable isotope (in counts per minute) versus time (in minutes).

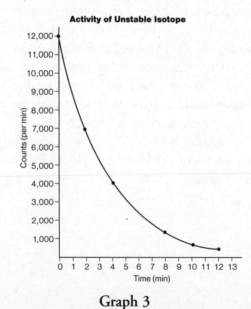

Graph 3

17. Based on Graph 1, what could one conclude?

    A. Any nucleus with an equal number of neutrons and protons is unstable.

    B. There are no stable isotopes with atomic numbers greater than about 83.

    C. A nucleus in which the number of neutrons equals twice the number of protons tends to be stable.

    D. An isotope of some element X, $^{70}_{30}$X, is unstable.

18. A nuclear scientist plans to study the decay series of different unstable nuclei. Which of the following would not be a good candidate for study?

    F. $^{152}_{58}$Ce

    G. $^{210}_{84}$Po

    H. $^{235}_{92}$U

    J. $^{55}_{25}$Mn

19. Which conclusion is consistent with Graph 2? The formation of $^{207}_{82}$Pb from $^{235}_{92}$U:

    A. is possible with a series of alpha decay reactions only.

    B. requires a minimum of 12 separate nuclear reactions.

    C. must include the isotope $^{219}_{86}$Rn as an intermediate daughter.

    D. must include a minimum of four beta decay nuclear reactions.

20. What is the half-life of the isotope represented by Graph 3?

    F. 2.5 minutes

    G. 5.0 minutes

    H. 6.5 minutes

    J. Cannot be determined from the graph

21. Suppose a small amount of radon is trapped in the basement of a house, which is sealed to prevent additional radon from entering. If the half-life of the radon is 3.82 days, what fraction of the original amount will be present in the basement after 11.46 days?

    A. $\dfrac{1}{8}$

    B. $\dfrac{1}{4}$

    C. $\dfrac{1}{3}$

    D. $\dfrac{1}{2}$

PASSAGE V

Enzymes are proteins that function as catalysts in biochemical reactions. The reactant that an enzyme acts on is called its *substrate*.

Here is how an enzyme works: A restricted region of the enzyme molecule, called its *active site*, binds to the substrate. Typically, the site is composed of amino acids and appears as a groove on the surface of the enzyme molecule. There is a compatible fit between the shape of the active site and the shape of the substrate. During a reaction, a substrate molecule enters the active site and the enzyme changes shape slightly to envelope the substrate in a snug fit. At this stage, the enzyme plus substrate is called an enzyme-substrate complex. Some of the amino acids in the active site then catalyze the conversion of substrate to product. The product now departs from the active site, leaving the enzyme unchanged and free to act on another molecule.

The general equation for enzyme reacting with substrate is as follows:

$$E + S \Leftrightarrow E\text{-}S \text{ Complex} \rightarrow E + P$$

where E = enzyme, S = substrate, and P = product.

Notice that the reaction to form the *E-S* Complex is reversible. The substrate may not stay bound to the enzyme.

The catalytic mechanism that causes the reaction to go forward has several components.

- Initially, the substrate is held in place by weak interactions, such as hydrogen bonds and ionic bonds.
- These weak interactions induce slight shape changes in the enzyme that strengthen the binding to the substrate and weaken the bonds in the substrate.
- The active site donates or accepts protons, aiding in the formation of product.
- Thus, the catalyst lowers the energy of the reaction to form product by creating an alternative chemical pathway for the reaction.

In a typical reaction, 1 enzyme molecule may act on about 1,000 substrate molecules per second. Since enzymes are left unchanged, a small number can have a large effect by acting on many substrate molecules in catalytic cycles. The rate at which a given amount of enzyme converts substrate to product is partly a function of initial concentration of substrate—the more substrate molecules, the more frequently they access the active sites of enzyme molecules. There is a limit. At some point, the concentration of substrate will be high enough that all the enzyme molecules are engaged. The reaction rate will stabilize. When the enzyme population is saturated, the only way to increase productivity is to add more enzyme.

An *enzyme inhibitor* is a substance that prevents enzyme activity. There are two types of enzyme inhibitors: competitive and noncompetitive.

Biochemists agree on the mechanism whereby competitive inhibitors block a reaction. A competitive inhibitor mimics the substrate and competes with it for the active site of the enzyme. A competitive inhibitor is able to compete because its shape resembles that of the substrate molecule. Once attached to the enzyme, the inhibitor does not react. The effect of a competitive inhibitor can be overcome by adding more substrate molecules.

The equation for a competitive inhibitor is

$$E + I_c \Leftrightarrow E\text{-}I_c \text{ Complex}$$

where I_c is a competitive inhibitor.

Biochemists disagree on the mechanism whereby noncompetitive inhibitors block a reaction.

Biologist 1

A noncompetitive inhibitor is a molecule that does not compete at the active site of an enzyme. Instead, it binds to an enzyme at a different site, a side group in the protein chain. This binding alters the shape of the active site, making the site incompatible with the shape of the substrate. The substrate molecule is therefore unable to attach itself to the enzyme molecule. This reaction is occasionally reversible and can be represented as follows:

$$E + I_{nc} \Leftrightarrow E\text{-}I_{nc} \text{ Complex}$$

where I_{nc} is a noncompetitive inhibitor.

Biologist 2

A noncompetitive inhibitor is a molecule that binds itself to an enzyme at a site other than the active site. When the substrate subsequently attaches to the active site of the enzyme, the catalytic mechanism is disrupted, preventing the reaction to form product from taking place. The presence of the noncompetitive inhibitor molecule on the enzyme prevents the change in shape of the enzyme that is required to strengthen the binding between enzyme and substrate and weaken the chemical bonds of the substrate. There is therefore no subsequent lowering of the energy of reaction, and product cannot be produced. The action of the noncompetitive inhibitor is irreversible and can be represented as follows:

$$E + S + I_{nc} \rightarrow E\text{-}S\text{-}I_{nc} \text{ Complex}$$

22. What can be determined from the information presented in the passage?

    F. A substrate is a catalyst that reacts with an enzyme to create a product.
    G. The active site of a substrate molecule is the same shape as an enzyme molecule, allowing the substrate to bond with the enzyme.
    H. An enzyme is a catalyst that speeds up a chemical reaction by lowering the energy of the reaction.
    J. An enzyme-substrate complex is an intermediate compound that acts as a catalyst in the chemical reaction to produce a product from the substrate.

23. Which of the following distinguishes a competitive inhibitor from a noncompetitive inhibitor?

    A. A competitive inhibitor attaches to an enzyme at its active site. A noncompetitive inhibitor attaches to an enzyme at a site different from the active site.
    B. A competitive inhibitor attaches to the substrate, preventing the enzyme from attaching to the substrate. A noncompetitive inhibitor attaches to the enzyme.
    C. A competitive inhibitor's attachment to an enzyme is always irreversible. A noncompetitive inhibitor's attachment to an enzyme is always reversible.
    D. In the presence of an unlimited amount of inhibitor and substrate, a competitive inhibitor blocks the formation of any product while a noncompetitive inhibitor allows formation of some product.

24. Which of the following could explain why just a small amount of enzyme is sufficient to produce a chemical reaction with a large amount of substrate?

    F. The catalytic mechanism of the enzyme is much faster than the rate of chemical reaction to form product.
    G. An enzyme molecule has multiple active sites and can process many substrate molecules simultaneously.
    H. An enzyme molecule is small and sleek and can move at a faster rate than a substrate molecule, which is large and bulky.
    J. Since an enzyme molecule is unchanged by the chemical reaction that produces product, a single enzyme molecule can repeat its cycle and react with many different substrate molecules.

25. Which of the following assertions about noncompetitive inhibitors is consistent with Biologist 2's theory?

    A. The binding of the noncompetitive inhibitor to the enzyme causes the shape of the enzyme's active site to change.
    B. The presence of a noncompetitive inhibitor causes the chemical bonds of the substrate to weaken.
    C. The presence of a noncompetitive inhibitor on an enzyme places the substrate in close proximity to additional protons it may need for reaction.
    D. Despite the presence of a noncompetitive inhibitor on an enzyme, the shape of the enzyme's active site is compatible with the shape of the substrate.

26. Which of the following reaction equations is consistent with Biologist 1's theory of an enzyme (E) and its substrate (S) in the presence of a noncompetitive inhibitor (I)? The product is represented as P.

   F. $E + S + I \Leftrightarrow E\text{-}I$ Complex $+ S + P$
   G. $E + S + I \Leftrightarrow E\text{-}I$ Complex $+ S$
   H. $E + S + I \Leftrightarrow E\text{-}S\text{-}I$ Complex
   J. $E + S + I \Leftrightarrow E\text{-}S\text{-}I$ Complex $+ P$

27. Based on the information in the passage, which of the following graphs represents, for a fixed amount of enzyme, the rate of an enzyme–catalytic reaction as the concentration of substrate increases? (You may assume that no inhibitors are present.)

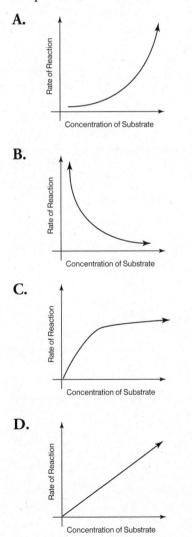

   A.

   B.

   C.

   D.

28. An example of an enzyme inhibitor is malonate ions inhibiting the enzyme succinic dehydrogenase. The enzyme acts as a catalyst in converting succinate ions to fumarate ions. The catalytic reaction is:

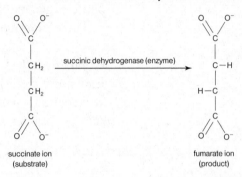

   succinate ion (substrate)   fumarate ion (product)

   The reaction is inhibited by malonate ions:

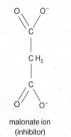

   malonate ion (inhibitor)

   The similar shape of the malonate ion to the succinate ion lets the malonate ion bind to the active site. However, the lack of the $CH_2\text{-}CH_2$ bond in the center of the ion stops any further reaction from taking place. Which of the following is a true statement about this example?

   F. The malonate ion is a competitive inhibitor because it competes with the succinate ion for the active site on the succinic dehydrogenase enzyme.
   G. The malonate ion is a competitive inhibitor because it competes with the fumarate ion for the active site on the succinic dehydrogenase enzyme.
   H. When malonate ions are added to succinate ions in the presence of succinic dehydrogenase, no fumarate ions will be produced.
   J. When malonate ions are added to succinate ions in the presence of succinic dehydrogenase, a succinic-dehydrogenase-malonate ion complex is formed in an irreversible reaction.

PASSAGE VI

An industrial process used to produce steel also produces polluting emissions released to the atmosphere. The pollution consists of gaseous compounds of nitrogen (N), sulfur (S), and phosphorus (P). In addition, dust particles generated in the process form part of the polluting emissions.

Three experiments were performed to reduce the emissions.

Experiment 1

Emissions were passed between electrified metal plates. The plates attracted dust particles and removed them from the emissions. The percent of particles removed at different voltages is shown in Graph 1.

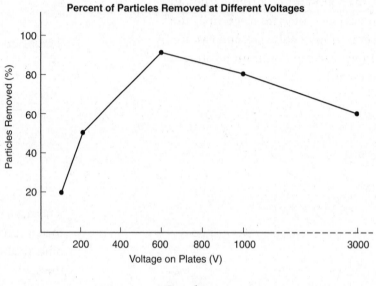

Graph 1

Experiment 2

Emissions were passed through filters of different pore sizes to trap dust particles. Reductions in particulate emissions were measured, and the data are shown in Graph 2.

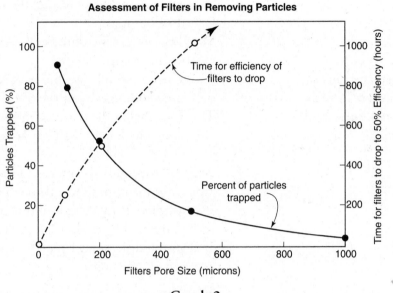

Graph 2

Experiment 3

A chemical method of reducing pollution was used. Emissions were passed through solutions of concentrated alkali (solutions of OH^- ions). The percentage of three pollutants removed at different alkali concentrations is shown in Graph 3.

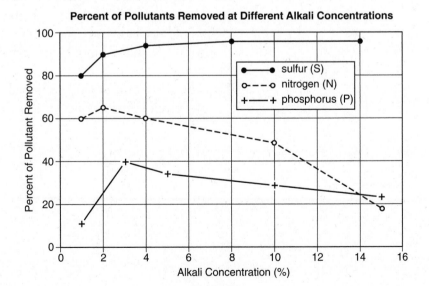

Graph 3

29. Which voltage was found to be most effective for removal of particulate matter from industrial emissions?

    A. 100 V
    B. 600 V
    C. 1,000 V
    D. 3,000 V

30. If emissions contained equal amounts of sulfur, phosphorus, and nitrogen, which concentration of alkaline solution would remove the most pollution?

    F. 1%
    G. 3%
    H. 10%
    J. 15%

31. According to Experiment 2, which of the following statements best describes the relationship, if any, between pore size and filter durability?

    A. The greater the pore size, the longer the filter lasts.
    B. The smaller the pore size, the longer the filter lasts.
    C. There is no relationship between pore size and longevity of the filter.
    D. The smaller the particles in the emissions, the longer the filter lasts.

32. Suppose the industrial process releases emissions into the atmosphere through a long exhaust pipe. If the length of this pipe were to be increased by a factor of 3, what effect, if any, would the longer pipe have on the removal of emissions?

    F. The particles would consolidate and become larger, leading to greater effectiveness in removal by filter.
    G. The voltage would be magnified by the increased length of pipe, leading to greater effectiveness in removal by electrified plates.
    H. The percentage of pollutants removed by passing emissions through alkali would decrease since the alkali solution would be diluted in a longer exhaust pipe.
    J. The effect cannot be determined from the given information.

33. Assume that the lifetime of a filter means the number of hours before its efficiency drops to 50%. Based on the data shown in Graph 2, which is a valid conclusion?

    A. A filter with a pore size of at least 800 microns would remove most of the polluting particles and have a lifetime of over 1000 hours.

    B. A filter with a pore size of 400 microns would remove fewer than half of the polluting particles and have a lifetime of less than 50 hours.

    C. A filter with a pore size of 200 microns would remove about half of the polluting particles and have a lifetime of about 500 hours.

    D. A filter with a pore size of 100 microns would remove most of the polluting particles and have a lifetime of less than 100 hours.

34. Which of the following could be a follow-up experiment that combines the electrical and chemical methods of removing pollution from industrial emissions?

    F. Pass the emissions through a filter placed in the exhaust pipe, and then bubble them through an alkali solution.

    G. Determine the size of particles as they pass out of the exhaust pipe and into the atmosphere.

    H. Pass the emissions across electrified plates, and then bubble them through an alkali solution.

    J. Place a filter at the end of the exhaust pipe to capture emissions that are first passed across electrified plates.

When a brick is in free fall somewhere on Earth, if air resistance is ignored, the only force acting on the brick is its weight, *W*.

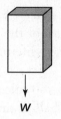

The mass of the brick, *m*, in kilograms, is constant everywhere in the universe. However, its weight, *W*, depends on the gravitational acceleration of Earth, *g*, which is 9.8 meters per second squared (9.8 m/s^2). The equation linking weight and mass is $W = mg$ newtons (N), where $1\text{N} = 1 \text{ kg} \cdot \text{m/s}^2$

Experiment 1

Planet *A* has a different gravitational acceleration than Earth. In a hypothetical experiment to determine the gravitational acceleration on Planet *A*, an astronaut weighs several objects whose masses are known. The data he obtains are plotted on a graph. Graph 1 below shows the line of best fit for the data.

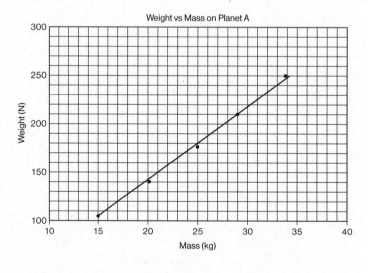

Graph 1

Back on Earth, consider a brick on a surface. There are now several additional forces acting on it.

Case 1: The brick is not moving, and a horizontal force, F_a, is being applied.

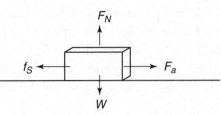

F_N is the *normal* force, the force perpendicular to the surface, which equals the weight of the brick and acts in the opposite direction to the weight. The force of static friction, f_S, works in the opposite direction to the applied force. The maximum value of f_S is the value of F_a just as the brick starts to move. This maximum force of static friction, $f_{S,max}$, is proportional to the normal force: $f_{S,max} = \mu_s F_N$, where μ_s is the coefficient of static friction.

Case 2: The brick is moving with constant velocity.

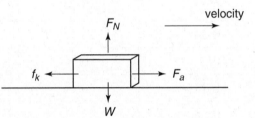

F_a is the force applied to keep the velocity constant.

f_k is the force of kinetic friction, which opposes the sliding of the brick and works in the opposite direction to the applied force.

When the velocity is constant, $f_k = -F_a$ and $f_k = \mu_k F_N$, where μ_k is the coefficient of kinetic friction.

Students in a physics class performed two experiments to calculate μ_s and μ_k, the coefficients of static and kinetic friction for a brick moving on wood.

Experiment 2

A spring scale was attached to a brick on a wooden table. The spring scale was used to apply and measure the force required to start the brick sliding. The force applied was parallel to the table. The highest reading taken before the brick moved was a measure of $f_{S,max}$. This measurement was recorded, and the experiment was repeated with bricks of the same material and different weights.

Experiment 3

The same setup was used as for Experiment 2. This time the brick was pulled along the table with constant velocity, with care being taken to keep the scale parallel to the table. The reading on the scale in this experiment was a measure of the force of kinetic friction, and this measurement was recorded for several different weights. The table below shows one student's results for Experiments 2 and 3.

Weight (N) $W = -F_N$	Maximum Static Friction (N) $f_{s,\,max}$	Coefficient of Static Friction $\dfrac{f_{s,max}}{F_N}$	Kinetic Friction (N) f_k	Coefficient of Kinetic Friction $\dfrac{f_k}{F_N}$
17 N	4 N	0.24	4 N	0.22
34 N	9 N	0.26	8.5 N	0.25
51 N	14 N	0.27	13.7 N	0.27
68 N	16 N	0.24	15 N	0.22
85 N	17 N	0.20	16 N	0.19
102 N	21 N	0.21	20 N	0.20
119 N	24 N	0.20	23 N	0.19

35. Based on the graph of the data for Experiment 1, the gravitational acceleration on Planet *A*, in meters per second squared (m/s^2), is closest to which of the following?

   A. 0.33 m/s^2
   B. 0.75 m/s^2
   C. 1.33 m/s^2
   D. 7.5 m/s^2

36. The gravitational acceleration on Earth is 9.8 m/s^2. If an object on Planet *A* weighed 150 N, which of the following would be closest to its weight on Earth?

   F. 205 N
   G. 150 N
   H. 21 N
   J. 2 N

37. According to the results in the table, what is the relationship between μ_s and μ_k, the coefficients of static and kinetic friction for brick on wood?

   A. $\mu_s > \mu_k$
   B. $\mu_s \gtrsim \mu_k$
   C. $\mu_s < \mu_k$
   D. There is insufficient data to make a conclusion.

38. Suppose a wooden block were pulled at constant velocity on a wooden surface and its force of kinetic friction, f_k, were measured. If an identical wooden block were attached to the first block and the experiment repeated, the force of kinetic friction, f_k, would:

   F. stay the same.
   G. be doubled.
   H. be halved.
   J. be quadrupled.

39. Suppose all of the students who performed Experiments 2 and 3 got comparable numerical results for μ_k, the coefficient of kinetic friction. Which of the following generalizations for kinetic friction would appear to be false?

    A. The force of kinetic friction is independent of the speed of the object on the surface.

    B. The force of kinetic friction is independent of the area of contact between an object and its surface.

    C. The force of kinetic friction is independent of the weight of the object on the surface.

    D. The force of kinetic friction is dependent on the type of material of both surfaces.

40. Which of the following represents a graph of maximum static friction, $f_{s,max}$, versus the normal force, F_N, for two surfaces in contact?

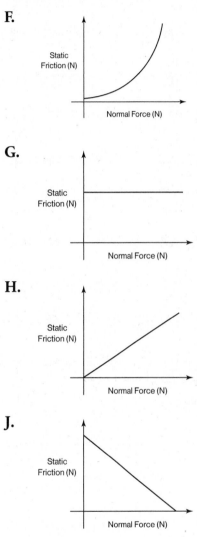

F.

G.

H.

J.

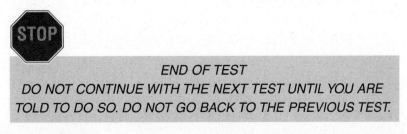

END OF TEST
DO NOT CONTINUE WITH THE NEXT TEST UNTIL YOU ARE
TOLD TO DO SO. DO NOT GO BACK TO THE PREVIOUS TEST.

Answer Key
PRACTICE SCIENCE TEST

1.	(B)	11.	(B)	21.	(A)	31.	(A)
2.	(G)	12.	(J)	22.	(H)	32.	(J)
3.	(B)	13.	(C)	23.	(A)	33.	(C)
4.	(F)	14.	(G)	24.	(J)	34.	(H)
5.	(C)	15.	(C)	25.	(D)	35.	(D)
6.	(F)	16.	(F)	26.	(G)	36.	(F)
7.	(D)	17.	(B)	27.	(C)	37.	(B)
8.	(H)	18.	(J)	28.	(F)	38.	(G)
9.	(A)	19.	(D)	29.	(B)	39.	(C)
10.	(F)	20.	(F)	30.	(G)	40.	(H)

Science Answers and Explanations

PASSAGE I (SOLUBILITY)

1. **(B)** The trend in Graph 1 is that as temperature increases, solubility of gases decreases. Thus, choice (B) is the correct answer, while choice (A) is incorrect. The other choices are also contradicted by the data.

    Choice (C): A counterexample is cerium sulfate, whose solubility *decreases* with increasing temperature.

    Choice (D): All of the solids shown, except for cerium sulfate, increase in solubility with increasing temperature.

2. **(G)** According to Table 1, the maximum amount of sodium chloride that will dissolve in 100 mL of water at 90°C is 38 grams. Therefore, in half the amount of water, only half of 38 grams will dissolve.

3. **(B)** The solubility of NaCl is almost constant with temperature increase, at about 36g/100 mL. The only graph that shows this is choice (B). The other choices are incorrect.

    Choices (A) and (C): These show an increasing trend instead of an almost constant trend.

    Choice (D): This is the worst choice since the numbers in the table for NaCl are slightly increasing, not decreasing as is shown in this choice.

4. **(F)** From a depth of about 0 to 15 meters, there are about 4 mg per liter of dissolved oxygen (O_2). Deeper than 15 meters, the O_2 level falls off sharply. From 20 meters and deeper, no oxygen is recorded. Thus, the quantity of dissolved oxygen decreases as depth increases. Note that even though there is a region where the amount of dissolved oxygen stays constant, this is the best answer among those given. The other assertions are all false.

    Choice (G): The quantity of sulfide (HS^-) is 0 until a depth of about 23 meters, at which point the amount increases. For example, at a depth of about 35 meters, the HS^- reading is about 2,400 mmol L^{-1}.

    Choice (H): Ammonia (NH_3) is undetectable until a depth of about 20 meters, when the quantity of NH_3 starts to increase.

    Choice (J): At a depth of about 10 meters, the temperature starts to decrease.

5. **(C)** According to the passage, solubility of O_2 decreases as temperature increases. Hot water discharged into the lake would raise the temperature and reduce the amount of dissolved oxygen, possibly harming the aquatic organisms, which need dissolved oxygen to survive.

PASSAGE II (CHICKEN FEED)

6. **(F)** The successful experiment to produce fly larvae used pig manure. The unsuccessful experiment used cattle manure, so choice (G) is incorrect. Choices (H) and (J) are wrong because bagasse and silk cotton tree wood were used to produce termites.

7. **(D)** From Table 1, you can see that the termite yield from Method 2, the setup that used cartons, was 133 g/carton, versus 97 g/hole for Method 1. Each of the other statements is false.

Choice (A): Since both Methods 1 and 2 used some kind of fish waste (actual fish waste in Method 1 and fish waste water in Method 2), you cannot conclude from the passage that fish waste was an essential ingredient in the production of fly larvae. You would need to do a controlled experiment to make that conclusion.

Choice (B): The experiment that used cattle manure, Method 1, produced a negligible yield of fly larvae. This was therefore an ineffective method.

Choice (C): Method 1 for termites, the holes (no cartons), produced 97 grams of termites per hole (Table 1). Although this was not as effective as Method 2 (with cartons), it is false to say, "It was not possible to harvest termites," if the colonies were not in boxes.

8. **(H)** It is reasonable to assume that other insects were in the ground that could attack the termites in their natural habitat. The carton setup, however, was sealed off from other insects. The explanations in the other choices are implausible.

Choice (F): First, nothing was placed into the boxes to prevent rotting. Second, termites thrive on wood and ate through the wood provided in each setup.

Choice (G): The holes were not exposed to sunlight. They were under shady trees and covered with jute sacks to keep them dark.

Choice (J): Termites in both setups were protected by being covered. Nevertheless, rain was desirable to keep the environments humid. The interiors of the cartons were kept damp and dark.

9. **(A)** All of the numbers for this question are shown in Table 2. Ash values for termite and larvae samples are 8.3% and 6.6%, respectively. These are lower than the 41.7% for the fish meal. The statements in choices (B), (C), and (D) are all directly contradicted by the numbers in Table 2.

10. **(F)** From Table 3, the amounts of daily intake of maize were 28.7g, 26.0g, and 26.2g, which are comparable amounts. The corresponding intakes of metabolizable energy were 0.42 MJ, 0.44 MJ, and 0.46 MJ, which are also comparable amounts. This means that there was no obvious correlation between maize consumed and metabolizable energy consumed. The assertions in the other choices agree with the data presented in Tables 3 and 4. They are therefore wrong answers!

Choice (G): The daily crude protein intake for the control group was 5.6 g, higher than the 3.5 g and 3.4 g for the other two groups; yet the metabolizable energy intake was comparable. This suggests that the metabolizable energy intake was independent of the crude protein consumption.

Choice (H): The consumption of metabolizable energy per kg gain was 46.1 MJ for the control group, 48.9 MJ for the termite group, and 42.2 MJ for the fly larvae group. Yet the corresponding daily consumptions of metabolizable energy were 0.42 MJ, 0.44 MJ, and 0.46 MJ, respectively. This suggests that the energy consumed per kg of weight gain was independent of the daily intake of metabolizable energy.

Choice (J): Irrespective of what they consumed, the energy consumptions of the three groups were comparable.

11. **(B)** From Table 4, protein intake/kg gain was 312g for FLG and 615g for CG; yet weight gain for FLG was 10.9g and weight gain for CG was 9.1g. So the statement in choice (B) is supported by the table. All of the other choices are contradicted by the table.

Choice (A): Rates of weight gain were higher for FLG than for CG and TG.

Choice (C): To see which feed conversion ratio was "best" means to find the lowest number, the one that represents the smallest amount of feed needed for a 1 kg weight gain. From Table 4, notice that the feed conversion ratio was best for FLG.

Choice (D): The chicks in FLG consumed less metabolizable energy per kilogram of weight gain.

PASSAGE III (MUMPS)

12. **(J)** Notice from Figure 1 that the first onset of symptoms is on day 12. So on day 11, the person should be asymptomatic.

13. **(C)** The part of the graph that shows where the person is infectious is the candy-striped rectangle. Notice that it extends precisely from days 12 through 18 after exposure.

14. **(G)** The bar graph of Figure 2 represents the number of cases reported for each month in 2005. Since there is no bar for April, no case was reported for that month. Each of the other assertions is incorrect.

Choice (F): The line graph of Figure 2 shows the average of number of cases reported for each month. Since this line does not dip to 0 for April, the number of cases for April during 2000–2004 was not 0.

Choice (H): There is no information about the national average in Figure 2, so you cannot make assertions about it.

Choice (J): The value for the 5-year average in November is not a whole number (it looks slightly less than 1). Therefore, the assertion of equality is incorrect.

15. **(C)** You can get this answer in two ways. First, you are told that there were 47 cases of mumps reported in California in 2005 and that 21%—slightly more than one-fifth—were in Los Angeles County. $\frac{1}{5}$ of 47 ≈ 9. Slightly

more than 9 is 10! The second method of getting the answer is to find the sum of the bars in the bar graph, shown for 2005:

Number of cases = 1 + 1 + 3 + 2 + 1 + 1 + 1 = 10.

16. **(F)** From Figure 1, notice that the fever ends on day 16 and the antibody level starts rising on day 16. The other conclusions are not valid, based on Figure 1.

Choice (G): The person's antibody level starts rising on day 16. The headache, however, can persist past day 16 (according to the bar for headache in the diagram).

Choice (H): The person is infectious from day 12 until day 18. This overlaps the time that the antibody level starts rising.

Choice (J): The person first has symptoms 12 days after exposure. Antibody levels do not start rising until day 16.

PASSAGE IV (RADIOACTIVE DECAY)

17. **(B)** The set of stable nuclei does not extend beyond about 83 protons. It is therefore reasonable to conclude from the graph that no stable nuclei are beyond atomic number 83. The other three assertions are all contradicted by the graph.

Choice (A): Here is a counterexample: a nucleus with 10 protons and 10 neutrons lies in the stable region.

Choice (C): No points in the stable region represent a nucleus in which the number of neutrons equals twice the number of protons.

Choice (D): In the notation $^{70}_{30}X$, 30 is the atomic number (number of protons) and 70 is the mass number (sum of protons and neutrons). Therefore, the number of neutrons is 40. From the graph, a nucleus with 30 protons and 40 neutrons is stable.

18. **(J)** Studying the decay series of a nucleus that is likely to be stable does not make sense. Choices (F), (G), and (H) all represent isotopes that are outside the stability region shown in Graph 1. Manganese, or $^{55}_{25}Mn$, is likely to be stable (25 protons and 30 neutrons fall within the stability region).

19. **(D)** Based on Graph 2, it is not possible to follow the arrows without going right horizontally ($\rightarrow$) at least 4 times. Each rightward arrow represents a beta decay reaction. Each of the other choices is incorrect.

Choice (A): If this were true, there would be no rightward moves. However, you need at least 4 rightward moves.

Choice (B): No matter which path you take, the minimum number of moves is 11. Try it!

Choice (C): Notice that $^{219}_{86}Rn$ is an *optional* path. One can instead follow a path via the isotope $^{219}_{85}At$, from which an alpha decay could occur, bypassing $^{219}_{86}Rn$.

20. **(F)**

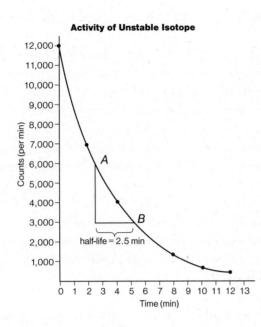

Activity of Unstable Isotope

Take any two points on the graph, such as *A* and *B*, where the counts per minute reading at point *A* is double that at point *B*. For example, let *A* be at 6,000 counts/minute and *B* be at 3,000 counts/minute. The time, in minutes, separating these points is about 2.5 minutes. Therefore, the half-life is 2.5 minutes, the time taken for the count activity to be halved.

21. **(A)** 11.46 represents 3 half-lives of radon.

After 1 half-life, there will be $\frac{1}{2}$ of the original amount left.

After 2 half-lives, there will be $\frac{1}{2}$ of $\frac{1}{2}$, that is $\frac{1}{4}$, of the original amount left.

After 3 half-lives, there will be $\frac{1}{2}$ of $\frac{1}{4}$, that is $\frac{1}{8}$, of the original amount left.

PASSAGE V (ENZYMES)

22. **(H)** The opening paragraph of the passage defines an enzyme as a catalyst. After a substrate bonds with an enzyme, the catalytic mechanism involves lowering the reaction energy that allows the reaction to go forward. The other assertions are all incorrect:

Choice (F): A substrate is not a catalyst. It is the substance that the catalyst acts upon.

Choice (G): A substrate molecule does not have an active site, an enzyme does.

Choice (J): An enzyme-substrate complex is an intermediate compound in the reaction. It is not, however, a catalyst. The enzyme is the catalyst.

23. **(A)** Both biologists agree that a competitive inhibitor attaches to the enzyme at its active site whereas a noncompetitive inhibitor attaches to the enzyme at a different site. The other assertions about inhibitors are incorrect.

Choice (B): Both types of inhibitors attach themselves to the enzyme, not the substrate.

Choice (C): The biologists both agree that the action of a competitive inhibitor is reversible. The equation shows a two-way arrow. From the passage, it is not known whether the action of a noncompetitive inhibitor is reversible. Biologist 1 asserts that it can be, while Biologist 2 asserts that it never is.

Choice (D): In the case of a competitive inhibitor, some product can be formed, depending on whether the substrate or inhibitor attaches to the active site of the enzyme. A noncompetitive inhibitor prevents any product from being formed.

24. **(J)** From the passage, note that 1 enzyme molecule can act on about 1,000 substrate molecules per second since the enzyme remains unchanged after reaction. All of the other choices make spurious claims that are not supported in the passage.

25. **(D)** The key to Biologist 2's theory is that the shape of the active site is not sufficiently altered by a noncompetitive inhibitor to prevent a substrate molecule from attaching to it. This means that the shapes of both the substrate molecule and active site are compatible for a bond to be formed. None of the other assertions is consistent with Biologist 2's theory.

Choice (A): If the shape of the active site is changed, then a substrate molecule would not be able to attach to the enzyme, contradicting Biologist 2's theory.

Choices (B) and (C): Causing bonds of the substrate to weaken and making protons available to the substrate are features of the catalytic mechanism. However, according to Biologist 2's theory, this mechanism is stopped from going forward by a noncompetitive inhibitor. Therefore, neither choice (B) nor (C) is compatible with Biologist 2's theory.

26. **(G)** According to Biologist 1's theory, the substrate is unable to bind with the enzyme. So eliminate choices (H) and (J), which show an *E-S-I* Complex. Choice (F) is wrong because it shows formation of product. The noncompetitive inhibitor blocks the substrate from reacting with the enzyme. Therefore, no product should be shown.

27. **(C)** Since 1 enzyme molecule can act on about 1,000 substrate molecules per second, the greater the concentration of substrate, the greater the rate. (You should eliminate choice (B), which shows a decreasing function.) When the enzyme population is saturated, then adding more substrate will have no effect on the rate. The rate levels out and becomes constant. This is shown in choice (C). Choices (A) and (D) are incorrect because even though they are increasing, they show no leveling out of the rate when the enzyme population is saturated.

28. **(F)** The inhibitor, a malonate ion, binds to the active site, which is a feature of a competitive inhibitor. A noncompetitive inhibitor binds to the enzyme at a *different* site. Each of the other choices is false.

Choice (G): The inhibitor never competes with a product. It competes with only the substrate.

Choice (H): Since malonate ions are competitive inhibitors, the substrate may "win" the competition and bind to the active site of the enzyme. In this case, product (a fumarate ion) will be produced because the catalytic reaction can proceed.

Choice (J): The reaction with a competitive inhibitor can be reversible. That is what makes the statement false. The complex formed when the enzyme binds with the inhibitor is correctly stated to be a succinic-dehydrogenase-malonate ion complex.

PASSAGE VI (POLLUTION)

29. **(B)** According to Graph 1, the maximum amount—90%—of emission particles were removed when the electric plates were at about 600V. Each of the other voltages show a lower percentage of particle removal.

30. **(G)** From Graph 3, see that the maximum amount of phosphorus removal occurs at a 3% alkaline solution. At 3%, amounts of sulfur and nitrogen removed are very close to their respective maxima. The other choices are incorrect.

Choice (F): 1% is well below maximum for each of the three pollutants.

Choice (H): 10% is well below maximum for nitrogen and phosphorus and is not high enough for sulfur to outweigh the others.

Choice (J): 15% represents a minimum value for nitrogen removal and a value below the maximum for phosphorus. Even though it is a maximum value for sulfur removal, this does not compensate for the low percentages of removal for nitrogen and phosphorus.

31. **(A)** From Graph 2, notice that when the pore size is very small, close to 0, the filter loses half of its efficiency in less than 100 hours. In contrast, when the pore size exceeds 600 microns, the filter takes more than 1,000 hours to lose half of its efficiency. The statements in the other choices are false.

Choices (B) and (C): As the pore size increases, the life of the filter increases.

Choice (D): The particle size was not addressed in the experiment.

32. **(J)** No experiment described in the passage examines the effect of lengthening the emissions exhaust pipe. You therefore cannot reach any conclusions about it. Also, no information is in the passage about whether pollution treatments happen before emissions reach the pipe, which would make the length of the pipe irrelevant.

33. **(C)** In Graph 2, the solid line shows the percentage of particles trapped by the filter. When the pore size is 200 microns, the corresponding percentage of particles trapped is 50%. The dotted line shows the number of hours before the filter loses half of its efficiency. A pore size of 200 microns corresponds with a time of 500 hours. Thus, this choice is correct. The other choices contradict the data in the graphs.

Choice (A): When the pore size is 800 microns or above, fewer than 10% of the particles are removed.

Choice (B): When the pore size is 400 microns, the lifetime of the filter is about 800 hours.

Choice (D): When the pore size is 100 microns, the lifetime of the filter is about 250 hours.

34. **(H)** The follow-up experiment aims to combine electrical and chemical methods of removing pollution, which choice (H) does. Reject each of the other choices:

Choice (F): No electricity is involved.

Choice (G): Neither electricity nor a chemical method is used.

Choice (J): No chemical method is used.

PASSAGE VII (FRICTION)

35. **(D)** Since weight is the product of mass and acceleration, $W = ma$, the gravitational acceleration, a, is given by the slope of the line. For points P and Q, shown below, slope $\approx \dfrac{30}{4} = 7.5$. Be careful that you use the correct units. Horizontally, each block length represents 1 kg. Vertically, however, each block length represents 10 N.

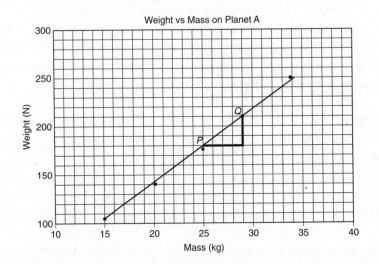

36. **(F)** If an object on Planet A weighs 150 N, its corresponding mass would be 21 kg. (Read this directly from the graph.) The mass is constant everywhere in the universe. Use the following equation to calculate weight on Earth.

$$W = mg = (21)(9.8) \approx (21)(10) = 210N$$

Thus, the closest weight from the answer choices would be 205 N. Notice that if you trusted your answer to the previous question, you could take a shortcut. The weight on Earth would be $\dfrac{9.8}{7.5}$ times the weight on Planet A.

This is about $\dfrac{4}{3}$. When you estimate $\dfrac{4}{3}$ of 150, you again get about 200 N.

37. **(B)** The middle column, $\dfrac{f_{s,\text{max}}}{F_N}$, represents the coefficient of static friction, μ_s.

The last column, $\dfrac{f_k}{F_N}$, represents the coefficient of kinetic friction, μ_k.

If you compare the values in the middle and last columns, the coefficient of static friction is generally greater than the coefficient of kinetic friction for any given weight. Notice, however, for a weight of 51 N, the students' measurements led to the two coefficients being equal. So, *based on the table*, $\mu_s \geq \mu_k$.

38. **(G)** Suppose the weight of one wooden block is m. Its normal force, F_N, is equal to its weight, mg. Also, $f_k = \mu_k F_N = \mu_k mg$.

When an identical block is added to the first, the mass becomes $2m$. Therefore, the new force of friction, f_{k2}, can be calculated as follows:

$$f_{k2} = \mu_k(2mg)$$
$$= 2\mu_k mg$$
$$= 2f_k$$

Thus, the force is doubled, which you may have guessed. One of the keys to answering this question is to realize that μ_k for wood on wood is constant.

39. **(C)** From the table, you should see that changing the weight of the object changes the force of friction. Each of the other statements is true and therefore a wrong answer!

Choice (A): Students were not told what velocity to use, just to keep the velocity constant. Yet they obtained comparable values for the coefficient of kinetic friction. This suggests that the force of kinetic friction is independent of the speed.

Choice (B): Since the force of kinetic friction depends on the normal force F_N, which in turn equals mg, only the mass apparently influences the force, not the orientation of the object on the surface. Thus, the two setups below should yield the same result.

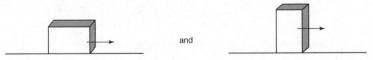

Choice (D): This is a true statement but is not based on the students' experiments. The force of friction calculated by the students is specific for brick on wood. Since the students did not experiment with different materials, they have no basis on which to judge whether choice (D) is true or false. By using common sense, however, they might guess that if a "slippery" surface (like oiled steel) were used instead of wood, the coefficient of kinetic friction (and therefore the force of kinetic friction) would be smaller.

40. **(H)** Since $f_s = \mu_s F_N$, where μ_s is a constant, the relationship is linear. You can therefore eliminate choice (F). As F_N increases, the maximum force of static friction also increases. Thus, eliminate choices (G) and (J).

Appendixes

APPENDIX A: SOME USEFUL MATH FORMULAS

You do not need to memorize many formulas for the ACT Math Test, since they will be provided as parts of questions. Nevertheless, here are some formulas that you should review before the test.

1. Area of a trapezoid with bases b_1 and b_2, and height h: $A = \frac{1}{2}h(b_1 + b_2)$

2. Area of a rhombus with diagonals d_1 and d_2: $A = \frac{1}{2}(d_1 d_2)$

3. Area of an equilateral triangle with side s: $A = \frac{s^2\sqrt{3}}{4}$

4. Sum of angles in a polygon with n sides: $S = (n-2)180°$

5. Sum of exterior angles in a polygon with n sides: $S = 360°$

6. Area of a sector with radius r and central angle $m°$: $A = \frac{m}{360} \cdot \pi r^2$

7. Arc length of a sector with radius r and central angle $m°$: $A = \frac{m}{360} \cdot 2\pi r$

8. The nth term, a_n, of an arithmetic sequence with first term a and common difference d: $a_n = a + (n-1)d$

9. The nth term, a_n, of a geometric sequence with first term a and common ratio r: $a_n = ar^{n-1}$

10. The sum of n terms, S_n, of an arithmetic series with first term a and nth term a_n: $S_n = \frac{n}{2}(a + a_n)$

11. The sum of n terms of an arithmetic series with first term a and common difference d: $S_n = \dfrac{n}{2}[2a + (n-1)d]$

12. The sum of n terms of a geometric series with first term a and common ratio r: $S_n = a \cdot \dfrac{1 - r^n}{1 - r}$

13. The sum of the first n positive integers: $S_n = \dfrac{n(n+1)}{2}$

14. The number of permutations of n objects taken r at a time: $_nP_r = \dfrac{n!}{(n-r)!}$

15. The number of combinations of n objects taken r at a time: $_nC_r = \dfrac{n!}{(n-r)!\,r!}$

16. The surface area of a cube with edge e: $S = 6e^2$

17. The surface area of a rectangular prism (box) with edges l, w, and h:
$S = 2(lw + lh + wh)$

18. The surface area of a cylinder with base radius r and height h: $S = 2\pi r^2 + 2\pi rh$

19. The volume of a cone with base radius r and height h: $V = \dfrac{1}{3}\pi r^2 h$

20. The volume of a pyramid with base area B and height h: $V = \dfrac{1}{3}Bh$

21. The surface area of a sphere with radius r: $S = 4\pi r^2$

22. The volume of a sphere with radius r: $S = \dfrac{4}{3}\pi r^3$

APPENDIX B: SOME USEFUL SCIENTIFIC UNITS

You are not expected to know scientific units for the ACT science test. Nevertheless, here are some units that may be used in the passages on the test. Being familiar with them may make the test a little easier. The units below are a modern form of the metric system, called SI (International System) units.

SI Prefixes

Prefix	Symbol	Meaning
nano-	n	10^{-9}
micro-	μ	10^{-6}
milli-	m	10^{-3}
centi-	c	10^{-2}
deci-	d	10^{-1}
kilo-	k	10^{3}
mega-	M	10^{6}
giga-	G	10^{9}

Some Basic Units

Unit	Name	Symbol	Meaning
Length	meter angstrom	m Å	10^{-10} m
Mass	gram	g	
Time	second	s	
Temperature	kelvin Celsius	K °C	
Amount of substance	mole	mol	6.02×10^{23} molecules
Capacity	liter	L	10^3cm^3
Luminous intensity	candela	cd	
Illuminance	lux	lx	cd / m^2
Velocity			m / s
Acceleration			m / s^2
Force	newton	N	$\text{kg} \cdot \text{m} / \text{s}^2$
Energy or work	joule calorie	J cal	N · m 4.184 J
Power	watt	W	J / s
Frequency	hertz	Hz	cycles / s
Pressure	pascal bar	Pa	N / m^2 10^5Pa
Electric current	ampere	A	
Electric charge	coulomb	C	A · s
Electrical potential	volt	V	J / C
Electrical resistance	ohm	Ω	V / A